Sport for Development, Peace, and Social Justice

Sport for Development, Peace, and Social Justice

Robert J. Schinke, Ed.D.
Laurentian University

Stephanie J. Hanrahan, Ph.D.
University of Queensland

Editors

Fitness Information Technology
A DIVISION OF THE INTERNATIONAL CENTER FOR PERFORMANCE EXCELLENCE

262 Coliseum, WVU-CPASS
PO Box 6116
Morgantown, WV 26506-6116

Library of Congress Card Catalog Number: 2011938923

ISBN: 978-1-935412-34-2

Cover images: All images courtesy of Dreamstime.com; earth image © Artman; ball players © Federico Donatini; runners © Daniel Korzeniewski; soccer goalie © Petesaloutos; hockey player © Designpicssub; cyclist © Melinda Fawver; jumper © Jianbingless; rowers © Corepics Vof; children © Lindas 131

Cover Design: 40 West Studios
Production Editor: Jennifer Bowman
Copyeditor: Mark Slider
Typesetter: 40 West Studios
Proofreader: Geoffrey C. Fuller
Indexer: Geoffrey C. Fuller
Printed by: Data Reproductions Corp.

10 9 8 7 6 5 4 3 2

Fitness Information Technology
A Division of the International Center for Performance Excellence
West Virginia University
262 Coliseum, WVU-PASS
PO Box 6116
Morgantown, WV 26506-6116

800.477.4348 (toll free)
304.293.6888 (phone)
304.293.6658 (fax)
Email: fitcustomerservice@mail.wvu.edu
Website: www.fitinfotech.com

Contents

CONTENTS

Sport as a Possible Intervention: An Introduction

1

Robert J. Schinke and Stephanie J. Hanrahan

Sport has been acknowledged widely for its motivational value for some time. There are many stories of athletes who have clawed their way from life on city streets and employed sport as a means to better themselves. Boxing, basketball, track and field, and football seem to be sport disciplines where socio-economics, class, and race are less important than ability and determination. Sport often serves as a level playing field (we guess that is where the saying originated) where people can just play, enjoy, and excel.

Individuals participate in sport for many reasons. Only a minority of athletes seek to achieve fame and fortune. Some engage in sport for the pure fun of it. According to incentive motivation, there are seven main types of experiences that participants believe are important and available from sport: a) affiliation—being socially reassured that one is acceptable or worthwhile; b) power—having the opportunity to influence others' attitudes, interests, or opinions; c) independence—having the chance to do things on one's own without the help of others; d) stress—the excitement, pure action, and adrenalin that can be found in some sporting activities; e) excellence—doing something well for its own sake or being better than others; f) success—the extrinsic rewards that sport can provide (e.g., recognition); and g) aggression—being able to subdue, intimidate, or dominate others (Kirk, Nauright, Hanrahan, Macdonald, & Jobling, 1996). Through sport, people not only compete against, but perform amongst others who have gravitated to the same context in search of something. Playing and competing amongst people of like mind offers the possibility of friendship, shared interests, shared enjoyment, and shared experience, often within a positive context. Sport then serves as more than a means to an end; it is also a process that can enrich people.

Participating in sport can result in many individual benefits. Physically, regular participation in sport can reduce risk of heart disease; help with weight control; improve cholesterol levels; increase energy; prevent bone loss; improve strength, endurance, and flexibility; prevent/control diabetes; increase immunity to minor illnesses; and increase longevity (Mostofsky & Zaichkowsky, 2002). Psychologically, regular participation in sport can reduce depression, reduce state and trait anxiety, improve mood, buffer future stress, improve self-esteem, decrease anger, improve cognitive functioning, enhance emotional well-being, improve the quality of sleep, and increase motivation to make positive lifestyle changes (Mostofsky & Zaichkovsky).

Nevertheless, few have really considered the potency of sport beyond these individual components (most of which could be argued to be the result of any physical activity, not just sport) to consider groups of people and the communities in which they live. We need to look more closely at what sport can offer pockets of society, be they regional, socio-economic, cultural, or several of these considerations combined. Sport development (SD) strikes at the heart of such a discussion. Sport, we propose, can offer the possibility of solutions where change might be needed, be it within an impoverished community or among a sub-population at risk for differential associations, substance abuse, or disease. Through SD projects, those involved might learn behaviors and values through a thoughtfully designed context, that later spur changes among membership such as in the case of a shift from violence to peace. Sport then, may serve as a remedy to societal ills, risks, and hardships, assuming such programs are thoughtfully conceived and made available where and when they are needed to those who need them most.

Sport development (SD) is an emerging topic that crosses disciplinary boundaries. Authors engaging in SD, as you will see, come from the domains of sport management, sport sociology, sport and exercise psychology, and also cultural studies of sport. The approaches taken by academic researchers and practitioners drawn to this new area of study and practice vary, and their endeavors offer up a number of potentially potent strategies for youth, adults, cultural communities, and people from challenged socio-economic backgrounds. SD projects move people well beyond academic knowledge to attempt solutions built in response to some of the world's most pressing challenges. Hence, a natural bridge becomes possible and, we would propose, necessary among those from academia and the community.

But how might one tackle such a broad area of discussion and learn what is needed to create and maintain a successful SD project? Few, if any, SD courses are presently offered at universities. Search course calendars and you will be hard pressed to identify even a single course exclusively devoted to the topic. Instead, you will likely find traditional courses housed within the areas of sport management, sport sociology, sport pedagogy, sport and exercise psychology, and sport sociology. We agree that these traditional human kinetics courses are needed within all of the aforementioned domains, however we propose that SD courses are equally important to students, professionals, and societies, especially in the present day whilst the world appears to be challenged by many social problems. Within SD, discussions will often move beyond conventional boundaries and the confines of a single sport discipline. Instead, people engaged in SD are asked to join forces through an interdisciplinary approach with researchers, practitioners, and community members. The objective is to engage widely in societal challenge/hardship/problems that urgently require resolution and develop initiatives right at the ground level.

Though few, if any, courses in SD are presently provided to aspiring academics and practitioners, the editors and authors in this book wish to challenge readers to broaden the scope of what they think can be achieved through sport and to consider teaching and encouraging this emerging trajectory. To do so, we all need to learn what needs to be learned and then pass on that knowledge where it is most needed. Demands for special topics courses are a hard sell to administrators, especially within the present economy. Nevertheless, as a counterpoint, especially within dire circumstances, people need hope and actions instilled into the contexts where they work, play, and live. It is our hope that SD, first as a special topic, eventually becomes a mainstay in academia, accessible to aspiring practitioners and academics. SD projects can serve as catalysts to change, and what can be achieved through them is only limited by the scope of our vision.

Over the past five or six years, we (Robert and Stephanie) have slowly shifted our visions to research and practice that loosely might be considered SD-related topics. Stephanie's interest in the area of SD began several years before Robert's when she started working with Australian Aboriginal performing artists (Hanrahan, 2004). As part of her work in applied sport psychology/performance enhancement, Stephanie began to look holistically at what might be achieved through physical activity, including the building of confidence and the affirmation of culture, especially among disadvantaged and/or oppressed populations. When Stephanie began her applied work with Indigenous performing artists, she had no idea that through the performing arts, many of her clients sought to overcome cultural mistrust. Dance, theater, and singing became liberating activities, where the Aboriginal performing artists could excel in a multicultural context. Imagine if such lessons were taught en masse to interested youth from cultures and communities where silencing and subversion have erased opportunities and the belief in the possibility of self-determination.

Robert's applied research has been with several culturally oppressed populations, though primarily Canadian indigenous peoples to this point in his career. Initially, Robert's objective was to shine a light on culturally safe sport and exercise psychology practice among the specific population. As a motivational consultant to elite athletes, he has been well aware that the sport psychology offered in many academic contexts is mainstream in approach and therefore not culturally safe across clients from different regions and socialization. Though Robert and his colleagues believe they are successfully branding a domain termed *cultural sport psychology,* their best collaborations have been at the grass roots level with youth and sport service providers, on an Aboriginal reserve (i.e., a designated land where an Aboriginal community resides). The opportunity to engage in an SD project began when Robert was invited to work with his Aboriginal co-researchers on an applied project with an adventure leadership experience crafted as part of the research. Since then the focus of their work has been on developing youth opportunities through sport and physical activity programming on one reserve. Now, the research team is looking to expand their horizons to other reserves wishing for a similar SD opportunity. The youth leadership training the team has been part of continues, and most recently, it has been shifted from academically supported to self-sustaining and self-governed by the reserve.

There is no telling what sort of calling will entice readers to engage in an SD project, or how it will come about. What we can say with confidence is that once you have experienced the richness of such efforts, it will be difficult to consider research and practice that does not offer wide-reaching and tangible benefits. At the heart of each of us is a desire to contribute to a community and be part of its advancement. The present book and the four trajectories that are featured are meant to exemplify the possible avenues for SD research and practice. We would anticipate that what follows in terms of possible trajectories over time will not be definitive, nor exhaustive. Hopefully, new trajectories will be created to match with societal challenges and shifts. Hence, if the simplicity of the forthcoming book is critiqued in the coming years, that would be fine with us, so long as the interest in the area gains in traction.

BOOK TRAJECTORIES

We believe that the breadth of content of this book only teases at the large number of potential topics and projects available to SD scholars and practitioners. As readers can well imagine, the domain of SD is, presently, mostly uncharted. The vast amount of possibilities in terms of location, population, and topic only broaden the potential that presently exists. Consequently, the sections and chapters ought to be regarded as catalytic and not definitive. In the present book we feature four trajectories that seem to reflect much of the SD literature currently available. These four trajectories are *peace and reconciliation, social justice initiatives, health and well-being,* and *corporate social responsibility.* Each of these four types of SD will be briefly described.

Peace and Reconciliation

Peace is not only exemplified by the absence of violence, as Marion Keim articulates in Chapter 2. Peace is defined through proactive strategies developed to restore relationships among people previously or presently in conflict. The four chapters in the first section feature either societies that are presently enmeshed in conflict or societies that are somewhere on the path to peace. Within the section, Alexis Lyras, the author of Chapter 3, describes an international project supported by the International Olympic Committee. A few of the features represent national initiatives, such as those exemplified in Chapter 2 in relation to post-apartheid South Africa, and the work of Roni Lidor and Boris Blumenstein in Chapter 4, where focus is placed on the search for better relations among Israeli and Arab youth through sport. The remaining chapter in the section features work undertaken by Robert Schinke and colleagues at the Canadian local level on an Indigenous reserve (Chapter 5). The scope of the four projects vary from grand to small, but the objective across the projects exemplifies how people with reasons to distrust can reach a shared objective and, through either sport or activity, seek to overcome socio-historical injustices.

Social Justice

The second section pertains to social injustice and how inequities are presently being remedied through SD projects. When perusing this section there is no denying that social injustices continue, even in progressive countries such as Canada. As you will find, social injustices happen in large urban areas and also in remote locations. In Chapter 6 Douglas Hartman takes a close look at highly publicized inner-city youth sport programs. In Chapter 7, Audrey Giles and Mehgan Lynch look through a critical lens at SD projects. The intent of the authors of Chapter 7 is not to create skepticism about SD projects, but rather, to propose a higher degree of awareness among readers about where SD projects can (and might) fall short in their objectives. Chapter 8 features Barbara Ravel's reflections about work with one group of people located at the margins of society—people with alternative sexual orientations. Chapter 9 features the work of Ted Fay and Eli Wolff, who complete the book's trajectory with a focus on sport opportunities for people with disabilities.

Health and Well-being

Within the third section the focus shifts to positive development in the form of physical health and well-being. Though some of the groups featured might also be found in other sections, here the focus is on physical and psychological development through sport and physical activity. In Chapter 10 Stephanie Hanrahan considers how programs incorporating physical games can instill positive worth and life satisfaction among youth in an orphanage. The focus then shifts in Chapter 11 to the work of Glyn Roberts and his colleagues who, over several years, have worked with youth and employed a sport context to educate them about life skills and AIDS awareness. What follows in Chapter 12 is a comprehensive review of youth research. From Dan Gould and colleagues' thorough analysis of the literature, the reader can find possibilities for the next generation of SD projects with youth. The section closes with Jay Coakley's reflections in Chapter 13 about how positive life development for youth can be built through SD projects.

Corporate Social Responsibility

The final section is devoted to the topic of corporate social responsibility. As readers will see when perusing several of the contributions, there are challenges when one seeks to create a bridge between a corporation and a community. Corporations, however, offer important financial resources with which communities can develop effective programming. Hence, in the chapters devoted to this section, the focus is shifted away from the recipient of the SD program, and instead, placed on those funding SD endeavors, be they corporations or municipal governments. In Chapter 14 Michael Giardina and C. L. Cole consider how a professional football organization in New Orleans provided housing for the homeless after Hurricane Katrina. In Chapter 15 Laura Misener and Daniel Mason reflect upon what is left after a major games event for the residents of the host city in terms of lodging and infrastructure. Jeffrey Stinson and Dennis Howard then consider the social responsibility of large American universities. Sport in such institutions is sometimes regarded as big business, and so the authors of Chapter 16 raise evocative questions regarding the responsibilities of varsity sport to the larger university community. Shane Pegg and Ian Patterson end the section by considering what works and what doesn't work from the vantage of the corporations who support SD projects. From their work, the reader is provided with a glimpse into what SD fundraisers need to know if they seek to establish a partnership with a corporation.

HOW TO USE THIS BOOK

This book is intended as a catalyst for administrators, coaches, and academics fascinated by SD in theory and application. Within SD, there will likely be a trajectory that captivates you more than others. Within the trajectory of interest, you will also likely find one or a few topics that really speak to you and encourage reflection and, hopefully, the creation of new ideas that can be shared with others in academia and the community in your region. Should you be a practitioner or community member, you will find in the forthcoming chapters different approaches, not only in terms of context, but also in terms of disciplinary approach. As we have indicated, some chapters are written by sport administrators, others by academics found in the disciplines of sport sociology, sport psychology, and cultural studies of sport. Though each approach is worthy in its own right, it might well be that some of the best answers to come will be from partnerships formed across disciplines using a holistic approach. Dare to consider not only the merits of any idea in context, but also its potential metamorphosis into a new SD project, built in relation to an emerging social/community challenge. Hence, it is our hope that this book stimulates concrete solutions among practitioners and community stakeholders, as well as their collaboration.

We also propose that this book is relevant to the academic readership. For scholars, the present compilation might be referenced in relation to SD projects that also feature applied research in the area. Several of the invited authors were asked to showcase their research projects, not only in terms of application, but also in terms of methodology and scientific results. Such work opens up and, we hope, encourages consideration of the potential partnerships that can be achieved when academic and applied minds meet. For such consumers the topic of a given chapter might stimulate ideas of how an applied methodology might intersect with a societal challenge and stimulate a creative solution, where sport becomes the conduit.

More generally, the authors of each chapter were tasked with the challenge of writing about their projects in a manner where people from any discipline or walk of life might appreciate its content. We suggest that you start off by deciding what interests you about SD literature before you jump into any chapter and begin reading. If you are fascinated by culture, there are several chapters that will intrigue you. You might be interested by a topic where the targeted population is youth at risk. If that is your interest, there are a few chapters provided to satiate. You might be interested more generally in one of the aforementioned trajectories. If that is the case, we have attempted to maintain balance in the number of chapters so that you can read several chapters devoted to your trajectory of interest. More generally, choose whatever chapter topic interests you, and allow your mind to wander to the possibilities that can, but presently do not exist for SD projects in your area.

REFERENCES

Kirk, D., Nuaright, J., Hanrahan, S., Macdonald, D., & Jobling, I. (1996). *The socioculutral foundations of human movement.* Melbourne: Macmillan.

Mostofskty, D. L., & Zaichkovsky, L. D. (Eds.) (2002). Medical *and psychological aspects of sport and exercise.* Morgantown, WV: Fitness Information Technology.

Developing Peace through Community Sport in Multi-ethnic South African Contexts

Marion Keim

"Sport has the power to change the world, the power to inspire, the power to unite people in a way that little else can...[S]port can create hope...[I]t is an instrument for peace." (Nelson Mandela, 1993)

Sport can be seen as a reflection of society, its miseries and success stories, its socio-economic challenges and its values. What better example than South Africa during the glow of the world's biggest football event, the 2010 FIFA World Cup? The World Cup was the first time such a major international sporting event had been held on the African continent, and now there is public aspiration among South Africans of hosting the Olympic Games in the future (Newstime, 2010). The World Cup was an amazing moment for South Africa where sport had been divided through racial lines under South Africa's apartheid government for decades. Sport has always been an important element of the country's culture and has played a crucial role in the struggle for a democratic South Africa.

Questions posed locally and globally: What does this mega soccer event mean to the country and to its people? What socio-economic effect will it have at the grassroots level for ordinary South Africans? What does it mean with regards to development and peace in the local communities and what does it mean with regards to social transformation and nation building for South Africa as a whole? Hopes are high that the 2010 FIFA Football World Cup will have played a key role in the country's sporting history, not only leaving behind an infrastructure and economic benefits, but also a social legacy that enhances nation-building and promotes a peaceful nation. In this chapter I will try to give some insight into the South Africa context and will look at the role sport can play in enhancing and facilitating the development of South Africa's youth and South Africa's communities in terms of building peace at the grassroots level through locally developed and driven initiatives.

SOUTH AFRICA

South Africa is a country in transition, only a decade and a half into democracy. The country displays diversity in cultures, religious beliefs, and languages, with 11 official languages being recognized in one of the most modern constitutions, "The South African Constitution of 1995." South Africa is ethnically diverse with a majority of 79.5 % of its population being of Black African ancestry, divided among various ethnic groups speaking different African languages, nine of which having official status (Statistics South Africa, 2009). The country is also home to the largest European, Indian, and racially mixed communities. For centuries the country suffered under colonialism and apartheid. In the 20th century, after years of internal protests, activism, and insurgency by Black South Africans and their allies, finally in 1990, the South African government began negotiations that led to dismantling of discriminative laws, including in the sphere of sport. In 1994 the first democratic elections took place with Nelson Mandela appointed as South Africa's first democratically elected president.

SPORT AS A CATALYST FOR CHANGE IN SOUTH AFRICA

Sport historically played a crucial role as a dynamic part of civil society in the abolishment of apartheid. As early as the 1950s Black South African sport organizations were pointing out to the world that the racial exclusivity of White sport organizations violated the principle of equality as enshrined in the Olympic Charter. The following principles guided official government policy until 1971, although informally these principles were instituted beyond 1971 (see Archer & Bouillon, 1982):

1. Whites and Non-Whites must organize their sport separately.

2. No mixed sport would be allowed within the boarders of South Africa.

3. International teams competing in South Africa against White South African teams must be all-White.

4. Non-White sportsmen and -women from abroad could compete against Non-White South Africans in South Africa

5. Non-White organizations seeking international recognition must do so through already recognized White sport organizations in their code of sport.

6. The Government would refuse travel visas to "subversive" non-White athletes who sought to discredit South Africa's image abroad or to contest the Government's racial policies.

7. At the 1953 IOC conference in Baden-Baden, South Africa was excluded from the Olympics due to its apartheid policy, which included the complete racial (by law) segregation of sport in South Africa. This exclusion meant that South Africa was not present at the Tokyo Olympics in 1964, nor in subsequent Olympics until 1992.

In the following two decades an array of factors forced the apartheid government to modify its stand on segregation. These factors included the principle of equality with reference to race, religion, or creed in international sport; the great social importance of sport to "White" South Africa; and the effective campaign of the South African Council of Sport for the international isolation of South Africa's racially exclusive "White" sport associations (Keim, 2003). Subsequently in the 1980s and 1990s the opposition to apartheid in sport had gathered enough national and international momentum to gain a victory over segregation in sport. In 1994 for the first time the new democratic government's "(Draft) White Paper" on Sport assured access to sport to all sportsmen and women in South Africa regardless of their skin color (Department of Sport and Recreation, 1995). Allison (2000) remarked,

> In few countries could institutions of civil society (such as sport) outflank and manipulate what appears to be a powerful state in this manner; in no other country, perhaps, could sporting institutions have played so large a part in forming the direction that the state would take. (p. 69)

When South Africa returned to the Olympic Games in Barcelona in 1992, the Olympic Movement was the first to welcome a non-racial South Africa, under the leadership of Nelson Mandela. Nelson Mandela was present at the Olympic Games in Barcelona and has been a strong supporter for sport and the Olympic movement and is a patron of Olympic Truce (which is the status of peace between countries enacted before, during, and after the Olympic Games, an Olympic tradition that allowed athletes to travel safely from their countries to the games and back home).

SOUTH AFRICA TODAY—CURRENT SOCIAL CHALLENGES

Since apartheid ended in 1994, there is a post-conflict and current conflict situation in South Africa, with the world's highest murder and rape rates and increasing xenophobic attacks. South Africa has the highest Gini Coefficient in the world, (the Gini coefficient measures the inequality of income or wealth), the largest number of people with HIV in the world, and increasing tension in civil society sparked by faltering service delivery and governmental corruption.

Apartheid's legacy persists in the form of ongoing separation between racial groups — White, Black, Colored (Asian and mixed-race heritage)—and deep mistrust between individuals. Apartheid destroyed the fabric of trust that holds South African society together, and it has not yet been repaired (Harris, 2003; Hassim, 2009). A social phenomenon factoring into the conflict is the lack of togetherness expressed between different cultural groups. "Conceptions of race and belonging are central both to the violence of South Africa's past and the relative peace of its present" (Pillay, 2005, p. 11). The vast majority of South African children and youth still live in formerly segregated Black and Colored communities, with almost no recreational activities, nor opportunities for healthy multicultural activities to interact and make friends across the cultural divide.

Sport is another area where the challenges in the current South African context are visible. These challenges include limitations in the following areas (see Keim, 2003, 2006):

- Multicultural sport teams beginning at the community level, led by coaches and trainers who are able to navigate team building as a process that includes all parties and creates mutual respect between cultures and races.

- Integration programs between schools.

- Public support, political acceptability and viability, and cooperation between organizations and multicultural exchanges.

- Support for physical education in all primary and high schools.

- Development of facilities for basic and further training.

- Cooperation between schools and sports clubs.

- Convenient conditions for public participation, including accessible transportation, infrastructure, and facilities.

- Close cooperation between different government departments such as the Departments of Sport and Education to ensure a united education and sport policy.

- Coordination of public institutions and structures of government, organized sport, providers of social services, and leisure activities with regard to development.

- Involvement of the media in asking critical questions about sport in South Africa and discussing the use of sport as a tool for social transformation.

- Improvement in the situation of women in sport.

- Introduction of a form of assessment to ensure that stated social and transformational goals for sport and community development are met.

- Development of a national policy framework that incorporates sport and recreation and physical activities into community development policies and peace-building initiatives.

There are no "quick fix" solutions for South Africa's problems. Coordinated approaches are needed to overcome the injustices and hurt of the past and facilitate healing and building of trust. Sport can be one of the tools to facilitate the healing process and thus contribute to community development, social transformation, and peace building.

THE CONCEPTS OF PEACE AND PEACE BUILDING

We succeeded to take our last steps to freedom in conditions of relative peace. We commit ourselves to the construction of a complete, just and lasting peace. ...We enter into a covenant where we shall build the society in which all South Africans, both black and white, will be able to walk tall, without any fear in their hearts, assured of their inalienable right to human dignity—a rainbow nation at peace with itself and the world. (Nelson Mandela, Inauguration Speech, May 10, 1994)

Building peace is a long-term process including activities to build and promote peace and overcome violence (Pfaffenholz, 2003). Galtung (1964) distinguished between *negative peace,* referring to the absence of violence, and *positive peace,* the restoration of relationships and the integration of human society through the creation of social systems that serve the needs of the whole population. More recently, he proposed a holistic approach to peace building in the form of *3 Rs: Reconstruction* of people and places, *reconciliation* of relationships, and *resolution* of issues and animosities (Galtung, 1998). Developing peace is therefore also about identifying and understanding the notion and nature of factors obstructing peace within a crosscultural and multidisciplinary context (e.g., underlying unjust and discriminatory structures and practices). The objective is not simply to eliminate or control these factors, but rather to facilitate a change process focused on the identified factors and thus striving towards positive, sustainable peace.

An interesting aspect is to compare the Western World's and the South African concepts of peace. The term *peace* derives from the Latin word "pax" and is, in the Western World, generally understood as "a contractual relationship that implies mutual recognition and agreement" (Miller, 2005, p. 56). Others see peace as a "political condition that ensures justice and social stability through formal and informal institutions, practices and norms" (Miller, p. 55). In isiXhosa, one of the eleven official South African languages, the word for peace is "uxolo" which covers a state of inner tranquility and an atmosphere of peace, but also implies asking for forgiveness. In the context of South Africa's recent history, sport has been used as a tool for forgiveness.

Efforts to promote peace building, forgiveness, and healing were much discussed in post-Apartheid South Africa. One attempt by the new government to move forward towards peace building, healing, forgiveness, unity, and ubuntu, the African concept of humanness, was the Truth and Reconciliation Commission. The Promotion of National Unity and Reconciliation Act (Act NO. 34, 1995, p.1) reads as follows:

> . . . [T]he Constitution states that the pursuit of national unity, the well-being of all South African citizens and peace require reconciliation between the people of South Africa and the reconstruction of society; . . . [T]he Constitution states that there is a need for understanding but not for vengeance, a need for reparation but not for retaliation, a need for ubuntu but not for victimization. (SDC, 2005)

In post-apartheid South Africa, sport has been seen by politicians, sports officials, and many ordinary people as a means to overcome race and class barriers and to forge social transformation, a national identity, and development. The former Minister of Sport and Recreation (and later Minister of Community Safety) Stephen Tshwete, believed that "Sport exerts an immeasurable influence as a unifying force for reconciliation and for the process of nation-building" (Interview 24 June 1994, in Keim 2003, p. 171).

THE POWER OF SPORT

Peace can be built through various approaches and activities, sport being one of them. Sport can assist in the creation of a social system that serves the needs of its population (especially but not exclusively, the youth), and it can contribute to the 3 Rs, especially in the area of reconciliation of relationships because sport has the advantage of "speaking a simple language" and creating role models. Sport can change attitudes, increase peoples' self esteem, and help the disadvantaged to discover and experience their own strengths (Keim, 2003). Research conducted in South Africa in the early 1990s indicated that in 1994 South Africans believed in the ability of sport to influence the transformation process in a positive way and to contribute to the creation of a national identity (Keim). The role of soccer was repeatedly mentioned.

Nelson Mandela experienced the power of sport during his imprisonment on Robben Island and also more generally in the struggle against the apartheid system in South Africa. He has recognized the important role of sport in providing a platform to unite people of different cultural, political, and religious backgrounds, and thus for peace building and social transformation in post-apartheid South Africa. Unforgettable was the moment when he and Archbishop Desmond Tutu both wore the Springbok jersey at the 1995 Rugby World Cup, celebrating with the nation the victory of the South African team only one year after the country's first democratic election. The act of wearing the Springbok jersey of an all-White Afrikaaner team was considered a defining moment on the country's path to peace and nation building.

Both Mandela and Tutu, as the spiritual leader, believe in the power of sport. Tutu, who is the patron for the Kicking for Peace initiative, maintained,

> Through properly organized sport we can learn to play together with respect and with laughter, we can learn to all be on the same team and in the process we can contribute to building a new South Africa that is a just nation for all (Archbishop Tutu, in Keim, 2003, p. 9).

Mandela's speech at the "Signatures for the Truce" event in Athens, on June 19, 2002, touched on the problems facing our societies and communities especially, but not exclusively, in South Africa.

> Sport, and the example and influence of leading athletes, can make an impact in tackling some of our serious social problems. These include the restoration of the culture of teaching and learning in our schools, and the reintegration of the so-called marginalized youth into the mainstream of society. Likewise with the problems of violence and drug abuse. The Olympic Truce to be observed during the Olympic Games eloquently demonstrates the positive influence that sport can make. I heartily welcome the central themes of the Games: global peace, strengthening of family ties and general upliftment of young people. I know the message will touch a chord in all our hearts. (p. 8)

It should be noted that the above view places a somewhat idealistic lens on the International Olympic Committee's contribution to societal betterment through sport. Some have correctly disputed this belief and instead proposed that the Olympic truce is an ideal aspiration, and not much else. Nevertheless, the promise of hope and unity through sport is something much needed in South Africa.

Translating the Vision of Sport into Community Action

Through community research, Keim (2003) revealed that, if administered properly, sport is seen as a potential and manifold benefit to South African communities. Sport as a tool for peace building and community development should not only be seen as competitive, but also as a recreational activity holistically applied and inclusive of all ages, genders, population groups, abilities/disabilities. Whereas government approaches to peace building are mostly conducted as top-down, civil society actors mainly use bottom-up approaches, beginning within communities, by their people.

The following South African sport initiative is a grass roots approach by civil society to build peace from the bottomup. It incorporates the idea of sport as a tool for peace building driven by the spirit of Coubertin's Olympic Truce and takes it to the level of community action as suggested by Mandela. The example below affirms that sport as a tool for peace building is not a myth. Rather, peace through sport can be a reality if certain factors are taken into consideration, such as promoting role models of different cultural groups, multilingual educators, integration programs between schools, awareness campaigns supported by media, and multicultural sports programs with special attention to choice of venue, time, transport, and coaches (Keim, 2003).

Western Cape Network for Community Peace and Development

The Kicking for Peace initiative is a soccer program run by the Western Cape Network for Community Peace and Development, a unique collaboration of 40 NGOs, local communities, and the University of the Western Cape, supported by the provincial government and the City of Cape Town. The Network is a collectively guided independent and registered non-profit provincial umbrella organization of 40 NGOs working in the field of conflict resolution, youth, women, community development and peace building, and sport in the Western Cape. Its members share common values and so empowerment, youth development, peace building, conflict management, democracy, sustainable development, human dignity, diversity, integrity, transparency, accountability, and nondiscrimination became binding principles. These common values (see Network Constitution, 2007) help to create conflict-free and sustainable communities and provide a platform from which the Network can work.

The activities of the Network are geared towards building conflict resolution and peace-building capacity in civil society as well as the building of stronger relationships between civil society, academic institutions, and government. The active exchange of ideas, approaches, and work experiences in the field happens at regular meetings, every six weeks. Joint initiatives such as community programs, training, youth projects like the Kicking for Peace Soccer initiative of the "Sport for Peace" Network program, and research, are priorities for the Network. The Network aspires to become a replicable model for other provinces and provides guidance for others to establish similar networks in a creative and collaborative way. The outcomes of the Network's efforts since its inception in 2005 include the establishment and support of a provincial network for organizations, academic institutions, and government departments striving for community peace and development.

The Network assisted in the analysis of training needs as well as the training capacity of current Network partners and in accessing service providers who can offer training and any other support with regard to community peace and development. Through the provision of regular seminars and forums, the Network discusses areas of interest and build strong relationships amongst similar organizations. Other outcomes include the mobilization of communities to address issues of gang violence, violence against women and children, youth at risk, social transformation, healing, and the implementation of community-based programs for children and youth involving sport as a means for conflict prevention and transformation, peace building, and social change.

The Network uses sport as a tool for community development, social transformation, and peace building and established a Sport for Peace program in 2006. In its Sport for Peace program the Network is guided by the visions of Pierre de Coubertin and Nelson Mandela. It uses sport as a training tool for an active, healthy life style, but also as a vehicle for fostering sportsmanship, friendships, citizenship, and social inclusion. A combined sport and life skills program emphasizes the important role sport can play as a means for empowerment and personal development, and for social transformation and reconstruction, crime prevention, peace building, and democracy.

Apart from Coubertin's belief in the value of sport, these findings are also reflected in the work of many international authors and sport and government agencies over the last three decades, including Coakley (1978), Jarvie and Macquire (1994), Swanepoel (1997), Allison (2000), The Magglingen Call to Action (see United Nations, 2005), Swiss Agency for Development Cooperation (2005), Keim (2006), and Vanden Aauweele et al. (2006). Nevertheless, there is limited international, national, and local qualitative and quantitative research to ensure that internationally stated social and transformational goals for sport, peace building, and community development are being met. In addition there is my own critique about the limited inclusion of civil society organizations and community members in research processes themselves (see Keim, 2009).

Taking into account the outcomes and findings stated above, the Network embarked on the Kicking for Peace Project, a soccer program for children and youth from diverse communities. This project includes civil society as part of the research process and works in partnership with the University of the Western Cape in the planning, implementation, monitoring, and evaluation stages of its holistic sport and life skills program.

Kicking for Peace

Kicking for Peace is a grassroots initiative using sport to develop skills and attitudes that help build a just, peaceful society. It brings together boys and girls from volatile, formerly segregated communities in South Africa to share the joys of soccer and learn life skills that transform them into citizens equipped to live together peaceably and for all to participate cooperatively in the peaceful development of our nation. Children in these communities have few extracurricular programs, little supervision, and minimal contact with the world outside their townships. Kicking for Peace reduces violence by giving youth something to belong to without joining a gang. Multicultural soccer teams provide a healthy alternative to drugs and crime.

The project offers multilingual activities using sport as a tool for conflict resolution, peace building, and social transformation. Essential skills are taught for a just and harmonious society to build bridges across racial divides through soccer. These life skills modules include conflict transformation skills, communication, problem solving, leadership, community development, and peace building skills. The youth learn about fair play and about managing conflict and communicating with peers from different backgrounds, where few extramural activities or recreational programs are taking place. Their capacities for trust, love, and dedication grow as they develop respect for themselves and others from whom they were forcibly separated. Attitude change is measured though participatory evaluations conducted in cooperation with the University of the Western Cape. A focus of this initiative is to use soccer as a vehicle to bring different communities together leading to nation building and reconciliation. The Network believes *Kicking for Peace* will assist in the social transformation of South Africa's communities and at the same time spread the enthusiasm of soccer to all communities in the Western Cape. Preliminary results suggest a change of awareness among the participants. The participants indicated the program helps them to "get to know one another, to respect other players and people, to learn trust and work as a team, to be peaceful and communicate with respect" (Keim 2009, p. 86).

The project's long-term goal is to build a South Africa that is free of prejudice and violence. In addition, accredited training in conflict resolution and coaching courses are offered with the University of the Western Cape. In 2009, 60 coaches and mentors were trained, and in 2010, 150 sports youth leaders were trained in conflict resolution and leadership skills as part of the City of Cape Town's 2010 Leadership Program. These training programs have affected a total of 50 communities, each with approximately 300,000 inhabitants, fostering tolerance and understanding, whilst nurturing cooperation.

Lessons Learned: Practical Insights from the *Kicking for Peace* Project

When working in a place that has yet to recover from violent conflict, segregation, and social or ethnic exclusion, it has been proven crucial for the Network to involve parties from all cultural groups. The Western Cape Network for Community Peace and Development is a unique grassroots network that brings together South Africa's disenfranchised Black populations with White and Colored groups.

The project's success depends on being able to reach across sociohistorical and cultural divides that have demarcated South African communities for decades. By initiating the project through a network of 40 NGOs and other entities, the project can reach more deeply into communities and achieve greater participation than a single NGO could have. Every hour spent in sport and life skills training is an hour not spent in activities that undermine youth's lives, such as drugs, gangsterism, and crime. The model is easily replicable in other South African provinces and internationally with the potential to serve millions of children.

The Network facilitates a process of social healing and giving voice to people who have been historically silenced and separated by apartheid. The objective of *Kicking for Peace* is to build new confidence, respect, and trust among youth and adults. Operating the project through a broad-ranging, multicultural network is the best way to achieve that objective. This multicultural setup supports the project's fundamental goal of restoring true democracy and a peaceful and caring society in South Africa.

THE WAY FORWARD

The overall aim of peace building is to prevent violent outbreaks of conflicts or to make a sustainable transformation of violent conflict into peaceful actions (Pfaffenholz, 2003). Many challenges remain to be addressed, and many problems remain unsolved that would speed up the process of community development and peace building in South Africa. Sport has a meaningful function for social transformation, community development, and peace building in South African society. Whether sport can, in fact, fulfill this function and play this challenging role of a community-developing, peace-building vehicle depends, to a large extent, on the specific way in which sport is organized and presented. On its own, sport cannot reverse poverty or prevent crime or violence, solve unemployment, stop corruption, and respect human rights. The establishment and support of a provincial and even national network for organizations, academic institutions, and government departments striving for community peace and development is therefore vital.

In my view there is too little research and therefore too little recognition of how both recreational and professional sport at the community level are used as a positive force for reconstruction, development, reconciliation, and peace. To counteract the negative effects of poverty, violence, and crime, we need innovative and effective interventions to actively promote community development and peace building and thus create safer communities. Those in influential sport positions have yet to come to terms with the important influence they have and can have on South African society.

Consequently, more public discussions are needed, such as the roundtable panel discussion of the Helen Suzman Foundation in May 2010 where the following questions were raised that remain vital to all of us who work in the sport and development field: What are the challenges that exist globally in building effective and successful sporting initiatives that can enhance social cohesion and peace building, and how can these challenges be overcome?

As the host of the 2010 FIFA World Cup South Africa attracted increased attention and widespread public interest. The degree to which sport becomes a key part of the solution to pressing social and developmental challenges depends on global and local role players as well as the residents of South Africa. The World Cup is supposed to leave a legacy with regards to infrastructure, tourism, and also nation-building whilst creating a common identity. I would like to end with a quote from our former President Nelson Mandela,

> A united, non-racial, non-sexist and democratic South Africa is the best hope for handing over such a society to our children. It is a vision which we promote vigorously. It is a vision which we invite you to examine, to refine and to enrich. It is, if necessary, a vision which we invite you all to surpass. (1991, p. 13)

REFERENCES

Allison, L. (Ed.). (2000). *Taking sport seriously*. (2nd ed.). Oxford, UK: Meyer & Meyer Sport.

Archer, R., & Bouillon, A. (1982). *The South African game: Sport and racism*. London: Zed Press.

Coakley, J. J. (1978). *Sport in society: Issues and controversies*. St. Louis, IL: Mosby.

Department of Sport and Recreation, South Africa. (Eds.). (1995). *White paper (Draft). Sport and recreation in South Africa. A national policy framework*. Pretoria: Government Printer.

Galtung, J. (1964). An editorial. *Journal of Peace Research 1*, 1-4.

Galtung, J. (1998). *Peace by peaceful means: Peace and conflict, development and civilization*. Oslo: International Peace Research Institute.

Harris, B. (June, 2003). *Spaces of violence, places of fear: Urban conflict in postapartheid South Africa*. Paper presented at the conflict and urban violence panel. Cartagena, Columbia.

Hassim, S. (2009). After apartheid: Consensus, contention, and gender in South Africa's public sphere. *International Journal of Politics, Culture and Society, 22*, 453-464.

Helen Suzman Foundation. (31 May, 2010). Round table panel discussion on Sport and Nation building. Johannesburg, South Africa.

Jarvie, G., & Maguire, J. A. (1994). *Sport and leisure in social thought*. London: Routledge.

Keim, M. (2003). *Nation-building at play—Sport as a tool for social integration in post-apartheid South Africa*. Oxford, UK: Meyer & Meyer Sport.

Keim, M. (2006). Sport as opportunity for community development and peace building in South Africa. In Y. Vanden Auweele, C. Malcom, & B. Meulders (Eds.), *Sport and development* (pp. 97-106). Leuven, Belgium: Uitgeverij Lannoo Press.

Keim, M. (2009) *Translating Olympic truce into community action in South Africa—Myth or possibility in Olympic truce-peace and sport* (pp. 77-89). Olympia, Greece: International

Olympic Truce Centre.

Mandela N. (1991). *Vision für Südafrika.* Speech at the opening of the IDASA conference in Johannesburg: Der Überblick 4/91, Frankfurt, Germany.

Mandela N. (1993). *Mandela, Nobel Peace Prize.* Retrieved from http://igbarb19.wordpress.com/2009/09/

Mandela, N. (May 10, 1994). *Inauguration speech.* Retrieved from http://www.anc.org.za/ancdocs/history/mandela/1994/inaugpta.html

Miller, C. E. (2005). A glossary of terms and concepts in peace and conflict studies. *University for Peace, Africa Programme.* San Jose, Costa Rica: University for Peace.

Network Constitution. (2007). Constitution of the Western Cape Network for Community Peace and Development, unpublished document, Cape Town.

Newstime. (July 12, 2010). *S A Olympic bid in the pipeline.* Retrieved from http://www.newstime.co.za/Sport/SA_Olympic_bid_in_the_pipeline/7607/8

Pfaffenholz, T. (2003). *Community-based bottom-up peacebuilding.* Life and Peace Institute, Nairobi, Kenya: Modern Lithographic.

Pillay, S. (2005). The radical imagination of peace: Belonging and violence in South Africa's past and future. *African Journal on Conflict Resolution, Vol. 5,* 11- 33. Durban, South Africa: The African Centre for the Constructive Resolution of Disputes (ACCORD).

Statistics South Africa. (2009). Statistics South Africa statistical release P0302. Retrieved from http://www.statssa.gov.za/PublicationsHTML/P03022009/html/P03022009.html

Swanepoel, H. (1997). *Community development: Putting plans into actions.* (3rd ed.). Pretoria, South Africa: J. L. Van Schaik.

Swiss Agency for Development Cooperation. (Eds.). (2005). The *Promotion of National Unity and Reconciliation* (Act, NO. 34 of 1995) Retrieved from http://www.info.gov.za/acts/1995/a34-95.pdf

United Nations. (2005). *The Magglingen Call to Action 2005.* Retrieved from http://www.un.org/sport2005/newsroom/magglingen_call_to_action.pdf

Vanden Aauweele, Y., Malcom, C., Meulders, B., Avis, P., Bosmans, M., Keim, M., et al. (Eds.). (2006). *Sport and development.* Leuven, Belgium: Uitgeverij Lannoo Press.

The Doves Olympic Movement Project: Integrating Olympism, Development, and Peace

Alexis Lyras

It is universally accepted that sport, under certain conditions, can play an important role in promoting a culture of peace. The United Nations (UN) General Assembly unanimously adopted a resolution entitled "Building a peaceful and better world through sport and the Olympic ideals" at its 54th Session on November 24, 1999 (IOC, 2000). The following extract from the address of Secretary General of the UN to the World Conference on Education and Sport for a Culture of Peace sets out clearly the UN's collective view on the matter:

> Be it team competition or individual athletics, sport has long displayed an inspiring ability to overcome national, political, ethnic and cultural differences. Sport, in short, is an instrument of understanding among people. It is a vehicle for education about the world at large. It can be especially powerful in instilling in children and young people universal values such as respect and tolerance (IOC, 1999).

Since 1999, a number of UN agencies, the European Union, the International Olympic Committee, and a number of national and international sport and humanitarian organizations have urged the use of sport practices as a medium of resolving a number of challenges that youth face globally (e.g., juvenile delinquency, racism, crosscultrual intolerance).

Sport, however, can also be considered a double-edged sword with positive and negative outcomes (Bairner, 1999; Hardy, 1996; Horne, 1996; Martens, 1993; Rees, 1996), especially in countries where conflict exists (Saunders & Sugden, 1997; Sugden, 2006; Sudgen & Harvie, 1995). Given that the institution of sport can influence both stability and conflict, we often see sport practices that can bring a community together or lead to discord. Sport programs and policies that aim to leverage youth development and educational objectives should be driven by theory and grounded in evidence (Lyras, 2007, 2009, 2010).

Through this chapter a case study approach will be used, analyzing an alternative, theory-driven, research-oriented sport initiative working for peace and development in Cyprus, called Doves Olympic Movement Project (Doves Project). The purpose of this chapter is to provide the theoretical foundations and assumptions on which the methodology of the Doves Project was grounded (Lyras, 2003, 2007; Lyras, Yiannakis, & Kartakoullis, 2005, 2006, 2007), and then discuss the implications of similar Sport for Development and Peace (SFDP) projects around the globe. Information about the context and the historical background of the Cyprus conflict will also be provided.

SPORT FOR DEVELOPMENT AND PEACE: A COMPLEX SOCIAL PROBLEM-SOLVING PROCESS

Sport for Development and Peace (SFDP) projects deal with challenges that entail social, psychological, societal, institutional, and political complexities (Lyras, 2007). Therefore, the social and political context of each situation and each country should be carefully considered in the design and implementation of any sport intervention aimed at achieving reconciliation and change (Lyras, 2007, 2009; Sugden, 2006, 2007; UN, 2003, 2005). Consistent with these guidelines, a holistic and detailed representation of the social context of the Cyprus society will be presented to evaluate and understand the effects and the limitations of the Doves Project in Cyprus, and potentially conceptualize similar implications in other regions.

The present chapter adheres to a threefold model in an attempt to present the complexity of the Cyprus problem. The following section (a) provides historical and political background information about Cyprus, (b) describes the components and assumptions of the Doves Project methodology, and (c) discusses the theoretical linkages between the methods used in the Doves initiative and the existing scientific body of knowledge.

HISTORICAL CONTEXT OF THE CYPRUS PROBLEM

People are trapped in history, and history is trapped in them.
—James Baldwin

Cyprus has a long history of interethnic conflict between Greek Cypriots, who represent the 77% of the population of the island, and Turkish Cypriots who represent 18% of the legal population of the island. For almost four decades Cyprus has been a divided island. Greek and Turkish Cypriots have been living in their own separate communities with minimal contact or communication. Compounding this state of affairs is that the two communities are also separated by differences in religion, ethnicity, and language. This separation has contributed to a level of mistrust, fear, and insecurity, which has made it difficult for the two communities to live and work together in peace. The complexity and the controversies of the Cyprus problem at both the national and the international level have kept both communities segregated and in a state of hostility for more than 40 years.

The unsettled political aspects of the Cyprus problem create an unstable situation on the island and present obstacles to the development of both communities. One of the biggest roadblocks to progress in interethnic relations, however, can be attributed to the divergent historiographies of the two groups. According to Papadakis (1998, 2003, 2004, 2008), the structure of the divided nation, the national commemorations of each community (Greek and Turkish Cypriot), and the way history is taught in schools are constructed in a way that reproduces social memories of intercommunal conflict, nationalism, opposition, fear, hate, and insecurity.

Papadakis (1998, 2003, 2004, 2008) also stated that the memories of the Cypriots are constructed and transferred from one generation to another in a way that reproduces images of war, conflict, and insecurity. Such settings promote the construction of two completely different narratives based on opposing perspectives and contradictory rationales. The descriptions below are intended to provide the content of the "national histories" that promote what Papadakis called the sense of the "self righteousness" of each community.

The history of Cyprus, simplistically described by Greek and Turkish Cypriots, clearly indicates the distinctions that exist between the two communities. A Turkish Cypriot would say:

> Greek Cypriots always wanted unification with Greece and never accepted us as citizens of this island. For more than a decade (from 1960 until 1974) we lived in fear and hostility. The Greek Cypriots never accepted the idea of coexistence and they made every effort they could to isolate us and get us out of their way. Coexistence was impossible. In 1963 we were put in enclaves for our own

safety. Life before 1974 was terrible and we were often afraid that we might lose our lives. Greek Cypriots always viewed us as second-class citizens and Turkey made a "peaceful operation" to protect us from "ethnic cleansing." In 1983 we established a separate government and we have been seeking international recognition since then. Greek Cypriots want to exclude us from receiving the benefits of the European Union and they don't want to live with us or share with us any kind of political and economic power. We should also get all the benefits of the EU and Greek Cypriots shouldn't put obstacles in our way. We voted *yes* to the UN and Secretary General Annan's peace plan for a solution to the problem, but we doubt that Greek Cypriots truly seek co-existence.

A Greek Cypriot would probably state:

Cyprus is a Greek island that has been occupied by Turkish troops since 1974. The island's Greek identity can be easily identified through the cultural heritage of the island. We survived through the years of Ottoman and British rule and even if *"enosis"* (unification) with Greece was not possible due to the circumstances of the international scene, we gained our independence in 1960. Turkey was always "in our way" and Turkish troops invaded in 1974. Since then we have been trying to find a solution for the Cyprus problem. Turkish Cypriots took our homes and have been trying to obtain legitimacy for their so-called "government." They pretend that they want a solution of the Cyprus problem because now we are members of the European Union. Through hard work and education we managed to become members of the European Union and now Turkish Cypriots want to be friends with us to take advantage of the benefits of the European Union. Turkish Cypriots do what they are told to do and Turkey controls their "government." We rejected the UN plan for a solution in 2004 because we cannot trust the army that invaded and killed our people, and surely, a solution that does not secure all fundamental human rights is unacceptable. They opened the checkpoints not because they love us but because they want to get the benefits that our government provides them (medical services and financial support). They just want to get a passport so that they can obtain the benefits from the European Union. For thirty years, the Turkish Cypriots didn't want any interaction; now they pretend that they want us. Turkish Cypriots get the benefits that we provide to them, but at the same time they want to "legitimate" the division of the island.

Such positions are a fairly accurate portrayal of the mainstream attitudes and beliefs of the Greek and Turkish Cypriots. These paraphrased descriptions, based on personal experience and a variety of Turkish and Greek Cypriot sources, attempt to provide a comprehensive and balanced picture.

CYPRUS, THE EUROPEAN UNION, AND THE DOVES PROJECT

In May 2004, Cyprus joined the European Union. The European social model provides new perspectives for the members of both the Greek and Turkish Cypriot communities to help develop practices based on common interests and goals. Building trust between the young Greek and Turkish Cypriots is a crucial factor that could greatly contribute to laying the foundations for helping to resolve the many problems that confront both communities in Cyprus. The Cyprus problem remains unresolved and the members of the Greek and Turkish Cypriot communities live separately in the absence of understanding, trust, and social integration.

The use of sports programs as a medium to reach children has not been widely used in Cyprus (Lyras, 2003, 2004, 2005). The Doves Project (Lyras, 2001, 2003), an educational sport initiative based on Olympism (sports and cultural enrichment activities), was pioneered to help bring the two communities together to achieve personal and social change. The curriculum of the Doves Project (Lyras, 2003) uses the Olympism model (a blend of sports, education, cultural enrichment activities, and Olympic ideals) and is divided into two major theme areas. The first theme refers to *physical activities* and includes various sports, a treasure hunt, hiking, dance, and music. Physical activities are not performance oriented, with little emphasis on winning, and are mainly used as a vehicle toward achieving educational objectives. The second theme refers to a number of multidisciplinary *educational topics* that provide students with skills and knowledge in diverse areas of their lives. The educational topics include workshops and activities that speak to human rights issues, the Olympic spirit, conflict management, environmental awareness, health and well-being, and technology. Such a multidisciplinary context is intended to help facilitate fundamental practices for peace building, international cooperation, understanding, and enhance global awareness (Amara, Aquilina, Henry, & Taylor, 2005; Fountain, 1999; Mechikoff & Sullivan, 2001; Reich & Pivovarov, 1994; United Nations, 2003, 2005).

Assumptions of the Doves Project

In this section, learning theory and cognitive and social psychology are used as the theoretical basis to provide the assumptions and rationale of the proposed methods and activities used in the Doves Project to effectively reduce conflict and tension between the Cypriot youth.

Intergroup contact: Principles that facilitate positive psychological outcomes. During the first years after World War II, social scientists increased their efforts to provide scientific guidelines that help prevent racism, discrimination, and cross-group intolerance. Allport (1954), who was among the first scientists to provide a substantial theoretical framework regarding intergroup contact, suggested that contact between diverse groups (any group of people who share similar characteristics such as sex, ethnic, or racial factors) is the most effective tool for reducing racism, prejudice, and discrimination. In situations where there is a lack of interaction and intergroup contact "prejudice and conflict grow like a disease" (Brameld, 1946, p. 24, as cited by Pettigrew & Tropp, 2006). According to Allport, cross-group contact can be positive and effective only when certain criteria are satisfied. These criteria refer to (a) equal status among the members of the groups; (b) common goals as the purpose and the framework of the contact; (c) intergroup cooperation that would help the diverse groups reach their goals; and (d) the support from the authorities, structures, and institutions of a society. Recent findings add (e) "friendship potential" as the fifth principle (Pettigrew, 1998; Pettigrew & Tropp, 2006).

These principles are considered important factors that help individuals develop positive emotions and cognitions with out-group members, but they do not guarantee positive intergroup contact (Pettigrew, 1998; Pettigrew & Tropp, 2006). In other words, the presence of the four intergroup contact principles (e.g., equal status, common goals, intergroup cooperation, support from authorities) does not ensure the decrease or elimination of prejudice. Instead, these principles only facilitate the process of breaking down the barriers of stereotypes and prejudice. Research indicates that there is an absence of substantial evidence regarding (a) the process of the development of positive emotions and cognitions toward out-group members, and (b) the extent to which the positive outcomes from cross-group contact can be generalizable to people with similar characteristics (Pettigrew, 1998; Pettigrew & Tropp, 2006).

Sternberg developed two theories that explain the process of how relationships are formed, helping us understand how emotions and cognitions interact and interplay: the triangular theory of love (Sternberg, 1986, 1994; Sternberg, Hojjat, & Barnes, 2001) and the duplex theory of hate (Sternberg, 2003). Both theories state that in any kind of relationship there are three distinctive components: passion, intimacy, and commitment. According to these theories, individuals construct a story about a person or a group of people through their education, their peers, and their families. According to the story people possess, they approach other people with positive or negative emotions (passionate to love or to hate). The cognitive dimensions (e.g., stereotypes, values, beliefs, behaviors) are distinctly different from the affective indicators and depend more closely on the quantity and quality of the contact (Sternberg, 1986, 1994, 2003; Sternberg et al., 2001). In group contact, individuals either verify their existing stories of who is "good" or "bad" or re-construct new stories with more positive emotions and cognitions. Through interaction, individuals test their existing cognitive stories and then make a conscious decision that relates to the level of intimacy (close relationship or casual) and commitment (dedicated to love, to hate, or to kill). In other words, individuals, in any kind of relationship, make a continuous negotiation of passion, intimacy, and commitment.

Prejudice, according to Pettigrew and Tropp (2006), has two distinctive dimensions, the affective and the cognitive. These two psychological dimensions have different "mechanics" because empathy and positive feelings about an out-group member are more easily developed compared with the cognitive indicators of inter-group tolerance (Pettigrew & Tropp). The cognitive dimension of prejudice is considered a more complex process and might require the possession of higher mental functions. Affective outcomes, on the other hand, can more easily be generalized to out-group members when compared with cognitive outcomes (Pettigrew & Tropp). This information can be useful because it helps us understand that feeling good, safe, and secure are the first building blocks for interacting with the "unknown." Such conditions reduce intergroup anxiety and help individuals to be creative and develop higher mental and psychological functions (Maslow, 1970, 1971, 1998).

Humanistic foundations of development. According to the most established theorists of human development, people need a safe and autonomous environment, love and esteem, relatedness, and competence to meet their potential (Maslow, 1970; Ryan & Deci, 2000). People also need to think beyond "self," understand concepts that go beyond what they see and touch, and develop higher mental processes that enable them to develop their ideologies, have a vision, be creative, care about universal issues, and meet their potentials (Corsini 1994; Maslow, 1970; Vygotsky, 1978). During this developmental process, a person has continuous internal and external conflicts. To resolve such conflicts, people choose friends and select mentors that potentially can help them construct themselves, their beliefs, and their morality (Corsini, 1994; Vygotsky, 1978).

A relationship exists between personal and moral development and the development of higher mental processes (Maslow, 1970, 1971, 1998; Ryan & Deci, 2000; Sternberg, 2003). A self-actualized person should be able to think and act beyond self and nation, understand the need of a holistic co-existence in a global world, understand and accept diversity, and act toward meeting his or her potential. Such behaviors require the application of higher mental processes and the ability to find solutions to everyday problems (Sternberg, 2003).

It is difficult to specify all the measurable and intangible variables that need to be achieved to promote peace in divided communities and situations such as Cyprus. The intercommunal conflict of the island and the limited interethnic interaction, have contributed to limited interethnic tolerance between the Turkish Cypriot and Greek Cypriot communities. The recent history of the world teaches that segregation based on race, religion, and ethnicity facilitates and perpetuates the more negative dimensions of humanity as manifested in various forms of hate, revenge, ethnic cleansing, and genocide (Allport, 1954; Pettigrew, 1998; Pettigrew & Tropp, 2006; Sternberg, 2003). According to Sternberg (2003), a society can resist segregation practices by applying "one's intelligence and experience toward a common good through balancing one's own, other and institutional interests over the short and long terms" (p. 234).

Humanistic and social psychologists often suggest that through the development of a common "self-righteousness" we can establish stability, coexistence, understanding and tolerance for anything that is different from us (Allport, 1954; Pettigrew, 1998; Pettigrew & Tropp, 2006; Sternberg, 2003). Human beings, however, need to satisfy basic physiological and psychological needs to be able to self-actualize, to grow and develop, and to accept themselves and others (Maslow, 1970, 1971, 1998; Ryan & Deci, 2000).

Doves Project 2005-2010: Moving from Theory into Practice

Based on the posited foundations and inspired by the philosophy and the objectives of Olympism, Lyras and colleagues developed the first sport educational initiative that was implemented in Cyprus, named Doves Olympic Movement (Doves Project). The Doves Project was founded in 2001 and aims to provide evidence-based non-traditional educational sport practices to resolve a number of social problems such as crosscultural intolerance, juvenile delinquency, isolation of marginalized populations, and racism. Through the Doves Project, sport and education stakeholders and youth from diverse socioeconomic backgrounds, genders, religions, and ethnicities come together and engage in activities that facilitate character development and promote social inclusion. The program was designed with support provided by the Olympic Solidarity (Lyras, 2001, 2003) and the Cyprus Research Foundation (Lyras, 2007). During the last five years the Doves Project (2005-2010) implemented a number of initiatives that were funded by United Nations Development Program, United Nations Office of Program Services, and United States Agency for International Development (Lyras et al., 2005, 2006, 2007).

In the summer of 2005, the Doves Olympic Movement conducted the first bi-communal educational sport initiative in Cyprus. Most of the Doves Project participants acknowledged that, "this summer program was a very strong verification that human beings have no differences" (Lyras, 2005, p. 3). Participants also mentioned that "everybody feels that one week is not enough. In the camp we established strong relationships; we became one big family and we should continue to see each other after the camp" (Lyras, 2005, p. 3). Such expressions indicate that sports, in an educational and non-political setting, have the potential to empower individuals and societies. It seems that sports, under certain conditions, have the power to prepare the ground for a better future of the youth of Cyprus.

Since 2005 the Doves Project participants have implemented community-based initiatives related to the protection of the environment, enhancement of social inclusion of people with disabilities and underprivileged youth, and the development of active citizens who think, care, and act beyond community and national boundaries. Over the last five years, more than 700 Turkish and Greek Cypriot Youth and 50 instructors from both communities have been brought together in an educationally sound environment, through the Doves Project. The participants developed friendships and created a small community of active citizens with increased beliefs that they can contribute in the reconciliation process of their island.

Doves Project Programs and Activities

Since 2005, five youth camps have been conducted in Cyprus (International Youth Camps 2005, 2006, 2007, 2008, 2009 and Winter Leadership Camp 2007), where youngsters from the two main communities of the island got together and participated in Olympism activities. The majority of the Doves Project participants did not have previous bi-communal experience and never had the opportunity to experience interaction with people from the other community. Outcomes from research performed over the last five years indicate that both Greek Cypriot and Turkish Cypriot participants increased their (a) social perspective taking (thinking and caring about others, which is the basis of conflict resolution), (b) cross-cultural friendship and tolerance, (c) self- and academic efficacy, and (d) global citizenship knowledge, attitudes, and behaviors. Research also indicated that the majority of both the participants and instructors agreed that they were able to transfer what they had learned through the program to real world situations. Further, the Doves Project activities enabled participants to improve their conflict resolution skills, their abilities to consider perspectives of others, and implicitly or explicitly their understanding of the issues in Cyprus.

The Doves Project is not limited to weekly summer camps, but aims to provide ongoing activities to sustain positive changes. The annual program starts with a precamp experience where youth, instructors, and the organizers come together to create the structure of the summer camps and include the elements they consider essential. All individuals involved in the process actively participate in designing the program by participating in committees according to their interests that determine the way activities will be implemented. This participatory approach enables the program to draw from multiple sources of expertise and creativity, and ensures the program meets the interests and needs of the population. Providing the opportunity to participate in the initial stages of preparation helps individuals (youth, volunteers, and instructors) take responsibility for the implementation of the program and creates a feeling of ownership for the program, which then results in a passion and commitment to make it work. During this preparation phase, there is also an effort to include the parents, who are invited to attend informative workshops and orientation meetings.

Another component of the program is that the Doves Project aims to empower the youth by providing opportunities in which participants can become active citizens and act upon their environment after the camp is over. Given this foundation, during the summer camps participants get together and develop an action plan regarding a thematic area that interests them. The young people identify situations in the Cypriot society that need to be addressed, think of ways to address them, and come up with an action plan that participants are committed to implement throughout the year. Such methodology not only enables participants to become active citizens and transfer their skills into real life situations, but it also enables youngsters who otherwise consider themselves "enemies" to work together to achieve a common goal. Examples of such activities include tree plantings in burned areas of Cyprus, participation in charity events to raise money for a cause, and creation of a plan for dissemination of re-usable bags in the communities. Another example of youth activism is a project funded by the European Union that was initiated by the Doves Project Youth during their after-camp activities, where youth wrote a grant proposal to implement an island-wide project to increase the awareness of the society in Cyprus about the difficulties people with disabilities face in their everyday lives.

During the years 2006-2008, the Doves Project also developed a pioneer sport unit, called "Sport, Education and Development Unit" (SEDU). The SEDU was implemented in collaboration with a municipality in the capital of Cyprus. Through the SEDU, children had the opportunity to play sports; learn about life-skills, health, and well-being issues; and engage in individual and collective initiatives. The purpose of the SEDU was to provide a program that used sports as a vehicle for personal development and social change, which was facilitated by engaging the youth of the island in educationally focused sport activities that were based on the principle of balance between a healthy mind and a healthy body (*"mens sana in corpore sano"*). The after-school educational initiative aimed to promote sportsmanship and interpersonal relationships. Through this initiative, more than 120 participants met daily within the SEDU and practiced their favorite sport activities (both sport activities that are well known in Cyprus as well as sport activities that are not traditionally performed in Cyprus). The program also incorporated a cultural component. The participants participated in dancing, theatre, music, and painting. During the weekends the participants were exposed to many other non-traditional sports activities, such as rock-climbing, skiing, shooting, archery, and canoeing. The educational part of the program was implemented through discussions during the daily meetings (emotional education, conflict resolution, peace education), as well as during the weekends with lectures/presentations from experts on themes that are of interest to youth, such as sports and violence/ hooliganism, nutrition of athletes, anorexia-bulimia, Olympic values, sport psychology, technology, how to be safe on the road, and environmental awareness. The implementation of SEDU and the lessons learned through the Doves Project provided significant documentation that is currently being used by Cyprus youth and sport and education stakeholders (Cyprus Ministry of Education, Cyprus Sport Organization, Youth Sport Clubs, and municipalities) in an attempt to engage youth researchers and practitioners in collective efforts to reform physical education curricula, sport programs, and community-based initiatives.

SUMMARY, CONCLUSIONS, AND RECOMMENDATIONS

Although sport initiatives in Cyprus, under certain conditions, can provide opportunities to build peace and stability, the current political situation and existing status quo of the island are obstacles to the interaction and integration of the Cypriot youth from all the communities. Through the Doves Project, and projects with similar objectives, youth can have the opportunity to gain the essential attributes for peace and stability (e.g., life-lasting skills, relationships, attitudes, behaviors). Such skills can potentially become a valuable "anti-war-antivirus-software," which should be scientifically tested for its effectiveness.

The main objective of the Doves Project was to design, implement, and assess SFDP programs that can be replicated in other countries, by developing a theory-driven, evidence-based model that could serve as "social medicine" for a number of social issues we face globally. Based on the evidence gained through the Doves Project and grounded on the posited theoretical frameworks, Lyras (2007, 2009) developed a blueprint with program recommendations that can potentially help researchers and practitioners effectively design and assess SFDP programs. The proposed Sport for Development and Peace Model can serve as a blueprint to be applied by youth, sport, and education stakeholders (Lyras, 2007, 2009) because it provides guidelines and recommendations that were identified as factors that leveraged the Doves Project objectives (content, process, and outcomes). According to Lyras (2009), if we claim that sport can serve as "good medicine" for a number of social issues, then social scientists should use scientific assessment procedures to identify the ideal content, process, and outcomes. The content might include what sports and educational themes should be included in sport for development initiatives. The process would be composed of the methodology developed to maximize the effectiveness of every sport experience. Finally, the outcomes might include the kinds of behavioral and cultural change that can be promoted and the kinds of social and psychological indicators that can be assessed. The answers to these temporal considerations should be grounded in theory and evidenced from the field (i.e., real life setting; Lyras, 2007, 2009).

A blueprint of the propositions, the principles, and the practical recommendations on how sport can leverage positive educational outcomes can be found in Table 1. The proposed blueprint is currently being used by the Street Soccer USA Research Team (16 U.S.

TABLE 3.1. Global Standards on Sport for Development and Peace: Tested Elements of Effective Programming
(Lyras, 2007, 2009)

Impact Assessment	Organization	Sport	Education	Cultural Enrichment
Apply scientific monitoring and evaluation methodology (validated instruments, detached data analysis, and objective interpretation) Assess the effects of SFDP programs and policy across time and space Use a mixed methods approach and collect data from multiple sources of information (triangulation-reports, pre-post questionnaires, audiovisual data, journals, focus groups) Assess organizational components and identify attributes that leverage positive outcomes Identify organizational components that hinder positive change and development Identify and assess SFDP related social, psychological, and societal indicators Apply research ethics at all stages and respect local sensitivities (conflict, political complexity, and implications)	Increase social capital through ongoing training of all engaged stakeholders Foster an inclusive, collaborative environment designed to promote the development of innovative sport-for-development programs, products, and services Facilitate transformational leadership Ensure sustainable resources and institutionalize innovative organizational culture Build the capacity of and empower local stakeholders based on their needs and unique potentials Establish synergies with local and international SFDP stakeholders (e.g., universities, NGOs, policymakers, practitioners) Use inclusive decision making to promote individual and collective actions	Apply sport practices based on moral values and principles (existence of vision and philosophy) Create inclusive mixed teams (ethnicity, gender, competence level) Merge traditional with non-traditional sports and physical activities (e.g., soccer, treasure hunt, martial arts) Provide a variety of sport and physical activities to attract and sustain a representative population Use the principles of the educational component (Sport for Development Theory) Encourage coaches and instructors to serve as educators, positive role models, and agents of positive change Facilitate conditions for optimal engagement (peak and flow experiences) by keeping a balance between skills and challenge	Create child-oriented conditions for positive learning experiences Create reward system to reinforce positive attitudes, thoughts, and behaviors (social cognitive theory, role playing, cognitive and behavioral approaches, positive role models) Facilitate conditions for optimal engagement in every sport and non-sport activity (peak and flow experiences) Use real life sport and non-sport challenges to achieve educational objectives (constructivist pedagogy and problem-based learning) Create groups with similar interests Empower individuals by assigning preference and interest-based roles Promote empathy, care, and creative thoughts and actions in every sport and non-sport activity	Enrich sport intervention curricula with cultural activities (e.g., arts, music, dance, theater, poetry, short movie making) Apply multidisciplinary framework with global and local issues (e.g., human rights, global environment, international relations, peace and cross cultural understanding, technological literacy) Make mental and practical associations between sports and real life experiences (e.g., human rights, environmental issues, community based initiatives, life skills, spirituality) Create clusters to initiate community-based creative engagement and participation Use Olympism as a framework of inclusion, inspiration, and engagement Create positive entertaining experiences and facilitate innovation and outreach Embrace local culture and promote global perspective and appreciation

city multisited sport for homeless initiative), the Youth I.D.E.A.L.S. (EU-USA International Interinstitutional Youth Initiative), the 2011 World Scholar Athlete Games, and the 2011 International Youth Sport Summit (international Olympism for peace youth programs) to assess program and organizational effectiveness. The proposed model could also be applied in other regions around the globe (e.g., EU, USA, Caribbean, Africa) to effectively monitor and evaluate SFDP projects. Although the initial framework of the Doves Project was developed to serve as a model for interethnic tolerance and positive transformation of conflict into creative actions, the interdisciplinary human-centered theoretical foundations and program recommendations of the Sport for Development and Peace Model can potentially transcend the application of similar programs, research, and initiatives to accommodate universal youth needs and challenges.

Note: The formalization and the design of the initial concept of the Doves Olympic Movement project were made feasible with support from the Olympic Solidarity (International Olympic Committee). All the activities of the Doves Project were funded by UNDP-ACT and USAID and part of the research project was supported by the Cyprus Research Foundation. The views expressed in this publication are those of the author and do not necessarily represent those of the United Nations or its Member States, UNDP, USAID, IOC, or the Cyprus Research Foundation.

REFERENCES

Allport, G. W. (1954). *The nature of prejudice.* Reading, MA: Addison Wesley.

Amara, M., Aquilina, D., Henry, I., & Taylor, M. (2005). *Sport and multiculturalism.* Brussels, Belgium: European Commission, DG Education and Culture.

Bairner, A. (1999). Soccer, masculinity and violence in Northern Ireland: Between hooliganism and terrorism. *Men and Masculinities, 1,* 284-301.

Corsini, R. J. (1994). Piaget's theory. In *Encyclopedia of Psychology 1,* 86-89. New York: John Wiley & Sons.

Fountain, S. (1999). *Peace Education in UNICEF.* Working Paper. New York: UNICEF.

Hardy, L. (1986). Psychological stress and children in competition. In G. Gleeson (Ed.), *The growing child in competitive sport* (pp. 157-172). London, England: Holder & Stoughton.

Horne, J. (1996). Kicking racism out of soccer in England and Scotland. *Journal of Sport and Social Issues, 20,* 45-68.

International Olympic Committee. (1999). Peace cannot be built overnight. *Olympic Review, XXVI-28,* 34. Retrieved from http://la84foundation.org/OlympicInformationCenter/OlympicReview/1999/OREXXVI28/OREXXVI28zk.pdf

International Olympic Committee. (2000). Olympic truce. *Olympic Review, XXVI-30,* 19-22. Retrieved from http://www.la84foundation.org/OlympicInformationCenter/OlympicReview/1999/OREXXVI30/OREXXVI30o.pdf

Lyras, A. (2001). *Sport for development: The philosophy of sport of the millennium.* Unpublished manuscript, Nicosia, Cyprus.

Lyras, A. (2003). *Doves Olympic Movement: Pilot study for interethnic conflict management and cultural development.* Unpublished manuscript, University of Connecticut, Storrs, CTUSA. Proposed from the Olympic Solidarity to be included in the International Olympic Committee's extranet.

Lyras, A. (2005). *Doves Olympic Movement Summer Camp 2005: Training Manual.* Unpublished manuscript submitted to UNOPS/UNDP, Nicosia, Cyprus.

Lyras, A. (2007). Characteristics and psycho-social impacts of an inter-ethnic educational sport initiative on Greek and Turkish Cypriot youth. Unpublished dissertation. University of Connecticut, Storrs.

Lyras, A. (2009). *Sport for peace and development theory.* Unpublished manuscript. Paper shortlisted for a research award by the European Association for Sport Management. Amsterdam, Netherlands, September 2009.

Lyras, A. (2010). *Measuring success: Sport for development and peace monitoring and evaluation.* Keynote address at the Power of Sport Summit, International Association of Sport for Development and Peace, Boston, MA, June 2010.

Lyras, A., Yiannakis, A., & Kartakoullis, N. (2005). *Doves Olympic Movement Summer Camp 2005.* Grant awarded from the United Nations Office of Project Services.

Lyras, A., Yiannakis, A., & Kartakoullis, N. (2006). *Doves Olympic Movement Camps 2006-2008.* Grant awarded from the United Nations Development Programme.

Lyras, A., Yiannakis, A., & Kartakoullis, N. (2007). *Building a common future through sport and education.* Grant awarded by the United Nations Development Programme.

Martens, R. (1993). Psychological perspectives. In B. R. Cahill & A. J. Pearl (Eds.), *Intensive participation in children's sports* (pp. 9-17). Champaign, IL: Human Kinetics.

Maslow, A. H. (1970). *Motivation and personality* (2nd ed.). New York: Harper & Row.

Maslow, A. H. (1971). *Farther reaches of human nature.* New York: The Viking Press.

Maslow, A. H. (1998). *Toward a psychology of being.* New York: John Willey & Sons, Inc.

Mechikoff, A. R., & Sullivan, S. (2001). Peace through sport and religio athletae: Antiquated ideas or viable options? *The Sport Journal, 4*(4). Retrieved from http://www.the-sportjournal.org/2001Journal/Vol14-No4/peace.asp

Papadakis, Y. (1998). Greek Cypriot narratives of history and collective identity: nationalism as a contested process. *American Ethnologist, 25,* 149-165.

Papadakis, Y. (2003). Nation, narrative and commemoration: Political ritual in divided Cyprus. *History and Anthropology, 14,* 253-270.

Papadakis, Y. (2004). Discourses of "the Balkans" in Cyprus: Tactics, strategies and constructions of "others". *History and Anthropology, 15,* 15-27.

Papadakis, Y. (2008). *History education in divided Cyprus: A comparison of Greek Cypriot and Turkish Cypriot schoolbooks on the "History of Cyprus"*. Oslo, Norway: International Peace Research Institute (PRIO).

Pettigrew, T. F. (1998). Intergroup contact theory. *Annual Review of Psychology, 49,* 65–85.

Pettigrew, T. F., & Tropp, L. (2006). A meta-analytic test of intergroup contact theory. *Journal of Personality and Social Psychology, 90,* 751-783.

Rees, C. R. (1996). Race and sport in global perspective: Lessons from post-apartheid South Africa. *Journal of Sport and Social Issues, 20,* 22-32.

Reich, B., & Pivovarov, V. (1994). *International practical guide on the implementation of the recommendation concerning education for international understanding, co-operation and peace and education relating to human rights and fundamental freedoms*. Paris: UNESCO.

Ryan, M. R., & Deci, L. E. (2000). Self-determination theory and the facilitation of intrinsic motivation, social development and well-being. *American Psychologist, 55*(4), 68-78.

Saunders, E., & Sugden, J. (1997). Sport and community relations in Northern Ireland. *Managing Leisure, 2,* 39-54.

Sternberg, R. J. (1986). A triangular theory of love. *Psychological Review, 93,* 119–135.

Sternberg, R. J. (1994). Love is a story. *General Psychologist, 30,* 1–11.

Sternberg, R. (2003). A duplex theory of hate: Development and application to terrorism, massacres, and genocide. *Review of General Psychology, 7*(3), 299-328.

Sternberg, R., Hojjat, M., & Barnes, M. (2001). Empirical tests of aspects of a theory of love as a story. *European Journal of Personality, 15,* 199-218.

Sugden, J. (1991). Belfast united: Encouraging cross-community through sport in Northern Ireland. *Journal of Sport and Social Issues, 15,* 59-80.

Sugden, J. (2006). Teaching and playing sport for conflict resolution and co-existence in Israel. *International Review for the Sociology of Sport, 41,* 221-240.

Sugden, J. (2007). Football for peace in context. In J. Sugden & J. Wallis (Eds.), *Football for peace: Teaching and playing sport for conflict resolution in the Middle East.* Chelsea School Research Centre Series. Meyer & Meyer, Aachen.

Sudgen, J., & Harvie, S. (1995). *Sport and community relations in Northern Ireland.* Coleraine: University of Ulster.

United Nations. (2003). *Sport for development and peace: Towards achieving the millennium development goals.* Report from the United Nations Inter-Agency Task Force on Sport for Development and Peace. Retrieved from https://www.un.org/wcm/webdav/site/sport/shared/sport/pdfs/task%20force%20report%20english.pdf

United Nations. (2005). *The Magglingen call To action 2005.* Retrieved from http://www.un.org/sport2005/newsroom/magglingen_call_to_action.pdf

Vygotsky, L. S. (1978). *Mind in society.* Cambridge, MA: Harvard University Press.

Soccer as a Mediator for Fostering Relationships and Building Peace among Jewish and Arab Players

4

Ronnie Lidor and Boris Blumenstein

Israel is a multicultural state composed of slightly more than seven million residents, among them about 5.5 million Jewish citizens, 1.5 million Arab citizens, and 300,000 immigrants, mostly from Africa and Europe, who have not yet registered as Israeli citizens (Statistical Aspects of Israel, 2006). The Jewish and Arab citizens are spread across the country. Most villages and cities of small-to-medium size are populated by only Jewish or only Arab residents. Nevertheless, in the big cities in the country—Jerusalem (the capital), Haifa, and Tel-Aviv—Jews and Arabs live together, albeit mostly in separate neighborhoods.

Israel is surrounded by four Arab countries—Egypt to the south, Jordan to the east, and Lebanon and Syria to the north. Israel has diplomatic relations with two of these countries—Egypt and Jordan, meaning that Israeli citizens can travel to Egypt and Jordan and citizens of Egypt and Jordan can visit Israel. Unfortunately, with the other two Arab countries—Lebanon and Syria—Israel does not have diplomatic relations, but instead, relations that are hostile and unstable. In addition to the unstable relations with Lebanon and Syria, Israel has had a long-term political conflict with the Palestinian population living in Gaza and the West Bank. Needless to say, the unpredictable political climate that exists in this part of the Middle East negatively influences the lives of both the Jewish and Arab populations in Israel, mainly by increasing the political and social tensions between the two.

Since the establishment of the State of Israel in 1948, the Jewish and Arab citizens who live in the country have been struggling to find the most expedient way of maintaining cooperation between the two groups (Ben-Porat, 1993; Sorek, 2010). It has been one of the goals of nearly every government elected in Israel since its establishment to enable both the Jewish and Arab populations to achieve this objective. Indeed, the Jewish and Arab populations have basically maintained normal lives. Nevertheless, there have been few social-political links between them. Two examples of the existing separation between the Jewish and Arab populations are (a) Jewish and Arab children go to separate schools (there are only a few schools around the country that offer academic and social programs for Jewish and Arab children together) and (b) the adult Jewish and Arab populations rarely interact socially with each other, hindering any real opportunities for promoting positive relationships between the two populations. The separation between the Jewish and Arab populations can also be seen in various endeavors, among them business, politics, and primary education.

There is one context, however, where professional and social cooperation seem to exist between the two populations—in the game of soccer. Soccer is the most popular sport among both the Jews and Arabs in Israel (Lidor & Blumenstein, 2009; Sorek, 2010). It is the only sport in the country where both Jewish and Arab athletes practice and play together on a regular basis, true for beginning and young players as well as for adult professional players. For example, sport clubs in Division 1 (the highest competitive leagues in the Israeli sport system) in basketball, team handball, and volleyball in Israel are typically composed of only Jewish and foreign (individuals who do not carry Israeli citizenship) players. No Arab athletes play in these divisions, and the national teams for these sports in Israel also do not include Arab players. In soccer, however, usually two or three Arab athletes play for each club in Division 1. In addition, Arab players play regularly for the Israeli national team. Apparently, soccer is one of the domains in Israel where full cooperation between Jews and Arabs can be witnessed (other areas are academics, art, medicine, music, and theater). In this chapter we discuss the assumption that this cooperation helps to foster positive relationships and build peace between Jewish and Arab athletes in Israel.

The purpose of this chapter is fivefold: First, to briefly describe the structure of the sport system in Israel and the status of soccer in the Jewish and Arab populations. Second, to describe the psychological approach used by one sport psychology consultant (SPC) who worked with Jewish and Arab soccer players in two different frameworks—an academy for young players and a professional soccer club, both in Israel. Third, to describe the educational and social activities of a number of non-profit programs established in Israel for building peace between Jewish and Arab children and youth through supervised, non-competitive soccer activities. Fourth, to discuss the need for systematic data collection and data analysis associated with the sport psychology program and the educational programs described in our chapter, so that additional relevant information on the contribution of such programs aimed at promoting relations between Jewish and Arab players can be obtained. Fifth, to suggest a number of practical implications for those who work with Jewish and Arab soccer players in Israel.

SPORT IN ISRAEL

As in most countries, sport in Israel is an important aspect of the national culture. About 60 sports are played in Israel, at both the competitive and recreational levels. Since 1952, Israeli athletes have participated in the Olympic Games, and the first Olympic medals were awarded to an Israeli athlete in the 1992 Barcelona Games (silver and bronze medals in judo). In each subsequent summer Olympics, Israeli athletes have won medals in individual sports, such as kayaking, judo, and windsurfing. Israeli athletes have also consistently participated in World and European Championships, having won medals in events such as judo, shooting, and track and field.

Sport in Israel has been financially supported by both the public and private sectors (Lidor & Bar-Eli, 1998). For example, Olympic sports in Israel have been supervised by the Elite Sport Department since its establishment in 1984, and are sponsored both financially and ideologically by two bodies—the Ministry of Education, Sport and Culture and the Israeli Olympic Committee (Blumenstein & Lidor, 2008; Lidor & Blumenstein, 2009). The main objective of the Elite Sport Department is to provide elite athletes, and particularly Olympic athletes, with the optimal physical and psychological conditions they need to attain a high level of athletic excellence. Elite athletes in individual sports, such as fencing, judo, kayaking, sailing, surfing, swimming, and wrestling, are the main beneficiaries of the Department. The professional services of the Department, including psychological consultations, are offered not only to the athletes themselves but also to their coaching staff.

Nevertheless, ball games in Israel, particularly the ones that attract the most attention from the media and the public at large—basketball, soccer, team handball, and volleyball—are mainly sponsored by leading private enterprises. Little money comes from the public sector (i.e., governmental bodies) for these sports. The activities of the clubs sponsored by the private companies are business oriented, meaning that the players are considered to be employees in a private company and their main objectives should be to produce "good products"—victories and titles—to engender economic profit. The globalization trend, evident around the world, can also be observed in Israel; the clubs are composed of international players from different continents (e.g., Africa, Asia, Europe), and these players help the teams qualify for major international sporting events to increase the clubs' revenues. Soccer in Israel is a compelling example of the worldwide trend of elite athlete migration (see also the case of hockey in Canada; Schinke, Gauthier, Dubuc, & Crowder, 2007).

SOCCER IN ISRAEL

Soccer is the most popular sport in both the Jewish and Arab populations in Israel, in terms of the number of spectators watching the games, the television ratings, and the budgets allocated (Sorek, 2010). Recreational and competitive soccer clubs can be found in almost every city in the country. Although the game is played by both female and male athletes, it has clearly been dominated by the male teams.

The Israel Football Association is the official body organizing all competitive soccer activities in the country, both at the national and international levels. At the national level, there are five divisions for competitive soccer: Division 1 (the highest competitive level) and Division 2 (the second competitive level) are composed of 16 and 12 professional clubs, respectively. All the athletes who play for these clubs are considered to be professional athletes who make their livings from playing soccer. Divisions 3 to 5 are semi-professional, meaning the athletes who play for these clubs are not paid high salaries and therefore must have other sources of income.

These five divisions have been dominated by Jewish clubs. During the last two decades of the 20th century and the first decade of the 21st century, however, there has been a remarkable increase in the number of Arab clubs playing professional and semi-professional soccer. For example, in the beginning of the 1990s, 21 Arab clubs played in the professional and semi-professional divisions in Israel (seven percent of the total number of clubs playing in these divisions at that time). A decade later, there were 41 Arab clubs playing in these divisions (about 35% of the total number of clubs playing competitive soccer in Israel; The Israel Football Association, 2010). In almost every Jewish club there are two to three Arab players on the roster, and in many Arab clubs, particularly those playing in Divisions 1 and 2, there are three to four Jewish players on the rosters. For example, three Arab players played for *Hapoel Tel-Aviv*, the club that won the National Championship during the 2009-2010 season. The same number of Arab players played for *Maccabi Haifa*, the second best team in Israel during the same season. In *Maccabi Ahi Nazareth*, an Arab club that played in Division 1 in the 2009-2010 season, seven Jewish players were on the roster, four of whom were starters.

Both Jewish and Arab players also play for the national team. It is true that the national team is dominated by Jewish players, however two to three Arab players consistently play for the team and often are starters. When the national team plays a home game, the crowd is typically composed of both Jews and Arabs, all supporting the national team, but usually dominated by Jewish fans. The separation that is seen in daily life between the Jewish and Arab populations can also be seen in the stadium. The Jewish fans and the Arab fans prefer to sit separately while watching the games of the national team, with the Arab fans sitting in one area of the stadium and the Jewish fans sitting in other areas. No verbal or physical disputes are seen between the Jewish and Arab fans.

Because Jewish and Arab players play together for many soccer clubs in Israel, there have been several attempts in these clubs to use soccer's authentic environment to promote relationships between these players through a sport psychology intervention. It was the clear purpose of all those involved in the clubs—players, coaches, and members of the management—to bridge cultural disparities and create a positive climate among all players, to unite the players so that they would perform as one unit. In the following section we describe the principles of a sport psychology program used by an applied consultant (SPC) with Jewish and Arab players.

EDUCATIONAL AND SPORT PSYCHOLOGY CONSULTATIONS FOR YOUTH AND PROFESSIONAL JEWISH AND ARAB PLAYERS

Jewish and Arab players compete not only for professional soccer clubs in Israel, but also for the soccer academies for youth players (ages 13-18) founded by these clubs. A number of the soccer clubs playing in Division 1 in Israel have hired an SPC who provides psychological consultations for their professional players, as well as for the youth players playing in their academies. In this section we describe the experiences of one SPC, the second author, Boris Blumenstein, who has about 30 years of experience working with beginning and elite athletes in Russia and Israel. Boris earned his PhD in sport psychology in Russia and worked for a number of years with elite Russian athletes. After immigrating to Israel, Boris began providing sport psychology consultations to elite Israeli athletes. His experience working in two different cultures, and particularly two different sport cultures, helped him to gain sensitivity to the educational, psychological, and social needs of athletes who immigrated to Israel or who grew up in different cultures. Boris worked with two soccer teams (in different seasons) composed of both Jewish and Arab players: youth players playing for one soccer academy and professional players playing for one club in Division 1.

Working in an Academy for Jewish and Arab Youth Soccer Players

For one season Boris worked with youth players playing for the academy of one club located in a medium-sized city in the southern part of Israel. There were about 120 players in the academy, all males, of ages 13 to 18 years. In addition to the practice sessions, the players played one official game in leagues organized by the Israel Football Association, according to the age groups of the players; there were leagues for the 13–14-year-old players, the 15–16-year-old players, and the 17–18-year-old players. Boris worked regularly with only 12 players (seven players were 17–18 years old, four were 15–16, and one player was 14), who were assigned to him by the head coach of the academy. Among these players, 11 were Jewish and one was Arab. These players were selected to work with him because they were considered the most talented players in their age groups. He met with the players in either individual or group sessions. In this part we will focus on how Boris worked with the players in the group sessions, because his initiatives in fostering relationships between the Jewish players and the Arab player only took place in the group sessions. Information on the context of the individual sessions and the interventions used in these sessions can be found in Lidor, Blumenstein, and Tenenbaum (2007).

The objective of the group sessions was to discuss with the young players a number of issues related to team values, among them team cohesion, leadership, and fair play. The group sessions were planned to enable the SPC to increase mutual understanding and promote relationships among the players. Therefore, the issue of playing on a soccer team that is composed of both Jewish and Arab players, such as in most of the teams playing in the academy, was brought up in the group sessions. In these sessions, Boris presented video clips of games played by elite soccer teams in Israel in which both Jewish and Arab players played together. He also used short video clips of elite soccer clubs that took part in the European Championships League (a yearly tournament in which only the teams that win the championship in their national leagues, as well as a number of top teams playing in leading soccer leagues in countries such as Italy, Spain, and the United Kingdom, are allowed to participate), which included players from all over the world representing different countries and cultures. Boris emphasized to the athletes that on the field all players should play as one unit to help the team achieve a high level of proficiency. His goal was to facilitate shared over-arching objectives among the players based on the team's projected performance level.

In the group meetings Boris asked the young players to provide some background information about their families: the names of their family members, the occupations of their parents, how many brothers and sisters they had, and how their families perceived their sport activity. He asked the Jewish players to speak about their family traditions, because not all the parents or the grandparents of the players shared similar backgrounds and cultures. For example, although some of the parents of the Jewish players were born in Israel, others were immigrants from different continents, such as Africa, Asia, or Europe, and therefore they had different customs and traditions (e.g., types of food, music preferences, clothing styles). Likewise, the Arab player was asked to share with the Jewish players the traditions of his family. He taught them some Arabic and asked them to listen to his favorite singers. For some of the meetings a player's parent was invited to talk about some unique traditions of his family. The invited parents typically brought their traditional food for the players to taste. With these actions, the SPC provided the players with the opportunity to get to know each other better. It was Boris's objective to emphasize that there were not only cultural differences between the Arab player and the Jewish players, but also among the Jewish players themselves. He wanted to demonstrate to the players that cultural differences could exist not only in two different populations (e.g., Jewish and Arab), but also in one culture (e.g., Jewish).

During the season, a number of meetings were held with only the parents of the players. The attendance was full for almost all of these meetings. Boris talked with the parents about three main issues: (a) coach-parents' relationship, (b) the psychological-emotional support required from the families to help the players cope with the demands they face during their soccer activities, and (c) how to help the players organize their afternoon time effectively, so that they will be able to maintain their soccer activities and also allocate the required time to meet the school's academic demands (e.g., doing their school assignments and preparing for exams). He encouraged the parents to share their feelings and thoughts with him about their children's involvement in the academy. Throughout the season, a number of parents of the Jewish players approached Boris. However, the parents of the Arab player did not. He attempted a number of times to convince them to meet with him, but without success. They may have felt uncomfortable talking with him about their son, either due to the cultural gap existing between Jews and Arabs in Israel, or due to language barriers (they were not fluent in Hebrew). Boris felt sympathetic towards for the parents of the Arab player. He remembered that in his first years in Israel after leaving Russia he had difficulties in communicating with the Israeli people, due to the cultural and language barriers. He recognized that also for the parents of the Arab players there might have been challenges pertaining to language barriers, cultural barriers, and probably other social barriers.

Working with Professional Jewish and Arab Players

While working with a professional soccer club, Boris provided consultation to one team of 22 male players. The team was composed of 16 Jewish players, four foreign players who came from Africa and Europe and were Christians, and two Arab players who were Muslims. Boris used a similar approach to the one he used when working with the young soccer players in the academy in his consultations with the professional players: individual and group sessions were conducted on a weekly basis. As stated previously, in this chapter we are focusing on the psychological work done in the group sessions to describe the efforts made by Boris to promote relationships between the Jewish and Arab players.

Five of the Jewish players were starters on the team, as were the two Arab players who played for the team. The remaining four starters were foreign players. To create positive and supportive relationships between the players, Boris employed four main strategies when conducting group sessions: creating a professional dialogue between the players, discussing the relationship between players and fans, talking about the playing of the national anthem, and discussing the possibility of terror attacks.

Creating a Professional Dialogue Between Players

Boris encouraged the players to exchange ideas relating to their performances on the field. The foreign players as well as the Jewish and Arab players were encouraged to exchange their ideas. In the group meetings Boris repeatedly told the players that they were all professionals who had one major goal—to help the team achieve its goals. He proposed that all the players speak only the "language of soccer," namely that all cultural differences and political conflicts be set aside. From the beginning of the sport psychology sessions, the players cooperated with Boris. They agreed that adopting this kind of approach would help them communicate better on the field, and hopefully off the field as well. Boris showed the players video clips of elite clubs in Europe (Chelsea from the United Kingdom and Real Madrid from Spain), in which players from different cultures and nationalities played together successfully to achieve a high level of proficiency. He wanted to make a clear point – all the players were professional athletes and well-paid individuals who must work together as one unit. Without team commitment their individual goals as well as the team goals would not be reached.

Boris knew that achieving team commitment would not be an easy goal for this soccer team. Because the Jewish and Arab players came from different cultures and religions, and some of them were raised by families who might have been hostile to the "other culture," he was careful in implementing his interventions. When working with these players, he mainly emphasized their commitment to their team. He did not try to convince them to be committed to the society at large or to the country. He was not naïve about the difficulties in transferring the interventions used in the group sessions to other aspects of the players' lives. Although he was well aware of the separation between the Jewish and Arab populations in Israel, he wanted to ensure that this separation would be minimized as much as possible in all activities associated with the team. His feeling was that the Jewish and Arab players who played for the team also wanted to minimize the existing separation among them.

Discussing Problematic Relationships between Players and Fans during Away Games

Boris talked with the Arab players about playing in front of hostile Jewish fans and with the Jewish players about playing in front of hostile Arab fans. In the season in which he worked with the soccer team, Division 1 was composed of 13 Jewish clubs and one Arab club, and therefore the Arab players had to play many away games in front of Jewish fans, and the Jewish players had to play at least one away game in front of Arab fans. Boris worked with both the Jewish and Arab players on how to handle situations in which the fans demonstrated behavioral patterns of verbal violence toward the players. He discussed with them a number of actions that could be performed by the players, among them standing physically close to each other during hostile acts by the fans. In addition, he suggested to the players that each time we are interviewed by the Jewish or Arab press they should speak out against fan hostility. One of the Jewish players suggested that before the start of the game all the players would stand together in a big circle linking their arms around each other's back, giving the captain of the team the opportunity to provide any last-minute motivational words for the upcoming game. He explained that he had seen this circle in some of the basketball games he had watched on television. He thought that creating a circle would help the team feel united and would demonstrate that they were playing as one team. Another player suggested that they also use the structure of a circle before the start of the second half of the game. Boris accepted this proposal, as did the other players.

Talking with Arab Players about Their Emotions when the Israel National Anthem is played

The Israeli anthem "Hatikva" ("The Hope") focuses on the desire of the Jewish people to be free and live in the land of Israel. Because the song focuses only on the will of the Jewish people, the Israeli Arab population asserts that the anthem does not represent them (Lidor & Blumenstein, 2009). Therefore the Arab population does not join the Jewish population in singing the anthem. Because the Israeli anthem is played prior to official games in Division 1, Boris provided the Arab players with some relevant information associated with the anthem, such as how much time it would take to sing it, as well as advising them on what to do during this period of time (e.g., using imagery or self-talk). He emphasized that they were not required to join the Jewish players in singing the anthem, but only to stand respectfully with the team during the playing of the anthem. He suggested that when they stood on the field with the team, they could think about the upcoming game and shift their attention to what they had to do during the game.

Frankly speaking, Boris did not know what the Arab players were thinking during the time the anthem was played. He realized that it might be difficult for them to stand there quietly and listen to the anthem. He attempted to provide them with tips on what they might think about before the beginning of the game. In the group meetings he did not question the Arab players about their actual thoughts during the time the anthem was played, and he also did not discuss with the Jewish players the fact that the Arab players did not sing the anthem. He realized that both the Jewish and Arab players were sensitive to this issue, and he did not want to turn this heated topic into a bigger political-social debate.

Discussing the Possibility of a Terror Attack with Jewish and Arab Players

Unfortunately, during the time Boris worked with the professional players, a number of terror attacks occurred in the country. When these events occurred he maintained his regular psychological program. He typically gathered the two Arab players with a number of Jewish players or some of the foreign players with some of the Jewish players. He started each group session by practicing a relaxation technique, accompanied by soft music. After practicing relaxation for about 15 minutes, he asked the players to sit on the floor and share their feelings about the terror attacks. No political debates were allowed during these sessions. Furthermore, both the Jewish and Arab players were asked not to talk politics upon arrival at the stadium. Boris asked the players to practice and prepare themselves for the upcoming game by regularly attending the sport psychology sessions.

It was difficult for Boris to conduct sport psychology sessions when terror attacks occurred. Although both the Jewish and Arab players were used to terror attacks, none of them behaved in their normal manner when a wave of terror hit the country. All were busy thinking about the situation, listening to the special news reports, or talking about them with their friends and families. It was indeed difficult to focus solely on soccer. Nevertheless, because practices were not cancelled or postponed, all players were required to continue their training schedule, including the individual and group sport psychology sessions. It was for the benefit of the players to resume practices, because it helped them to cope better with the terror situation. All the players affirmed this policy of the club and maintained their training schedule.

EDUCATIONAL PROGRAMS FOR PEACE BUILDING THROUGH SOCCER

In the previous section we described our psychological approach as used by Boris when working with Jewish and Arab professional soccer players. Since soccer is also a very popular activity in Israel among children and youth, the game can be used as an educational mediator for building peace among young Jewish and Arab players. In the following section, we present educational and social activities of cooperative soccer programs that are offered in Israel for young players from the Israeli and Arab populations.

There are a number of non-profit programs in Israel that aim to organize soccer activities for children and youth from both the Jewish and Arab communities, as well as for Jewish and Arab children from Israel and children from the Palestinian Authority. These programs are sponsored by either national or international bodies established uniquely for the purpose of using the game of soccer as a mediator for peace building among young Jewish and Arab players. The programs offer organized and supervised activities either on a year-round basis or only during the summer break (July-August), emphasizing cooperative activities among players and attempting to minimize as much as possible a competitive atmosphere among the participants. For the purpose of this chapter, three programs for peace building through soccer are described: the *Twinned Peace Soccer Schools Project,* the *Mifalot's Sport for Education, Development, and Peace Program,* and the *Football for Peace Program.*

Twinned Peace Soccer Schools Project—Sport in the Service of Peace

The Twinned Peace Sport Schools Project, launched in 2002, annually engages 1,500-2,000 children aged 6-14 from twinned communities in Israel and the Palestinian Authority (Pitch for Peace, 2006). In each locality, the Peres Center for Peace has established a soccer or basketball school and provides the children with weekly sports training, peace education activities, and inter-language learning. The children meet with their twinned school for monthly joint Israeli-Palestinian activities and other special events.

There has been an acute need for a program such as the Twinned Peace Soccer Schools Project, because in disadvantaged communities in Israel and the Palestinian Authority there are limited opportunities for organized sporting activities, as well as limited sport equipment and facilities. Therefore, the program serves this need while engaging the children in peace-building activities with the "other side."

The primary long-term objective of this program is to foster values that favor peace and coexistence between young Israelis and Palestinians by diffusing stereotypes and improving attitudes toward the "other." By using the tool of sport, it is believed that a relationship between young Israelis and Palestinians will be built, as well as a relationship with the families of the participants in the program. In addition, the objective of the program is to improve appreciation for the values of peace. The secondary objectives are to provide a forum for the improvement of fitness; to develop the participants' physical, cognitive, and social skills; to foster understanding and internalization of the concepts of sportsmanship and teamwork; and to increase motivation, confidence, and leadership skills.

The Twinned Peace Soccer Schools Project was developed specifically to achieve objectives related to peace building and self-development through sport over a significant period of time. The program is implemented from September to June (parallel to the academic year) and encourages entrants to continue their participation for a number of years to successfully foster a profound appreciation of peace and to achieve other aims related to fitness improvement and self-development.

The program is composed of four phases. Phase 1, soccer and fitness training, involves Israeli and Palestinian children meeting separately in their own communities twice a week for 90-minute sessions with local coaches. Phase 2, peace education and instruction, focuses on issues such as conflict resolution, improving listening skills, inclusion and exclusion, and similarities and differences. During this phase the youngsters get the chance to learn about the other side's culture, customs, and holidays. Peace education is implemented directly into the joint soccer training and fitness sessions, innovatively using the ball in the context of teamwork and cooperation games. Among the instructional principles emphasized in the joint soccer and fitness sessions are that the Israeli and Palestinian children will always be assigned to mixed groups, Israeli and Palestinian coaches will always work together with the mixed groups, no emphasis will be placed on winning or scoring while playing soccer, and positive reinforcements will be provided by the coaches to all children participating in the sessions, regardless of their nationality or culture. Cooperative games, with and without a ball, are regularly played by the mixed groups during each soccer and fitness session. Peace education is also implemented in the joint sporting and social activities phase (phase 4) using the same methods. The groups participate in ice-breaking exercises in mixed Israeli-Palestinian teams with the aid of simultaneous translation by the coaches, who work together in Israeli-Palestinian pairs.

Phase 3, inter-language learning, promotes the instruction of Arabic for the Israeli participants and Hebrew for the Palestinian participants. Phase 4, joint Israeli-Palestinian social and sporting activities, takes place on a monthly basis. The structure of these joint meetings includes peace education activities, teamwork and cooperation games, and playing soccer. The youngsters always play in mixed Israeli-Palestinian teams to mitigate direct competition and encourage values of teamwork, equality, and mutual appreciation. During the joint sessions, basic vocabulary is taught in Hebrew and Arabic to advance communication and understanding.

Mifalot's Sport for Education, Development, and Peace Program

Mifalot is the largest and most diverse organization in the Middle East that promotes the use of sport for fostering development and peace. Founded in 1997 by the owners of *Hapoel Tel-Aviv* (one of the biggest sport clubs in Israel), the vision of the organization is to take full advantage of the potential and power of soccer to build active, compassionate, and cohesive communities, and to support the sustainable development of an open, just, and engaged society (Mifalot's Sport for Education, Development, and Peace Program, 2007). The primary objective of this organization is to serve the educational and social needs of children and youth throughout the region. The organization seeks to provide children and youth with opportunities to learn, grow, and excel, and to participate in the development of their community and their world.

Mifalot has over 300 programs that use soccer to teach life skills to children with special needs, promote the integration and inclusion of newly-arrived immigrants, create bonds of friendship between Israelis and Palestinians, and provide much-needed assistance to children living in at-risk, disadvantaged, or isolated environments. About 20,000 children and youth across the region participate in Mifalot's programs throughout each year.

Mifalot also attempts to engage political institutions, the corporate sector, the general public at large, and the international community to ensure that attention is directed to the most pressing social issues in the region and that resources are provided to communities in urgent need. Rather than being perceived as a marketing ploy or public relations campaign, Mifalot is perceived by its funders, supporters, and partners as an earnest and effective use of sport to promote development and peace.

There are four fundamental objectives for each of the educational programs offered by Mifalot: (a) to provide equal access to quality sport and educational opportunities for children and youth in need; (b) to teach and empower children and youth with essential life skills and values; (c) to develop local leaders and promote stronger families within partner communities; and (d) to promote peace, inclusion, and coexistence across different cultural, religious, ethnic, and social groups. These four objectives guide Mifalot's work in Israel, the Palestinian Territories, and around the world.

Thirteen years of experience has given Mifalot a clear understanding about the areas where the organization is most effective. As an organization committed to solving local issues via local solutions, efforts have been made toward a number of development arenas, including early childhood development, social integration, and peace.

Early childhood development and education. The organization has more than 100 active programs around the region using soccer as a powerful incentive to work hard and do well in school. These educational soccer programs provide the children with the needed tutorial and homework help, as well as a safe place for after-school programs. For children living in at-risk or isolated environments, such as children in state-run institutions, the organization fills the gaps in education by providing unique instructional programs for teaching life skills, nurturing a love of learning and promoting a healthy and active lifestyle.

Social integration and inclusion. The organization reaches out to socially excluded groups and uses sport to teach life skills as well as foster relationships between different communities. The organization works with recreational centers and schools to provide sport and educational activities designed to help children with special needs, new immigrants, and political refugees, and to open new paths for inclusion in mainstream society.

Coexistence and peace. To foster a culture of peace and coexistence, the organization uses soccer to bridge social, religious, and ethnic divides. Mifalot's peace programs encourage new friendships among Jewish Israelis, Arab Israelis, Palestinians, Bedouins, Druze, Christians, refugees, Ethiopian immigrants, and Kibbutz (small cooperative farming settlements) children.

Football for Peace

The Football for Peace (F4P) Program is a joint program initiated by the University of Brighton (United Kingdom) and the British Council, focusing on the use of value-based soccer coaching to build bridges between neighboring Jewish and Arab cities in Israel (Sugden, 2007). The program is aimed at making a modest contribution to the peace process between Israel and its neighbors. More specifically, there are four objectives for the program: (a) to provide opportunities for social contact across community boundaries; (b) to promote mutual understanding among Jewish and Arabs who are engaged in the program; (c) to engender in those participants in the program a desire for and commitment to peaceful coexistence; and (d) to enhance soccer skills and technical knowledge.

In addition to the abovementioned four objectives, F4P emphasizes five learning principles (Lambert, 2007): (a) neutrality—those who participate in the program (i.e., players, coaches, parents, administrators) are not allowed to express their ideological and political agendas; (b) equity and inclusion—all participants are treated equally and those who would like to take part in the organized activities can do so regardless of their ethnicity, race, religion, gender, or ability; (c) respect—the appreciation of one's own individuality and the values of others (e.g., teammates and players from the opposing team, coaches, parents) in a context of social diversity; (d) trust—learning to have faith in the abilities of others to mutually carry out their roles and responsibilities, in ways that also contribute to the well-being of their teammates; and (e) responsibility—understanding that an individual's behaviors demonstrated in practices and games also have an effect on the performance and experiences of others.

The F4P program takes place during the school summer break in Israel (i.e., July) in the northern part of Israel—the Galilee, where Jewish and Arab communities are geographically closest to each other and where they maintain a normal day-to-day relationship (Nujidat, 2007). Not only children, but also administrators and coaches, are recruited from both Jewish and Arab cities in the Galilee area. The administrators and coaches involved in the F4P program participate in a special preparation program conducted in two locations. A number of months before the initiation of the program all the Jewish and Arab people involved in the program fly to the United Kingdom for about two weeks to meet at the campus of the University of Brighton, where the administrators and coaches are exposed to the educational foundation of the F4P program, and where the coaches become familiar with the soccer activities that will be performed during the practice sessions. A number of days before the practice sessions begin, the administrators and coaches gather in a selected hotel in one of the cities in the Galilee area, where final preparations for the initiation of the program are made. Evaluative sessions are conducted at the end of the program to analyze the activities performed. Based on this analysis, instructional ideas for the planning of the next F4P program are proposed.

FOSTERING RELATIONSHIPS AND BUILDING PEACE THROUGH SOCCER—THE MISSING LINK

In the previous two sections we presented a sport psychology intervention and educational programs aimed at fostering relationships and building peace among Jewish and Arab players. Both the sport psychology program and the educational programs have been conducted for a number of years. The management of the soccer clubs that hired the SPC valued his work and believed he had helped their young and adult players perform better on and off the field. In addition, the non-profit bodies that ideologically, and more important financially, supported the educational programs considered that these programs had exerted a positive influence on the social interactions among Jewish and Arab children.

Nevertheless, to increase our understanding of the contributions of the described educational and psychological programs in fostering relationships and building peace among Jewish and Arab players, a more systematic approach of data collection and data analysis should be adopted. It is difficult to assess the value of such programs without the use of a database that would be collected prior to the beginning of the programs, during the conduction of the programs, and more importantly, after the end of the programs. More specifically, we propose that the following two actions be taken into account by SPCs and policy makers to account for the missing link in the described programs—the research.

First, data should be collected on the effectiveness of the sport psychology programs provided to elite Jewish and Arab soccer players in Israel. In this chapter, we described the experiences of one SPC who worked with beginning and elite Jewish and Arab players. As far as we know, only the experiences of this SPC when working with Jewish and Arab players have been reported up to now (see also Lidor & Blumenstein, 2009). Nevertheless, neither quantitative nor qualitative data have been collected on the usefulness of the described principles and interventions of the sport psychology program, with one of its objectives being to promote relationships between Jewish and Arab players. For example, in-depth interviews focusing on the use of the described interventions as a tool to promote relationships between Jewish and Arab players should be conducted with the players themselves, their family members, and the coaching staff. Systematic observations in practices and games should be performed to follow patterns of overt behaviors demonstrated by Jewish and Arab players when interactions occur between them. In addition, obtaining data from the community or discussion circles, and other action research strategies (see Schinke et al., 2009) can also be used to examine the contribution of educational and psychological programs in fostering relationships between Jewish and Arab players.

Second, studies should be conducted on each of the programs that have been developed to build peace between Jewish and Arab players in Israel. Indeed, qualitative data were collected on several aspects of the F4P program (e.g., Liebmann & Rookwood, 2007; Sugden, 2006, 2008). For example, based on interviews conducted in the field with the participants in this program, Sugden (2006) reported that if educational programs such as the F4P are locally grounded, carefully thought out, and professionally managed, they can make a modest contribution to wider efforts being carried out to promote conflict resolution and peaceful co-existence. Nevertheless, no data on the other two programs—Twinned Peace Soccer Schools Project and Mifalot: Sport for Education, Development, and Peace—can be found. We suggest that the soccer activities performed by Jewish and Arab players be systematically observed and analyzed. In addition, in-depth interviews with the children and their parents and with the coaching staff should be performed to obtain relevant information about their perceptions of the programs. The interviews should be conducted not only prior to the beginning of the programs and during them, but most importantly, after the end of the programs. It is of particular interest for policy makers to assess the long-term contributions of the programs to the process of peace building. It should be noted that the authors of this chapter and a number of colleagues are now seeking to bridge research and practice in the area of development through sport in Israel. It is our goal to assess the actual contribution of these emerging psychological and educational programs aimed at fostering relationships and building peace among Jewish and Arab athletes.

PRACTICAL IMPLICATIONS FOR SPCS AND EDUCATORS WHO WORK WITH JEWISH AND ARAB PLAYERS IN ISRAEL

Four practical implications are suggested for those who work with Jewish and Arab soccer players. First, because soccer is a popular activity in both the Jewish and Arab populations, efforts should be made by coaches, school teachers, and policy makers to encourage children from the two populations to participate *together* in soccer activities. Public recognition should be provided to those programs that succeed in recruiting children from the two populations. Second, SPCs and instructors who work with Jewish and Arab players should document their practical work and collect relevant data that can help them assess the usefulness of their programs. Third, the programs aimed at fostering relationships and building peace between Jewish and Arab players should attract attention not only from those involved in the programs but also from the public at large, particularly key figures in politics and business, to promote the idea that professionally-managed soccer activities can be used not only as a sport activity per se, but also as an educational psychological tool for solving conflicts among individuals, such as the conflict between the Jews and Arabs. Fourth, preparation programs should be specifically developed for practitioners who work with young soccer players from the Jewish and Arab populations. Practitioners from both populations should participate together in these programs. They should be provided with the opportunity to interact professionally and socially in order to (a) get to know each other, and (b) establish trust and open relationships with each other before starting to work with the young players. These preparation programs should be composed of both enrichment sessions (e.g., Jewish culture, Arab culture, and foundations of cultural and social sport psychology) and soccer activities (e.g., those in which cooperative games are emphasized).

REFERENCES

Ben-Porat, A. (1993). *State and capitalism in Israel*. Westport, CT: Greenwood Press.

Blumenstein, B., & Lidor, R. (2008). Psychological preparation in the Olympic village: A four-phase approach. *International Journal of Sport and Exercise Psychology, 6*, 287-300.

Israel Football Association. (2010). Retrieved from www.israel-football.org.il

Lambert, J. (2007). A values-based approach to coaching sport in divided societies—The football for peace coaching manual. In J. Sugden & J. Wallis (Eds.), *Football for peace?—*

The challenges of using sport for co-existence in Israel (pp. 13-33). Oxford: Meyer & Meyer Sport.

Lidor, R., & Bar-Eli, M. (1998). Physical education in Israel: An overview. *The Chronicle of Physical Education in Higher Education, 9,* 14-15.

Lidor, R., & Blumenstein, B. (2009). Working with elite athletes in Israel. In R. J. Schinke & S. J. Hanrahan (Eds.), *Cultural sport psychology* (pp. 141-152). Champaign, IL: Human Kinetics.

Lidor, R., & Blumenstein, B. (in press). Sport psychology consultations for professional soccer players—working with diverse teams. *Athletic Insight.*

Lidor, R., Blumenstein, B., & Tenenbaum, G. (2007). Psychological aspects of elite training programs in European basketball: Conceptualization, periodization, and planning. *The Sport Psychologist, 21,* 353-367.

Liebmann, S., & Rookwood, J. (2007). Football for peace? Bringing Jews and Arabs together in Northern Israel. *Journal of Qualitative Research in Sports Studies, 1,* 11-18.

Mifalot's Sport for Education, Development, and Peace Program (2007). Retrieved from www.mifalot.co.il

Nujidat, G. (2007). A view from the Israeli Sports Authority. In J. Sugden & J. Wallis (Eds.), *Football for peace?—The challenges of using sport for co-existence in Israel* (pp. 141-154). Oxford: Meyer & Meyer Sport.

Pitch for Peace (2006). *Twinned Peace Football Schools Project.* Tel Aviv: The Peres Center for Peace.

Schinke, R. J., Gauthier, A. P., Dubuc, N. G., & Crowder, T. (2007). Understanding athlete adaptation in the National Hockey League through an archival data source. *The Sport Psychologist, 21,* 277-287.

Schinke, R. J., Peltier, D., Hanrahan, S. J., Eys, M. A., Recollet-Saikonnen, D., Yungblut, H., Ritchie, S., Pickard, P., & Michel, G. (2009). The progressive integration of Canadian indigenous culture within a sport psychology bicultural research team. *International Journal of Sport and Exercise Psychology, 7,* 309-322.

Sorek, T. (2010). *Arab soccer in a Jewish state—The integrative enclave.* UK: Cambridge University Press.

Statistical Aspects of Israel (2006). Retrieved from www.cbs.gov.il

Sugden, J. (2006). Teaching and playing sport for conflict resolution and co-existence in Israel. *International Review for the Sociology of Sport, 41,* 221-240.

Sugden, J. (2007). Introduction: Football for peace in context. In J. Sugden & J. Wallis (Eds.), *Football for peace?—The challenges of using sport for co-existence in Israel* (pp. 1-12). Oxford: Meyer & Meyer Sport.

Sugden, J. (2008). Anyone for football for peace? The challenges of using sport in the service of co-existence in Israel. *Soccer & Society, 9,* 405-415.

Working through Distrust with a Canadian First Nation through Sport Research

Robert J. Schinke, Duke Peltier, Leslee Anne Fisher,
Amy T. Blodgett, Lawrence Enosse, and Mary Jo Wabano

The word itself "research" is probably one of the dirtiest words in the indigenous world's vocabulary. When mentioned in many indigenous contexts, it stirs up silence, it conjures up bad memories, it raises a smile that is knowing and distrustful…. The ways in which scientific research is implicated in the worst excesses of colonialism remains a powerful remembered history for many of the world's colonized peoples. (Linda Smith, 1999, p. 1)

Globally, there has been an acknowledgement that indigenous peoples have been marginalized—perhaps even targeted[1]—through a wide number of colonizing practices, including colonization through research. Mainstream researchers involved in colonizing might suggest that their oversights/omissions are inadvertent whilst working with a culture other than their own and supplanting local with mainstream research practices. There is nothing wrong with using mainstream research practices when participants hold mainstream worldviews. When participants and researchers are mainstream in their standpoints, the voices of both members are respected within the exchange. Nevertheless, when researchers are learning from/working with participants from exploited populations, mainstream research practices silence, and in the process push or sustain voices at the margins. Smith (1999) articulated that research is a location where power is abused, and, as such it must also be a location where inequities are remedied. We propose that Smith's views about research must also be considered within sport science research. In this chapter, we describe Wikwemikong Unceded Indian Reserve members' previous experiences working with mainstream researchers (although it should be noted that a member's experiences do not represent the entire reserve, necessarily). We also invite readers to examine the seven year long research collaboration between Wikwemikong and researchers from Laurentian University, the shift in the method and focus of our research as a result of becoming culturally reflexive in our practice, and our shared partnership. Finally, we make suggestions related to culturally reflexive practice for future researchers.

Waneek Horn-Miller, a Canadian Aboriginal Olympian from water polo, spoke at the 2002 North American Indigenous Games Sport Research Conference about her athletic experiences in mainstream sport contexts (see Brant, Forsyth, Horn-Miller, Loutitt, Sinclair, Smith, et al., 2002). During a panel discussion, Waneek pondered about a sport psychology and a sport psychologist coming from her worldview as an Aboriginal of Mohawk heritage. Waneek continued that the aforementioned wish "would be my dream" (p. 67). When the reader considers Waneek's request, on one level there is the call for a sport psychology that reflects her standpoint as a Canadian Aboriginal athlete from Mohawk descent. Considering the athlete's words a little more closely, it also becomes abundantly clear that a culturally safe sport psychology approach for Waneek seemed to be a dream, a world away from her firsthand experience with sport science. The inequity Waneek experienced was on a sociocultural level, when her Aboriginal practices were not known in advance of intervention by the mainstream sport psychology consultant. The same approach to sport science provision in practice has mirrored the sport science research domain on which it was founded (Ryba & Schinke, 2009). Unfortunately, there is already considerable evidence that research can and often does silence voices from the margins (Ryba & Schinke).

The focus in our chapter is on what can be achieved through research in terms of reconciliation. Just as research can silence, so too can research forefront the voices and cultural identities of co-researchers and participants. The benefits in and through research are immense: Research can reverse marginalization, build trust amongst cultures, and restore friendships (Schinke, Watson, Enosse, Peltier, & Lightfoot, 2010). What follows is a chapter based upon seven years of collaborative research with a First Nation in Canada, co-facilitated by the first and second authors, one from a university setting, one from Wikwemikong Unceded Indian Reserve. Further, this chapter represents collaboration in one First Nation community only. The reader must remember that each marginalized group is entitled to a unique/contextually relevant approach as mainstream researcher and oppressed community meet on level ground.

WIKWEMIKONG UNCEDED INDIAN RESERVE

Wikwemikong is located on the eastern side of Manitoulin Island in northeastern Ontario, Canada. It spans across Georgian Bay and Lake Huron with the reserve area totaling 413 square kilometers. The on-reserve population is over 3,000 people, making Wikwemikong the largest community on Manitoulin Island. As the first permanent settlement there, Wikwemikong has retained much of its rich history and traditional culture. The community is recognized as Canada's only Unceded Indian Reserve, meaning that its people have not relinquished title of their land to Canada's government (Manitoulin Island, 2005).

From what our co-authors understand, the Wikwemikong people remember many negative experiences of when "White researchers" stepped onto Wikwemikong territory and conducted research on its members and in the community, uninvited. Rita Corbiere, a Wikwemikong elder, recalled an experience when she was a public schoolteacher several decades ago. Rita noticed a white-skinned person walking through the corridors of her workplace with a pen and notepad in hand. The person seemed to be observing the students and taking notes, much as one would in quality assurance. As Rita continued to describe the event that unfolded—she was clarifying what her formative research experience was with academics—she bristled with irritation. When Rita asked what the White researcher was doing, he responded: "I'm doing research." The researcher was subsequently asked to physically leave the school. Rita's view was that researchers often step onto Wikwemikong territory uninvited as they proceed with their work. What ensues is a disrespect of local culture where consultation is expected from the beginning.

One might question whether Rita's experience would happen in present day. Rita has been in retirement and serving as a community elder for several years now. Nevertheless, just last week while the first author was co-presenting at a national ethics conference with a co-researcher and co-author from Wikwemikong, a similar experience was shared that had happened just a few weeks earlier (January, 2010). Lawrence Enosse, a member of our Wikwemikong–Laurentian research team bumped into a European visitor to the region of Northern Ontario. The visitor was videotaping and taking pictures on Wikwemikong territory, and Lawrence asked what the visitor was doing. The response was that the visitor was engaging in research for a forthcoming documentary. Lawrence responded that he was unaware of any such documentary. The researcher responded sheepishly that no harm would come to Wikwemikong. Underlying the researcher's belief was that Lawrence should take him at face value. Even though Lawrence asked the researcher to stop filming, the visitor remained on Wikwemikong territory the entire week, ignoring Lawrence's request. As Lawrence shared the story with Robert it was clear that the people of Wikwemikong have become increasingly wary about with whom they share their knowledge and also who is allowed to physically conduct research on the reserve. In accordance with the *Canadian Institute of Health Research Guidelines for Research Involving Aboriginal People*

(2007), Aboriginal reserves are entitled to protect their cultural practices and knowledge. If only mainstream researchers would respect such rights. It seems that even in the present day, researchers continue to disrespect Aboriginal participants.

There now exists a process to initiate research within Wikwemikong and of its people. Potential projects are required to seek approval from the Council of Wikwemikong Unceded Indian Reserve through a recommendation by a mandated committee or board, dependent upon the area that is to be studied. The committee or board is tasked with vetting all research projects where researchers wish to step onto Wikwemikong's grounds, or whenever Wikwemikong Band members are invited onto research projects either as co-researchers or as participants/co-participants. The vetting process that now exists in Wikwemikong is necessary and, sadly, reactive to past research experiences and is also proactive in terms of future experiences.

THE WIKWEMIKONG—LAURENTIAN RESEARCH TEAM

Our team first met in Spring, 2004, when Robert and his academic co-applicants were awarded research funding by the Social Sciences and Humanities Research Council of Canada. The project was a Research Development Initiative conceptualized to spur a culturally reflexive movement in sport psychology termed "cultural sport psychology." Robert is a sport psychology consultant who works with elite amateur and professional boxers from a variety of cultures. The clients Robert has encountered in the field have included athletes from the Caribbean, Eastern Europe, North Africa, Asia, Central America, the Near East, and athletes born in Canada of British, French, and Aboriginal descent (Schinke, 2007). From his experiences, Robert found that athletes often appreciate a culturally informed approach during their sport psychology sessions. Further, Robert found that many of his Aboriginal clients disengaged from the national boxing team after only one season due to a mono-cultural approach, where cultural identities of those outside the mainstream were subverted. Consequently, the goal through the research was to develop a sport psychology relevant among Canadian Aboriginal elite boxers. Robert hoped to share his findings with coaches and sport scientists through formal dissemination.

When the project was funded Robert was invited to present his work to members from Wikwemikong's Council, local Elders, and other stakeholders. Until the moment the presentation began, Robert anticipated that he was informing Wikwemikong of the project and its potential importance for academics, as a type of update. After a brief presentation/ lecture with a full complement of Power Point slides, the community members began to ask questions. The questions and ensuing discussion was about the salience of the project to Wikwemikong. Though Robert was unaware of the potential consequences from the discussion, had the members decided the project was not meaningful in Wikwemikong, the community might have opted out of the research. Of note, a second reserve initially supported the research project and did in fact opt out. Luckily for Robert, those attending, including the Chief, a few elders, Duke Peltier, and Lawrence Enosse, chose to collaborate. Through agreeing to collaborate on the project, the community of Wikwemikong agreed to invest considerable time and effort educating the project team's mainstream academic co-researchers about culturally relevant and safe research practices in the community.

Meetings such as the one Robert experienced are opportunities for growth amongst mainstream researchers seeking to engage Aboriginal communities. Initial meetings are opportunities for community members and academics to meet and discuss the implications of research projects in advance of formal commitments. Recently, a research project was brought forward to Wikwemikong for support, and the mainstream researchers chose not to attend the initial meeting whilst the community considered the research project. The Wikwemikong committee tasked with evaluating the project halted their deliberation and requested that the academics attend in person. When the Wikwemikong consider supporting research projects they ponder many aspects such as (a) do the mainstream researchers approach the community in an open manner, inviting comprehensive involvement in the study?; (b) does the project allow for capacity-building amongst Wikwemikong community co-researchers?; (c) is the project (and the academics) respectful of local customs?; (d) is the project relevant in Wikwemikong, given the community's current directions/objectives?; and finally (e) are community members willing to work with the mainstream academics on the project to ensure proprietary rights and the integration of local Aboriginal worldviews? When the community halted their evaluation on the research project discussed in the immediate paragraph, the mainstream researchers who initially chose not to attend quickly realized that within Wikwemikong-partnered projects, the academics would have to work outside of their traditional silos. Departures from conventional research habits include the building of meaningful collaborations from the beginning and also a long-term commitment to the Wikwemikong, potentially beyond the mandate of any single project (see Blodgett, Schinke, Peltier, Fisher, Wabano, Pickard, et al., 2010).

The relationship among our blended team of researchers advanced steadily as trust built within the team and also with the Wikwemikong people (see Blodgett, Schinke, Fisher, Wassengeso-George, Peltier, Ritchie, & Pickard, 2008). When Schinke, Hanrahan, and Catina (2009) unpacked a number of basic considerations for culturally informed research and practice, they identified time as a critical part of inter-cultural discussion. Our team's mainstream academics are typically governed by clock-based time. We expect to complete funded projects within the two- to three-year timeline permitted by the funding agencies that sponsor our work. Typically, mainstream researchers work on research projects, keeping in mind the calendar year. At the end of a three-year project, the research project culminates in published contributions and a report to the granting agency. Thereafter, relations often cease with participants and co-researchers as academics shift focus and pursue new projects. Problems arise contributing to distrust within mainstream academic and Aboriginal community research teams when an adherence to a definitive beginning and end of a research project guides the chronology of commitments, especially as commitments end. Within Wikwemikong, community members are governed by event-based time, where relationships are built and maintained over the long term, with meetings serving to update and deepen relations (Schinke, Blodgett, Ritchie, Pickard, Michel, Peltier, et al., 2009). Consequently, at the end of a three-year project, assuming that the people of Wikwemikong enjoy a given research partnership, the team is expected to continue their collaboration through either the continuation of an existing project or the development of a new project, informed by lessons from the previous project (Schinke, Hanrahan, Eys, Blodgett, Peltier, Ritchie, et al., 2008). Research relationships need not have a beginning and an ending. Rather, research should be built around a commitment by co-researchers to work together, learn from each other, and refine practices and questions over the long term, perhaps even over the researchers' entire careers.

RECIPROCATING THROUGH THE SHIFTING FOCUS OF RESEARCH

As mentioned previously, our research team has worked together since 2004. The team began researching the practices of Canadian Aboriginal elite athletes from across Canada. The project was among the first formal sport psychology investigations into cultural practices for populations that are not mainstream and Eurocentric. Eurocentrism is a view that all people are governed by the same culturally informed worldview (Ryba & Wright, 2005). The origins of Eurocentrism reflect European values, where the individual is prioritized over the group. Researchers and applied practitioners in domains such as sport psychology have adhered to the tenets of Eurocentrism, likely because people are educated in universities from knowledge generated by mainstream researchers. In sport psychology as in psychology generally (Riggs, 2004), the approach to research and practice has been entirely mainstream, with theories of individuality such as self-efficacy, learned helplessness, self-determination, and self-regulation informing much of the discourse (Schinke, Hanrahan, & Catina, 2009). Consequently, by asking Canadian Aboriginal participants how to develop a meaningful sport psychology approach, as was suggested by Waneek Horn Miller, a larger discussion was spurred in the sport sciences. The intent through research was to develop a Canadian Aboriginal sport psychology, though arguably when one groups all people of a culture together, the approach is reductionist and overly simplistic (Andersen, 1993).

Our research team committed several mistakes within our formative efforts. Our oversights have been outlined elsewhere (e.g., Schinke, Peltier, Hanrahan, Eys, Yungblut, Ritchie, et al., 2009) and reflected limited understanding on the part of the mainstream academic researchers. For example, the research methods our team employed initially were conventional mainstream qualitative strategies, including semi-structured interviews, thematic analysis, and conventional validity guidelines. The Aboriginal co-researchers in our team were tolerant of the mainstream approach employed in the research. Duke, Lawrence, and a third colleague, Chris Pheasant, waited with patience while the mainstream academics found that mainstream methods would not invite full engagement from local participants. The Wikwemikong co-researchers then waited for the academic co-researchers to return to the group in search of better ways to glean in-depth knowledge. There was no certainty that the two-year completion date for our first project would signal a shift to culturally informed methods. Nevertheless, in keeping with views toward non-interference (Martin-Hill & Soucy, 2007), the Wikwemikong co-researchers waited patiently while the mainstream academics learned a more thoughtful way of engaging with community co-researchers and co-participants. The shift in orientation from mainstream to culturally reflexive methods has enhanced relationships among the researchers, and also the research team's relationship with Wikwemikong. Had the team not evolved in our approach, the initial silencing of Wikwemikong customs and values would have been overlooked, and such silencing would not have been remedied through our research. Rather, the team would unintentionally have supported colonizing practices through our research practices.

More recently, our team has shifted focus and tackled a social challenge in Wikwemikong: Barriers and consequent engagement of youth in sport and recreation programming. The shift in topic matter has increased the relevance of our work efforts in Wikwemikong. The earlier project has evolved into a new project, with the shift of topic matter affirming what is most important at present in Wikwemikong. The shift in research focus from our initial work to our project with youth marked an important moment in the project team's efforts. The new project evolved over the course of a research meeting as Duke Peltier and Robert Schinke ate lunch. The earlier project with elite athletes was progressing well, and the work was receiving formal acceptance within academia. Publishing novel work was important to Robert and also to Duke. Duke's view was (and continues to be) that Wikwemikong receives international exposure through our collaborations and the collaborations among other research teams engaging with Wikwemikong, where research manifests in international publications and presentations. Nevertheless, Duke's wish, which was also the wish of the community co-researchers, generally was that any future research should be immediately relevant in the daily lives of people on the reserve. Excavating deeper into the shift in research, there was a shift in the relationships within the team. Duke was a former elite athlete, as was Lawrence. Both men, however, were working with youth when they chose to serve as community co-researchers during the team's earliest project about elite athletes. Duke and Lawrence have been committed to youth sport initiatives for some time given the number of health risks associated with a sedentary lifestyle. Risks among the Wikwemikong include rates well above the national average in terms of substance abuse, diabetes, and incarceration (Health Council of Canada, 2007). Consequently, the community members' interest in youth became the new direction for the research team. The consequence was enhanced goodwill among the team's members, especially when the academic researchers agreed to shift their research focus away from their own personal interest of elite sport.

SHIFTING METHODOLOGY

Researchers are often unaware that the methodologies they employ are culturally informed. In qualitative methods, there are a wide array of strategies from which a researcher might choose, including an approach relevant when partnering in research with Aboriginal communities: Participatory action research (PAR). PAR is "an orientation to research that focuses on relationships between academic and community partners, with principles of co-learning, mutual benefit, and long-term commitment, and incorporates community theories, participation, and practices into the research efforts" (Wallerstein & Duran, 2006, p. 312). The research methods our team began with (aforementioned) were mainstream and Eurocentic, meaning that the approaches were developed from within academic circles and then taken into field research. Our team employed collaborative efforts from the beginning, though the extent of collaboration initially sought from Duke, Lawrence, and Chris was relatively minor (Schinke, Peltier, et al., 2009). Assistance was sought in the refinement of interview questions, when making sense of themes that surfaced throughout analyses, and in terms of publishing and presenting. Our academic co-authors believed that the feedback sought from Wikwemikong initially was "collaboration." Nevertheless, when our project team re-considered our research focus and re-directed our efforts towards youth sport and physical activity, we also reconceptualized our approach to research.

Our team's step forward was through the implementation of a talking circle in place of a focus group interview. Though both data collection strategies are efforts where people from a collective orientation might feel at ease, talking circles signaled the embracing and respect of local practices in our work. Unlike focus groups where often mainstream researchers lead discussion, in talking circles, discussions were led by the community co-researchers. Those who chose to engage in the open invitation to participate sat in a circle, with each member invited to either contribute or decline before passing tobacco or a talking stick to the next person, moving clockwise around the circle (see Picou, 2000; Running Wolf & Rickard, 2003). Finally, unlike focus groups, the talking circles only ended when there was nothing more to be said among the group, affirming an event, in place of a clock-based approach to time.

During a talking circle, a co-participant passed Robert a piece of paper to articulate her view regarding the difference between his White academic and her community and collective worldviews. On the piece of paper were two diagrams (see Figure 5.1). The first diagram featured a web of interconnected circles, with the diagram resembling a spider's web. The community member's sketch for the second diagram was that of an individual in authority with people placed in unilateral contact to the right, reflecting their decreasing levels of power. From the diagram, Robert realized that his approach was top-down and authoritative and the view of the co-participants in the circle reflected a collective orientation, where people inter-related, with each person offering the circle unique expertise (i.e., there was no single authority; knowledge and expertise were collectively owned by Wikwemikong). Since that first talking circle, every aspect of what our team has done reflects a shared voice, with each member bringing her/his expertise to the group. From our collective approach to research, the team has developed collaborative data analysis strategies where terminology and the grouping of data are developed onsite in Wikwemikong (see Schinke, Yungblut, Blodgett, Peltier, Ritchie, & Recollet-Saikonnen, 2010). Our team has also developed a vignette, which is a form of narrative, written collaboratively by the Wikwemikong co-researchers (Blodgett, Schinke, Peltier, Wabano, Fisher, Eys, et al., 2010). The purpose of the vignette was to empower the Wikwemikong co-researchers to voice their research experiences and recommendations in their own words, and to forefront local indigenous perspectives amongst those from the mainstream. The research team has clearly shifted towards more culturally safe and relevant methods among Wikwemikong

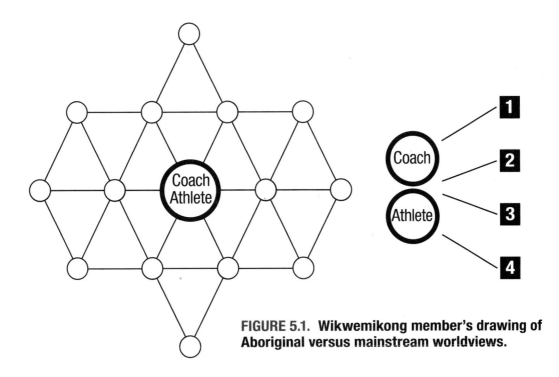

FIGURE 5.1. Wikwemikong member's drawing of Aboriginal versus mainstream worldviews.

co-researchers, and developed a better approach to research within the context. Neverthe-less, it should be noted that the shifts in research methods would not have been possible had Duke, Lawrence, Chris, and Rita withheld their elaborate knowledge of relevant PAR research within Wikwemikong. The knowledge among our research team was developed in Wikwemikong and shared with the academics as a means of fostering deeper partner-ships based on understanding and also as a strategy for initiating meaningful projects that are culturally affirming. Through similar collaborative efforts, researchers in other inter-cultural community research teams can also employ or develop approaches to meaningful research within the relevant context.

A SHARED PARTNERSHIP

Recently, two members of our research team co-presented at a national research ethics conference. Lawrence and Robert were invited to speak about cultural missteps dur-ing research with Aboriginal co-researchers and co-participants. The presentation was devised to feature the worldviews of both co-presenters with Lawrence and Robert speak-ing to each slide from Wikwemikong community and mainstream academic perspectives. The presentation went extremely well, with slightly more time apportioned for Lawrence, given that he has experienced many culturally insensitive research projects as a partici-pant, co-researcher, and also as a member of his community's research evaluation commit-tee. Lawrence addressed questions throughout the presentation and also at its end. Those attending were interested in learning from Lawrence, given his Aboriginal community standpoint, about how to work ethically during inter-cultural research. Contrasted with our efforts earlier in the conference, a team of mainstream academic and Aboriginal com-munity members (not Wikwemikong) also co-presented. The academic researchers spoke almost the entire presentation, inviting perfunctory-sporadic comments from their com-munity co-presenters. Though on paper the second presentation was collaborative, most of the information conveyed represented the views only of the academics.

A shared partnership should extend beyond collaborating superficially, into com-plete engagement and equal voice within presentations, and also within publications. Our research team has always co-presented, though much like the contrasting project we just described, initially, most of the information we conveyed was by the mainstream aca-demic co-researchers. Although the community co-researchers in our team have undeni-ably enjoyed traveling to international venues over the course of the funded projects, only recently have they felt the have provided great depth to the presentations. The community co-researchers have always held the knowledge of how best to describe a Wikwemikong worldview. With confidence, built from active engagement in writing and presenting, it seems that the community co-researchers are quickly becoming the project team leaders. The academic co-researchers are also changing their roles as they offer some expertise in data management and authoring as well as the human resources to seek funding and manage research students (research and all of the commitments it entails is part of their employment). Consequently, our co-researchers are all engaged in research tasks, though only members from Wikwemikong can speak from a community perspective. The engagement and subsequent ownership by Wikwemikong in the research has transformed our project team (see Cho & Trent, 2006; Lather, 1986) and has become the most salient measure of our success as researchers.

CONCLUDING REMARKS

The work we have outlined within this chapter is part of an ongoing collaboration among co-researchers from Wikwemikong Unceded Indian Reserve and sport science researchers from the academic community. The experiences we have shared reflect efforts where the goal has been to progressively create research projects meaningful within our region for Aboriginal youth participants. Furthermore, the collaborative processes have been geared at creating social change locally, from within the reserve. The research team is now in our seventh year of collaborating, and the two successive projects we considered here are meant to reflect evolution on the part of our members. The academic researchers continue to learn from Duke, Lawrence, Chris, and Rita about how research needs to happen in Wikwemikong. Our academic White researchers initially believed that we understood how to engage in inter-cultural research with community members on the reserve. As the Wikwemikong co-researchers take on a progressively more active role within the team, it is becoming clearer that how we have proceeded to this point and from the innovation that has resulted, we are only scratching the surface. The opportunities that are starting to avail are the result of a long-term commitment and could not have materialized from one fleeting research project. With time and openness comes trust, though trust only happens over time (and by time, we do not mean by a definitive clock).

Further, although we did not start out envisioning that this project would serve as a resistance strategy to the oppression that can sometimes occur in mainstream research, we now realize that this might have happened. Like Heldke and O'Connor (2004), we advocate for using coalition-building—in this case, amongst mainstream university academics and Aboriginal community members as co-researchers—as a resistance strategy against the usual "divide-and-conquer" mentality that has been in place historically when White mainstream researchers have entered First Nation spaces. Working together, we've come to realize that we've disrupted the "usual" approach. In the words of Matsuda (2004), we are also reminded that coalition-building should not be based on always "feeling comfortable." We believe that research with traditionally marginalized peoples should be uplifting and protectionary versus value-neutral and comfortable for those in the mainstream.

Finally, we believe that such work should continue to be done in collaboration with First Nations peoples. As Matsuda suggested (2004):

> [A]nalysis done from on high, that is, from outside rather than inside a structure of subordination, risks misunderstanding the particularity of that structure. Feminists have spent years talking about, experiencing, and building theory around gender. Native Americans have spent years developing an understanding of colonialism and its effect on culture. That kind of situated, ground-up knowledge is irreplaceable, and a casual effort to say, 'OK, I'll add [another facet] to my analysis,' without immersion into [situated] practice is likely to miss something. (p. 736)

It is our hope that future researchers can benefit from the mistakes and growth we have undergone.

RECOMMENDATIONS FOR RESEARCHERS WORKING THROUGH CULTURAL DISTRUST

Stemming from our seven-year research collaboration between mainstream academics and Aboriginal community members, we offer some general suggestions for other researchers working through cultural distrust. The recommendations are presented from both the mainstream and Aboriginal authors' standpoints.

Mainstream Perspective

- Initial community meetings should be viewed as opportunities for mainstream researchers to learn about the community and people with whom they are seeking to engage in a given project. Researchers should be receptive to the contextual information that is often shared in these meetings, including local priorities and concerns that are relevant to community members, the formal research protocols that are in place, and the key people who would be instrumental in moving a project forward locally. By taking in such information in the initial community meetings, researchers show that they are genuinely interested in learning how to work with the community to meet local expectations and needs.

- A PAR approach should be used to engage community members as equal and active partners in a project, therein contributing to a re-balancing of power relations amongst the community and academic co-researchers. This local engagement strategy reflects a transformative process in empowering community members to transition out of passive participant roles and into researcher roles where they are responsible for leading relevant project aspects from within their community.

Aboriginal Perspective

- Research relationships should be maintained long term. Although traditionally, research relationships are established for the duration of a funded project and then fizzle at the project conclusion, there is often a greater commitment expected when working with marginalized community members. Research relationships should be built around a mutual commitment by co-researchers to work together, learn from each other, and ultimately work toward improving the community context, beyond the scope of a single research project.

- Research projects must be relevant to community members and should explore transformative possibilities for improving the local context. Projects should be developed from within the community to align with local needs and priorities, rather than from the academic agendas of mainstream researchers.

- Mainstream researchers should be open to gaining capacity from the local knowledge of community members, ongoing. A new repertoire of strategies steeped in community perspectives and traditions may be gained as research relationships are deepened, open dialogues are engaged, and community members feel comfortable sharing their views. Accordingly, mainstream researchers must be open and flexible to a research process that constantly evolves through better contextual understanding.

REFERENCES

Andersen, M. B. (1993). Questionable sensitivity: A comment on Lee and Rotella. *The Sport Psychologist, 7,* 1-3.

Blodgett, A. T., Schinke, R. J., Fisher, L. A., Wassengeso-George, C., Peltier, D., Ritchie, S., & Pickard, P. (2008). From practice to praxis: Community-based strategies for Aboriginal youth sport. *Journal of Sport and Social Issues, 32,* 393-414.

Blodgett, A. T., Schinke, R. J., Peltier, D., Wabano, M. J., Fisher, L. A., Eys, M. A., et al. (2010). Naadmaadmi: Reflections of Aboriginal community members engaged in sport psychology co-researching activities with mainstream academics. *Qualitative Research in Sport and Exercise, 2,* 56-76.

Blodgett, A. T., Schinke, R. J., Peltier, D., Fisher, L. A., Wabano, M. J., Pickard, P., et al. (2010). May the circle be unbroken: The recommendations of First Nation community members engaged in participatory action health research with mainstream academics. Submitted for publication.

Brant, R., Forsyth, J., Horn-Miller, W., Loutitt, J., Sinclair, C., Smith, M., et al. (2002). North American Indigenous Games Sport Research Panel. In R. Brant & J. Forsyth (Eds.), *2002 North American Indigenous Games Conference Proceedings* (pp. 67-70). Winnipeg, Canada: University of Manitoba Press.

Canadian Institutes of Health Research. (2007). *CIHR guidelines for health reseach involving Aboriginal people.* Ottawa, Canada: Author.

Cho, J., & Trent, A. (2006). Validity in qualitative research revisited. *Qualitative Research, 6,* 319-340.

Fisher, L. A., & Anders, A. (2010). Critically engaging with sport psychology ethics through cultural studies. In T. Ryba, R. Schinke, and G. Tenenbaum (Eds.), *The cultural turn in sport and exercise psychology* (Chapter 6). Morgantown, WV: Fitness Information Technology.

Health Council of Canada. (2007). Aboriginal Health 2006 Annual Report. Retrieved June 10, 2008, from www.healthcouncilcanada.ca

Heldke, L., & O'Connor, P. (2004). *Oppression, privilege, & resistance: Theoretical perspectives on racism, sexism, and heterosexism.* Boston, MA: McGraw Hill.

Lather, P. (1986). Research as praxis. *Harvard Educational Review, 56,* 257-277.

Manitoulin Island. (2005). Visit Wikwemikong. Retrieved November 21, 2007, from http://www.manitoulin-island.com/wikwemikong/

Martin-Hill, D., & Soucy, D. (2007). *Ethical guidelines for Aboriginal research elders and healers roundtable.* Report by the Indigenous Health Research Development Program to the Interagency Advisory Panel of Research Ethics.

Matsuda, M. (2004). Standing beside my sister, facing the enemy: Legal theory out of coalition. In L. Heldke and P. O'Connor (Eds.), *Oppression, privilege, & resistance: Theoretical perspectives on racism, sexism, and heterosexism* (pp.732-738). Boston, MA: McGraw Hill.

Picou, J. S. (2000). The "talking circle" as sociological practice: Cultural transformation of chronic disaster impacts. *Sociological Practice: A Journal of Clinical and Applied Sociology, 2,* 77-97.

Riggs, D. W. (2004). Challenging the monoculturalism of psychology: Towards a more socially accountable pedagogy and practice. *Australian Psychologist. 39,* 118-126.

Running Wolf, P., & Rickard, J. A. (2003). Talking circles: A Native American approach to experiential learning. *Multicultural Counseling and Development, 31,* 39-43.

Ryba, T. V., & Schinke, R. J. (2009). Methodology as a ritualized eurocentrism: Introduction to the special issue. *International Journal of Sport and Exercise Psychology, 7,* 263-274.

Ryba, T. V., & Wright, H. K. (2005). From mental game to cultural praxis: A cultural studies model's implications for the future of sport psychology. *Quest, 57,* 192-212.

Schinke, R. J. (2007). A four-year chronology with national team boxing in Canada. *Journal of Sport Science and Medicine, 6,* 1-7.

Schinke, R. J., Blodgett, A., Ritchie, C., Pickard, P., Michel, G., Peltier, D., et al. (2009). Entering the community of Canadian Indigenous athletes. In R. J. Schinke & S. J. Hanrahan (Eds.), *Cultural sport psychology: From theory to practice* (pp. 91-102). Champaign, IL: Human Kinetics.

Schinke, R. J., Hanrahan, S. J., & Catina, P. (2009). Introduction to cultural sport psychology. In R. J. Schinke & S. J. Hanrahan (Eds.), *Cultural sport psychology: From theory to practice* (pp. 1-12). Champaign, IL: Human Kinetics.

Schinke, R. J., Hanrahan, S. J., Eys, M. A., Blodgett, A., Peltier, D., Ritchie, S., et al. (2008). The development of cross-cultural relations with a Canadian Aboriginal community through sport psychology research. *Quest, 60,* 357-369.

Schinke, R. J., Peltier, D., Hanrahan, S. J., Eys, M. A., Yungblut, H., Ritchie, S., et al, (2009). The progressive move toward indigenous strategies among a Canadian multicultural research team. *International Journal of Sport and Exercise Psychology, 6,* 309-322.

Schinke, R. J., Watson, J. W., Enosse, N., Peltier, D., & Lightfoot, N. (2010). Cultural missteps and ethical considerations with Indigenous populations: Preliminary reflections from Northeastern Ontario, Canada. *The Journal of Academic Ethics.* In Press.

Schinke, R. J., Yungblut, H. E., Blodgett, A., Peltier, D., Ritchie, S., & Recollet-Saikonnen, D. (2010). The role of families in youth sport programming within a Canadian Aboriginal community. *The Journal of Physical Activity and Health, 3,* 156-166.

Smith, L. T. (1999). *Decolonizing methodologies: Research and Indigenous peoples.* Dunedin: University of Otago Press.

Wallerstein, N. B., & Duran, B. (2006). Using community-based participatory research to address health disparities. *Health Promotion Practice, 7,* 312-323.

ENDNOTE

[1] Some researchers (e.g., Fisher & Anders, 2010) have suggested that *marginalization* is not a strong enough word to connote the inherent racism and colonialism that people of color and those who have alternative gender and sexual orientations face in a racist, sexist, homophobic, and heteronormative society. They use the term *targeted* instead to reflect this position.

Rethinking Community-based Crime Prevention through Sports

Douglas Hartmann

n the 1990s, a new wave of social interventions appeared on the American urban landscape: community-based, sports-oriented crime prevention programs. Touted as innovative, inexpensive, and remarkably effective approaches to crime prevention and targeted typically at racial minorities, these initiatives came in a variety of types and sizes. Some were small, single-sport programs located in schools or operated at community centers. Others were city-wide, multi-sport summertime projects, and still others were run by sports experts at Olympic training centers or sports foundations. They ranged from police athletic leagues to prison boot camps and used sporting practices as diverse as basketball, calisthenics, martial arts, and motor-cross. But whatever the specifics, the idea of using sport to prevent crime (and reduce risk) was both popular and well-publicized, and helped shape an entire generation of sports-based social programming in the United States and elsewhere (Pitter & Andrews, 1997; see also: Cameron & MacDougall, 2000; Nichols, 2007).

For all of this publicity and positivity, however, sports-based crime prevention was not well thought through or understood. For example, although relatively inexpensive in and of themselves, such programs were often the ironic, unintended result of the cutbacks and privatization of public parks and recreation facilities in many locales (Crompton, 1998; Crompton & McGregor, 1994; Schultz, Crompton, & Witt, 1995), and sports-based initiatives certainly couldn't replace all social services that were being eliminated or reconstituted as neo liberalism took shape in American metropolitan areas (Harvey,

2005; Wacquant, 2009). Also, these programs were often predicated on troubling images and stereotypes of minority populations (for analysis, see Cole, 1996; Hartmann, 2001; for a broader critique of the racialized character of neoliberalism, see Goldberg, 2008). Moreover, in spite of the supposed novelty of these projects, there was actually a long legacy of such programs stretching back at least to the urban playground movement of the early 20th century that used physical activities to combat the perceived deviance and delinquency of the children of new immigrants (Cavallo, 1981). Perhaps most problematic, empirical evidence that these programs actually served to reduce risk or prevent crime was sparse at best.

To the extent that formal evaluations or scholarly analyses of sport-based crime prevention existed, they were mostly program-based case studies lacking in the comparisons and controls that proper, systematic assessment requires. The most comprehensive and rigorous survey of the American literature at the time (Sherman, Gottfredson, MacKenzie, Eck, Reuter, & Bushway, 1998) listed only one scholarly study that focused explicitly on recreation-based programs (Howell, 1995), and its findings about community-based, after-school recreation programs were limited and contradictory. Documentation and assessment was also lacking outside of the United States (for a British example, see Utting, 1996). It is also worth noting that numerous, well regarded risk prevention programs run by organizations such as the Boys and Girls Clubs, 4-H, or the YMCA include athletic activities, but these initiatives tend not to be sport-based or even use physical recreation as a point of entry.

I am not suggesting that community-based sports programs did not or, for that matter, cannot contribute to crime prevention and risk reduction. Rather, the point is that little was known about sports-oriented crime prevention when these programs were first launched. This limited knowledge, I believe, suggests that these programs were not always implemented properly and thus may not have had the outcomes that were expected—which may, in turn, help account for our inability to systematically document positive, pro-social effects.

Fortunately, in the last decade or so a new body of scholarly work has emerged to help us better understand sports-based crime prevention and how such programming can be most effectively implemented and administered. It is now well documented, for example, that sport is a powerful tool for outreach, recruitment, and retention of program participants (Hartmann & Wheelock, 2002; Sotiriardous, Shilburg, & Quick, 2008). The theoretical foundations of how sports-based programming can contribute to crime prevention are now more firmly grounded and thoroughly conceptualized (Coakley, 2002; Hartmann, 2003; Holt, 2008; Martinek & Hellison, 1997; Nichols, 2007; Witt & Crompton, 1997), and case studies have helped us understand who is most likely to benefit from such interventions (Correira, 1997; Nichols, 2004; Zarrett, Lerner, Carrano, Fay, Peltz, & Li, 2008).

Researchers are also beginning to appreciate the broader public and symbolic importance of these programs in the cities and communities in which they are implemented. And although documenting the effectiveness of such initiatives still remains a challenge, a more sophisticated framework for measurement and assessment is now in place (Baldwin, 2000; Nichols & Crow, 2004; Witt & Crompton, 1997).

This chapter draws upon a decade of my own research on one of the most prominent and highly politicized of such sport-based crime prevention initiatives—the late night, basketball-based programs known as midnight basketball—to illustrate and elaborate several key points that have emerged from recent research in this area. These points include a) the role of sports and leisure activities in recruitment and retention of otherwise hard-to-reach populations; b) the theoretical principles underlying successful, individual interventions; and c) the public visibility and symbolic value of such sports-based initiatives at the wider, community level. Working through these points in the context of the broader ideas about development through sport that are the focus of this volume will provide an understanding of what sports-based crime prevention programs can reasonably be expected to accomplish, how they can be better evaluated, and ultimately, how they can be more effectively implemented.

MIDNIGHT BASKETBALL BASICS

The midnight basketball concept originated in the late 1980s. (The basic background information on midnight basketball is drawn from original archival research and interviews, and my own previous writings.) Midnight basketball was the brainchild of a man named G. Van Standifer, a retired systems analyst and former town manager in Glenarden, Maryland, who had become convinced that one of the keys to the problems of poor, inner-city young men was the absence of safe, constructive activities during what he believed to be the high crime, late-night hours. Standifer's solution was to organize a basketball league that would operate in his Washington, D.C., area community between 10:00 PM and 2:00 AM Standifer's basketball-based program was intriguingly simple and inexpensive: it operated only during summer months and had three core components: first, that the target participant group was young men between the ages of 17 and 21; second, no game could begin before 10 o'clock at night; and third, that two uniformed police officers had to be present and visible at each game. The basic idea was that a sports program would provide an alternative to the non-productive or even destructive activities of the street.

With statistics and support from local law enforcement, Standifer claimed great success for his program—a 30% reduction in late-night crime in his community in its first three years of operation. A Prince George's County corrections chief, for example, claimed, "I haven't seen a single one of these basketball players back in my jail since the program began" (quoted in Hartmann, 2001, p. 347). After seeing a story about the program in the

New York Times, public housing officials in Chicago began planning a league of their own. It was this league that brought the idea of midnight basketball to national attention.

In the fall of 1989 the Chicago Housing Authority—with a matching grant of $50,000 from the Department of Housing and Urban Development under the direction of Jack Kemp, a former Congressman who had made his reputation as a professional football star and cheerleader for the Reagan administration's supply-side economics—organized leagues in two notoriously troubled housing projects (the Rockwell Gardens and the Henry Horner Homes). Within weeks, the Chicago leagues were featured on ABC's *Good Morning America,* one of NBC television's national NBA broadcasts, and in dozens of newspapers and magazines across the country. On the strength of the public support of and widespread attention to the Chicago project, Standifer created Midnight Basketball Leagues, Inc., and began to sanction affiliated programs all over the United States. Within three short years, the organization became the National Association of Midnight Basketball, Inc., and included 38 official midnight basketball programs in major metropolitan areas all across the country. Each chapter, according to the parent organization, was a "non-profit, community-based organization adhering to formal training, rules, and regulations" based upon the original Standifer model.

Over the course of the following decade, dozens more communities adopted midnight basketball programs and hundreds of copycat programs appeared (Schultz et al., 1995). Indeed, sport sociologists Robert Pitter and David Andrews (2007) described midnight basketball as the "paradigmatic" project for the entire "social problems industry" that emerged in the last decade of the 20th century on the American sporting scene. Midnight basketball was and is unique in several respects. Its target population was clearly older than that of most youth-oriented programs and largely dominated by African American young men in most communities. These leagues also proved to be far more controversial and widely politicized than other such sport-based social initiatives (Wheelock & Hartmann, 2007). But even with these caveats in mind, midnight basketball and my research on midnight basketball illustrate many of the key points about the benefits and potential drawbacks of sports-based crime prevention.

OUTREACH AND RECRUITMENT

Probably the best place to begin rethinking the preventionist potential of youth sports programs such as midnight basketball is with the elements that every program necessarily begins with: outreach and recruitment. Not only are outreach and recruitment the first concern of any social policy initiative (you can't have a social program without participants), it is the one area in which midnight basketball programs and all sports-based crime prevention initiatives have been able to clearly document their effectiveness and success. This unique ability to recruit and retain otherwise hard-to-reach populations has been true for the all of the various midnight basketball programs I have studied or with which I have been otherwise associated. Consider the case of a basketball-based program I worked with in Minneapolis, Minnesota, in the late 1990s called "Stay Alive."

I had initiated research with Stay Alive with the idea of using the program as a model to assess (and hopefully document) the effectiveness of basketball-based programs. My attempts in this regard failed rather miserably. The problem wasn't that my research assistants and I were unable to document any systemic positive effects (though we weren't); the problem was that we never really got to ask the question in the first place. The program was so poorly organized and operated that we were unable to conduct even a basic analysis of its effects, positive or problematic (Hartmann & Wheelock, 2002). Nevertheless, the one area that was an exception to these failures and disappointments was in the Stay Alive league's ability to reach out and recruit the otherwise hard-to-reach target population of Native American and African American men aged 18-25.

In 1999, the first year for which we had full data, the Stay Alive program served some 256 players. Of these, 75% had a residence in the city of Minneapolis proper, 60% were African American, and 28% were Native American. (The rest were either White, Hispanic, or claimed a "multi-racial" ethnicity). The majority (i.e., 57%) of participants were within the program's 17-30 year old target range. These numbers were a bit lower than program administrators had hoped, but were explained by the presence of several teams of 15- and 16-year-old youth who had entered the league in hopes of finding older, more physically mature and experienced competition. Perhaps more important and far more positive, at least 45% of participants 18 or older in the league had criminal history records with the Minneapolis Police Department.

These demographic characteristics may not sound like a lot, but they constituted a huge accomplishment in the context of the homicide prevention program of which Stay Alive was part in the city of Minneapolis. The basketball program was originally only one of a dozen pilot programs that were given small grants in the first year of the campaign. The Stay Alive program was not only continued but expanded because it was the only one of the pilot programs that came close to reaching out and engaging the difficult-to-reach 18–25-year-old minority male population that had been identified by city researchers as the focal point of the homicide explosion. That is not to suggest that city bureaucrats were convinced Stay Alive would be an effective homicide prevention program; only that basketball was the only activity they had going that could claim to do anything remotely proactive in terms of bringing young men of color into a structured, safe environment.

This case is, in my experience, reading, and research, not at all unusual. For all of the challenges of sports-based risk reduction initiatives, I have rarely heard of a program shutting down for lack of participants. To the contrary, recruitment is one of the things that no one seems to question. Indeed, the claim that sport is a powerful tool for outreach and recruitment is so common sense and taken for granted among sport scholars and sport policy makers that it is rarely analyzed anymore. Sometimes the lack of such evidence and examination raises concerns for the analyst; in this case, however, I think it indicates an area in which sports-based crime prevention is an unquestioned success (see also Witt & Crompton, 1996).

Of course, recruitment is only just the beginning of any successful intervention. Once participants are brought into a program (any program), the question quickly becomes: what does the program do with them now that they have gotten them in the door? What does the program actually do? These questions are where the policy challenge really begins, and the need for better understanding is most pressing for both program implementation and evaluation.

THEORIZING SPORT'S ROLE IN PREVENTION

One of the first things that anyone working in and around sports-based prevention programs learns is that there are many different visions of what prevention is and how sport is believed to contribute to it. Probably most common and important are the ideas related to direct, individual-level interventions and effects. Midnight basketball's effect on at-risk young people was not explicitly theorized by the funders and operators who brought it into being; however, at least two different rationales (or underlying justifications) that informed and inspired the initiative can be identified.

One of those draws upon basic conceptions of deterrence and prevention as a matter of physical containment, surveillance, and control. The idea, in short, is that as long as participants are involved in a controlled physical activity, they cannot be involved in delinquency and offending. Their energies and risk-oriented proclivities are thus controlled and diverted toward other pursuits, pursuits that are physically contained and that have the additional benefit of being exciting, challenging, and physically demanding. This containment-and-control rationale for sports-based programs as crime prevention is probably what made midnight basketball so popular among conservatives in the late 1980s and early 1990s. "Keep 'em off the street" was a simple but concrete social control notion, consistent with the larger push toward more prisons and police as the key to crime prevention in urban areas.

The second rationale that animated midnight basketball supporters was informed by a more ostensibly proactive, development-oriented set of ideas. It was the traditional, idealistic notion that sport participation is associated with character-building, self-discipline, and socialization. The assumption here is that simply playing sports builds self-esteem and social skills that teach otherwise undisciplined and disorderly young people principles of social order and self-control. Containment and control, in this conception, is exercised by individuals themselves through their own socially-directed self surveillance.

Both of the approaches have roots in the conception of crime prevention and social intervention as matters of containment, surveillance, and control that has taken hold in the neoliberal era (e.g., Wacquant, 2009). In previous work I have argued that the unique synthesis of these two different visions of using sport for crime prevention was what made the concept of basketball at midnight so popular and compelling when it was first introduced to the public (Hartmann, 2001). The obvious tensions between these two approaches also help account for the political controversy that unfolded around midnight basketball in the context of the 1994 American crime bill debates (Wheelock & Hartmann, 2007). But as approaches to individual level risk reduction, both visions have fundamental problems.

The containment-and-control approach is limited as a crime prevention strategy by the basic limitations of midnight basketball programs: the number of at-risk people they serve and the nature and extent of their programming. For example, Standifer's original program in Maryland counted only 60 participants in its first year of operation, and still had only 84 in the year it was "discovered" by the national media. Similarly, the widely celebrated Chicago plan called for only 160 participants. Although this number may have been impressive as a basketball league, it paled in comparison with the estimated 6600 "at-risk young adults" residing in the housing projects in which the program was located (not to mention the hundreds of thousands at-risk young people not in public housing). Simply put, these programs do not serve enough individuals to make a significant dent in crime and delinquency rates. Even if they served more participants, most sport-based crime prevention programs operate only a few days a week for a limited number of weeks in a year, meaning that the extent of actual, physical containment and control is quite limited.

The shortcomings of the approach that posits sport as a builder of character and social skills are a bit more complicated, but at their root is the idealistic belief that simply playing sports is inherently and inevitably an effective, pro-social (and anti-risk) influence. This point is precisely what a generation of sport scholarship has taught us to question and challenge. Contrary to most popular assumptions, sport participation is not automatically a positive social force. It can be that, but if a program is not properly run or has poor leadership and role models, it can also have the opposite effect. Sport-based programming is better understood, like any other tool or technology, as an "empty form" (MacAloon, 1995)—a practice that can be positive, but can also be a problem if the energies involved are not directed and channeled appropriately. Too often, this understanding has not been in place for midnight basketball programs, rendering their actual intervention into the lives of at-risk young people limited only to physical containment and control.

The implication is that the success of a sport-based social interventionist program is largely determined by the strength of its non-sport components, what it does with young people once they are brought into the program through sport. The literature on sport and development—the larger focus of this volume—helps elaborate this point. In the sport and development literature, scholars have distinguished between "sport plus" and "plus sport" programs (Coalter, 2009; Levermore & Beacom, 2009). On the one hand, "sport plus" initiatives "give primacy to the development of sustainable sports organizations, programmes and development pathways" (Coalter, p. 58) and then go on to address broader social issues. The "plus sport" model puts the sport/social intervention relationship the other way around, "giv[ing] primacy to social and health programmes where sport is used, especially its ability to bring together a large number of young people, to achieve some of their objectives" (Coalter, p. 58).

Clearly, this latter orientation and approach (see also Levermore 2009) is most proper and appropriate if a sport-based program is to be a significant force in the struggle against crime and delinquency. This framing also makes it easier to understand why many of the best, most effective programs include specific programming for education, mentorship, and skills training as well as what Witt and Crompton (2003) have called value-directed personal development. Time and again, case studies have revealed that the programs that are most promising and successful as crime prevention programs are those that incorporate non-sport, development-oriented elements (see, for examples: Hartmann, 2003; Nichols, 2007; Witt & Crompton, 1996). The main investment of any sport-based crime prevention program should be in its non-sport elements, in individual development, education, job training, and the like. Sport can't and shouldn't be dropped from the equation. After all, it functions as the essential "hook." Nevertheless, getting participants in the door is only one part of a successful outreach program. You also have to keep them in the program. In addition, you have to get them actively involved and interested and invested in the program as a whole, especially in its preventionist elements.

COMMUNITY-LEVEL EFFECTS

What can easily disappear from focusing on individual-level intervention and treatment (fundamental as that is) is the claim that midnight basketball advocates initially trumpeted in introducing their programs to the public in the 1990s: namely, that sports-based crime prevention can have broad, community-level effects, effects that extend well beyond the limited number of participants they directly service and serve. It is easy to be skeptical or downright dismissive of such claims. Indeed, a closer look at the claims Standifer made about his Prince Georges County Program (that they reduced crime by 30%) reveals little more than a spurious correlation where the implementation of midnight basketball simply coincided with declining crime rates throughout the region. Even the most extensive basketball-based programs operated only a few nights a week for a couple of months a year, and served no more than 200 individuals.

Still, it is important not to discount the possibility of community-level effects. Since James Coleman's (1961) classic study of the influence of interscholastic athletics on high schools and teenage culture, sport scholars have known that sport has social consequence and cultural power that extends far beyond those individuals directly engaged in competitive physical activity. Sports-based programs such as midnight basketball are typically among the most visible and popular crime prevention programs any agency or community can offer. Surely, the prominence of these initiatives and the positive publicity typically associated with them has some kind of broader, community-level consequence or outcome.

Using some basic quantitative data and techniques, a colleague of mine and I took a first step toward addressing the possibility of community-level effects empirically (Hartmann & Depro, 2006). Our research strategy was fairly simple and straightforward. We identified cities that were early adopters of official midnight basketball programs and then plotted changes in their average violent and property crime rates across the period from 1985 to 2001 against the rates for cities without midnight basketball (all other American cities with populations over 100,000).

Our analysis yielded a number of revealing results. One was that cities that adopted official midnight basketball leagues had consistently higher rates of property and violent crime for the period 1985 to 2001 as compared with cities without the programs. They also tended to have a higher percentage of ethnic and racial minority residents. These findings are interesting in themselves, though they probably say more about the social and demographic characteristics of cities inclined to experiment with an unproven and unlikely program such as midnight basketball than about the effectiveness of such initiatives.

Of course, our real interest in generating these plots was not adoption but the effect on crime rates—and here is where things got really interesting. In a nutshell, our statistical analyses and tests showed that the crime rates in cities that adopted midnight basketball appeared to decline somewhat faster than in cities without the programs (i.e., the gap between the two groups of cities appears to narrow over the crucial 3-year period) and that these results were statistically significant (which is to say that the relationships hold even when controlling for key factors that might otherwise explain these results). We were able to confirm that cities that adopted midnight basketball programs experienced greater declines in crime rates than those cities that lacked midnight basketball leagues.

These results held for both violent crime rates and property crime rates, and the magnitude of these effects was striking. Using econometric statistical techniques, we estimated that cities that were early adopters of midnight basketball programs saw a drop of approximately 90 offenses per 100,000 population compared to non-midnight basketball counterparts for violent crime rates. The results for property crime rates were even more impressive. We calculated that midnight basketball cities saw a drop of approximately 390 offenses per 100,000. Effects of this scope cannot be attributed to individual-level mechanisms that are the emphasis of the theoretical literature on sports-based social interventions and most effectiveness evaluation. Even adding in the possibility of "spillover" effects to friends and acquaintances not actually in the programs, basketball leagues in the early 1990s were simply too limited in size, scope, and population served to account for the magnitude of the effects reported here.

Given the nature of the statistical methods employed in this analysis, it is important not to overstate the direct, causal claims about the effects of midnight basketball on community crime rates. To wit: we cannot say that midnight basketball was directly responsible for the relatively steeper declines in crime in cities that were early adopters of midnight basketball. Nevertheless, there does appear to be some kind of association or correlation there, a relationship that holds even after standard social and demographic factors known to affect community crime rates are included and accounted for. Moreover—and this is the key point—there are mechanisms that can account for these community-level relationships and associations, mechanisms that suggest the broader import and influence of sports-based crime prevention.

One factor that can help explain these patterns has to do with the packaging or bundling of crime prevention initiatives—more specifically, that midnight basketball programs were usually not the only crime prevention initiatives undertaken in these communities, but rather were part of an entire package of community-based risk reduction and crime prevention programs of which midnight basketball was one high-profile component. The effects we observed were not the result of midnight basketball alone but rather of a whole package of crime prevention programs initiated in these communities. Cities that adopted midnight basketball programs tended to have not only distinct demographic profiles, but also unique city-level spending levels and priorities. This interpretation is supported by early adopter cities tending to be Black, having high police expenditures per capita, and having populations with low home ownership. These characteristics are not surprising considering that midnight basketball programs were frequently adopted in cities that were examining low-cost alternatives to policing and championed as ways to increase social capital stocks in cities with indicators suggesting communities were less connected because of expected mobility (i.e., low shares of homeownership). This explanation minimizes the direct effect of midnight basketball, but raises interesting questions about the configuration of such prevention policy packages in general and the role sports-based initiatives might play in such a policy climate.

A second factor contributing to these results involved media and communication mechanisms—what might be called "publicity effects" (Johnson & Bowers, 2003)—especially because they operate at the local, neighborhood level. The public attention devoted to high-profile prevention programs such as midnight basketball can influence community crime rates in one of two ways. On the deterrence side, public attention to midnight basketball programs might send a message to potential criminals of a new emphasis on crime prevention and the extent to which law enforcement and other public officials are willing to go in the fight against crime, thus creating a rational deterrent for would-be criminals. On the more proactive side, the creation of popular, high-profile programs such as midnight basketball can send a positive message to community members of a new emphasis on community outreach and empowerment, one that builds trust and commitment to the community.

The former explanation is, of course, the more typical in the field currently and frequently the subject of highly publicized debate. On the other hand, the latter, less-developed proactive explanation has implications and consequences that are far less understood but important to think through. The creation of popular, community-based programs such as midnight basketball might incline all community members (not just those in the program) to be less likely to commit crimes, not for fear of being caught, but because they feel more directly connected to their communities and more positively served by law enforcement and social services. Indeed, what we found regarding the particularly significant effect on property crime rates seems consistent with this explanation because midnight basketball may serve to help generate a wide and diffuse sense of community solidarity and trust that serves as a buffer against the individualistic and antisocial sentiments and behaviors that otherwise contribute to crimes against property and the community at large.

The explanations I have offered here are only speculative; a good deal more research must be conducted before we can firmly establish the magnitude of these effects and the mechanisms that account for them. Nevertheless, what is most important here is that we are provided with some evidence that, against a great deal of public and scholarly skepticism, midnight basketball appears to be associated with decreased city-level property crime rates. Perhaps we should not be so quick to dismiss community-level effects of sports-based crime prevention programs such as midnight basketball that might appear, on the face of it, to be rather limited in scope and design. Moreover, these findings suggest that analysts would do well to focus on the intangible, indirect ways in which these results may be achieved. More specifically, these programs need to be implemented in combination with other risk reduction initiatives and be attentive to the intangible, community-building effects that might come with the positive collective sentiments that they may help to generate and sustain. Certainly in a climate of limited resources requiring innovative, cost-effective solutions, these possibilities deserve serious consideration from funders, policy makers, service providers, and program evaluators alike.

CONCLUSIONS AND CAUTIONS

As popular and pervasive as sport-based crime preventions programs such as midnight basketball have become in recent years, the vast majority of these well-intended initiatives have lacked a coherent conceptual foundation, not to mention basic empirical evidence of their effectiveness. As a result, such programs far too often simply provide an excuse for athletic administrators to secure funding for otherwise limited sports facilities or programs, or are used as a community relations ploy by public officials trying to make it look like they are taking steps to deal with the problems of urban crime, violence, and public safety without actually committing new resources, energy, or attention to the relevant communities. Such shortsighted and even cynical visions not only compromise the immediate influence and effectiveness of the interventionist aspects of these initiatives, they leave such efforts vulnerable to public criticism and cutbacks (such as the attacks on midnight basketball in the context of debates over the federal crime bill in 1994).

In this chapter I have tried to use some of what I have learned working in and around midnight basketball initiatives to counter these problematic tendencies and trends, or put somewhat more positively, to lay out some of the basic principles and understandings on which all sport-based risk reduction initiatives should be founded. I have highlighted three points in particular. One is that sport is a powerful tool for outreach, recruitment, and retention of individual program participants. Another point had to do with the public visibility and symbolic value of sport-based crime prevention at the community level. I suggested that sport-based programming can be an important part of a whole package of community-based approaches to crime prevention and can play a significant role building broad-based trust and support for such initiatives. A final point, the second discussed above, is a bit more conceptual and complicated, involving the kinds of individual-level interventions that are likely to be successful and who is most likely to benefit from them.

Although sport can be a powerful social force, its effects are not (counter to traditional idealistic beliefs) automatically or inevitably positive when it comes to individual-level risk reduction and crime prevention. Indeed, sport is best understood as a tool for development and social intervention whose influence depends upon the ends toward which it is directed, how it is implemented, and the context in which it is deployed. This conceptualization has obvious and concrete implications for program design, implementation, and operation. The success of any sport-based intervention program is largely determined by the strength of its non-sport components and what it does with young people once they are brought into the program through sport. That said, I don't want to suggest that the sport-based components of such programs can be ignored, taken for granted, or minimized. To do so would be to risk losing the very hook that brings young people into the program and inspires their ongoing and energetic participation. Rather, I insist that there needs to be a balance between the sport-based and the non-sport-based aspects of a program, where sport is just one part of a whole package of resources and social supports requiring a level of investment and intensive, day-to-day involvement far beyond that of most sport-based intervention programs. Rather than having it easier than other youth workers, sport-based program organizers have a unique double burden requiring that they must be proficient at both sport and social intervention.

With all of these challenges and complexities in mind, it is important to stress one final point: whatever sport-based social intervention programs may have to contribute to improving the lives of urban youth, we must be careful not to expect too much from them, not to treat them as a magic bullet or miracle elixir. Crime prevention and social intervention are complex and challenging enterprises even under the best of circumstances, with abundant resources, and the most comprehensive and advanced programming. Given their typically limited resources and scheduling, sport-based programs by themselves, even when brilliantly conceived and properly implemented, will not always succeed. They will fail more often than not. To believe anything else not only overestimates the social force of sport, it underestimates the difficulties of meaningful social intervention and change. A failure to understand these realities and limitations has implications far beyond sport. Indeed, unrealistic expectations for sport-based interventions can actually serve to reinforce and exacerbate the problems faced by at-risk urban youth by deflecting public attention away from deeper social sources of their problems. "If we are not cautious," as Jay Coakley (2002) has put it, such programs

> …may unwittingly reaffirm ideological positions that identify young people, especially young people of color as 'problems' and then forget that the real problems are deindustrialization, unemployment, underemployment, poverty, racism and at least twenty years of defunding social programs that have traditionally been used to foster community development in ways that positively impact the lives of young people. (p. 23)

REFERENCES

Baldwin, C. K. (2000). Theory, program, and outcomes: Assessing the challenges of evaluating at-risk youth recreation programs. *Journal of Park and Recreation Administration, 18*, 19-33.

Cameron, M., & MacDougall, C. (2000). Crime prevention through sport and physical activity. *Trends and Issues in Crime and Criminal Justice*, No. 165. Canberra: Australian Institute of Criminology.

Cavallo, D. (1981). *Muscles and morals: Organized playgrounds and urban reform, 1880-1920.* Philadelphia: University of Pennsylvania Press.

Coakley, J. (2002). Using sports to control deviance and violence among youths: Let's be critical and cautious. In M. Gatz, M. A. Messner, & S. J. Ball-Rokeach (Eds.), *Paradoxes of youth and sport* (pp. 13-30). Albany, NY: SUNY Press.

Coalter, F. (2009). Sport-in-development: Accountability or development? In R. Levermore, & A. Beacom (Eds.), *Sport and international development* (pp. 55-75). Hampshire, England: Palgrave Macmillan.

Cole, C. L. (1996). American Jordan: P.L.A.Y., consensus and punishment. *Sociology of Sport Journal, 13,* 366-397.

Coleman, J. S. (1961). *The adolescent society: The social life of the teenager and its impact on education.* New York: Free Press.

Correira, M. (1997). Boot camps, exercise and delinquency: An analytical critique of the use of physical exercise to facilitate decreases in delinquent behavior. *Journal of Contemporary Criminal Justice, 13,* 94-113.

Crompton, J. L. (1998). Forces underlying the emergence of privatization in parks and recreation. *Journal of Park and Recreation Administration, 16*(2), 88-101.

Crompton, J. L., & McGregor, B. (1994). Trends in the financing and staffing of local government park and recreation services. *Journal of Park and Recreation Administration, 12*(3), 19-37.

Goldberg, D. T. (2008). *The threat of race: Reflections on racial neoliberalism.* New York: Wiley-Blackwell.

Hartmann, D. (2001). Notes on midnight basketball and the cultural politics of race and at-risk urban youth. *Journal of Sport and Social Issues, 25,* 339-371.

Hartmann, D. (2003). Theorizing sport as social intervention: A view from the grassroots. *Quest, 55,* 118-140.

Hartmann, D., & Depro, B. (2006). Rethinking sports-based community crime prevention: A preliminary analysis of the relationship between midnight basketball and urban crime rates. *Journal of Sport and Social Issues, 30,* 180-196.

Hartmann, D., & Wheelock, D. (2002). Sport as prevention? Minneapolis' experiment with late-night basketball. *CURA Reporter, 32*(3), 13-17.

Harvey, D. (2005). *A brief history of neoliberalism.* New York: Oxford University Press.

Holt, N. L. (Ed.). (2008). *Positive youth development through sport.* London: Routledge.

Howell, J. C. (Ed.). (1995). *Guide for implementing the comprehensive strategy for serious, violent, and chronic juvenile offenders.* Washington, DC: U.S. Department of Justice, Office of Juvenile Justice and Delinquency Prevention.

Johnson, S. D., & Bowers, K. J. (2003). Opportunity is in the eye of the beholder: The role of publicity in crime prevention. *Criminology and Criminal Policy, 2*(3), 201-228.

Levermore, R. (2009). Sport-in-international development: Theoretical frameworks. In R. Levermore, & A, Beacom (Eds.), *Sport and international development* (pp. 26-54). Hampshire, England: Macmillan.

Levermore, R., & Beacom, A. (2009). Sport and development: Mapping the field. In R. Levermore & A. Beacom (Eds.), *Sport and international development* (pp. 1-25). Hampshire, England: Palgrave Macmillan.

MacAloon, J. (1995). Interval training. In S. L. Foster (Ed.), *Choreographing history,* (pp. 32-53). Bloomington, Indiana: Indiana University Press.

Martinek, T. J., & Hellison, D. R. (1997). Fostering resilience in underserved youth through physical activity. *Quest, 49,* 34-49.

Nichols, G. (1997). A consideration of why active participant in sport and leisure might reduce criminal behaviour. *Sport, Education and Society, 2,* 181-190.

Nichols, G. (2004). Crime and punishment and sports development. *Leisure Studies, 23,* 177-194.

Nichols, G. (2007). *Sport and crime reduction: The role of sports in tackling youth crime.* London: Routledge.

Nichols, G., & Crow, I. (2004). Measuring the impact of crime reduction interventions involving sports activities for young people. *Howard Journal, 43*(3), 227-236.

Pitter, R., & Andrews, D. L. (1997). Serving America's underserved youth: Reflections on sport and recreation in an emerging social problems industry. *Quest, 49,* 85-99.

Schultz, L. E., Crompton, J. L., & Witt, P. A. (1995). A national profile of the status of public recreation services for at-risk children and youth. *Journal of Park and Recreation Administration, 13*(3), 1-25.

Sherman, L. W., Gottfredson, D. C., MacKenzie, D. L., Eck, J., Reuter, P., & Bushway, S. D. (July, 1998). *Preventing crime: What works, what doesn't, what's promising. Research in brief.* Washington, DC: National Institute of Justice.

Sotiriardous, K., Shilburg, D., & Quick, S. P. (2008). The attraction, retention/transition, and nurturing process of sport development: Some Australian evidence. *Journal of Sport Managements, 22,* 247-272.

Utting, D. (1996). *Reducing criminality among young people: A sample of relevant programmes in the United Kingdom.* London: Home Office Research and Statistics Directorate.

Wacquant, L. (2009). *Punishing the poor: The neo-liberal government of social inequality.* Durham, NC: Duke University Press.

Wheelock, D. & Hartmann, D. (2007). Midnight basketball and the 1994 crime bill debates: The operation of a racial code. *The Sociological Quarterly, 48,* 315-342.

Witt, P. A., & Crompton, J. L. (1996). *Recreation programs that work for at-risk youth.* Philadelphia, PA: Venture.

Witt, P. A., & Crompton, J. L. (1997). The protective factors framework: A key to programming for benefits and evaluating results. *Journal of Park and Recreation Administration, 15*(3), 1-18.

Witt, P. A., & Crompton, J. L. (2003). Positive youth development practices in recreational settings in the United States. *World Leisure Journal, 45,* 4-11.

Zarrett, N., Lerner, R. M., Carrano, J., Fay, K., Peltz, J. S., & Li, Y. (2008). Variations in adolescent engagement in sports and its influence on positive youth development. In N. L. Holt (Ed.), *Positive youth development through sport,* (pp. 9-23). London: Routledge.

Postcolonial and Feminist Critiques of Sport for Development

Audrey R. Giles and Meghan Lynch

7

port for development initiatives are becoming increasingly popular throughout the world. Primarily targeting marginalized individuals, such as youth, women, and persons with disabilities, sport for development programs pursue a variety of goals (Levermore & Beacom, 2009). In 2006, the 176 projects listed on the International Platform for Sport and Development's website aimed at both general and specific objectives, including conflict resolution and intercultural understanding; building physical, social, sport, and community infrastructure; educating communities about HIV/AIDS; empowerment; economic development; and poverty alleviation (Levermore, 2008). Likewise, the Sport for Development and Peace International Working Group (SDPIWG, 2007) report highlighted sport for development initiatives in the areas of basic education and child development, health promotion and disease prevention, conflict resolution and peace education, and community development (Stewart-Withers & Brook, 2009). Although so-called developed countries (e.g., Canada, Australia, United States) commonly use sport to assist with international development and relations (Levermore, 2008), sport for development program examples can also be found in marginalized regions of developed countries, such as on First Nations reserves in Canada (Kidd, 2008). Rapid growth within the area of sport for development has not occurred without a number of critiques being leveled against such initiatives. In this chapter, we use postcolonial and feminist theories to situate sport for development within broader critiques of development and offer suggestions for the ways in which this burgeoning field might be strengthened.

SITUATING SPORT FOR DEVELOPMENT WITHIN DEVELOPMENT

Sport has long been considered by many countries to be a successful means to foster development, particularly in bridging gaps and unifying disparate groups of people (Kidd, 2008; Levermore, 2008). Sport has also been viewed, however, as being capable of creating and even increasing the unequal relations between those who are able to exercise power and those who are marginalized (Stoddart, 1988). Although excellent sport for development initiatives exist, we argue that some programs, especially those that involve foreign donors, serve to extend and/or re-inscribe imperial and colonial legacies, particularly in terms of uneven relations of power. We are not suggesting that sport for development practitioners and policy makers are ill-intentioned. Rather, we suggest that many programs and policies could be improved if they engaged with critiques that have been made concerning development in general and sport for development in particular, especially those offered by feminist and postcolonial scholarship. Feminist and postcolonial theorists have problematized many aspects of development, offering much to the burgeoning field of sport for development.

Though recently making significant strides in popularity, the origins of social development through sport can be traced back to the 19th century (Kidd, 2008; Levermore & Beacom, 2009). Throughout the history of British imperialism, the transfer of predominant beliefs regarding social behavior, standards, relations, and conformity could be found to occur through sport (Stoddart, 1988) and fit all five characteristics that form the "core ideology" of imperialism: militarism, royalism, creation of national heroes, the cult of personality, and the racial ideas of social Darwinism (Levett, 2010). In recent years, governments in the Global North (the term used in development literature to refer to wealthy countries) have used sport to help with international development initiatives, while governments in the Global South (the term in development literature to refer to poor countries) have used sport as a way to deliver health and education initiatives on a national level (Levermore & Beacom). Over the past decade, steady growth has been noted in the sport for development movement (Hayhurst, 2009; Stewart-Withers & Brook, 2009), beginning primarily in the 1990s, when high profile athletes were encouraged to improve sport's tarnished image following doping and bribery scandals (Kidd). It was not until 2001, however, when the formalization of the use of sport as a tool for social development began at the United Nations (UN) level with former President of Switzerland, Adolf Ogi, being appointed as the first Special Advisor to the UN Secretary General on Sport for Development and Peace (Nicholls, 2008).

Shortly after, in 2002, the UN Secretary General commissioned an interagency task force to examine the use of sport for development and peace in a systematic manner (Nicholls, 2008). Then in 2003, the General Assembly of United Nations passed motion 58/5 entitled "Sport as a means to promote education, health, development and peace" (United Nations General Assembly, 2003), which recognized the role sport could make towards achieving Millenium Development Goals (Brady, 2005; Nicholls). Over the next few years, the use of sport for development slowly gained popularity with mainstream contributors to development initiatives (i.e., non-governmental organizations [NGOs], governments, development agencies). Sport for development's emerging popularity was particularly noted following the declaration by the UN that 2005 be the "International Year of Sport and Physical Education" (Levermore & Beacom, 2009). Since then, the UN has worked to bring greater international prominence to sport for development, while also promoting the notion that national governments of recipient countries play important roles in the success of any program (Akindes & Kirwin, 2009). The UN, national governments, and civil society have shown improvements in working together to develop policies and recommendations on sport for development (Stewart-Withers & Brook, 2009).

The need to improve these attempts at working together illustrates the ways in which some sport for development projects initially failed, and in some cases continue to fail, to address many of the critiques associated with development in general. Indeed, sport for development is not called sport for cultural self-determination or sport for political representation. Instead, the use of the word development identifies such initiatives as being part of the broader political processes associated with development.

Development is a process of social and material change that in the 19th century was viewed as natural and part of an evolutionary process (McEwan, 2009). After the 19th century, development was used by imperial powers to create social order. McEwan has cogently traced the history of development theories and approaches since 1945. The approach of the 1950s and 1960s was characterized by modernization theories, but by the 1970s dependency theories became more popular. From the 1980s onwards, the neo-liberal focus on issues such as local knowledge, gender in development, culture and development, and sustainable development began to inform development agendas. Although space allowances prohibit us from engaging in detailed descriptions of each of these approaches, what is clear is that development is not neutral (Kabeer, 1994), but is instead attached to historical and political ideologies and legacies, particularly those associated with the ideology of imperialism and the practice of colonialism. These ideologies, legacies, and practices are often absent from discussions concerning sport for development, because many sport practitioners lack detailed knowledge of development processes (just as many development practitioners have limited knowledge concerning sport).

POSTCOLONIAL THEORY

The conditions, both discursive and material, produced by colonialism facilitated the need for development, which has been subsequently critiqued by a variety of theorists, including postcolonial and feminist scholars. Postcolonial theory refers to a broad set of approaches, strategies, and concepts that are used to understand imperialism's and colonialism's legacies. According to Johnston, Gregory, and Smith (1994), "[c]haracteristic features of the colonial situation include political and legal domination over an alien society, relations of economic and political dependence and exploitation between imperial power and colony, and racial and cultural inequality" (p. 75). Postcolonial theorists examine the influence of "the imperial process from the moment of colonization to the present day" (Ashcroft, Griffiths, & Tiffin, 1989, p. 2). Importantly, the "post" in postcolonial does not refer to a time "after" colonialism, but rather "responds to experiences of colonization and imperialism" (Battiste, 2004, p. 1) and marks the continuing struggle for decolonization (Frankenberg & Mani, 1993). Postcolonial theorists have different areas of focus depending on the geographic and social contexts in which they live and/or conduct their research. In general, though, postcolonial theorists are especially concerned with issues related to race, diaspora, power, culture, and empire (for excellent descriptions of the development of postcolonial theory, see McEwan, 2009; Young, 2001).

Feminist theory has had a significant influence on the ways in which postcolonial theory and development are understood (Young, 2001). Black feminist theorists such as hooks (1984) and Lorde (1984) have challenged the ways in which Anglo-Western women's experiences have been generalized to represent all women's experiences and have forced White Western feminist theory to confront its racist tendencies (Lewis & Mills, 2003). Feminist postcolonial scholars, with Mohanty (1988) and Sen and Grown (1987) perhaps being the best known, have offered powerful critiques of the ways in which both development theory and White Western feminists have constructed a generic "Third World woman": a homogenous Other who is poor, helpless, and often disease-ridden.

McEwan (2009) has argued that until recently, postcolonial theory and development have rarely been put into conversation with each other; certainly, the same can be said of feminism, postcolonial theory, and sport for development (for some notable exceptions see Hayhurst, 2009; Nicholls, 2008; Nicholls & Giles, 2007; and Nicholls, Giles, & Sethna, 2011). Thus, in this chapter, we put these domains into conversation with one another. Specifically, we examine and extend critiques of discourses of limited evidence concerning sport for development's efficacy, the rhetoric of partnerships and participation in sport for development, the deficit approach that informs sport for development efforts, and claims of empowerment through sport for development.

LIMITED EVIDENCE

A major point of discussion within the sport for development literature is a fundamental one: does it work? Unfortunately, there is scant evidence that demonstrates sport to be an effective means for development (Stewart-Withers & Brook, 2009). Although we know that sport has the power to convene diverse groups of people and can, in some places, be harnessed to create positive change (Nicholls, 2008), we also know that there is a huge youth drop-out rate for sport within developed countries (Hedstrom & Gould, 2004), that sport is a space where masculine privilege and violence are often condoned (Levermore, 2008), and where girls and women are marginalized and even abused (Brady, 2005). Is it possible, then, to expect sport for development initiatives to ameliorate problems for marginalized peoples and communities when sport has been a space of contestation and discrimination for many in relatively privileged parts of the world? If so, what evidence do we have and need to support such claims?

Nicholls et al. (2011) have recently argued that the "lack of evidence" discourse concerning sport for development initiatives' effectiveness results from the marginalization of sport for development practitioners' voices. Nicholls et al. (2011) pointed out that both UNICEF (2005) and the SDPIWG (2007) have stated that there is a need to build a stronger evidence base to prove sport for development's efficacy. Evidence, however, appears to only be accepted if it is scientific and/or academic in nature, and not evidence from grassroots sport for development practitioners. Through the use of the example of Kicking AIDS Out, a network of organizations that use peer education and sport to facilitate HIV/AIDS education, Nicholls et al. argued that peer educators' contributions to sport for development are deemed insufficient for contributing to program and policy decisions in sport for development, and that the subjugation of their knowledge is a result of colonial legacies that render the Black female peer educators' experiences and knowledge not as evidence, but as mere anecdotes. Nicholls et al. revealed that another one of the main reasons for the continued production of the limited evidence discourse was barriers to the co-creation of knowledge, which stems from the gulfs that exist between grassroots practitioners on the ground and policymakers and funders. These gulfs involve not only distance, but often myriad factors including gender, race, language, and economic status. The authors further argued that although gaps between practitioners and policymakers and funders are common in many other types of policy environments, the differences in relations of power between practitioners and policymakers and donors exacerbate the situation considerably and consequently hinder attempts at knowledge cocreation.

Others have argued that the source of the problem concerning the limited evidence of sport for development's efficacy stems from elsewhere. A widespread issue in the sport for development literature is the unclear terminology used in program descriptions (Hayhurst, 2009). Reviewing documents and frameworks concerning sport for development, Brady (2005) found insufficient precision in terminology that then led to conceptual flaws in both program design and the measurement of outcomes. Countering this critique, Levermore and Beacom (2009) argued that sport for development programs' outcomes simply cannot be measured, because they involve concepts such as national unity, self-esteem, or how success in competitive sport can help portray a country in a positive light. There also exists the challenge of Western researchers studying complex phenomena in non-

Western cultural settings (Kay, 2009), which can result in researchers ignoring the important context and interactions in which outcomes occur and evidence emerges (Coalter, 2009). Stewart-Withers and Brook (2009) suggested that to better address the complex issues that inform sport for development programs, it is crucial that qualitative research be used, because numbers alone are incapable of conveying the complex nexus in which sport for development-driven change may occur.

The evidence that many identify as being absent from sport and development is that produced by academics and development agencies (Brady, 2005; Levermore, 2008; Nicholls, 2008; Willis, 2000). Stewart-Withers and Brook (2009) identified several possible reasons for why sport is neglected by certain realms in academia, such as sport being characterized by many as being male-dominated and exclusive. Sport has additionally received criticism for being tied to issues of drug abuse, homophobia, marginalization of women, and intensifying social conflict and social inequality (Levermore; Stewart-Withers & Brook). Sport may also not be taken seriously as a vehicle for change, because it is perceived by many to be more about being active and having fun or building sporting infrastructure as opposed to achieving development goals, which results in sport being considered a low priority compared to other, more traditionally accepted initiatives (Stewart-Withers & Brook). Finally, exaggerated claims by the media of sport being a cure-all have done little to help the acceptance of sport for development by academia and development agencies (Levermore, 2008). Essentially, sport has been painted by some as an unimportant distraction amidst realities of the Third World (Willis, 2000), and overstated as being a panacea by others (Levermore).

Evidence from formal evaluations of non-governmental organizations' (NGOs) efforts is also minimal (Brady, 2005). The evaluation of sport for development programs over the past decade reveals that little has been done to evaluate the long-term effects of programs, with evaluations instead favoring the study of short-term effects and the quantification of data (Akindes & Kirwin, 2009; Kay, 2009). Compounding the limited evidence discourse is limited access to evaluations and funding reports produced by donor agencies presenting challenges for academics who attempt to study sport for development, while academic evaluations have been deemed inaccessible by some development practitioners (Nicholls, 2008). Nevertheless, partnerships between NGOs and academics are beginning to emerge in evaluating sport for development initiatives and thus building an apparently legitimate evidence base (e.g., Sport for Life and Johns Hopkins University). Partnerships between donors and recipients of sport for development, however, have been identified as being more difficult.

PARTICIPATION AND PARTNERSHIPS

Postcolonial (e.g., Young, 2001) and feminist (e.g., Hesse-Biber, Leavy, & Yaiser, 2004) scholars have recognized the need for peoples whose lives are the focus of various forms of supposed improvement and intervention to be included in all stages of change processes. In particular, these groups of scholars have identified the need to move beyond the rhetoric of participation and inclusion—buzzwords that are often included in grant applications because it is now politically untenable to omit them, though programs and research often fail to live up to the expectations these words evoke (Pisani, 2009). Nagar and Ragu (2003) have noted that NGOs have increasingly taken over work in the social service sector, especially for political hot potatoes that governments do not want to take on for fear of condemnation (e.g., condom use and harm reduction for intravenous drug users). These authors have pointed out that as "the work of development shifts into the realm of primarily donor-driven NGOs, the emerging issues are many and contentious" (p. 2), including, dismayingly, the shifting of recipients' dependence on governments to dependence on NGOs.

Sport for development programs have also been criticized for being driven more by the needs of donors and funding agencies, as opposed to recipients' needs. Recipients are typified as "passive recipients" of sport for development (Hayhurst, 2009) rather than active participants in identifying their own needs and shaping interventions. Communities are typically not included in the planning of sport for development programs, which results in some programs making more sense to donors than recipients (Kidd, 2008). In addition, most sport for development programs are delivered to communities instead of being conceptualized within them; those targeted by projects are rarely heard (Darnell, 2007). For example, Akindes and Kirwin (2009) noted the problem of NGOs entering a region and promoting their own football programs instead of forming collaborations with local residents and organizations. Sport for development policies and initiatives have also been accused of being driven by political agendas and the interests of donors who provide funding (Darnell, 2007). With a focus on gaining more funding, determining how to actually involve recipients in a meaningful way has been neglected. As a result, fundamental inequalities form between those delivering and those receiving sport for development initiatives, with policy target groups becoming the subjects of, rather than partners in, policy and program development (Stewart-Withers & Brook, 2009). Unfortunately, as Hayhurst (2009) noted, these issues remain hidden, because sport for development documents are typically filled with participatory language that covers patterns of organizational hierarchy and control, and fails to address the asymmetrical power relations involved in such partnerships.

What are the dangers of donor-driven priorities rather than those developed through partnerships? Perhaps one of the best examples is the United States President's Emergency Plan for AIDS Relief (PEPFAR). A $15 billion (USD) international initiative devised by George W. Bush's administration, PEPFAR has had over half of its funds channelled through NGOs (Pisani, 2009), including those engaged in sport for development. For example, designed by researchers at Johns Hopkins University, the PEPFAR-funded "Sport for Life" (SFL) program is a school-based sport for development program. Originally launched in June 2004 in Ethiopia, three years later the program was operating in 1,660 schools (PEPFAR, 2009) and in 2006 commenced in Côte d'Ivoire (Embassy of the United States, 2007). Focused entirely on HIV/AIDS prevention, SFL uses soccer as a vehicle to engage youths in grades 7 and 8 to "use their creative and athletic talents to develop life skills and reduce their HIV/AIDS risk" (PEPFAR, 2009, p.160). The program's curriculum is designed based on the assumption that targeted youths are not sexually active (PEPFAR). Thus, the SFL curriculum aims to impart knowledge and skills, such as decision making, communicating with parents, preparing for the future, and delaying sexual debut, which are hypothesized to protect them from acquiring the disease (Embassy, 2007; PEPFAR).

Importantly, according the United States Government's website, PEPFAR funds cannot be used in any setting for marketing campaigns that target youth and that promote condom use as the form of primary intervention for HIV prevention" (PEPFAR, 2009). Although, granted, PEPFAR "allows high risk" youth *outside* of the school setting to access information concerning condoms as an intervention for HIV prevention, it is conceivable that youth, a vulnerable demographic for contracting HIV (UNAIDS, 2001), are being inculcated with information concerning the benefits of abstinence, which has been shown to be largely ineffective (Barnett & Parkhurst, 2005), and skills that though likely valuable and hypothesized to protect youth, are not as effective as condoms in reducing the transmission of HIV (Vermund, Allen, & Abdool Karim, 2009). Thus, rather than being encouraged to be culturally appropriate, healthy, sexual beings who engage in practices that are associated with decreases in HIV transmission (i.e., condom use), youth in the SFL program are instead delivered programming that serves the ideological needs of conservative Americans.

Recipients of development efforts, including those in sport for development, are intelligent, capable people who often live in cultural and social contexts that are notably different than those in privileged regions of the West. Nevertheless, development recipients are "rendered passive" (Fraser, 1989, p. 174) and have their voices silenced in favor of donors and aid workers who are deemed to be best situated to identify and ameliorate apparent deficits in recipients' lives. Donor-driven approaches are thus ill-suited to respond to postcolonial and feminist critiques of the need to privilege local voices and practices. What is often taken to be development, including sport for development, might more correctly be defined as intellectual imperialism (Alatas, 2000) that is based on a deficit approach.

DEFICIT APPROACH

One of the key features of imperialism is its tutelage component, where "the people dominated are considered a kind of ward" (Alatas, 2000, p. 23) of the imperial power. Alatas described how through imperialism-dominated groups are "taught certain things... asked to do certain things...[and] are organized towards certain ends and purposes laid out by the subjugating power" (pp. 23-24). Certainly, imperialistic approaches to sport for development are based on a deficit model, where sport for development is used to improve those who do not live up to Western society's ideals.

A variety of deficit models have been traditionally employed to create and assess interventions, sport-based or otherwise (Epstein, 1999). Though these models differ in areas such as data collection and measures, they share the common objective of a focus on identifying problems in people or situations (Epstein). Although a deficit approach is useful in its ability to diagnose specific problems, this approach has been questioned in terms of its capacity to create effective, long-term interventions (Cox, 2006; Lappalainen, Savolainen, Kuorelathti, & Epstein, 2009). Due to its focus on identifying problems, a deficit model of assessment has been criticized for reinforcing a negative bias of people and their situations (Wright & Lopez, 2002). People are stigmatized as a result of focusing entirely on their weaknesses and deficits in their environments (Cox). Using a deficit approach, people are labeled according to what are deemed to be their problematic symptoms and issues, and are thus caricatured as being their weaknesses (Rashid & Ostermann, 2009), rather than complex individuals who live in an equally complex world. For these reasons, the need to consider the variety of characteristics people possess and to use models that do not focus exclusively on problem identification and symptom treatment have been recognized as important in creating effective interventions (Cox; Wright & Lopez).

Sport for development programs are often deficit-based, in that donor NGOs, governments, or religious groups identify a problem that they believe to be in need of fixing and then develop or support a program that is designed to fix that problem. When the "problem," however, is that recipients do not mimic privileged Westerners in their cultures, beliefs, and associated practices and are then compelled to make changes that align them with Westerners to receive services or interventions, the situation recreates colonial power relations that many in the Third World have fought, often with their lives, to abolish. Rowlands (1995) has contended that the view of "'development-as-Westernization' has come to dominate to such a degree that [it] has become virtually impossible for any different possibility even to be imagined" (p. 12). Indeed, when sport for development programs' ideal outcomes appear to be the recipients of development more closely approximating the lives and beliefs of those in the West, we must question how and for whom the programs are actually designed to help and/or empower.

EMPOWERMENT

One of the most commonly employed, yet vaguely defined, terms employed in development programs is *empowerment* (Malhotra & Schuler, 2005; Rowlands, 1995). The lack of clarity involved in the concept of empowerment begins with the *power* portion of the term. The term power itself can take on a variety of meanings depending on the type of power, the definition drawn upon, and the effects of power on society (Rowlands). Accordingly, the meaning of empowerment is intrinsically tied to how one is interpreting the term power (Rowlands), and thus needs to be understood as a term that is historically, politically, and culturally bound. In regions of the world that have experienced colonization, power relations within sport for development exist in an already charged atmosphere.

In feminist development literature, the empowerment of others is a concept that has been described as being problematic and challenging. Definitions of empowerment have come mainly from work in industrialized countries (Rowlands, 1995), even though the meaning of empowerment shifts over time and context (Eyben & Napier-Moore, 2009). Although empowerment can be defined in such simplistic terms as increasing people's access to decision-making processes, from a feminist perspective, empowerment involves deeper issues of relations of power and ensuing oppression (Rowlands). Because the abilities of a particular group of people are socially constructed, development programs that take an empowering approach should do more than focus on beneficiaries participating in decision-making processes, and instead examine issues of power relations inherent to social construction (Rowlands). Development programs that do not tackle issues of ideological and institutional change present little hope for sustaining empowerment and social transformation (Batliwala, 2007), which were the original goals of feminist approaches to empowerment.

In the 1980s, women's empowerment grew to be defined as a multidimensional concept that recognized how broader structures of class, race, ethnicity, and religion affect women's position in developing societies (Batliwala, 2007). Since the 1990s, however, empowerment has often become unfortunately nothing more than a buzzword used by a variety of development agencies and programs, without any clarity regarding what exactly it encompasses or how it can be applied (Batliwala). Consequently, although many development initiatives claim to support women's empowerment, they typically lack the multifaceted understanding of the term (Batliwala).

Though several groups have identified empowerment as an outcome of various sport for development programs (e.g., UNICEF, Right to Play), the ways in which empowerment has measured and the ways in which empowerment has or has not been rooted in local understandings of the term have been vague. To strengthen assertions of sport for development's utility in empowering people, especially girls and women, further clarity is needed in descriptions of the mechanisms of this empowerment and also the ways in which, if at all, Western, hegemonic understandings of empowerment are challenged.

Current approaches to empowerment have been found to focus on developing individual power, achievement, and status (Batliwala, 2007; Eyben & Napier-Moore, 2009), attributes that have a close association with capitalist ideology and for which measurement is problematic. Contemporary development programs also use the term *empowerment* synonymously with the term *participation* (Batliwala). The conflation of empowerment with participation is problematic, however, because with a narrow focus on participation, which we have shown above is often not extending beyond rhetoric, contextual issues remain beyond the control of the beneficiaries of the development programs and the structural reforms required for social change are left untouched (Botchway, 2001).

The sport for development context within Canada serves as an example of the ways in which sport for development can serve as a band-aid solution. Aboriginal peoples within Canada have been and continue to be subjected to colonial legislation (i.e., the Indian Act), policies and practices, which has served to ghettoize Aboriginal housing, health care, and education. Given the current federal policy climate, in which important determinants of Aboriginal health are chronically underfunded (First Nations Education Council, 2009; Young, 2003), it is curious that the federal Department of Canadian Heritage would support Motivate Canada, an organization that in turn supports sport for development initiatives in Aboriginal communities. Small-scale funding of sport for development programs does little to promote structural reforms that are needed for Aboriginal peoples to be in the situation where they have sufficient resources to self-identify their own development objectives and initiate related programs.

CONCLUSIONS

Though the past decade has seen much growth, far more change is needed in the field of sport for development if it is to live up to its high expectations. As demonstrated in this chapter, for sport for development to grow, it is crucial for sport for development leaders to learn from development literature outside of the sport setting to avoid now well-known pitfalls. In particular, sport for development needs to be driven by those who are to be on the receiving end of development initiatives. Such change needs to go beyond the rhetoric of participation, partnerships, and empowerment, and instead go to the core power issues that inform past and current development initiatives. For example, the organizers of a recent sport for development gathering in Canada failed to invite Inuit and Métis governments to the table. After the first author offered this critique, several people informed her that they believed that these nations were not ready to participate in discussions at the policy level, even though they are the very people that the programs target. Comments such as these only reinforce the need to use the tools that feminism and postcolonialism offer sport for development scholars and practitioners alike.

Another tactic that should be considered for youth in sport for development is a strengths-based approach. Contrary to the narrow, weakness-focused descriptions created by a deficit model, a strengths-based approach investigates what positive characteristics people possess to effectively deal with their own issues (Rashid & Ostermann, 2009). A strengths-based assessment focuses on the emotional and behavioral skills and characteristics that can help people feel accomplished, improve relationships, enhance coping skills, and promote development (Lappalainen et al., 2009). By looking beyond simply identifying and treating deficits and instead considering people's strengths, this approach emphasizes a view of people as possessing multifarious characteristics and living in diverse contexts (Cox, 2006; Epstein, 1999). By focusing on people's strengths, they can then be actively involved in ameliorating their lives (Cox; Epstein), which is essential, because when participants are actively included in processes of change, they are more likely to embrace the programs and interventions (Lappalainen et al., 2009). Although a strengths-based approach has been used frequently in areas such as clinical psychology (Rashid & Ostermann, 2009; Wright & Lopez, 2002), education and special education (Lappalainen et al., 2009; Nelson & Pearson, 1991), and family services (Dunst, Trivette, & Deal, 1994), it is an approach rarely explored in the context of sport for development.

A feminist, postcolonial, strengths-based approach that is supported by strong partnerships and political will has the potential to address the critiques of sport for development that we have described throughout this chapter. Such an approach will also help the sport for development field to mature and meet its considerable promise.

REFERENCES

Akindes, G., & Kirwin, M. (2009). Sport as international aid: Assisting development or promoting under-development in Sub-Saharan Africa? In R. Levermore & A. Beacom (Eds.), *Sport and international development* (pp. 219-245). Hampshire, UK: Palgrave Macmillan.

Alatas, S. H. (2000). Intellectual imperialism: Definitions, traits, and problems. *Southeast Asian Journal of Social Science, 28*(11), 23-45.

Ashcroft, B., Griffiths, G., & Tiffin, H. (1989). *The empire writes back*. London & New York: Routledge.

Barnett T., & Parkhurst, J. (2005). HIV/AIDS: Sex, abstinence, and behaviour change. *The Lancet Infectious Diseases, 5,* 590-593.

Batliwala, S. (2007). Taking the power out of empowerment—an experiential account. *Development in Practice, 17,* 557-565.

Battiste, M. (2004). Animating sites of postcolonial education: Indigenous knowledge and the humanities. Retrieved from http://www.usask.ca/education/people/battistem/pdf/csse_battiste.pdf

Botchway, K. (2001). Paradox of empowerment: Reflections on a case study from Northern Ghana. *World Development, 29,* 135-153.

Brady, M. (2005). Creating safe spaces and building social assets for young women in the developing world: A new role for sports. *Women's Studies Quarterly, 33*(1/2), 35-49.

Coalter, F. (2009). Sport-in-development: Accountability or development? In R. Levermore & A. Beacom (Eds.), *Sport and international development* (pp. 55-75). Hampshire, UK: Palgrave Macmillan.

Cox, K. (2006). Investigating the impact of strength-based assessment on youth with emotional or behavioral disorders. *Journal of Child and Family Studies, 15,* 287-301.

Darnell, S. (2007). Playing with race: Right to play and the production of whiteness in development through sport. *Sport in Society, 10,* 560-579.

Dunst, C. J., Trivette, C. M., & Deal, A. G. (Eds.). (1994). *Supporting and strengthening families: Methods, strategies, and practice.* Cambridge, MA: Brookline Books.

Embassy of the United States. Embassy Newscentre (2007). *Ivoirian soccer maestro becomes PEPFAR ambassador against HIV/AIDS.* Retrieved from http://abidjan.usembassy.gov/ivoirian_soccer_maestro_becomes_pepfar_ambassador_against_hiv/aids_.html

Epstein, M. H. (1999). The development and validation of a scale to assess the emotional and behavioral strengths of children and adolescents. *Remedial and Special Education, 20,* 258-262.

Eyben, R., & Napier-Moore, R. (2009). Choosing words with care? Shifting meanings of women's empowerment in international development. *Third World Quarterly, 30,* 285-300.

First Nations Education Council. (2009). *Paper on First Nations education funding.* Wendake, QC: Author.

Frankenberg, R., & Mani, L. (1993). Crosscurrents, crosstalk: Race, 'postcoloniality' and the politics of location. *Cultural Studies, 7,* 292-310.

Fraser, N. (1989). *Unruly practices: Power, discourse, and gender in contemporary social theory.* Minneapolis, MN: University of Minnesota Press.

Hayhurst, L. M. C. (2009). The power to shape policy: Charting sport for development and peace policy discourses. *International Journal of Sport Policy, 1,* 203-227.

Hedstrom, R., & Gould, D. (2004). Research in youth sports: Critical issues status. *Institute for the Study of Youth Sports.* Retrieved from http://www.educ.msu.edu/ysi/project/CriticalIssuesYouthSports.pdf

Hesse-Biber, S. N., Leavy, P., & Yaiser, M. L. (2004). Feminist approaches to research as process. Reconceptualizing epistemology, methodology, and method. In S. N. Hesse-Biber & M. L. Yaiser (Eds.), *Feminist perspectives on social research* (pp. 3-26). Oxford, Oxford University Press.

Hooks, B. (1984). Feminist theory from margin to center. Boston: South End Press.

Johnston, R. J., Gregory, D., & D. M. Smith (Eds.). (1994). *The dictionary of human geography* (5th ed.). Oxford: Blackwell.

Kabeer, N. (1994). *Reversed realities: Gender hierarchies in development thought.* London: Verso.

Kay, T. (2009). Developing through sport: Evidencing sport impacts on young people. *Sport in Society, 12,* 1177-1191.

Kidd, B. (2008). A new social movement: Sport for development and peace. *Sport and Society, 11,* 370-380.

Lappalainen, K., Savolainen, H., Kuorelahti, M., & Epstein, M. H. (2009). An international assessment of the emotional and behavioural strengths of youth. *Journal of Child and Family Studies, 18,* 746-753.

Levermore, R. (2008). Sport: A new engine of development? *Progress in Development Studies, 8,* 183-190.

Levermore, R., & Beacom, A. (2009). Sport and development: Mapping the field. In R. Levermore & A. Beacom (Eds.), *Sport and international development* (pp. 1-25). Hampshire, UK: Palgrave Macmillan.

Levett, G. (2010). Sport and the imperial city: Colonial tours in Edwardian London. *London Journal, 35*(1), 39-57.

Lewis, R., & Mills, S. (Eds.). (2003). *Introduction. In Feminist postcolonial theory* (pp. 1-24). London: Routledge.

Lorde, A. (1984). *Sister/outsider: Essays and speeches.* New York: The Crossing Press.

Malhotra, A., & Schuler, S. R. (2005). Conceptualizing and measuring women's empowerment as a variable in international development. In D. Narayan (Ed.), *Measuring empowerment* (pp. 71-88). Washington, DC: World Bank.

McEwan, C. (2009). *Postcolonialism and development.* London: Routledge.

Mohanty, C. T. (1988). Under western eyes: Feminist scholarship and colonial discourses. *Feminist Review, 30,* 61-88.

Nagar, R., & Ragu, S. (2003). Women, NGOs and the contradictions of empowerment and disempowerment. *Antipode: A Radical Journal of Geography, 35*(1), 1-13.

Nelson, C. M., & Pearson, C. A. (1991). *Integrating services for children and youth with emotional and behavioral disorders.* Reston, VA: Council for Exceptional Children.

Nicholls, S. (2008). *Playing games with power and privilege: Subjugated knowledge and sport for development* (Master's thesis). University of Ottawa, Ottawa, Ontario.

Nicholls, S., & Giles, A. R. (2007). Sport as a tool for HIV/AIDS education: A potential catalyst for change. *Pimatisiwin: A Journal of Aboriginal and Indigenous Community Health, 5*(1), 51-85.

Nicholls, S., Giles, A. R., & Sethna, C. (2011). Perpetuating the 'lack of evidence' discourse in sport for development: Privileged voices, unheard stories and subjugated knowledge. *International Review for the Sociology of Sport, 46,* 249-264.

Pisani, E. (2009). *The wisdom of whores: Bureaucrats, brothels, and the business of AIDS.* Toronto: Penguin.

President's Emergency Plan for AIDS Relief. (PEPFAR) *Populated Printable COP.* (2009). Retrieved from http://www.pepfar.gov/documents/organization/140327.pdf

Rashid, T., & Ostermann, R. F. (2009). Strength-based assessment in clinical practice. *Journal of Clinical Psychology, 65,* 488-498.

Rowlands, J. (1995). Empowerment examined. *Development in Practice, 5,* 101-107.

Sen, S., & Grown, C. (1987). *Development, crisis and alternative visions: Third World women's perspectives.* New York: Monthly Review.

Sport for Development and Peace International Working Group (SDP IWG) (2007, October 17). *Literature Reviews on Sport for Development and Peace.* Commissioned by Sport for Development and Peace International Working Group (SDP IWG) Secretariat. Toronto, Canada. Retrieved from http://www.righttoplay.com/news-and-media/Documents/Policy%20Reports%20docs/Literature%20Reviews%20SDP.pdf.

Stewart-Withers, R., & Brook, M. (2009). Sport as a vehicle for development: The influence of rugby league in/on the Pacific. *Massey Working Paper Series.* Retrieved from http://muir.massey.ac.nz/bitstream/10179/1070/3/wps3_Stewart-Withers_and_Brook.pdf

Stoddart, B. (1988). Sport, cultural imperialism, and colonial response in British empire. *Comparative Studies in Society and History, 30,* 649-673.

UNAIDS. (2001). Children and young people in a world of AIDS. Joint United Nations Programme on HIV/AIDS. Geneva: UNAIDS.

United Nations Children's Fund. (2005). *Adolescent development: Perspectives and frameworks. A summary of adolescent needs, an analysis of the various program approaches and general recommendations for adolescent programming. Learning series No. 1.* New York: Adolescent Development and Participation Unit Programme Division, United Nations.

United Nations General Assembly. Resolution 58/5. (2003). *Sport as a Means to Promote Education, Health, Development and Peace.* Retrieved from http://daccessddsny.un.org/doc/UNDOC/GEN/N03/592/54/PDF/N0359254.pdf?OpenElement

Vermund, S. H., Allen, K. L., & Abdool Karim, Q. (2009). *Current Opinion in HIV and AIDs, 4,* 266 – 273.

Willis, O. (2000). Sport and development: The significance of Mathare Youth Sports Association. *Canadian Journal of Development Studies, 21,* 825-849.

Wright, B. A., & Lopez, S. J. (2002). Widening the diagnostic focus: A case for including human strengths and environmental resources. In C. R. Snyder & S. J. Lopez (Eds.), Handbook of positive psychology (pp. 26–44). New York: Oxford.

Young, R. (2001). *Postcolonialism: An historical introduction.* Oxford: Blackwell.

Young, T. (2003). Review of research on Aboriginal populations in Canada: Relevance to their health needs. *British Medical Journal, 327,* 419-422.

Making Space for Gay Sport Participants

Barbara Ravel

8

Gay sport participants challenge the traditional heterocentric assumption that all sport participants are heterosexual. Moreover, their presence reinforces the idea that sport is a reflection of society where individuals with marginal sexualities have moved from the shadow of the closet to (relative) visibility. Although they were once declared mentally ill and their sexual relations condemned as being illegal, they are now protected by anti-discrimination policies (at least in Western countries) as well as recognized and celebrated by annual gay pride parades all around the world. In the sports world, the presence of non-heterosexual individuals has sometimes been accompanied by homophobia, which has led to the creation of special events for lesbian, gay, bisexual, and transgender athletes (LGBT), such as the Gay Games. Away from LGBT leagues and competitions, what are the experiences of non-heterosexual men and women in sport today? This chapter will first provide an overview of the situation for LGBT individuals in sports including an examination of several "out" high-profile athletes. Then, the results of a study on women with a non-conventional sexuality conducted in Québec will be presented. Finally, the chapter will offer practical recommendations intended for various actors in the sports world (e.g., coaches, administrators, researchers).

THE SITUATION FOR LGBT INDIVIDUALS IN SPORTS

"I could never have come out without first establishing myself and earning respect as a player. Rugby was my passion, my whole life, and I wasn't prepared to risk losing everything I loved." This quotation from Gareth Thomas, a Welsh professional rugby player who came out as a gay man in a British newspaper (Weathers, 2009), illustrates the situation for many LGBT athletes, especially among those who are famous, who perceive that there is a risk in coming out to their teammates and ultimately to the public. As one of the latest high-profile gay or lesbian athletes to come out, Thomas decided to do so at age 35 after a prestigious career, notably representing Wales in many international competitions and being the team's captain when Wales won the 2005 Six Nations Championship, rugby's most important European competition. Similar to Thomas's example, professional basketball star Sheryl Swoopes publicly came out as a lesbian in 2005 after four Women's National Basketball Association (WNBA) championships, three WNBA Most Valuable Player Awards, and three Olympic gold medals (Granderson, 2005). Another interesting parallel between Thomas and Swoopes is how they are represented in the media as conventionally masculine and feminine, respectively. Indeed, Thomas's "toughness" and success in the "macho" sport of rugby are particularly emphasized in his coming-out article (i.e., Weathers) through the author's narrative and the pictures chosen to illustrate the article (e.g., on the field with a tight-fitting rugby jersey showing his muscular upper body; bleeding after a play during a rugby match; hand in hand with his ex-wife; holding the Six Nations trophy in 2005). As for Swoopes, King (2009) who presented an analysis of the media coverage of the player's coming out argued that her image was definitely "feminine," with motherhood and her son often being mentioned as being of upmost importance to her. Comparing Swoopes to Martina Navratilova, King said,

> In contrast, Swoopes' image as the "exceptional" Black woman —hard working, nurturing, feminine, professionally successful—was well established by the time she came out. This, combined with a context that is characterized by greater tolerance for some versions of lesbianism within popular culture, helped to produce Swoopes as a figure who could be comfortably consumed by a predominantly White media and by White lesbian and other consumers. Were she butch, or darker skinned, or not in a stable relationship, her currency may have been compromised. (p. 282)

If Thomas and Swoopes are among the most recent professional athletes to come out, Martina Navratilova was the first big sport star to come out, excluding Billie Jean King, who was forced out and denied being a lesbian for years after. Illustrating one of the risks of coming out as a professional athlete that were articulated by Thomas, Navratilova came out in 1981 when she was 25 years old and had already won several Grand Slam singles and doubles titles, but nonetheless experienced important sponsorship losses in the process (Spencer, 2003). In her career spanning over three decades, Navratilova eventually benefited from the progressive openness of sport and society to homosexuality and secured major sponsorship deals, notably with Subaru and Olivia, a lesbian travel company, which marked the first time she was sponsored for "being gay rather than in spite of it" (Robson, 2005, para. 1).

Contrary to these star players and most others who have come out, Amelie Mauresmo and Matthew Mitcham came out at the beginning of their careers and before any major successes. The recently retired French tennis player Mauresmo came out in 1999 during a second round match at the Australian Open where she reached her first Grand Slam final at age 19. As the first French athlete to publicly come out, her coming out was highly publicized in the media at the time. But contrary to Navratilova, who may have lost millions because of her sexuality, all of Mauresmo's sponsors continued to support her after she came out. Though it may seem paradoxical, Mauresmo's openness about her sexuality from the beginning of her career is one of the reasons why she was popular, especially in France (Ravel, 2007).

Matthew Mitcham, a 20-year-old Australian diver and medal hopeful at the 2008 Beijing Olympic Games, publicly came out as a gay man a few months prior to the Olympic Games in an Australian newspaper (Halloran, 2008). He went on to capture gold in the 10-meter platform event while receiving the highest scoring dive in Olympic history in the process and becoming the only non-Chinese athlete to win gold in diving at the 2008 Games. Mitcham's athletic performance and recent coming out were arguably newsworthy, but by failing to mention his sexuality during their telecast of the diving competition, several television channels, including NBC, demonstrated the double standard in how the media deal with athletes' sexualities. While heterosexual athletes' sexuality is often part of the athlete's media coverage, the sexuality of non-heterosexual athletes tends to be omitted (Ravel, 2009). Despite a relatively homophobic coverage by mainstream media, Mitcham reported a warm welcome and support from Australian fans as well as fellow competitors (Dennett, 2008).

This acceptance could be explained by Anderson's theory of inclusive masculinity (2009) and his idea of diminishing "homohysteria"—*homohysteria* being defined as "the fear of being homosexualized" (p. 7). Anderson developed his theory based on ethnographic studies of American and British young men, athletes and non-athletes, and suggested that "in cultures of diminishing homohysteria, two dominant (but not dominating) forms of masculinity exist: One conservative and one inclusive" (p. 8). He proposed that "heterosexual men ascribing to an 'inclusive masculinity' demonstrate emotional and physically homosocial proximity. They include their gay teammates and are shown to value heterofemininity" (p. 8). It is in this sport context where homophobia ceases to be a guiding principle in the production of masculinity that Mitcham was able to come out without negative repercussions.

The picture that Anderson depicted of men's sport today, however, seems to contrast with what previous researchers on men in sports have reported (e.g., Hekma, 1998; Messner, 2007; Pronger, 1990). Most notably, men's sport, particularly team sports, is a space where heterosexual masculinity is reinforced through homophobic and misogynistic discourses. It is a place where non-heterosexual athletes are not welcome and women are denigrated, mostly by being depicted as sexual objects. But Anderson (2009) would also argue that diving is not a sport "at the center of masculine production" (p. 9), like football and basketball are. Nonetheless, Anderson's work on gay athletes and his theory of inclusive masculinity suggest that the situation for non-heterosexual male athletes is changing and that sport and society are moving toward a greater acceptance of non-normative sexualities.

Men's sports may be transitioning from a very homophobic space to one that is somewhat more open to the presence of gay athletes. Women's sports, however, have often been represented as being both homophobic and serving as a refuge for non-heterosexual women (e.g., Cahn, 1993, 1994; Griffin, 1998). This paradox was well summarized by Cahn's expression of "play it, don't say it" (Cahn, 1994, p. 185). As Cahn put it, "the athletic setting provided public space for lesbian sociability without naming it as such" (1993, p. 358). Her examination of the historical development of homophobia in U.S. women's sport revealed that silence around lesbian sexuality pervaded and that the appearance of heterosexual femininity was often necessary to continue playing sport as a woman in the middle of America's 20th century. Several decades later, similar results have been found by researchers on women in sport (e.g., Griffin, 1998; Hekma, 1998; Mennesson & Clement, 2003). Indeed, whether in France (Mennesson & Clement, 2003), Great Britain (Shire, Brackenridge, & Fuller, 2000), Holland (Hekma, 1998), or the United States of America (Griffin, 1998; Iannota & Kane, 2000), sport seems to be a space of socialization for lesbian athletes, yet it is also frequently influenced by homophobia, notably with conventional femininity often being required from athletes, regardless of their sexuality (e.g., Cox & Thompson, 2000; Forman & Plymire, 2005; Spencer, 2004).

ATHLETES WITH A NON-CONVENTIONAL SEXUALITY IN QUEBEC WOMEN'S SPORT

To further our understanding of the situation for LGBT athletes, a study was conducted in Montréal (Québec, Canada; Ravel & Rail, 2006, 2007, 2008), and its main results are presented here. In the study, our first objective was to provide empirical data on the situation of non-heterosexual athletes. Second, we had a theoretical objective as we intended to examine non-conventional sexualities and consequently the concept of sexuality more broadly. Finally, we designed the study so that it would give a voice to women who have historically been silenced because of their marginal identities. The participants of the study were 14 non-heterosexual White women living and playing sport in Montréal. Aged between 21 and 31 years of age, they were all Francophone women competing in different team sports (e.g., ice hockey, soccer) at various levels, from recreational to elite. They often participated in more than one sport and mostly played in mainstream leagues, although four of them participated in LGBT leagues. Data were collected through conversations with the participants. The conversation transcripts were first analyzed thematically. Then, a poststructuralist discourse analysis was performed, which consisted of identifying the multiple discourses circulating in the participants' narratives (Gavey, 1989; Weedon, 1987). By examining how the participants positioned themselves in relation to various discourses, we were able to highlight how they reproduced or challenged dominant ideas about sexuality and how circulating discourses influenced the way in which they constituted themselves as non-heterosexual individuals.

THE SITUATION FOR NON-HETEROSEXUAL WOMEN IN QUEBEC'S SPORT

First, the study was designed to provide empirical data on the situation of non-heterosexual women living and playing sport in Montréal. International accounts (e.g., Hekma, 1998; Iannota & Kane, 2000; Mennesson & Clement, 2003) revealed that, despite an increasing acceptance of non-conventional sexualities in sport more generally, various manifestations of homophobia are still found in the athletic world. These manifestations include invisibility of lesbian sexuality during public events in women's elite ice hockey in Canada (Theberge, 2000) and distancing from the words "lesbian" or "gay" in Great Britain (Shire et al., 2000) as well as New Zealand (Cox & Thompson, 2000). Another manifestation of homophobia that was reported in sport is the overt decision of certain teams to only recruit players who were perceived as heterosexual and to harass the non-heterosexual players on their team (Mennesson & Clement). It was therefore interesting to see if and how the fact that the data were collected in the city of Montréal would influence the results because Montréal is well known for its openness and acceptance towards diversity. Indeed, Montréal, Québec's biggest city, is often described as "gay friendly" or, as Podmore (2001) put it with regards to one of Montréal's neighborhoods, "a place where ethnic, social and sexual marginalities came together to create an 'alternative space'" (p. 342).

Data analysis revealed that the participants constructed sport as a space of resistance to heterosexism and emphasized the comfort and enjoyment related to being "out" in sport. Indeed, all the participants but two (and only in one of their teams) were open about their sexuality with their teammates. They also emphasized the great acceptance and, sometimes, even celebration of non-conventional sexualities in their sport environment, which is somewhat surprising because most played in mainstream leagues. The following quotation from Simone (pseudonym), a 29-year-old handball player, illustrated the open context for non-heterosexual athletes in women's sport in Montreal:

> Slowly we became closer and, I don't know, I must have told everyone, one by one, on the team. Then, since everybody knew, we were out and open about it. It was no longer an unspoken fact; it was out in the open so we'd come to team practices and we'd exchange stories. It was like "what about your girlfriend?"

The situation was, however, rather different in other social milieus (e.g., family, work) where invisibility and silence about their sexuality were more common. From the discourse analysis there was evidence that, although dominant (heteronormative) discourses were circulated in non-sport settings, marginal discourses about sexuality were circulated in sport. Montréal's supposedly "gay-friendly" atmosphere seemed to influence sport, at least women's sport, more so than other milieus, with women's sport appearing to be more welcoming to sexual diversity than society at large. Sandra's example nicely illustrates the openness of sport with regards to sexual diversity because her (mainstream) ice hockey league was the only public space in which she was able to be "out":

> We just watch a game, we talk to friends and I'll just put my arm around her [her girlfriend] shoulders, I'll just give her a little signal to say "look, I'm here." You know, to say "I'm able to show it [my affection] to you, I'm happy and it feels good to be able to express it." I feel comfortable touching my girlfriend in that environment, at hockey.

UNDERSTANDING NON-CONVENTIONAL SEXUALITIES

The study was also designed to further our understanding of non-conventional sexualities in women's sports. Before I reveal the results, it is important to point out the theoretical shift that has occurred in the study of marginal sexualities in sport. Although earlier studies on the subject tended to solely focus on the experiences of lesbian athletes (e.g., Cahn, 1993; Fusco, 1998; Krane, 1996), more recent researchers have highlighted the need to go beyond traditional conceptions of sexuality and the heterosexual/homosexual binary (e.g., Broad, 2001; Shire et al., 2000), thus expanding their examination of sexuality to other non-conventional sexualities (e.g., queer, butch). These more recent studies were designed with a theoretical framework inspired by feminist post-structuralism and queer theory and questioned the sport environment's heteronormativity as well as the fixed categories of sex, gender, and sexuality (e.g., Broad, 2001; Caudwell, 1999, 2003).

Our study was also inspired by feminist post-structuralism and queer theory. Along with other researchers using feminist post-structuralism, we have recognized the influence of language and discourses on the constitution of one's subjectivity (see also Weedon, 1987). It is through language and by positioning themselves in relation to multiple discourses that individuals constitute themselves as "subjects" in the post-structuralist sense of the term. Because they borrow elements of discourses that are dominant or marginal and sometimes contradictory, individuals show an unstable and changing subjectivity, which is a key element for post-structuralist theorists (Gavey, 1989; Weedon, 1987, 1999). Inspired by post-structuralist ideas, queer theorists have contested the hegemony of heterosexuality as the only "natural" or "normal" sexuality (Butler, 1990; de Lauretis, 1993). Moreover, they have proposed to destabilize the relation between sex, gender, and sexuality (e.g., the traditional relation woman-feminine-heterosexual) as well as the categories man/woman, masculine/feminine, heterosexual/homosexual (Butler, 1990; de Lauretis, 1993). As Weedon (1999) put it, the two poles of such binaries must be replaced by "a proliferation of differences which queer theory and politics refuse to hierarchize" (p. 73).

Non-heterosexual participants were recruited for our study with the purpose of examining how they constructed their "non-heterosexuality." The results depict how differently the participants constructed their sexualities. More specifically, although most participants positioned themselves as "gaie" (the French and feminine version of the English "gay"), others positioned themselves as lesbian or bisexual, or refused to attach any label to their sexualities. Even though different non-conventional sexualities were revealed during the conversations, *gaie* sexuality was often the umbrella term used to refer to non-conventional sexualities generally. The participants constructed *gaie* sexuality as a fun, young, and feminine version of lesbian sexuality. In doing so, they showed how their construction of sexuality was affected by their construction of gender. Precisely, by positioning themselves as *gaie*, the participants/athletes also positioned themselves as conventionally feminine and rejected the stereotypical image of the butch or "masculine" lesbian. Their discursive constructions of sexuality and gender appeared to be concurrently influenced by multiple discourses. Indeed, with their *gaie* sexuality, they reproduced marginal ideas about sexuality that challenged the hegemony of heterosexuality while also reiterating dominant discourses about gender and femininity that were derogatory (and homophobic) towards "masculine" lesbians. In other words, if it was okay to be *gaie,* but being too "masculine" (i.e., butch) was not well received and often mocked.

Moreover, several *gaie* participants along with other participants, especially those positioning themselves outside hegemonic or existing categories or refusing to label their sexualities, challenged traditional assumptions of sexuality. The following quotation from Simone, who positioned herself as lesbian in other parts of the conversation, represents how some participants disrupted the heterosexual/homosexual binary by contesting the idea of a stable sexuality and of exclusive desires for individuals of one gender:

I'm not completely gaie because I am attracted to men, more so than many lesbians that I know—the majority of them in fact. However, I know that fundamentally, I prefer women. I think I'm pretty open when it comes to my sexuality. I think that I'm more open than most people, whether gaie or straight.

The above quotation exemplifies unstable and shifting identities, which were often revealed in the narratives of the participants. In addition, multiple and competing discourses were identified in the participants' accounts and illustrated complex constructions of their sexualities. For example, the participants' narratives were based on discourses about sexuality that contested the hegemony of heterosexuality (even though they tended to normalize *gaie* sexuality as compared to other non-conventional sexualities). The participants also constructed their sexualities by borrowing elements from dominant discourses about gender, which valued traditional femininity over other expressions of femininity. The results therefore highlighted the utility of feminist post-structuralist and queer theories in interpreting the data collected through conversations with the participants. Indeed, our post-structuralist approach enabled us to see how complex the participants' constructions of their non-conventional sexualities could be and how influenced by multiple discourses they were. Moreover, adopting a queer perspective proved relevant because the participants often constructed their sexualities outside of hegemonic categories of sexuality and outside of the two poles of the heterosexual/homosexual binary.

Empowering the Participants

Finally, the study was conceived with the objective of giving a voice to and empowering women with non-conventional sexualities. To this end, the traditional interview format was replaced by conversations with the participants within which their experiences were greatly valued, power relations between the interviewer and the interviewees were minimized, and roles between the interviewer and the interviewee were expected to shift (Fontana, 2002; Jansen & Davis, 1998; Kvale, 1996). Moreover, I intended that each participant actively take part in the research process (Kvale, 1996) by reviewing the transcription of the conversation and adding to or deleting any part of the text to better reflect their thoughts on the issues discussed. I also asked the participants to comment on the results presented under the form of a fictional story, especially with regards to its resemblance to their own experiences. This last strategy was used to enhance the quality of the results (Harrison, MacGibbon, & Morton, 2001; Sparkes, 2002) and also provided an opportunity to give back to the participants as well as to re-engage them in the research process. In addition, having the interviewer share her experience as a queer woman and an ice hockey player facilitated communication and contributed to the blurring of boundaries between the interviewer and the interviewee. The following exchange between me and Nathalie (pseudonym), a 21-year-old ice hockey player, illustrates how mutual understanding (in this example common knowledge about Montréal's gay Village) and reciprocity enabled the creation of a positive climate during the conversation:

> Nathalie: I'd been in Montréal for 2 weeks and I went out with a bunch of girls
> from the team as well as some other girls. The first time I went out in Montréal
> I went to [a popular club in the Village]
> Barbara: That's a good start! [Laughs]
> Nathalie: Yeah. And, you know, we partied and all that. [...]

The conversations with the participants were conducted in French; therefore the quotations presented in various articles or chapters about this project were translated into English to become publishable data for an Anglophone audience. Nevertheless, several French expressions (even the acute accent on "Montréal" and "Québec") or references to Québec culture were kept, notably the original version of the word most participants used to describe their sexuality, *gaie*—the French and feminine version of the English "gay." This strategy was used to empower the (Francophone) participants involved in the study by not assimilating them into the Anglophone community that surrounded them as Francophone women in Canada and in North America more broadly.

CONCLUSIONS

One main result of the study that was presented here is that sport can be open to those who challenge heteronormativity, but less so to those who transgress gender boundaries. This result echoes one of the key findings of a U.K. research report entitled *A Review of Sexual Orientation in Sport* (Brackenridge, Alldred, Jarvis, Maddocks, & Rivers, 2008) within which it was argued that "much of the prejudice and negativity around LGBT issues in sport can be traced back to the application of gender stereotypes and perceptions of masculinity and femininity" (p. 55). Moreover, we revealed how sexuality may not be as fixed as once believed and therefore cannot only be understood in terms of hegemonic categories of sexuality. In this respect, it appears relevant to include diverse sexual minorities in research/ interventions related to LGBT issues, rather than to only focus on gay men or lesbians.

Although the above results are encouraging with regards to the improving situation for LGBT athletes, they are obviously influenced by the sample of women who participated in the study. The 14 women who were interviewed were all young, White, living in Montréal, and playing team sports. It is therefore important to note that these results do not necessarily reflect the situation of all LGBT individuals in sport, such as those living in non-Western countries and those playing at the highest level of competition. Indeed, famous LGBT athletes are still reluctant to come out of the closet during their careers, which may indicate that elite sport is not entirely welcoming to non-heterosexual athletes. Moreover, the popularity of the Gay Games and of LGBT sports leagues more generally suggests that LGBT athletes may still not feel as comfortable in mainstream athletic contexts. Nevertheless, their involvement in LGBT sports leagues may be due to participation in an explicitly and openly LGBT environment adding another dimension to sport that these athletes seek rather than to the existence of homophobia in mainstream sport. Finally, the situation for non-heterosexual individuals in sport is different for men and women because the stakes are not the same in men's and women's sports. Compared to women's sports, men's sports benefit from large media coverage and substantial financing. This greater media attention and sponsorship, in conjunction with the obligation to conform to traditional gender norms, makes it more difficult for men to come out as non-heterosexual athletes. Despite the existing barriers to coming out, sport appears to be more accepting of sexual diversity with more and more athletes (men and women) deciding to come out in sport.

PRACTICAL RECOMMENDATIONS

What can we do to create a more welcoming sports environment for LGBT individuals? First, educational programs or initiatives focusing on LGBT issues in sport exist and can help coaches, sports administrators, or other individuals involved in sport to be inclusive of sexual diversity. Riding on the wave started with the Olympic Winter Games held in Vancouver in February 2010, the organizers of the Canadian campaign for the International Day Against Homophobia (IDAHO) chose a sports theme for their 2010 campaign (Fondation Émergence, 2010a). The campaign entitled "Speaking about silence—Homophobia in the sports world" was an opportunity for the organizers to condemn sport being a space where marginal sexualities are often silenced and to break this silence by speaking about LGBT issues in sport. The 2010 IDAHO campaign circulated in Canadian mainstream media (e.g., Radio Canada, Canoe.tv) along with various articles on related topics on and around May 17, the date chosen to be the International Day Against Homophobia each year. This initiative is not the first in Canada, however; The Canadian Association for the Advancement of Women and Sport and Physical Activity (CAAWS) has been organizing workshops addressing homophobia in sport for years and offers various resources for sports leaders in the "Homophobia in Sport" section of their website (http://www.caaws.ca/homophobia/e/index.cfm). Moreover, two key documents on homophobia in sport have been published in Canada: *Seeing the Invisible, Speaking about the Unspoken: A Position Paper on Homophobia in Sport* (CAAWS, 2006) and "Homophobia in sport—Fact of life, taboo subject," an article by Demers published in the *Canadian Journal for Women in Coaching Online* (2006). Both manuscripts give practical advice for sports professionals/volunteers to eliminate homophobia from sport. Nevertheless, the leading educational program is certainly *It Takes a Team! Making Sport Safe for Lesbian, Gay, Bisexual, and Transgender Athletes and Coaches* (Griffin, Perrotti, Priest, & Muska, 2002), a U.S. "Education kit for athletes, coaches, and athletic directors" published by the Women's Sports Foundation. It provides an extensive coverage of LGBT issues in sport and notably offers several action guides targeted towards athletes, coaches, or other individuals involved in sports.

One common underlying assumption from these programs or initiatives is that they challenge heterosexism defined as "the belief that everyone is heterosexual and that heterosexuality is the only acceptable way of being" (Fondation Émergence, 2010b). One recurrent suggestion is the conception within sports federations or organizations of anti-discrimination policies that explicitly mention sexual orientation as a potential basis for discrimination. The anti-discrimination policy of the Quebec Major Junior Hockey League is representative in this respect. Lately, the 2010 IDAHO campaign targeting homophobia in sport included a declaration against any form of discrimination that can be found in the sports world (Fondation Émergence, 2010a). This declaration can be used by organizations as well as by individuals to show that they support a discrimination-free athletic environment. In addition to these anti-discrimination policies, the creation of an inclusive or positive space for LGBT individuals in sport is a key objective for sports leaders. The establishment of such a space can be facilitated by following the guidelines proposed by the Women's Sports Foundation in its *It Takes a Team* educational program or by the Canadian Association for the Advancement of Women and Sport and Physical Activity. For example, in the Action Guide for Coaches in *It Takes a Team,* coaches were encouraged to educate themselves about LGBT issues in sport, disapprove of derogatory comments towards LGBT people in the team's environment, and "treat all athletes and coaches fairly and respectfully regardless of their sexual orientation or gender expression" (Women's Sports Foundation, 2010). Two examples illustrate successful attempts to create a safe space for LGBT individuals in sport. First, it was reported in the position paper on homophobia in sport edited by CAAWS (2006) that "For the first time in Canada, the Commonwealth Games Association of Canada created a positive space for Team Canada at the 2006 Commonwealth Games in Melbourne, Australia" (p. 8) ensuring that LGBT Team Canada members knew that they were "welcome and supported in one of the most important competitions of their athletic careers" (p. 8). In the same vein, the first-ever Olympic Pride houses in Vancouver and Whistler during the 2010 Olympic Winter Games were created with the intent to "provide an open and welcoming venue for the LGBT community and their allies to celebrate together diversity and inclusiveness through sport" (Pride House, 2010). Such initiatives show how we can make space for gay (understood in the larger sense of the word) sport participants such as athletes, coaches, or sports fans, and how sport can be empowering for "out" athletes and other persons involved in sports. See Boxes 8.1 and 8.2 for suggestions regarding making space for gay sport participants in terms of both research and practice.

BOX 8.1. Suggestions for Researchers

- Increase research on athletes with non-conventional sexualities and genders (e.g., athletes from different countries, athletes competing in mainstream or LGBT leagues, transgender athletes).
- Increase the visibility of results from studies on LGBT issues in sport (e.g., interviews with the media, publications intended for a large audience and not only for an academic audience).
- Establish more connections with researchers outside of the sports world to ensure that research on sport is not cut off from the most recent works on sexuality.
- Establish more connections with the sports world (e.g., athletes, coaches, sports administrators).

BOX 8.2. Suggestions for Practice

- Educate yourself about LGBT issues in sport (e.g., consult electronic resources, attend workshops).
- Denounce all derogatory comments (e.g., homophobic, sexist, racist).
- Be inclusive when you speak and do not assume that everybody is heterosexual.
- Create a welcoming climate where diversity is valued and everybody can feel comfortable. For example, invite partners of LGBT individuals when partners are invited (e.g., social events, fundraising activities).
- Increase the visibility of non-conventional sexualities and genders (e.g., portraits in the media) and encourage open discussions about LGBT issues (e.g., between team members and coaches).
- Be knowledgeable about the existence of LGBT support groups in your area and share the information with individuals who might be interested.

REFERENCES

Anderson, E. (2009). *Inclusive masculinity: The changing nature of masculinities.* New York: Routledge.

Brackenridge, C., Alldred, P., Jarvis, A., Maddocks, K., & Rivers, I. (2008). *A review of sexual orientation in sport: sportscotland Research Report no. 114.* Edinburgh, Scotland: sportscotland. Retrieved from http://www.sportscotland.org.uk/ChannelNavigation/Resources/TopicNavigation/Collections/Research/A+literature+review+of+sexual+orientation+in+sport.htm

Broad, K. L. (2001). The gendered unapologetic: Queer resistance in women's sport. *Sociology of Sport Journal, 18,* 181-204.

Butler, J. (1990). *Gender trouble: Feminism and the subversion of identity.* New York: Routledge.

Canadian Association for the Advancement of Women and Sport and Physical Activity (CAAWS) (2006). *Seeing the invisible, speaking about the unspoken: A position paper on homophobia.* Ottawa, Canada: CAAWS. Retrieved from http://www.caaws.ca/pdfs/CAAWS_Homophobia_Discussion_Paper_E.pdf

Cahn, S. K. (1993). From the "muscle moll" to the "butch" ballplayer: Mannishness, lesbianism and homophobia in U.S. women's sport. *Feminist Studies, 19,* 343-368.

Cahn, S. K. (1994). *Coming on strong: Gender and sexuality in the twentieth-century women's sport.* Toronto: Maxwell Macmillan Canada.

Caudwell, J. (1999). Women's football in the United Kingdom: Theorizing gender and unpacking the butch lesbian image. *Journal of Sport and Social Issues, 23,* 390-402.

Caudwell, J. (2003). Sporting gender: Women's footballing bodies as sites/sights for the (re) articulation of sex, gender and desire. *Sociology of Sport Journal, 20,* 391-386.

Cox, B., & Thompson, S. (2000). Multiple bodies: Sportswomen, soccer and sexuality. *International Review for the Sociology of Sport, 35,* 5-20.

de Laurentis, T. (1993). Sexual indifference and lesbian representation. In H. Abelove, M. A. Barale, & D. H. Halperin (Eds.), *The lesbian and gay studies reader* (pp. 141-158). New York: Routledge.

Demers, G. (2006). Homophobia in sport—Fact of life, taboo subject. *Canadian Journal for Women in Coaching Online, 6* (2). Retrieved from http://www.coach.ca/WOMEN/e/journal/apr2006/index.htm

Dennett, H. (2008). A backward three-somersault tuck (with a twist). *The Advocate,* August 26. Retrieved from http://www.advocate.com/issue_story_ektid58427.asp

Fondation Émergence (2010a). 2010 *Campaign: Speaking about silence—Homophobia in the sports world.* Retrieved from http://www.fondationemergence.org/default.aspx?scheme=3886

Fondation Émergence (2010b). *What is Homophobia?* Retrieved from http://www.fondationemergence.org/default.aspx?scheme=1277

Fontana, A. (2002). Postmodern trends in interviewing. In J. F. Gubrium & J. A. Holstein (Eds.), *Handbook of interview research* (pp. 161-175). Thousand Oaks, CA: Sage.

Forman, P. J., & Plymire, D. C. (2005). Amélie Mauresmo's muscles: The lesbian heroic in women's professional tennis. *Women's Studies Quarterly, 33,* 120-133.

Fusco, C. (1998). Lesbians and locker rooms: The subjective experience of lesbians in sport. In G. Rail (Ed.), *Sport and postmodern times* (pp. 87-116). New York: State University of New York Press.

Gavey, N. (1989). Feminist poststructuralism and discourse analysis: Contributions to feminist psychology. *Psychology of Women Quarterly, 13,* 459-475.

Granderson, L. Z. (2005). Three time MVP "tired of having to hide my feelings." *ESPN The Magazine,* October 27. Retrieved from http://sports.espn.go.com/wnba/news/story?id=2203853

Griffin, P. (1998). *Strong women, deep closets: Lesbians and homophobia in sport.* Champaign, IL: Human Kinetics.

Griffin, P., Perrotti, J., Priest, L., & Muska, M. (2002). *It takes a team! Making sport safe for lesbian, gay, bisexual, and transgender athletes and coaches.* New York: Women's Sports Foundation. Retrieved from http://www.womenssportsfoundation.org/Issues-And-Research/Homophobia/Resources.aspx

Halloran, J. (2008). Out, proud and ready to go for gold. *Sydney Morning Herald,* May 24. Retrieved from http://www.smh.com.au/articles/2008/05/23/1211183107597.html

Harrison, J., MacGibbon, L., & Morton, M. (2001). Regimes of trustworthiness in qualitative research: The rigors of reciprocity. *Qualitative Inquiry, 7,* 323-345.

Hekma, G. (1998). "As long as they don't make an issue of it…": Gay men and lesbians in organized sports in the Netherlands. *Journal of Homosexuality, 35,* 1-23.

Iannota, J. G., & Kane, M. J. (2000). Sexual stories as resistance narratives in women's sports: Reconceptualizing identity performance. *Sociology of Sport Journal, 19,* 347-369.

Jansen, G. G., & Davis, D. R. (1998). Honoring voice and visibility: Sensitive-topic research and feminist interpretive inquiry. *Affilia: Journal of Woman and Social Work, 13,* 289-311.

King, S. (2009). Homonormativity and the politics of race: Reading Sheryl Swoopes. *Journal of Lesbian Studies, 13,* 272-290.

Krane, V. (1996). Lesbians in sport: Toward acknowledgment, understanding, and theory. *Journal of Sport & Exercise Psychology, 18,* 237-246.

Kvale, S. (1996). *Interviews: An introduction to qualitative research interviewing.* Thousand Oaks, CA: Sage.

Mennesson, C., & Clement, J. P. (2003). Homosociality and homosexuality: The case of soccer played by women. *International Review for the Sociology of Sport, 38,* 311-330.

Messner, M. A. (2007). *Out of play: Critical essays on gender and sport.* Albany, NY: State University of New York Press.

Podmore, J. A. (2001). Lesbians in the crowd: Gender, sexuality and visibility along Montréal's Boul. St-Laurent. *Gender, Place & Culture, 8,* 333-355.

Pride House (2010). *About Pride House.* Retrieved from http://www.pridehouse.ca/About-PRIDEhouse/tabid/75/Default.aspx

Pronger, B. (1990). *The arena of masculinity: Sports, homosexuality, and the meaning of sex.* New York: St. Martin's Press.

Ravel, B. (2007). *Examining a lesbian version of a virtual Navratilova-Mauresmo match.* Paper presented at the Annual Meeting of the North American Society for the Sociology of Sport, Pittsburgh, PA.

Ravel, B. (2009). "We can't cover everything": Matthew Mitcham, coming-out and the media. Paper presented at the *Annual Meeting of the North American Society for the Sociology of Sport,* Ottawa, Canada.

Ravel, B., & Rail, G. (2006). The lightness of being "gaie": Discursive constructions of gender and sexuality in Quebec women's sport. *International Review for the Sociology of Sport, 41,* 395-412.

Ravel, B., & Rail, G. (2007). On the limits of "gaie" spaces: Discursive constructions of women's sport in Quebec. *Sociology of Sport Journal, 24,* 402-420.

Ravel, B., & Rail, G. (2008). From straight to gaie? Quebec sportswomen's discursive constructions of sexuality and destabilization of the linear coming out process. *Journal of Sport and Social Issues, 32,* 4-23.

Robson, D. (2005). Raising a racket with Martina Navratilova: The legendary lesbian tennis star talks about her new role as Olivia's spokeswoman and dispatches travel wisdom from years on the sports circuit. *The Advocate,* July 5. Retrieved from http://find-articles.com/p/articles/mi_m1589/is_2005_July_5/ai_n15399813

Shire, J., Brackenridge, C., & Fuller, M. (2000). Changing positions: The sexual politics of a women's field hockey team 1986-1996. *Women in Sport and Physical Activity Journal, 9,* 35-64.

Sparkes, A. C. (2002). *Telling tales in sport and physical activity: A qualitative journey.* Champaign, IL: Human Kinetics.

Spencer, N. E. (2003). "America sweetheart" and "Czech-mate": A discursive analysis of the Evert-Navratilova rivalry. *Journal of Sport and Social Issues, 27,* 18-37.

Spencer, N. E. (2004). Sister Act IV: Venus and Serena Williams at Indian Wells: "Sincere fictions" and white racism. *Journal of Sport and Social Issues, 28,* 115-135.

Theberge, N. (2000). *Higher goals: Women's ice hockey and the politics of gender.* Albany, NY: State University of New York Press.

Weathers, H. (2009). British Lions rugby legend Gareth Thomas: "It's ended my marriage and nearly driven me to suicide. Now it's time to tell the world the truth—I am gay." *Daily Mail,* December 18. Retrieved from http://www.dailymail.co.uk/sport/rugbyunion/article-1237064/British-Lions-rugby-legend- Gareth-Thomas-Its-ended-marriage-nearly-driven-suicide-Now-time-tell-world-truth--Im-gay.html

Weedon, C. (1987). *Feminist practice and poststructuralist theory.* Oxford: Backwell.

Weedon, C. (1999). *Feminism and the politics of difference.* Malden, MA: Blackwell.

Women's Sports Foundation. (2010). *It takes a team! Action guide for coaches.* Retrieved from http://www.womenssportsfoundation.org/Content/Articles/Issues/Homophobia/I/It-Takes-a-Team-Action-Guide-for-Coaches.aspx

Examining the Spectrum of Inclusion and Opportunity in Sport for Persons with Disabilities

Ted Fay and Eli Wolff

This chapter is based, in part, on the previous remarks expressed by the authors at their Opening Address of the *Developments in International Disability Sport Law Symposium* hosted by the Boston University Law School on January 23, 2009. The topics in this chapter are intended to reflect a number of timely and complex issues facing local, regional, national, and international sport governing bodies in how to view, understand, integrate, and provide inclusion for athletes with a disability within their common practices, organizations, and events. Unfortunately, many sport governing bodies and sport systems continue to perpetuate the false premise that separate, segregated opportunities for sport, leisure, and cultural activities by persons with a disability are both desirable and equitable. The purpose of this chapter is to make an effort to help frame and more graphically display these disparities. The authors have developed a series of interlinking conceptual frameworks starting with how all individuals who participate in sport have multiple identities based on the context of a given circumstance or situation. Once self-identified, an individual then can be located in one or more segments of the Sport Opportunity Spectrum (SOS), which has at its foundation participatory play and recreational engagement leading to the pinnacle that is elite sport.

CREATING AN HISTORICAL CONTEXT

It is impossible to hypothesize and discuss the future for athletes with a disability in sport in the 21st century without providing some historical context regarding disability in sport issues in the 20th century. Prior to exploring some of the past and present realities, it is important to establish a common language. For the purposes of this chapter, the authors intentionally use the phrase "disability in sport" and not "disability sport" to highlight and illustrate the overarching emphasis on disability-related issues in sport contexts.

Disability sport is a relatively recent construct used by DePauw and Gavron (2005) in their book, *Disability and Sport,* to mean sports uniquely created for people with disabilities depending on the use of specific technology by all participants (e.g., wheelchairs, ice hockey sledges) or by substantial rule modifications and equipment requirements such as blindfolds by all participants (e.g., beep baseball and goalball). This typology may seem perfectly natural and useful for defining sport, but questions of who is eligible, what type of disability a participant must have, and whether or not it is substantially different in rules and practice from so-called able-bodied or mainstream sport are open to many different perspectives. Throughout the 20th century, sport opportunities for people with disabilities have been more traditionally organized by sport organizations designed for a specific disability type, rather than being sport specific such as their counterparts in the sport mainstream (Hums, Wolff, & Legg, 2003).

For example, national and international sport federations were created to focus on generalized types of disability identity groupings ranging from sensory disabilities (e.g., deaf and hearing impaired, blind and visually impaired) to mobility disabilities (e.g., spinal injury, amputees, neurological-related disabilities) to intellectual disabilities (Brittain, 2010). The oldest international sport governing body for people with disabilities is the International Committee of Sports for the Deaf (CISS) which held the International Silent Games in Paris in 1924 (DePauw & Gavron, 2005). The next international body was the International Stoke Mandeville Wheelchair Sports Federation (ISMWSF). This organization has held international games since 1952 and served as the organizing body for the first Summer Paralympic Games held in Rome in 1960 (International Wheelchair and Amputee Sports Federation, 2010). Other disability sport organizations that followed, such as the International Blind Sports Association (IBSA), Cerebral Palsy International Sports & Recreation Association (CPISRA), and the International Sport Organization for the Disabled (IOSD), have focused on mobility-related disabilities and led to the creation of the International Paralympic Committee (IPC) in 1989 (International Paralympic Committee, 2010). Special Olympics began in 1968 with the first International Special Olympics held in Chicago (Special Olympics, 2010).

The term *disability in sport* is therefore intended to focus on issues pertaining to labeling, identity, and classification systems used either to include or exclude based on self and/or organizational descriptors. *Disability* identity is a socially constructed paradigm promulgated through cultural and sport classification systems that can become an internalized, as well as externalized, paradigm similar to race and gender. When reflecting over the progression of civil and human rights in the 20th century, the challenges facing individuals with a disability are informed by comparison to similar struggles regarding race and gender. For example, a century ago in the United States it was not uncommon for certain organizations, including sport clubs and related institutions, to only admit Whites or males; such places were not at all accessible for individuals with a disability (Yellow Springs, 1981). Public bathrooms, theaters, swimming pools, and other facilities were segregated by race, gender, *and* disability (Watson, 1963). Major League Baseball was segregated according to race, and intercollegiate athletics were segregated by gender and often by race until the early 1970s (Davis, 2008; Fay, 1999).

These forms of racial and gender intolerance in sports persisted for the next half-century despite the accomplishments of many African-American male and female athletes throughout this time. The achievements of Jesse Owens, Joe Louis, Jackie Robinson, Babe Didrikson, Althea Gibson, Billie Jean King were the examples of outliers who succeeded in the face of tremendous odds and prejudice (Davis, 2008).

Barely a half-century ago, the 1960 Rome Olympics served as a nexus for an African-American woman, Wilma Rudolph, to captivate a nation with her gold-medal performances in the 100- and 200-meter sprints, despite lingering prejudice based on racial and gender prejudice at home, while at the same time, Sir Ludwig Guttman was also able to realize his dream with the staging of the first Paralympic Games in Rome (Brittain, 2010; Davis, 2008). It would be not until 1984, at the Los Angeles Olympic Games, that the International Olympic Committee would sanction a women's marathon race, the event having long been barred because of prejudice based on medical theories promulgated by male physicians that such an event would do harm to women's health (Lovett, 1997), as well as sanctioning the first-ever alpine skiing (Sarajevo) and track exhibition (Los Angeles) events within the Olympic Games for athletes with locomotor disabilities (Legg, Fay, Hums, & Wolff, 2009; Lovett, 1997). It was also a period of activism and advocacy that resulted in the first national teams being integrated with athletes with disabilities (US Skiing) including equal participation at national championship events (Fay, 1999).

During this period and leading into the early 1990s, global and national pressure mounted for more equity for athletes based on race, gender, and disability. During the late 1980s, national and international sporting events for athletes with disabilities began to be less about cultural games as part of a rehabilitation perspective and more about emerging elite competition. The International Paralympic Committee was created in 1989 and took control of all aspects of international competition for athletes with a disability with the exception of deaf and hearing-impaired athletes and athletes with an intellectual disability

(Brittain, 2010). The sports movement in the United States during this period was due in part to the motivations and desires of Vietnam War veterans (Disabled Sports USA, 2009).

With the passage of the *Americans with Disabilities Act* (ADA) of 1990 and the *Ted Stevens Olympic and Amateur Sports Act* (Stevens) in 1998, athletes with disabilities were hopeful that they would see significant increases with support from the US Olympic Committee (USOC) and other national governing bodies (NGBs) involved in both Olympic and Paralympic sport for participatory and distributive justice issues in sport (ADA, 1990; Stevens, 1998).

Unfortunately, this progression did not occur because new policies from the USOC and its related NGBs pushed for significant regression by limiting resources and sporting opportunities via a stated policy of organization and practical re-segregation (Fay, 1999). The decade between 2000 and 2010 has witnessed arguably bigger leaps in the resources, professionalism, legal challenges, and advances in sport technology with regard to sit-skis, prosthetics, sport wheelchairs, and related devices than the previous 90 years combined. Athletes with a disability such as Marla Runyon, Natalie duToit, Natalia Partyka (see Box 9.1), and Brian McKeever (See Box 9.2) have qualified and competed in both Olympic and Paralympic Games (DisabilityNow, 2009). Casey Martin sued and won his right as a professional golfer to compete on the PGA Tour using a motorized cart (*PGA Tour, Inc. v. Martin,* 2001). Tatyana McFadden sued and won the right to practice with and compete for her high school track team (*McFadden v. Cousin,* 2007). Scot Hollonbeck and others sued the USOC over equity and distributive justice issues (*Hollonbeck v. US Olympic Committee,* 2008).

BOX 9.1. Partyka Biosketch

International table tennis player Natalia Partyka of Poland was born without a right hand and forearm. Partyka was able to adapt and compensate for her disability and become good enough to not only compete and win consecutive Paralympic gold medals in singles competition in 2004 and 2008 as well as two silver medals in the team competition, she also qualified and competed for her native Poland in the team competition at the Beijing Olympic Games in 2008. She, along with Natalie du Toit from South Africa in distance swimming, became the first Paralympians to compete in both the Olympic and Paralympic Games in the same year. Partyka regularly competed in European and international table tennis competitions for athletes with disabilities as sanctioned by the International Paralympic Committee (IPC), as well as European and international competition sanctioned by the International Table Tennis Federation (ITTF). Her biography reveals a person whose individual multiple identity sport classification index (IMISCI) places her at the top of the sport opportunity spectrum (SOS). For more information on Natalia Partyka, as well as Natalie du Toit, one can go the following websites to begin a search about them.

http://en.paralympic.beijing2008.cn/news/special/features/n214591907.shtml

http://www.timesonline.co.uk/tol/sport/olympics/article4561216.ece

http://www.sports-reference.com/olympics/athletes/pa/natalia-partyka-1.html

Finally, Oscar Pistorius won his administrative appeal in the international Court for Arbitration in Sport (CAS) for the right to compete at the 2008 Beijing Olympic Games (*Pistorius v. International Amateur Athletics Federation*, 2008). During this last decade, other critical events have included the passage and ratification of the U.N. Convention on the Rights for Persons with Disabilities including its landmark Article 30.5 with its focus on sport, leisure, and cultural rights for persons with a disability (*Convention RPD*, 2007). This historical context brings us to the present and a new window to the future. We must ask what the next decade, quarter century, half century, or century will yield. Will the world and Olympic champions of the future look more like Oscar Pistorius and less like the fully-limbed Olympic sprinters of the present? Will there be a shift from the "norms of naturalism" to trans-humanism that will yield new paradigms and understanding of what is sport and who are athletes (Butryn & Mascucci, 2003; Wolbring & Fay, 2009)? To answer these questions effectively, people need to start by using a set of overarching conceptual frameworks related to an array of critical issues confronting individuals with disabilities as a means to challenge, assess, and publicly expose the prevailing traditions of sport governance and acculturated public opinion that serve to limit opportunities in sport.

BOX 9.2. McKeever Biosketch

Similar to Marla Runyon, Brian McKeever, who is a visually impaired athlete, became the first Paralympic athlete to qualify to compete in the Winter Olympic Games. Brian, who begin ski racing as a thirteen year old, began losing his vision due to Stargardt's disease at age nineteen. A three-time winter Paralympic athlete in cross country skiing and biathlon (2002, 2006, & 2010), McKeever won the Canadian Olympic trials in the 50-kilometer cross country ski event on his home course at Canmore, Alberta, the site of the cross-country and biathlon events at the 1988 Calgary Winter Olympic Games. With this victory, McKeever had won the right to be named to the Canadian Olympic Team as a cross country skier. Many thought that he had also won the right to start in the 50-kilometer event on the final day of Olympic competition, but he was denied the right to start due to a discretionary decision by the Canadian coaching staff. This set off a wave of negative response to this decision in both the public as well as the social media. Unlike Runyon, McKeever had a bittersweet end to his dream of representing his nation in Olympic competition.

Normally when racing in Paralympic events, Brian is guided by his older brother Robin, a former Canadian Olympic skier. This team of brothers won two gold and one silver in cross country skiing in 2002 at the Salt Lake City Winter Paralympic Games, along with a bronze in biathlon. They repeated again four years later in Torino at the 2006 Winter Paralympic Games and swept three gold in cross country at the 2010 Winter Paralympic Games in Vancouver. Thus, although Brian became the first Canadian athlete to be named to both Paralympic and Olympic teams for the Games in Vancouver, he was denied the right to become the first athlete in the world to compete in the Winter Paralympics and Winter Olympics in the same year. For more information on Brian McKeever, one can go the following websites to begin a search about him and his accomplishments.

http://seattletimes.nwsource.com/html/stevekelley/2011133447_kelley20.html

http://sports.espn.go.com/espn/page2/story?id=4915757

http://www.montrealgazette.com/sports/2010wintergames/McKeever+Olympic+dream+

INDIVIDUAL MULTIPLE IDENTITY SPORT CLASSIFICATION INDEX (IMISCI)

Many athletes who have a disability face a decision on whether to identify with a sport identity, a cultural identity, or both. All persons have an individual multiple identity classification index, whether they participate in sport or not. When sport becomes important this index becomes more complex and contextual. There are many cases of athletes with a disability who are "able" enough to successfully compete with and against athletes without the same disability or no apparent disability. Where do these athletes fit and how do they define or identify themselves? How athletes answer the basic question of "who am I?" relative to other athletes within a sport context is based on a number of factors, including their own awareness and definition of ableism. The following two quotes illustrate a spectrum of possibility:

> [Ableism is] the devaluation of disability [that] results in the societal attitudes that uncritically assert that [it] is better for a child to walk than roll, speak than sign, read print than read Braille, spell independently than use a spell-check, and hang out with non-disabled kids as opposed to disabled kids, etc. (Hehir, 2002, p. 3).

Ableism devalues people with disabilities and results in segregation, social isolation, and social policies that limit their opportunities for full societal participation. Unfortunately, persons with disabilities are also susceptible to internalizing stereotypes and negative beliefs. This process, which we call *internalized ableism,* is similar to internalized racism and sexism of other devalued people (Mackelprang & Salsgiver, 1998).

Identity is always contextual, but at the same time it is an outgrowth of culturally created social construction. It is dependent on each individual's abilities specific to a given time, location, set of unique circumstances, and context. In applying the IMISCI to fields of play, the index retains a complex array of personal- and sport-specific characteristics and/or relationships that when aggregated serve to define a person relative to a specific sport context, thus creating a context of eligibility that either provides access or denies access to the field of play (Fay & Wolff, 2006b). The Oscar Pistorius case is a perfect example of such application of the International Rules of Control (ICR) of a given sport governance system, namely the International Association of Athletics Federations (IAAF), which oversees and governs the sport of track and field for World Championships and Olympic events (*Pistorius v. International Amateur Athletics Federation,* 2008).

The IMISCI is the critical piece or interlocutor between sport classification systems, eligibility for event participation, and the exclusiveness or inclusiveness of sport opportunity spectrums. Natalie du Toit of South Africa participated in the 2008 Beijing Olympic Games in part because she qualified for the women's 10-kilometer swim without using her leg prosthesis. Thus, she was capable of meeting the performance standard without using a technological aid. The fact that she was at a disadvantage compared to her fully limbed competition was not relevant to the ICR of the International Swimming Federation—FINA (Longman, 2008). Natalia Partyka of Poland competed in the doubles table tennis competition at the 2008 Olympic Games in Beijing despite having only one hand. Once again, she was allowed to participate based on her ability to compete within the rules (Holt, 2008). Thus, determining who gets to compete depends largely on the eligibility and classification systems that are applied within a given sport governance system.

SPORT OPPORTUNITY SPECTRUM

The Sport Opportunity Spectrum (SOS) was created to show that sport opportunities for individuals with disabilities within a given society are often perceived by the majority of that society's population as more limited than the SOS for able-bodied athletes in the same society.

In this regard, sport governance systems intentionally use classification systems and performance standards as strategies and/or as a means to control participation within a given sport environment including creating different Sport Opportunity Spectrums for able-bodied athletes versus athletes with a disability. Athletes with a disability often reinforce the acceptance of different Sport Opportunity Spectrums than for able-bodied athletes through an acculturation process of internalized ableism.

In 2008, Fay and Wolff modified the *Criteria for Inclusion* to show in Figure 1 the assessment and grading of the efforts of a particular organization or governance system with respect to inclusion of athletes with disabilities ranging from governance to media to

Criteria for Inclusion
(at each stratification level and each stage of Organizational Continuum)

	OCSG Stages					
	EC	LSI	T	CM	TAD	VD
CI – 1: Governance (Mission and Policies)	1	2	3	4	5	6
CI – 2: Media and Information Distribution	1	2	3	4	5	6
CI – 3: Management	1	2	3	4	5	6
CI – 4: Funding and Sponsorship	1	2	3	4	5	6
CI – 5: Awareness and Education	1	2	3	4	5	6
CI – 6: Events and Programs	1	2	3	4	5	6
CI – 7: Awards and Recognition	1	2	3	4	5	6
CI – 8: Philosophy	1	2	3	4	5	6
CI – 9: Advocacy	1	2	3	4	5	6
Subtotals:	9	18	27	36	45	56

FIGURE 9.1: Criteria for Inclusion (Fay & Wolff, 2009)

sponsorship and funding. Thus, an organization that clearly acts and maintains its practices as an exclusive club (Stage I of the Organization Continuum (OCSG)) would have a score between 9 and 17, whereas if it were to progress to Stage II by showing lip service to inclusion, it would have a score between 18 and 26. This framework could be used to assess a nation's effectiveness in adopting Article 30.5 of the UN Convention on the Rights of Persons with Disabilities (*Convention RPD, 2007*).

A PLATFORM FOR ANALYSIS: CONCEPTUAL FRAMEWORKS, ACCESS TO SPORT, AND CHANGE

In this chapter we provide a broad analysis and discussion of the key issues based on the concept that all people have the right to access the fields of play. The following conceptual frameworks address critical issues confronting individuals with disabilities because they challenge persistent and prevailing traditions of sport governance and acculturated public opinion that serve to limit opportunities in sport. They help create a new super-critical context that identifies, analyzes, and frames levels of progression and regression towards understanding greater socio-cultural, political, legal, economic, environmental, and technological contexts of access, equity, and justice.

These conceptual frameworks have their basis in historical, sociological, and open-systems perspectives. People live in societies that consist of complex networks of identity relationships (e.g., race, ethnicity, gender, disability, sexual orientation, age, religion) that are socially constructed under historically specific conditions (e.g., race and slavery, ethnic cleansing and genocide, male hegemony) through which organizational structures reinforce the status quo acculturated belief system. Dominant political and cultural ideologies and social norms are pervasive, and thus cultural practices are not easily transformed even with the advent of new laws and government-induced policies (Sage, 1998). The frameworks that follow have been constructed to evaluate and access the progression and regression from highly discriminatory and segregationist practices to more equity-based and inclusionary practices.

In analyzing the societal change process, one must consider whether it is a series of random events or if it can be viewed as a strategic and therefore intentional process. As Malcolm Gladwell (2002) illustrated in his book, *The Tipping Point,* social phenomena and systems change defy linear or incremental analysis and reasoning. Instead, change is often a blend of weighted factors or variables that come together in a perfect storm-like concussion that precipitates major cultural shifts in societies as they become either more or less inclusive.

Fay (1999), in his work *Race, Gender, and Disability: A New Paradigm Towards Full Participation and Equal Opportunity in Sport,* established a new theoretical framework entitled Critical Change Factors Model (CCFM) to bring a large field of data under some level of control, coherence, and readability, which would minimize bias on the part of the researcher or analyst. Fay designed a set of ten core factors drawn from equity (including distributive and participatory justice), critical social (including agency), and open-systems theories. The prevailing logic behind the creation and selection of these specific principles was one of commonality or universality, rather than uniqueness to a specific identity group, organization, or sport. These factors were selected for their potentially broad application across identity groups and different sport governance structures and are drawn from an historical analysis of three different identity groups based on race, gender, and disability. These factors can also be used to determine differences in breakthroughs and progression towards inclusion at three primary stratification levels of (a) athletes, (b) coaches and middle-level management, and (c) senior executive or ownership of organization and/or franchise (Fay, 1999, 2009).

Finally, this model serves as a coding structure to determine a hierarchy of change factors that need to be in place for key stakeholders to advocate against a specific organization's practices. In weighing each critical change factor in the context of a given situation, the model looks to four categories. A Category I CCF is sufficient by itself to cause change; a Category II CCF is necessary but not sufficient by itself to cause change; a Category III CCF is supportive but not necessary or sufficient by itself to cause change; and a Category IV CCF is counter-productive because it causes a reversal or regression to increased integration and inclusion of an identity group (Fay, 1999, 2009).

This conceptual framework is an *access* paradigm that shows where a person or group resides within a dynamic organizational environment based on a self- or culturally imposed identity group label. This construct was modified from a model developed from research on workplace diversity by Esty, Griffen, and Hirsch (1995). *The Organizational Continuum on Workplace Diversity* was a unidirectional model that did not account for stratification levels of different types of employees (i.e., labor, management, and ownership). Fay has adapted and modified this model to represent this continuum as a dynamic environment that may be progressive, regressive, or static, ranging from exclusivity for a particular identity group (e.g., White males) to inclusivity embracing a wide spectrum of identity groups (Sage, 1998). This continuum helps map the progression of a given identity group within the context of time and place. It also allows one to discover that an organization might be progressive regarding the use and integration of labor, but less progressive in the levels of management and ownership (Fay, 1999, 2009).

The standard sport rules and operating principles that are expressed through the ICR of a given sport are based on creating the contexts and standards of eligibility, parameters of performance, metrics for the field of play, and classification of participants. Issues of fair play and how an apparent competitive advantage is determined are often based on subjective (phenomenological) criteria derived from the traditions of the sport rather than objective evidence or science-based criteria. In the Pistorius case, however, it became evident that the IAAF was determined to use its version of what able-bodied sport is as its norm and, as a result, it diminished the value sport has for people with disabilities (*Pistorius v. International Amateur Athletics Federation,* 2008).

The IMISCI, when applied to a specific sport context, helps create a context of eligibility as an element of classification, thereby either providing or denying access for a given athlete or team to the field of play within a specific set of parameters including event type, time, and location. The concept of sport eligibility is a social and organizational construct controlled by a set of designated organizations. The IMISCI provides a potential conceptual and practical framework and critical context to a sport governance system. The IMISCI clarifies what it means to provide fair access to an athlete to be eligible to qualify and therefore compete at the highest level of performance capability on the maximal number of fields of play. Once eligibility is determined, a qualification process and system can be put in place based on certain publicly disseminated criteria known to the potential participants (e.g., athletes) and their support groups (e.g., coaches, trainers) that have been accepted as the norms of the sport as created and managed by the relevant sport governance system.

There is often a nexus related to the administration of *open* versus *segregated* competition based on a set of specific discriminating characteristics that are either *personal* (e.g., gender, age, race, religion, disability group) or *performance* (e.g., minimum qualifying standards) identifiers that can confound sport governance systems over who has a right to compete and in what competitions. It is critical to note that classification of a given athlete or team is based typically on a uniform code outlined in the ICR for a given sport as overseen by a designated International Sport Federation and its member National Sport Federations or NGBs (IPC, 2010). Fear that economic resources prioritized to able-bodied individuals might be somehow diverted to athletes with a disability serves to perpetuate myths and stereotypes as to who should get to participate at certain levels of sport (*Hollonbeck v. US Olympic Committee,* 2008). This fear is often due to limited awareness, education, and expertise on the part of management professionals within sport governance structures in fully understanding the capability and level of athletic ability of a person with a disability. Pistorius's Cheetah legs provided the opportunity for him to participate in open competition because of his athletic body, not because of his extraordinary advantage as a perceived cyborg athlete (Butryn & Mascucci, 2003; Wolbring, 2009).

CONCLUSION: DIVERSE SPORT OPPORTUNITIES FOR PEOPLE WITH DISABILITIES

Part of the purpose of this chapter has been to add a discourse of ableism in challenging the hegemony of sport power elites similar to those that perpetuate racism and sexism as found in sport and in society. Work in all sectors needs to be done to help advance access, inclusion, equality, respect, legitimacy, and opportunity for people with disabilities in sport and in society. Through research, education, and advocacy activities, efforts to construct new and more diverse sport opportunities within existing mainstream systems of sport can begin to emerge.

Initiatives need to be developed that bring people with disabilities from the margins to become integral members of the sporting community. Ongoing research needs to be conducted examining the inclusion of people with a disability in sport. More educational awareness training on inclusion in sport and in society, as well as resources, need be developed to support sport organizations regarding the process of inclusion. Agencies from both the public and private sectors need to serve as facilitators to organize and bring individuals and groups to work together to promote the inclusion of people with disabilities.

In the past 10 years, more and more academics are beginning to focus their research in these areas and more widely present at regional, national, and international professional conferences. Advocacy groups and legal organizations have begun to facilitate and support the development of legal opinions for the plaintiffs in cases such as *PGA Tour, Inc., v. Martin,* (2001), *McFadden v. Cousin,* (2006), *Hollonbeck v. U.S. Olympic Committee,* (2008), and *Pistorius v. International Amateur Athletics Federation* (2008), as well as provide the platform for the ratification of *Article 30.5 of the UN Convention on the Rights for Persons with Disabilities.* Engaged and stimulating debate and dialogue still needs to be fostered among sport management professionals, academics, and policy makers.

Individuals and organizations need to continually work on integrating people with disabilities from the margins of society into their desired communities. Ongoing research needs to examine ways to facilitate and support the full inclusion of people with disabilities in sport. This research must be practiced through conscious reflection and evidence-based qualitative and quantitative analyses of the past and present to create arguments for systems change. Sport technology will force the re-conceptualization of the Sport Opportunity Spectrum in relation to new classification systems that reduce and end marginalization as the status quo while promoting legitimatization as the new inclusive paradigm.

Many questions, however, remain unanswered. What are the essential benchmarks and norms related to SOS that we need to know and explore? What data are missing? Where and from whom do we need to find it? What additional studies do we need to explore? Whose voices need to be heard? What role do the law, the sport humanities (e.g., sport sociology, philosophy, ethics, history), the sport sciences, and sport management disciplines have in informing theory and practice relative to SOS and classification systems for athletes with a disability? Does this research have potential relevance to other marginalized identity cultures involved in sport? A Triple A strategy of athletes, advocates, and strategic allies is needed to help break down barriers and reduce the fear factor present in the change towards a more inclusive and equitable society. We need personal narratives of pathfinders who have waged their own struggles to help frame the contest and create a game plan to illustrate how to effect change for greater equity and justice. Finally, we may have to be willing to break the rules of the game to create greater access to the fields of dreams.

REFERENCES

Americans with Disabilities Act of 1990, Pub. L. 101-336, 104 Stat. 327 (codified in scattered sections of 42 U.S.C.).

Brittain, I (2010). *The Paralympic Games Explained.* Routledge: New York.

Butryn, T. M., & Masucci, M. A. (2003). It's not about the book: A cyborg counter-narrative of Lance Armstrong, *Journal of Sport and Social Issues, 27,* 124.

Convention on the Rights of Persons with Disabilities, G.A. Res. 61/106, U.N.Doc. A/RES/61/106 (Jan. 24, 2007).

Davis, T. (2008). *Race and sports in America: An historical overview.* Legal Studies Paper No. 1141868. Available at SSRN: http://ssrn.com/abstract=1141868

DePauw, K. P., & Gavron, S. J. (2005), *Disability sport* (2nd edition). Champaign, IL: Human Kinetics Publishers.

DisabilityNow. (2009). *Games without frontiers.* Retrieved from http://www.disabilitynow. org.uk/living/features/games-without-frontiers

Disabled Sports USA (2009), *Guide to disabled alpine skiing competitions.* Retrieved from http://www.dsusa.org/programs-winter-competition-guideAlpine.html

Esty, K., Griffen, R., & Hirsch, M. S. (1995). *Workplace diversity: A manager's guide to solving problems and turning diversity into a competitive advantage.* Avon, MA: Adams Publishing.

Fay, T. G. (1999). *Race, gender, and disability: A new paradigm towards full participation and equal opportunity in sport.* Doctoral dissertation. University of Massachusetts Amherst.

Fay, T. G. (2009, June 11). *Reframing sport contexts: Labeling, identities, and social justice.* 2009 Play the Game Conference, Coventry University, Coventry, UK.

Fay, T. G., & Wolff, E. A. (2009 Summer). Disability in sport in the twenty-first century: Creating a new sport opportunity spectrum. *Boston University International Law Journal.* 27, 2.

Fay, T. G., & Wolff, E. A., (2006, November). *Disability in sport: Applying the opportunity spectrum.* North American Society for the Sociology of Sport (NASSS) Annual Conference, Vancouver, BC, Canada.

Galdwell, M. (2002). *The tipping point: How little things can make a big difference.* New York: Little, Brown & Co.

Hehir, T. (2002). Eliminating ableism in education, *Harvard Education Review, 72,* 1-3.

Hollonbeck v. U.S. Olympic Committee. 513 F.3d 1191. 1194-96 (10th Cir. 2008).

Holt, O. (2008). *Disabled Table Tennis Star Natalia Partyka Gives Doubters the Elbow. Mirror.* Retrieved August 14, 2008 from http://www.mirror.co.uk/sport/more-sport/2008/08/14/disabled-table-tennis-star-natalia-partyka-gives-doubters-the-elbow-115875-20696728/

Hums, M. A., Wolff, E. A., & Legg, D. (2003). *Examining opportunities for athletes with a disability within the International Olympic Committee: Criteria for inclusion.* Presentation at the 2003 Conference of the North American Society for Sport Management Annual Conference, Ithaca, NY.

International Wheelchair & Amputee Sports Federation (2010). *ISMWSF History.* Retrieved April 13, 2011, from http://www.iwasf.com/iwasf/index.cfm/about-iwas/history/ismwsf-history/

International Paralympic Committee (2010). *About the IPC.* Retrieved from, http://www.paralympic.org/release/Main_Sections_Menu/IPC/About_the_IPC/

Legg, D., Fay, T. G., Hums, M. A., & Wolff, E. A. (2009). Examining the inclusion of wheelchair exhibition events within the Olympic Games 1984-2004. *European Sport Management Quarterly, 9,* 3.

Longman, J. (2008). *Embracing the equality of opportunity.* New York Times, p. D1. Lovett, C. (1997). *Olympic marathon: A centennial history of the Games' most storied race.* Retrieved April 13, 2011, from http://www.marathonguide.com/history/olympicmarathons/chapter25.cfm

Mackelprang, R. W., & Salsgiver, R. O. (1998). *Disability: A diversity model. Approach in human service practice.* New York: Wadsworth.

McFadden v. Cousin, No. AMD 06-648 (D. Md. Apr. 17, 2006).

PGA Tour, Inc. v. Martin, 532 U.S 661, 666-67 (2001).

Pistorius v. International Amateur Athletics Federation, CAS 2008/A/1480, at 7-8 (May 16, 2008).

Sage, G. H. (1998). *Power and ideology in American sport: A critical perspective* (2nd edition). Champaign, IL: Human Kinetics Publishers.

Special Olympics (2010). *From backyard camp to global movement: The beginnings of the Special Olympics.* Retrieved April 13, 2011, from http://info.specialolympics.org/Special+Olympics+Public+ Website/English/About_Us/History/default.htm

Ted Stevens Olympic and Amateur Sports Act, 36 U.S.C. §§ 220501 et seq. (2000).

Watson v. City of Memphis, 373 U.S. 526, 530 n.2 (1963).

Wolbring, G., & Fay, T. (2009, November). *The world beyond Oscar: Intersection of sport, policy and practice.* Paper presented at the annual conference of the North American Society for the Sociology of Sport, Ottawa, Ontario, Canada.

Yellow Springs Exempted Vill. Sch. Dist. Bd. of Educ. v. Ohio High Sch. Athletic Ass'n, 647 F.2d 651, 675 (6th Cir. 1981).

Developing Adolescents' Self-worth and Life Satisfaction through Physically Active Games: Interventions with Orphans and Teenagers Living in Poverty

10

Stephanie J. Hanrahan

As mentioned in many other chapters in this text, youth activity involvement is related to positive development. In terms of well-being, activity involvement has been associated with high self-esteem, a sense of empowerment, strengthened initiative, as well as less anxiety and depression (Rose-Krasnor, Busseri, Willoughby, & Chalmers, 2006).

Although sport and other activities can be beneficial for all youth, I would like to focus on adolescents who are orphaned and/or living in poverty. I have selected this population for two main reasons. First, there are many underserved youth who do not have ready access to after-school enrichment programs, sporting clubs, or other extracurricular activities. Second, a lot of fund-raising efforts and existing volunteer programs designed to benefit underserved youth tend to focus on younger children (perhaps because they are cuter and provide better photo opportunities than teenagers, or maybe because of the belief that the younger participants are the more benefit they will get out of any programs).

In 2003 there were 12.4 million orphans in Latin America and the Carribbean (Joint United Nations Programme on HIV/AIDS, the United Children's Fund, and the United States Agency for International Development, 2004). More than half of all orphans are age 12 or older, and although adolescents may seem to be coping, they can experience depression, hopelessness, and increased vulnerability, which can lead to a sense of alienation, desperation, risk-taking behavior, and withdrawal (Joint United Nations Programme on HIV/AIDS et al.).

Orphans become vulnerable to physical and psychological risks. AIDS-orphaned children in Uganda were able to distinguish between their quality of life when their parents were alive and after they died (Sengendo & Nambi, 1997). As a result of being orphaned, children felt sad, depressed, and helpless, and developed a more external locus of control (Sengendo & Nambi). Similarly, adolescents living in poverty (or anyone who experiences continuously adverse circumstances) perceive a lack of control that often leads to feelings of helplessness, loss of hope, and diminished willpower (Lefcourt, 1976). Externally oriented individuals do not believe they are responsible for what happens in their lives (as opposed to internally oriented individuals, who feel they have the ability to control events and their behavior). If adolescents are feeling hopeless and have a minimal sense of internal control, they are unlikely to take steps to change their lives or participate in community initiatives. Therefore, it makes sense to figure out ways of enhancing life satisfaction and encouraging orphans and adolescents living in poverty to become active participants in their own lives. One way of addressing this issue is through games.

BENEFITS OF PHYSICALLY ACTIVE GAMES

Through sports and games children can learn to become sensitive to others' values and needs, handle dominance and exclusion, and manage emotions (Henley, Schweizer, de Gara, & Vetter, 2007). Games provide the opportunity for youth to learn self-control (which could be argued is relevant to an internal locus of control) and to express emotions in acceptable ways. Recreational programs vary in their effects on youth development. Adventure-based/active recreation programs are superior to social recreation programs in terms of creating enhanced attitudes and actions regarding trust and cooperation (Witman, 1987). In adolescents, physical activity on its own is related to perceived life satisfaction (Valois, Zullig, Huebner, & Drane, 2004), therefore it seems to be important that any program involving games is physical in nature.

In addition to the benefits of physical activity, games programs offer opportunities for participants to learn new problem-solving skills in managing their emotions and behaviors, and also enhance peer relationships (Henley et al., 2007). Problem-solving skills are, in turn, a strong predictor of improved resilience, "the process that enables some survivors of high risk environments to experience social competence, empathy, caring, problem-solving skills, critical and creative thinking, task mastery and a sense of purpose and connectedness in the face of adversity and distress" (Henley et al., 2007, pg, 53). Problem-solving skills also enhance the likelihood that life's challenges will be successfully resolved (Fok & Wong, 2005).

CHARACTERISTICS AND CONTEXTS OF EFFECTIVE PROGRAMS

From the above information it seems obvious that a program of physically active games involving a component of problem-solving that targets orphans and/or teenagers living in poverty could be beneficial. More information, however, is needed in terms of the structure or context of the program.

Petitpas, Cornelius, Van Raalte, and Jones (2005) indicated that programs designed to enhance adolescent psychosocial development (through sport) should be created within a context that (a) encourages participants to develop a sense of initiative; (b) allows youth to find valued roles within the group; (c) is voluntary, contains clear rules, and requires concerted effort over time; (d) is psychologically safe where participants are willing to take risks and learn from their mistakes; and (e) is challenging. Larson (2000) argued that structured, voluntary activities are conducive to the development of initiative (i.e., autonomous action) in adolescents. When participants are intrinsically motivated (e.g., find the activities to be fun) and are appropriately challenged, they have experiences of directing and regulating their actions in pursuit of one or more goals, which in turn, develops initiative (Larson).

Edwards, Mumford, and Serra-Roldan (2007) stated that to positively develop, youth need to experience support, empowerment (which requires safety and security), boundaries and expectations, and constructive use of time. Adolescents are more likely to take advantage of these developmental experiences if they have a commitment to learning, positive values, social competencies, and positive identity (Edwards et al.). Ideally, activity programs will not only meet the structural requirements mentioned above, but also nurture the aforementioned internal qualities (rather than expecting participants to arrive in programs already being confident, socially competent, and hungry to learn).

Another characteristic of youth programs that promotes positive development is when the environment fosters caring. The perceived quality of interpersonal relationships between adults and youths within the programs influence youths' regulatory skills to control emotions and empathy (Gano-Overway, Newton, Magyar, Fry, Kim, & Guivernau, 2009).

A GAMES PROGRAM WITH MEXICAN TEENAGER ORPHANS

I addressed many of these issues in a 15-session program I ran at Nuestros Pequeños Hermanos (NPH; Hanrahan, 2005, 2009). NPH cares for orphaned and abandoned children in nine Latin American countries. The main facility is in Miacatlán, Mexico, where there is a home for almost 1000 children (referred to as pequeños). I worked nearby in Cuernavaca where approximately 200 adolescent pequeños live and attend a vocational school. Through a flyer on the door to the comedor (dining area), I invited individuals to attend a program designed to teach skills that would help them with sport, work, music, or any other area of achievement. They were informed that there would be a combination of games and workshops. The director and sub-directors provided me with a list of pequeños who they felt needed help (e.g., those with behavior problems). The program ended up involving a few who read the flyer and badgered the administrators to be allowed to take part, but the majority was made up of teenagers who were told to attend (going against my original plan of participation being voluntary as suggested by Petitpas et al. (2005)

In total, 34 of the adolescents (14 girls and 20 boys) participated in the program. Ages ranged from 15 to 20 with a mean of 17.09 years. The teenagers had been at NPH between 1.16 and 16 years ($M = 6.97$ years). Some individuals had been at the Miacatlán facility since being an infant, and others had only come to NPH relatively recently. The more recent arrivals were not necessarily newly orphaned or abandoned. Some had previously been living on the street or in the large rubbish piles outside of Mexico City. To stay at the NPH facility in Cuernavaca, the adolescents are required to attend a vocational school to learn a trade to support themselves. Participants in my program were studying accounting ($n = 3$), childcare ($n = 6$), computers, ($n = 10$), electronics ($n = 5$), or tourism ($n = 10$).

The program involved 15 sessions (Monday through Friday for 3 weeks), with each session lasting approximately 90 minutes. Because of teenagers' attentional and behavioral tendencies in mixed company, the sessions were held separately for boys and girls. Separating groups based on gender was also appropriate because many of the games involved physical contact and may have been beneficial because of the machismo society of Mexico (e.g., I didn't think that males would be up front about discussing issues with confidence in front of teenage girls).

I supplied each pequeño with a folder for handouts and written exercises. It probably sounds like a minor detail, but I had about seven or eight different colors of folders. Allowing the teenagers to choose the color that they wanted was a simple way to begin to introduce an element of autonomy. I provided Australian stickers (e.g., koalas, crocodiles, kangaroos) as rewards for punctual attendance. I also used a variety of stickers (starting with relatively plain ones and getting more interesting as the program progressed) to reward sustained effort and completion of homework. I was surprised how even 18-20 year old males were excited about getting stickers.

Most sessions involved a combination of games, discussions, and handouts, with each session concluding with a thought for the day. The discussions and handouts related to optimal activation, concentration and attention, imagery, self-talk, time-management, and self-confidence. The games were first and foremost designed to be fun, but most also involved the development of trust, communication, and problem-solving skills (see Hanrahan & Carlson, 2000 for descriptions of some of the games). Soccer (i.e., fútbol and fútbol rápido), basketball, and racquetball were popular sports at the orphanage. As a result I used examples from these sports within the sessions. Not all of the participants were athletes, however, so examples were also taken from other relevant achievement domains (e.g., dancing, writing, studying, music).

To test the effects of the program on pequeños' self-worth and life satisfaction, I asked the teenagers to complete two questionnaires at the beginning of the first session and at the end of the final session. Harter's (1988) Self-Perception Profile for Adolescents and Diener, Emmons, Larsen, and Griffin's (1985) Satisfaction with Life Scale had thankfully already been translated into Spanish and found to have acceptable psychometrics (Atienza, Pons, Balaguer, & García-Merita, 2000; Pastor, Balaguer, Atienza, & García-Merita, 2001; see Hanrahan, 2005, for additional information about the psychometrics of the questionnaires). The teenagers were also invited in the final session to complete a one-page sheet with five open-ended questions with extra space to make any additional comments. They were asked to list three things they had learned in the program, what they liked most, what they liked least, what they would be most likely to remember from the program in one year, and what they had learned that they would use in their daily lives. See Hanrahan (2009) for information about the process of qualitative data analysis. For all assessment items participants used codes rather than their names, allowing pre- and post-measures to be matched up while maintaining confidentiality.

The teenagers attended an average of 8.82 of the 15 sessions (range 1 to 13). Absences were due to school examinations, illness, soccer games, dance rehearsals, dentist appointments (my program happened to overlap with the annual visit of a volunteer dentist), and of course, apathy or disinterest. Four participants never completed the post-test measures. Excluding the four participants who only attended one or two sessions, statistical comparison of the means showed that the program resulted in significant increases in life satisfaction and global self-worth (Hanrahan, 2005). Although the subsample was too small to use statistics, it is worth noting that global self-worth decreased for the four individuals who only attended one or two sessions, and their life satisfaction did not change.

Qualitative feedback about the program was positive. The most frequently cited responses about what they had learned were controlling the controllable, patience/tolerance, and specific mental skills (e.g., imagery, goal setting). "Control the controllable," was the first thought for the day in the program and set the tone. In one of the first sessions the adolescents were asked to list six things they could control and six things they could not control. They all had a complete list of things they could not control, but none, one, or two things that they felt they could control (e.g., "maybe my temper"). This initial sense of limited control is not surprising given the institutional environment in which they lived. They could not control what they ate, when they ate, what time they got up, what chores they were assigned, what clothes they owned (dependent on donations), or who their roommates were (some rooms contained over 30 teenagers in bunk beds). By the end of the program the pequeños could list over 20 things they could control (e.g., my thoughts, how I react to others, how much I try, what I do with my time, activation levels). Learning patience and tolerance was solely the result of the games, because at no time were their handouts, thoughts for the day, or pre-planned discussions about this topic.

The participants predicted that in one year they would remember goal setting, positive thoughts, how to have confidence in self and others, and the games. Again, the topic of confidence in others was never explicitly discussed; therefore, I can only surmise that regular participation in games that required trust and communication lead to this outcome. In their daily lives the adolescents felt they would use skills related to self-confidence and how to work effectively in groups. They were able to extrapolate for themselves the relevance of the teamwork required in some of the games to working in groups in other areas of their lives. The most-liked aspects of the program were the games, their personal successes and achievements, and sharing with the group. I believe that overcoming the challenges of many of the games led to their experiences of success (see also Larson, 2000). Sharing with the group probably would not have been a highlight for the teenagers without the creation of a psychologically safe environment, the encouragement of autonomy/initiative, and the activities that promoted team building and effective communication (see also Petitpas et al., 2005). The least-liked components were when they didn't play, when they had to write, and the negative attitudes of others.

In summary, the pequeños found the games to be fun, but in addition, participation in the program resulted in enhanced self-worth and increased life satisfaction. Life satisfaction is an important outcome variable. Positive judgments about life satisfaction lead to building resources, better regulation of negative affective experiences, and better health (Frederickson, 1998). Life satisfaction is positively correlated with positive social interactions, creativity, internal locus of control, and active involvement in the community. Poor life satisfaction is associated with depression, interpersonal rejection, anxiety, and aggressive behavior (Huebner, 2004). The majority of research in the area of life satisfaction in adolescents has been correlational. Huebner called for the use of life satisfaction as a treatment or intervention indicator. The results from the program at NPH indicate that life satisfaction can be positively affected through an intervention program. Future research needs to determine whether these increases are maintained, or if some type of booster program may be needed.

POVERTY AND SELF-REGULATION

In a study of school-aged youth living in poverty in the Unites States, Buckner, Mezzacappa, and Beardslee (2003) found that resilient youth had greater self-regulatory skills and self-esteem compared to the non-resilient youth. These findings were true even after controlling for differences in the experiences of negative life events and chronic strains. The association between self-regulation and resilience was true for females and males and for all ages (in this case 8–17 years; Buckner et al.). Self-regulation can be beneficial in terms of coping with stress in a proactive manner as well as coping with stressors after they have occurred, and involves both emotional and behavioral regulation. The ability to regulate one's emotions assists emotion-focused coping and the ability to regulate one's behavior facilitates problem-focused coping (Eiseiberg, Fabes, & Guthrie, 1997).

The ability to self-regulate is likely to undergo significant developmental change during adolescence (Lerner, 2005). In addition to changes at the individual level, there are also changes in the relationship between adolescents and their contexts, making adolescence a particularly pertinent time to study self-regulation. The mental skills that are included in the games program promote self-regulation and influence psychological well-being, particularly for children and adolescents (Petlichkoff, 2004).

THE GAMES PROGRAM IN THE CONTEXT OF POVERTY

After the initial program in Cuernavaca, I ran modified versions of the games program in two other towns in Mexico. These programs were designed to be 10 sessions in length (deleting time management as a topic area) and were offered to teenagers living in poverty. In Southern Baja California, Mexico, I ran two 2-week programs with the support of the Optimist International Baja California Sur Club. Optimist Clubs around the world are dedicated to "Bringing Out the Best in Kids." Each Optimist Club determines the needs of the young people in its community and conducts programs to meet those needs (Optimist International, 2010). The participants in the programs in Baja California can be described the following:

- Being of low socioeconomic status (in an area with a lot of tourism that although providing jobs has increased the cost of living (e.g., buses, food);
- Having parent(s) who had not finished primary school;
- Being children of single mothers (80%);
- Having a family income of 2000 pesos or less every two weeks (about US $400/ month);
- Having six family members (average);
- Living in poorly constructed homes (e.g., cardboard, corrugated iron) with 70% having the entire family living in a single room.

The Optimist Club had existing programs that encouraged children to stay in school. The Club provided uniforms, school supplies, school fees, and tutorial assistance on the condition that the students maintained a grade average of 8.5 out of 10. The Club at times found it difficult to persuade parents to allow their intelligent and hardworking children to remain in school, because if not in school the teenagers could work (e.g., in local hotels/resorts) and immediately provide income for their families. The program in one town ended up being for girls only and took place in a childcare facility after it had closed for the day. A local psychologist attended approximately half of these sessions. In the other town an arrangement was made with the local Red Cross where in exchange for a year's supply of toilet paper and soap for the building, the program could be run in their large meeting room. Because of limited time availability of the room and the adolescents (due to school), separate sessions for boys and girls were not possible, resulting in a mixed-gender group. In this second town a local social worker attended all sessions. A couple of adult Optimist Club volunteers attended a couple of the sessions in both towns. An overview of the 10-session program is provided in Table 10.1.

TABLE 10.1. Outline of the 10-Session Program

Session	Games[a]	Discussion/Activity	Handout	Thought for the Day	Homework
1	Ice breakers 10 things in common Ling Tag	Why I am here Object that best represents you—now and in six months	Factors that affect performance	Control the controllable	Six things you can control and six things you can't control
2	Have you ever... Knee tag	What have you controlled? Optimal activation Abdominal breathing and cue words Muscular relaxation	Self-reflection homework	Nobody can make you feel inferior without your consent. (Eleanor Roosevelt)	Self-reflection (e.g., what brings you joy, what would you really like to do in the working part of your life)
3	Human knot (with and without blindfolds) Pairs – fake n/ push	Self-reflection homework Things you controlled in the past couple of days	Goal setting	Step by step, there is no other way to achieve your goals	Progress towards personal goal or working on controlling something
4	Pendulum Blowing in the breeze 4-way thumb wrestling Toe tapper (pairs and group)	Share progress/obstacles in achieving goals Attention/concentration Breath and count Past, present, future Number grid	Number grid (for concentration exercise)	Always look for the positive	Write three positives that you experienced (big or small)

The qualitative evaluations in both towns were extremely positive, perhaps demonstrated by the high attendance rates for most participants. Statistically, there were significant increases in life satisfaction and self-worth for the participants in the all-female group (which were maintained in a 2-week follow-up). The results for the other town were in the desired direction, but did not quite reach significance. These findings may have been non-

Session	Games[a]	Discussion/Activity	Handout	Thought for the Day	Homework
5	Autumn leaves Balance activity Mirror	Positive experiences Progress towards goals Counting out loud backwards by 7s 20 questions	List of participants	There is no success without failure	Write a positive (warm fuzzy) about each participant
6	Triangle tag Imagery games	Collect homework Situations in which you were able to refocus attention Imaging with 5 senses	Imagery	I can accept failure. Everyone fails at something. What is important is to always try. (Michael Jordan)	Goals/controllables/ refocusing attention
7	Keep it up (balloons) Ball and chain	Personal progress Write and share imagery scripts Personal declaration of short term goal	Envelope with warm fuzzies (provide each participant with the positive statements from co-participants)	If you don't live every instant in your life, you lose it; live every moment	Work toward goal
8	Help me tag Nose and toes Mine field	Self-talk Create slogans	Self-talk	One of the slogans created by the group	10 affirmations
9	Electric fence Push to stand	Check affirmations are positive Practice saying affirmations out loud Possible uses of affirmations Examples of thought stoppage in past 24 hours Self-confidence	Self-confidence	One of the slogans created by the group	
10	Move person from A to B	Progress made during program Pairs—review main points of program and present		One of the slogans created by the group	

[a] Descriptions of many of the games can be found in Hanrahan and Carlson (2000).

significant because of the co-ed nature of the group or because of special outings (rewards for good grades) and activities (International Children's Day festivities) being held immediately before pre-test data were collected. The inclusion of a local psychologist and social worker allowed for these professionals to be introduced to the content and structure of the program. They were provided with extra copies of all handouts, and I have been told that they have introduced components of the program in their ongoing work.

Most recently I ran the program in two slums (villas) of Buenos Aires, Argentina, and an additional low SES town outside of Buenos Aires. This time I worked through LIFE Argentina. LIFE stands for "Luchemos part una Infancia Feliz y con Esperanza," meaning "We strive for a childhood with happiness and hope." LIFE is a non-profit, civil society organization that works with youth living in socially marginalized and extremely impoverished areas of Argentina. The majority of their existing programs (e.g., weekly supportive classes in mathematics, language, science, and English; recreational activities; birthday parties) predominantly target children in primary school. I used the same community centers/soup kitchens in which they hold the programs for younger children on days in which their existing programs were not running. Unlike the programs in Mexico where individuals were responsible for their own folders, I collected the folders every day in Argentina, because of their living conditions and the precedent set by existing LIFE programs for younger kids. In addition to the possibility of participants forgetting their folders, there was a good chance that folders would have been damaged or stolen or that non-participants may have come along just to get folders.

The program was held across seven weeks, with one or two sessions held at each of the three locations each week. The first location was in a clean soup kitchen with tables and benches and a small area on the sidewalk outside in which we played some of the games. Running activities outside was difficult because of the amount of traffic (both vehicular and on-foot), the heat (the middle of the South American summer), and regular interruptions. Although I had promoted the program as being for those ages 12 to 20, the participants were all girls and ranged in age from 8 to 16 (with a trio of 8 and 9 year olds being the most consistent attendees). One boy attended the first session of the program, but never came again. His absence may have been due to his being the only male, but I strongly suspect that he was dyslexic and believed (as perhaps did his family and teachers) that he was stupid (which he wasn't). The absence of assessment and support is demonstrative of the impoverished community.

The second location was a community center (used for religious services on weekends) with a single bare bulb in a dark, mosquito-infested room. Due to the dangerous neighborhood, all activities took place inside (often after a concerted effort to get the stray dogs to go outside to continue their fights). This group was co-ed but small, with ages ranging from 12 to 21. Because of a combination of transportation issues (it is unsafe to walk in that neighborhood, there is no public transportation within it, and taxi drivers refuse to go there) and the use of the room for pre-existing programs, only seven of the ten sessions were held at this location.

The third location was in a town outside of Buenos Aires and was held in the backyard of a house. This group ended up being all boys (ages 10-16), although at one point a few women in their 70s or 80s asked if they could join (a proposition I declined given that I did not think it would have been conducive to the boys expressing themselves freely (not to mention I couldn't picture the young boys and the older women playing games together).

Because of the limited space in all three locations, some games had to be modified or deleted. Although I generally don't recommend the program for participants younger than 12, there were a few younger children who thoroughly enjoyed the games and seemed to understand some of the skills content (although adaptation on my part was required). One incident that stands out in my mind took place during a discussion about confidence. Generally, when talking about confidence, adolescents describe confident people as having their heads up and shoulders back, and those with little confidence as looking down and having slumped shoulders. In these impoverished areas the description of confident people was no different, but the description of people with little confidence was those who are always looking left and right and being scared. Confidence went beyond the confidence to speak up or trust one's abilities in sport to the basic concept of having the gumption to walk down one's street. In discussions I have had about confidence with other groups fear is usually mentioned in terms of fear of failure, not fear of being killed. Generally, attendance was less consistent in these programs compared to attendance in Mexico. There was neither the institutionalized environment where participants all lived in a confined and accessible area, nor the luxury of all participants being top students as in Baja California (although some of the participants were highly intelligent). In addition to apathy and transportation issues, there were also childcare responsibilities (on more than one occasion there were 12 to 15 year olds who were looking after infants during the sessions). It is also difficult to compete against a brand new plastic wading pool (a Christmas present) in the shade on a hot summer day when the program takes place in a hot and stuffy room! Nevertheless the program was generally well received (I have received a few thank-you letters). I cannot make specific comments regarding results because I have not yet had the opportunity to analyze the data. I will need to keep in mind, however, the results of a study of quality of life in Buenos Aires neighborhoods. Cruces, Ham, and Tetaz (2008) found that satisfaction with one's neighborhood was a significant predictor of general life satisfaction. Factors associated with neighborhood satisfaction were the availability of public transport and the evaluation of safety, green areas, sidewalk maintenance, and cultural and sport activities (Cruces et al.). In two of the three places I worked there were no green areas and public transport was not readily accessible. Two of the three areas had no sidewalks, cultural and sport activities were minimal, and safety was a major concern. It would be interesting to learn whether improvements in any of these areas would be of greater benefit than a games program.

CONCLUSION

Although much more research is needed, the preliminary evidence indicates that a games program that incorporates the teaching of mental skills can increase the life satisfaction and self worth of orphans and teenagers living in poverty. In future work in Latin America I hope to involve a local university whereby university students continue running the program after I leave. Here, however, I will provide a list of suggestions or reminders that others who may be interested in delivering similar programs might find to be useful (Hanrahan, 2009):

- Be flexible regarding time. Cultures vary in their perceptions of the relevancy and importance of punctuality.

- Provide bottled water and/or snacks for participants. Doing so may increase attendance and enhance attention (particularly in the late afternoon).

- Use stickers as rewards. Deprivation and poverty may mean that even boys in their late teens will appreciate these tangible tokens.

- Run single-sex groups if possible.

- Provide paper and writing implements.

- Keep games as an integral part of the program.

- Encourage adolescents to work with each other. Allow input and discussion from them to ensure content is personally and culturally meaningful.

- Avoid reference to family when working with orphans.

- Recognize that participants may not know their actual birthdays.

- Appreciate the survival skills that the adolescents have developed.

- Have fun!

In summary, developing, implementing, and evaluating effective positive development programs for adolescents should be a high priority on the agendas of practitioners and researchers. After all, as stated by Lerner (2005, p. 55),

> Adolescents represent at any point in history the generational cohort that must next be prepared to assume the quality of leadership of self, family, community, and society that will maintain and improve human life. Scientists have a vital role to play to make in enhancing, through the generation of basic and applied knowledge, the probability that adolescents will become fully engaged citizens who are capable of, and committed to, making these contributions.

REFERENCES

Atienza, F. L., Pons, D., Balaguer, I., & García-Merita, M. (2000). Propiedades psicométricas de la Escala de Satisfacción con la Vida en adolescentes. [Psychometirc properties of the satisfaction with life scale in adolescents]. *Psicothema, 12,* 314-319.

Buckner, J. C., Mezzacappa, E., & Beardslee, W. R. (2003). Characteristics of resilient youths living in poverty: The role of self-regulatory processes. *Development and Psychopathology, 15,* 139-162.

Cruces, G., Ham, A., & Tetaz, M. (2008, September). *Quality of life in Buenos Aires neighborhoods: Hedonic price regressions and the life satisfaction approach.* (Latin American Research Network Working Paper #R-559). Buenos Aires: Universidad Nacional de La Plata.

Diener, E., Emmons, R., Larsen, R. J., & Griffin (1985). The satisfaction with life scale. *Journal of Personality Assessment, 49,* 71-75.

Edwards, O. W., Mumford, V. E., & Serra-Roldan, R. (2007). A positive youth development model for students considered at-risk. School *Psychology International, 28,* 29-45.

Eisenberg, N., Fabes, R. A., & Guthrie, I. K. (1997). Coping with stress: The role of regulation and development. In S. A. Wolchik & I. N. Sandler (Eds.), *Handbook of children's coping: Linking theory and intervention* (pp. 41-70). New York: Plenum Press.

Fok, M. S., & Wong, D. Y. (2005). A pilot study on enhancing positive coping behaviour in early adolescents using a school-based project. *Journal of Child Health Care, 9,* 301-313.

Frederickson, B. (1998). What good are positive emotions? *Review of General Psychology, 2,* 300-319.

Gano-Overway, L. A., Newton, M., Magyar, T. M., Fry, M. D., Kim, M. S., & Guivernau, M. R. (2009). Influence of caring youth sport contexts on efficacy-related beliefs and social behaviors. *Developmental Psychology, 45,* 329-340.

Hanrahan, S. J. (2005). Using psychological skills training from sport psychology to enhance the life satisfaction of Mexican orphans. *Athletic Insight, 7*(3). Retrieved from http://www.athleticinsight.com

Hanrahan, S. J. (2009). Using psychological skills training from sport psychology to enhance the life satisfaction of adolescent Mexican Orphans. In R. J. Schinke (Ed.), *Contemporary sport psychology* (pp. 171-180). New York: Nova Science.

Hanrahan, S. J., & Carlson, T. B. (2000). *GameSkills: A fun approach to learning sport skills.* Champaign, IL: Human Kinetics.

Harter S. (1988). *Manual for the Self-Perception Profile for Children.* Denver: University of Denver.

Henley, R., Schweizer, I., de Gara, F., & Vetter, S. (2007). How psychosocial sport & play programs help youth manage adversity: A review of what we know & what we should research. *International Journal of Psychosocial Rehabilitation, 12*(1), 51-58.

Huebner, E. S. (2004). Research on assessment of life satisfaction of children and adolescents. *Social Indicators Research, 66,* 3-33.

Joint United Nations Programme on HIV/AIDS, the United Children's Fund, and the United States Agency for International Development (2004, July). *Children on the brink 2004: A joint report of new orphan estimates and a framework for action.* New York: United Nations Children's Fund.

Larson, R. W. (2000). Toward a psychology of positive youth development. *American Psychologist, 55,* 170-183.

Lefcourt, H. M. (1976). *Locus of control: Current trends in theory and research.* Hillsdale, NJ: Lawrence Erlbaum.

Lerner, R. M. (2005). *Promoting positive youth development: Theoretical and empirical bases.* (White paper prepared for Workshop on Science of Adolescent Health and Development). Retrieved from Tufts University, Institute for Applied Research in Youth Development website: http://ase.tufts.edu/iaryd/documents/pubPromotingPositive.pdf

Optimist International (2010). *Optimist international: Friends of youth.* Retrieved from http://www.optimist.org/#

Pastor, Y., Balaguer, I., Atienza, F. L., & García-Merita, M. (2001). Análisis de las propiedades psicométricas del Perfil de Autopercepciones para Adolescentes (Harter, 1988) en adolescentes valencianos. [Analyses of psychometric properties of the Self-Perception Profile for Adolescents (Harter, 1988) in Valencian adolescents.] *IberPsicología, 6.1.1,* 1-21.

Petitpas, A. J., Cornelius, A. E., Van Raalte, J. L., & Jones, T. (2005). A framework for planning youth sport programs that foster psychosocial development. *The Sport Psychologist, 19,* 63-80.

Petlichkoff, L. M. (2004). Self-regulation skills for children and adolescents. In M. R. Weiss (Ed.), *Developmental sport and exercise psychology: A lifespan perspective* (pp. 269-288). Morgantown, WV: Fitness Information Technology.

Rose-Krasnor, L., Busseri, M. A., Willoughby, T., & Chalmers, H. (2006). Breadth and intensity of youth activity involvement as contexts for positive development. *Journal of Youth and Adolescence, 35,* 385-399.

Sengendo, J., & Nambi, J. (1997). The psychological effect of orphanhood: A study of orphans in Rakai district. *Health Transition Review, 7*(Supplement), 105-124.

Valois, R. F., Zullig, K. J., Huebner, E. S., & Drane, J. W. (2004). Physical activity behaviors and perceived life satisfaction among public high school adolescents. *The Journal of School Health, 74*(2), 59-65.

Witman, J. P. (1987). The efficacy of adventure programming in the development of cooperation and trust with adolescents in treatment. *Physician & Sports Medicine, 15,* 22-29.

Using Sport to Promote HIV/AIDS Education among At-risk Youths in Sub-Saharan Africa

11

Glyn C. Roberts, Cyprian Maro, and Marit Sørensen

hildren and adolescents in Sub-Saharan Africa are more at risk of contracting Human Immunodeficiency Virus (HIV) infections than in any other region worldwide (UNAIDS, 2010; UNICEF, 2004). Worldwide, the number of people living with HIV was estimated at 32.8 million at the end of 2009, and among them 22.5 million are estimated to live in Sub-Saharan Africa, with women making up 59% of those living with HIV in this region (Stover, 2004; UNAIDS, 2006, 2010). The majority of people living with HIV or Acquired Immunodeficiency Disease Syndrome (AIDS) in Africa are between 15–49 years of age, and over the years 14.8 million children are estimated to have lost one or both parents in Sub-Saharan Africa, of which 2.5 million are in Tanzania (Tanzanian Ministry of Health and Social Welfare, 2009; UNAIDS, 2010). The number of children under 15 years of age with HIV in the Sub-Saharan region increased from 1.6 million in 2001 to 2.3 million in 2009, making it one of the few regions where there has been no reduction since 2001 (UNAIDS, 2010). The number of new infections seems to be stable or decreasing in Africa in general, but is still very high, and there are great variations in HIV prevalence and number of people dying from AIDS among the African countries (UNAIDS, 2008). New infections are counted at 1.8 million in Sub-Saharan Africa in 2009, and young people (15-24 years) account for 45% of all new infections in any one year. In Sub-Saharan Africa, new infections in children under 15 years were estimated to be 300,000 in 2009 (UNAIDS, 2010).

Tanzania, a country with a population of 41 million, had a national HIV prevalence of 8.8% among youths and adults aged 15-49 years at the end of 2003, reduced to 5% in 2009. The reduction in prevalence was mainly among men (4.6%), not among women (6.6%) (Tanzania commission for AIDS, 2010). In general, youths are believed to account for approximately 60% of all the new HIV infections each year in Tanzania (Maro, Roberts, & Sorensen, 2009a). Unfortunately, because people do not get tested on a regular basis and HIV infection often goes unrecognized, there are probably many young Tanzanians who are unaware that they are HIV infected (Sangiwa, van der Straten, & Grinstead, 2000; Talle, Biswalo, Schreiner, & Klepp, 1995; Tanzanian Ministry of Health and Social Welfare, 2009). AIDS and HIV infection among young people has become a source of great concern and the need to reverse the trend is still regarded as critical (National AIDS Control Programme, Bureau of Statistics, & MEASURE project, 2004; UNAIDS, 2006, 2008, 2010; UNICEF, 2002).

Among young people, HIV is most commonly spread through unsafe sexual intercourse and, as a whole, heterosexual activity accounts for 85% of HIV transmission in Tanzania (Swai & Asten, 1991; Tanzania Commission for AIDS, 2010). Studies show a high level of sexual activity among young people in Tanzania (e.g., Caldwell, 2000; Klepp, Ndeki, Leshabari, Hannan, & Lymo, 1997; Ndeki, Klepp, & Mliga, 1994). The median age of first intercourse for Tanzanian youths is under 17 years for girls and 18 years for boys, and some children begin having sex as early as eight years of age (UNICEF, 2002). Studies show these early sexual experiences have been associated with inadequate use of condoms and having multiple sexual partners (Konings, Blattner, Levin, Brubaker, Siso, Shao, et al., 1994; Kraft, 1991; Tanzania Commission for AIDS, 2010). The consequences are quite profound: Not only have we seen a high rate of HIV infections among adolescents, but unwanted teenage pregnancies are also increasing in number. According to the 1996 Tanzania Demographic and Health Survey, 60% of young women have had a child by the time they reach 19 years of age, and teenage pregnancy rates increase from 3% at the age of 15 to 60% by the age of 19. The trend continues to the present day, therefore there is a growing necessity to target interventions to reduce the number of teenage pregnancies and to reverse the escalating HIV infection rate that specifically focus on youths (UNAIDS, 2006, 2008).

There is neither a vaccine nor a cure for AIDS. Consequently, efforts to reduce the incidence of AIDS have been focused on at-risk behavior reduction. As a response to the growing infections among youths, the Tanzania government developed AIDS educational packages for schools (e.g., Mgalla, Schapink, & Boerma, 1998; Rasch, Silberschmidt, Mchumvu, & Mmary, 2000; Tanzanian Ministry of Health and Social Welfare, 1995). The school-based HIV/AIDS education program has been implemented since the early 1990s with the intention of increasing knowledge about HIV and to provide education about HIV-related transmission and prevention. The focus on knowledge about HIV/AIDS is given priority on the assumption that ignorance of the virus and modes of transmission poses a risk and that increased knowledge will elicit the expected preventive actions (Lindegger & Wood, 1995) and that individuals will reduce risk of infection by personal application of the information (Choi & Coates, 1994). Formal settings such as churches, hospitals, schools, homes, and political arenas (rallies) are being used to deliver the messages for prevention. Many campaigns are conducted through TV and printed media outlets, including informational leaflets. When delivered personally, the information is given by adults such as nurses, doctors, teachers, and parents (National AIDS Control Programme et al., 2004).

Although it is feasible to train local teachers and health workers to provide HIV/AIDS education to Tanzanian primary school children (Klepp, et al., 1997; Mgalla et al., 1998; Rasch et al., 2000), many adults in Sub-Saharan Africa think AIDS education in schools is inappropriate and it is often not implemented. One study conducted among primary school pupils showed that schools were believed to be the least rated source for AIDS information (Ndeki, Klepp, Seha, & Leshabari, 1994) and that school teachers were rated as the significant others who pupils talked to least about HIV/AIDS prevention strategies. In addition, the national policy on AIDS refrains from emphasizing condom use for young people in primary school for moral reasons (Tanzanian Ministry of Health and Social Welfare, 1995). In Tanzania, conventional adult institutions such as religious agencies, schools, and families generally do not acknowledge that adolescents are sexually active and therefore do not recommend the use of condoms.

Despite having been in place for almost two decades, the efforts in Tanzania have not been successful in decreasing the rate of HIV infection in youths (e.g., UNAIDS, 2006; Sangiwa et al., 2000). Thus, after almost two decades, the HIV education and prevention strategies conducted through conventional adult-directed institutions such as schools, families, and religious bodies have been ineffective in reducing the rate of infection.

There is a further complicating factor: Tanzania primary school gross enrollment has declined by 1.4% per annum. The reasons are varied; one factor is the increase in AIDS orphans, with AIDS orphans less likely to attend schools. Furthermore, a recent report (UNICEF, 2004) using demographic health surveys from 1997 to 2001 indicated that 50% of children (aged 10-14) who have lost both parents and 30% who have lost one parent are not attending schools in Tanzania. Thus, many children in poor communities and half of all orphans are unlikely to attend school. As a result, in Tanzania the out-of-school children population is increasing in number. As families break down, and many children become orphans (1 in every 7 children in Tanzania is an orphan) and youths drop out of school, the efficacy of the AIDS education program through conventional adult institutions (e.g., schools) decreases dramatically. Thus, new approaches are needed that are effective for young people (Ndeki et al., 1994; Schueller et al., 2003) and there is a need to target youths through avenues other than schools.

In many countries, the use of mass media might be one way to target at-risk youths. But in Tanzania this option is not viable. Tanzanian people who are exposed to various media programs are a small percentage of the population (newspapers—11% women, 16% men; radio—34% women, 44 % men; TV—14% women, 20% men). Exposure to the media has decreased among young people 15-24 years of age with the lowest levels of exposure among women (National AIDS Control Programme et al., 2004). Coupled with children having an increased likelihood to be orphaned and thus not attending school, more and more children are at risk. As a result, there is an urgent need to re-think educational strategies aimed at at-risk youths (e.g., Klepp et al., 1997; Maro et al., 2009a; Schueller et al., 2003; Tanzanian Ministry of Health and Social Welfare, 1995).

Recommendations for HIV/AIDS prevention programs in Tanzania suggest that to be effective, any new approach to HIV prevention among youths must use the creative assets that youths have and involve youths in the delivery of services, development of the learning materials, and evaluation (e.g., Klepp et al., 1997; National AIDS Control Programme et al., 2004; Schueller et al., 2003). The recommendations also suggest that programs reach out to youths where they spend most of their time and use activities that youths value and with which they are familiar. In addition, it is recommended that programs employ peers as role models to serve as HIV/AIDS educators. We must recognize that peers play an important role in HIV/AIDS prevention (Downer, Levine, & Weaver, 2003), and in areas where peers have been involved in the delivery of HIV/AIDS education, the incidence of HIV cases has declined (UNAIDS, 2003). The recommendations are that we use familiar activities locally organized and use activities that youth value. The information should be given by relevant others (e.g., peers, respected adults such as coaches) because it is more likely to lead to success, and the information should be given with behavioral skill training because this type of training leads to less risky sexual practices. It is clear that peer interaction and support leads to safer sexual behavior (Boler & Aggleton, 2005; Bujra & Baylies, 2000; Family Health International, 2004; Klepp et al., 1997; NACP et al., 2004; UNICEF, 2004).

THE POTENTIAL OF SPORT

Considerable evidence now exists that children value activities other children value (e.g., Roberts, Treasure, & Conroy, 2007) and being on a sport team or engaging in sport activities with other children is one of the most highly valued activities for children (e.g., Duda, 1981). Children enjoy being on a sport team, value participating in sport, and experience the benefit of membership and affiliation with other children (e.g., Roberts, Treasure, & Conroy, 2007). And it has been demonstrated that through well-structured sport programs children can learn skills that serve them well in other areas of life (e.g., Danish 2002, Danish & Forneris, 2006). Sport is being increasingly recognized as a means of enhancing positive youth development and that through participation in sport, children can learn important life skills that are transferable to other spheres of life (e.g., Danish & Forneris, 2006). Sport is being increasingly recognized as a means of enhancing positive youth development and that through participation in sport, children can learn important life skills that are transferable to other spheres of life (e.g., Danish & Forneris, 2006). Sport is rapidly gaining recognition worldwide as an effective means of promoting education and health, which led the United Nations General Assembly to adopt resolution 58/5 and proclaimed 2005 the International Year of Sport and Physical Education (United Nations General Assembly, 2003). In particular, the United Nations has named sport as an effective platform to increase HIV/AIDS knowledge and awareness (United Nations, 2003). According to the UN, sport can improve physical health and well-being; teach essential values and life skills (e.g., cooperation, respect); be a positive force in childhood development; bridge social, political, and cultural divides; unite, motivate, inspire, and educate children; and strengthen links between children and adults (United Nations, 2003).

THE EMIMA PROGRAM

Based on these contentions, one of the co-authors (Cyprian Maro) initiated an experimental community-based sport program called EMIMA (which is "Elimu, Michezo na Mazoezi" in Swahili meaning Education, Sport, and Exercises) that was designed for disadvantaged youth in Dar es Salaam, Tanzania in 2001. The program uses peers as coaches for soccer skills and as a source of information, skills, and attitudes related to HIV/AIDS education. Life skills are incorporated into the practice activities and the objective of the EMIMA project is to assist at-risk children in acquiring sport skills and receive AIDS education and HIV prevention life-skills. Thus, the program used a popular youth activity to attract at-risk youths and used peer coaches as the instructors to deliver the educational information, knowledge, and skills through the sport program. In 2004, Dr. Maro decided to conduct an evaluation of the effectiveness of the EMIMA program and the evaluation became his doctoral project. We (Roberts and Sorensen) were his co-advisors for his doctoral program, and we initiated an experimental field study where we investigated the impact of the use of peer coaches to deliver HIV/AIDS education and the use of safe sex behaviors to at-risk youths.

The major purpose of this research was to investigate the relative effectiveness of the peer coach intervention through sport within the EMIMA program to deliver HIV/AIDS education and knowledge about the use of safe sex behaviors to at-risk youths. To determine the effectiveness, we compared the EMIMA educated youths to a group of youths of the same age (12-15 years of age) who underwent the standard school-based HIV/AIDS education. These youths were typical of the youths in Tanzania who were educated about HIV/AIDS through the normal educational practice in schools. We added a second control group of at-risk youths who did not experience the EMIMA program, and who were not within the school system in Dar es Salaam. These participants were quite literally street children, and many were orphans. The details of the research protocol and the detailed results may be found in studies published elsewhere (i.e., Maro et al., 2009a, 2009b).

Briefly, the research involved 1050 participants, 764 who completed both the pre-test and the post-test after the interventions. The participants were aged between 12 and 15 years of age. Three communities of Buguruni, Vingunguti, and Mtoni in Dar es Salaam, Tanzania, were involved in the study. These communities are where EMIMA programs have been active since 2001. Compared with other communities in Dar es Salaam, these communities are among the poorest, by all criteria. Social and health problems (including HIV and STDs) are common. The school dropout rate is also high in these communities. Many households are headed by a single parent, most often a woman but sometimes a child is the head of the household. Clearly, these were at-risk children.

There were 100 peer coaches recruited for the study. Fifty were randomly placed into the regular intervention that was the core of the EMIMA program, and 50 were placed into a mastery intervention group. For the mastery intervention group, we used the research that has investigated the effect of the motivational climate on cognition, affect, and behavior (e.g., Ames, 1992; Roberts et al, 2007). The mastery group peer coaches underwent additional training in how to implement mastery-oriented strategies into the peer coaching environment (see Maro et al, 2009b).

The most important factor was the training of the peer coaches to include HIV/AIDS prevention life skills in the practice sessions for the participants. For HIV/AIDS prevention, the training of peer coaches was conducted by EMIMA qualified staff according to the guidelines and manuals of the "Kicking AIDS Out" network (ref. www.kickingaidsout.net). The training consists of seminars and activities and peer coaches qualify to become peer coach level 1. The training takes six months, and the peer coaches in this study were fully trained Kicking AIDS Out peer coaches at level 1. Therefore, we had a group of 100 peer coaches who were trained in using the sport context to foster life skills related to AIDS prevention. The life skills were incorporated into the practice activities of the participants, and the peer coaches were instructed in how to coach soccer skills practice sessions that contain life-skills messages.

Before and after the interventions, participants completed questionnaires that asked basic demographic information, HIV-related knowledge, beliefs, attitudes, and risk behaviors. Such measures included, among other questions, attitude to condom use, condom knowledge and experience, subjective norms about condom use, abstinence, having an exclusive sexual partner, perceived behavior control in using a condom, and behavioral intention (intended condom use). These questions and scales were from a long set of questionnaires adapted from the Family Health International and World Health Organization's knowledge, attitudes, beliefs, and practices survey instruments for adolescents (World Health Organization, 1989).

The Findings of the Study

In the normal way, because many of these scales were adapted to the sport context, and were translated into Swahili, we conducted exploratory factor analyses on each scale to determine the factors and the items that contributed to the factors. In other words, we "cleaned" the data for further analyses. All scales were included in this process because they had adequate internal reliabilities ($\alpha > 0.70$). The descriptive data were interesting, only 4.5% of youths who were in school reported to be sexually active while 11% out of school and 13.5% from EMIMA reported to be sexually active. About 16.5% of children from the EMIMA, 13.5% from the schools, and the majority (63%) of the out-of-school children reported that their fathers were deceased. About 10 % of the children in EMIMA and in school, and 66% of the children out of school reported that their mothers were dead. These statistics mean that 7% of children in EMIMA, 3% of children in school, and 51% of children who were outside the school system were orphans. About 16% of children from EMIMA, 21% from school, and 85% of the street children reported that they did not live with their fathers. About 15% of children in EMIMA, 14% in schools, and 77% of children out of school reported not living with their mothers. Apart from the school children, these were children at-risk.

The main findings of the study were quite remarkable. We used multivariate analysis procedures and found that for knowledge about HIV/AIDS, there was no reliable difference between the EMIMA intervention groups and the children who were taught HIV/AIDS knowledge in the school system. The group at apparent risk were the children in the out of school control group who were significantly lower in their knowledge about HIV/AIDS and its modes of transmission. This finding was to be expected, and was no great surprise. But the real surprise was in the rest of the data!

The analyses with the variables that involved condom use in particular were revealing. When it came to the behavioral intention variables and the knowledge and attitudes toward condom use, the EMIMA intervention groups were considerably superior to the children educated in schools. Clearly, the HIV/AIDS education using peer coaching in sport was more effective than the national policy of school-based education. Interestingly, school education was no different to our street children control group in terms of knowledge about condom use. Even though the school children were more knowledgeable than the out-of-school children about HIV/AIDS and its mode of transmission, this knowledge was not transferred to knowledge of, attitudes toward, and behavioral intentions to use condoms.

The bottom line is that the use of peer coaches within the soccer coaching environment of the EMIMA program was effective in transmitting HIV prevention knowledge, cognitions, and perceived behavioral intentions to use a condom in the future for at-risk children. There were no significant differences between the in-school and the out-of-school groups except for the questions that pertained to condom use and future intentions to use a condom: The in-school children were more at risk than the out-of-school children! This result may have something to do with cultural and religious norms surrounding condom use! Even though condom use with children is officially recommended, it is clearly frowned upon by parents and church officials within Tanzania. It is believed that teaching children to use condoms is tantamount to condoning sexual activity. But the question arises immediately, because condom use is the most effective means of preventing HIV/AIDS, not to mention the epidemic of teenage pregnancies, why is condom use not more vigorously pursued?

The mastery coaching intervention was a little mixed in its effect. We did a manipulation check, and we found that the peer coaches were effective in creating a mastery climate, however it was only more effective than the standard EMIMA program for about half the variables. Interestingly, it was more effective for some of the condom-related variables (see Maro et al, 2009b).

We did find gender differences. The gender differences occurred at both pre-test and at post-test: Females are at greater risk especially with the condom-related variables. Nevertheless, the effect in the analyses was a main effect; the girls were systematically lower than the men. Although both girls and boys benefitted from the intervention, boys seemed to be more empowered on condom-related variables, they had more knowledge, and they intended to reduce risk behaviors by using a condom. In normal day-to-day life, females may have more difficulty in obtaining and using condoms because of the gender norms surrounding condom use. And this difficulty may be especially true in Tanzania because of the religious and cultural norms surrounding sexual activity for young female adolescents.

Conclusions of the Study

The research program evaluating the EMIMA program demonstrated the efficacy of the EMIMA Kicking AIDS Out program using sport to transmit the life skills about the implementation of safe sex knowledge and behaviors for at-risk youths in Tanzania. The use of peer coaches within the soccer coaching environment of the EMIMA program was effective in transmitting knowledge about HIV/AIDS and safe sex practices. Indeed, the EMIMA soccer program was reliably more effective than the traditional HIV/AIDS education through the normal school system for all knowledge, attitudinal, and behavioral variables investigated in the study (Maro et al., 2009). One important finding should be highlighted: The children who participated in HIV/AIDS education using peers in sport had higher intentions to use a condom in the first/next sexual intercourse in order to prevent HIV infections than the other groups. This finding illustrates that the sport-based approach is an effective means of communicating desirable information about safe sex behaviors to a population of at-risk adolescents.

Given the widely recognized potential risk of sexually transmitted HIV among disadvantaged youth and the grim statistics that reveal that the incidence of HIV/AIDS has not decreased for youths in Sub-Saharan Africa (Tamzania commission for AIDS, 2008; UNAIDS, 2010), the findings of the EMIMA program evaluation are especially noteworthy. Using peers within a popular activity for children, in this case soccer in Africa, by a long way the most popular sport in the region, is effective in transmitting important life skills. The EMIMA program focuses on changing the social and peer norms concerning at-risk sexual behavior avoidance and facilitates cognitive and behavioral skill acquisition through the regular practice of life-skill games in soccer. But the most important aspect of EMIMA is that it targets children who are truly at-risk.

Being an orphan, in particular an AIDS orphan, has a major societal and psychological effect on a child (Sengendo & Nambi, 1997). Because one has to pay to go to school in Tanzania, not having parents almost always condemns the child to be outside the school system. The current HIV/AIDS educational program in Tanzania is based in the school system, so the merit of the EMIMA program is that it targets these at-risk children who are not able to go to school. Thus, the importance of these programs is that they do make HIV/AIDS education available to children who are out of school. The program is a success, and given that we know that children in the age range of the EMIMA program benefit from participating in sport (e.g., Roberts, 2006) in terms of peer friendship, self-esteem, and so on, then participating in this program has tremendous psychosocial benefits in addition to the HIV prevention.

An interesting finding is that the school-based HIV/AIDS education program was little better than the "education" the street children received, presumably from their peers. But what was really surprising was that when it came to condom use, the most effective way of reducing the risk of HIV infection among youths, the school-based AIDS education was less effective even than that the street children received! Frankly, the HIV/AIDS education in schools in Tanzania actually puts the children going to school more at risk. The explanation may well be that the HIV preventive education in schools tends to be didactic by nature, taught in science lessons without actively engaging the pupils, and does not encourage behavioral change. These findings are a clear indication of the consequences of the policy by the authorities in Tanzania since the early 1990s of failing to emphasize the use of condoms in schools for moral reasons. HIV/AIDS education in schools is a controversial issue with many adults in Sub-Saharan Africa because they do not acknowledge youth sexual activity.

Clearly, targeting HIV/AIDS education in schools is one appropriate strategy. The efforts of the Tanzania government regarding AIDS education for young people, however, has been thwarted to some extent by the steady decline in the proportion of primary school aged children attending school, coupled with the high level of school dropouts (e.g.,

NACP et al., 2004). There is a great need to target young people at relatively early ages with effective youth-friendly interventions through avenues other than school. Interventions using peers in sport contexts may serve as an effective approach to further HIV/AIDS risk reduction interventions in Sub-Saharan Africa.

The EMIMA intervention program uses male and female trained peer coaches as HIV/AIDS educators using football skills and training to provide information, skills, and attitudes related to HIV education. Males coached males, females coached females. It is remarkable that even though soccer is a male-dominated sport in Africa as a whole, 25% of the peer coaches and participants were girls in the EMIMA program! Nevertheless, the evidence illustrates that both males and females benefited from the AIDS education interventions through the EMIMA program. The girls, however, were systematically lower on the cognitive and behavioral variables associated with HIV prevention knowledge and practices. The gender differences were systematic across all the groups. The findings reflect the deep-rooted gender inequitable norms within the Sub-Saharan African context.

Although using male and female peer coaches in increasing knowledge, attitudes, and behavioral beliefs for optimal HIV prevention was effective, the gender differences that remained demonstrate how strong the gender roles are within Tanzanian society. We implemented a culturally relevant and youth appropriate intervention using peer coaches in a youth friendly activity. Although the intervention was implemented through soccer, which is considered to be a masculine sport (Hargreaves, 2000), the female peer coaches challenged the gender social norms and attempted to empower females for effective HIV prevention. But the findings indicate how powerful the inequitable gender norms and gender roles within the society are. This inequity can only be seen as a debilitating factor in HIV prevention, especially in terms of condom attitudes and the intended use for females. In 2008, women comprised 60% of people living with HIV. Among the 15-24 age group, the staggering statistic is that women in Tanzania comprise 75% of those living with HIV (Tanzania commission for AIDS, 2008).

There is growing evidence that social norms that promote unequal gender roles increase the risk of women to contract HIV (Weiss, Whelan, & Rao Gupta, 2000). Sport participation and peer coaching by male and female peer coaches may empower youth, especially women, and reduce common problems related to unequal gender roles and sexuality (Miller, Sabo, Farrell, Barnes, & Melnick, 1998). Sport has rapidly gained recognition as an effective means and platform to increase knowledge and awareness, and reduce vulnerability for HIV/AIDS infection for both males and females (United Nations, 2003). Thus, using male and female peers in sport to inform young sport participants about HIV/AIDS through programs such as EMIMA is a promising avenue to reduce the HIV risk of infection as well as changing the gender social norms and promoting gender equity. Nevertheless, the evidence from this study suggests that simply expecting that participation alone is sufficient is wrong. We experienced gender differences, especially involving norms, attitudes, and intended behavior of the use of condoms, with women being more at risk than men. Thus, although the EMIMA-type approach may constitutes an important strategy to reduce risk of HIV infection among young people, and women in particular (see Mane & Aggleton, 2001; Pulerwitz, Barker, Segundo, & Nascimento, 2006; Weiss et al., 2000), clearly we have to develop and investigate specific strategies to enhance the empowerment of females within the Sub-Saharan context. One obvious avenue is to use female-oriented sport activities other than soccer. There is a need for community programs such as EMIMA to target both the in-school and out-of-school youths, males and females, because they are both at risk for HIV infection, with females being particularly susceptible.

The current context and culture in Sub-Saharan Africa require multicultural approaches to addressing HIV prevention issues in youth. Nevertheless, interventions that involve youth through familiar activities (whatever those may be) are effective in reducing at-risk behaviors and enhancing knowledge, attitudes, and behaviors for effective life-skills development, in this case HIV prevention. Clearly, community-based sport interventions can be successful in locating and enrolling youths with high-risk behaviors for HIV infection who may be missed by sampling in schools, clinics, and agency settings. To strengthen the effectiveness of interventions, it is important that subsequent research should investigate the relative effect of using peer coaches versus the use of sports as a vehicle to deliver life-skill messages and skills.

REFERENCES

Ames, C. (1992). Achievement goals, motivational climate and motivational processes. In G. C. Roberts (Ed.), *Motivation in sport and exercise* (pp. 161-176). Champaign, IL: Human Kinetics.

Boler, T., & Aggleton, P. (2005). *Life skills education for HIV prevention: a critical analysis.* London: Save the children and ActionAid International.

Bujra, J., & Baylies, C. (2000). Responses to AIDS epidemic in Tanzania and Zambia. In C. Baylies & J. Bujra (Eds.), *AIDS, sexuality and gender in Africa. Collective strategies and struggles in Tanzania and Zambia* (pp. 25-59). London: Routledge.

Caldwell, J. C. (2000). Rethinking the African AIDS epidemic. *Population and Development Review 26*(1), 117–135.

Choi, K. H., & Coates, T. J. (1994). Prevention of HIV infection. *AIDS, 8,* 1371-1389.

Danish, S. (2002). *SUPER (Sports United to Promote Education and Recreation) program: Leader and student activity book.* (3rd ed.) Richmond, VA: Life Skills Center, Virginia Commonwealth University.

Danish, S., & Forneris, T. (2006). Teaching life skills in schools. In M. Elias & H. Arnold (Eds.), *The educator's guide to emotional intelligence and academic achievement: Social-Emotional learning in the classroom.* Thousand Oaks, CA: Corwin.

Downer, A., Levine, R., & Weaver, M. (2003). *Critical reflections on human capacity development for HIV/AIDS prevention, care and support.* University of Washington: Centre for Health Education and Research.

Duda, J. L. (1981). A cross cultural analysis of achievement motivation in sport and the classroom. Unpublished doctoral dissertation, University of Illinois at Urban/Champaign.

Family Health International (2004). *Reaching out-of-school youth with reproductive health and HIV/AIDS Information and services.* Arlington, VA: Family Health International

Heargraves, J. (2000). *Heroines of sport: The politics of difference and identity.* London: Routledge.

Klepp, K. I., Ndeki, S. S., Leshabari, M. T., Hannan, P. J., & Lymo, B. A. (1997). AIDS education in Tanzania: Promoting risk reduction among primary school children. *American Journal of Public Health, 87,* 1931-1936.

Konings, E., Blattner, W. A., Levin, A., Brubaker, G., Siso, Z., Shao, J., et al. (1994). Sexual behaviour survey in a rural area of Northwest Tanzania. *AIDS, 8,* 987-993.

Kraft, P. (1991). Age at first experience of intercourse among Norwegian adolescents: A lifestyle perspective. *Social Science and Medicine, 33,* 207-213.

Lindegger, G., & Wood, G. (1995). The AIDS crisis: Review of psychological issues and implications *with special reference to the South African situation. South* African Journal of Psychology, 25, 1-11.

Mane, P., & Aggleton, P. (2001). Gender and HIV/AIDS: What do men have to do with it? *Current Sociology, 49,* 23-37.

Maro, C. N., Roberts, G. C., & Sorensen, M. (2009a). HIV/AIDS education in Tanzania: The experience of at-risk children in poorer semi-urban communities. *Vulnerable Children and Youth Studies, 4,* 23-36.

Maro, C., Roberts, G. C., & Sørensen, M. (2009b). Using sport to promote HIV/AIDS education for at-risk youths: An intervention using peer coaches in football. *Scandinavian Journal of Medicine & Science in Sports, 19,* 129-141.

Mgalla, Z., Schapink, D., & Boerma, J. (1998). Protecting school girls against sexual exploitation: A guardian program in Mwanza, Tanzania. *Reproductive Health Matters, 6,* 19-30.

Miller, K. E., Sabo, D. F., Farrell, M. P., Barnes, G. M., & Melnick, M. J. (1998). Athletic participation and sexual behavior in adolescents: The different worlds of boys and girls. *Journal of Health and Social Behavior, 39,* 108-123.

National AIDS Control Programme (NACP), Bureau of Statistics, & MEASURE project (2004). *AIDS in Africa during the nineties: Tanzania youth report.* Chapel Hill, NC: Carolina Population Center, University of North Carolina at Chapel Hill.

Ndeki, S. S., Klepp, K. I., & Mliga, G. R. (1994). Knowledge, perceived risk of AIDS and sexual behavior among primary school children in two areas of Tanzania. *Health Education Research, Theory and Practice, 9,* 183-191.

Ndeki, S. S., Klepp, K. I., Seha, A. M., & Leshabari, M. T. (1994). Exposure to HIV/AIDS information, AIDS knowledge, perceived risk and attitudes toward people with AIDS among primary children in Northen Tanzania. *AIDS Care, 6,* 183-191.

Pulerwitz, J., Barker, G., Segundo, M., & Nascimento, M. (2006). *Promoting gender-equity among young Brazilian men as an HIV prevention strategy.* Washington, D.C: Horizons Research Summary.

Rasch, V., Silberschmidt, M., Mchumvu, Y., & Mmary, V. (2000). Adolescent girls with illegally induced abortion in Dar es Salaam: The discrepancy between sexual behavior and lack of access to contraceptives. *Reproductive Health Matters, 8,* 52-62.

Roberts, G. C., Treasure, D. C., & Conroy, D. E. (2007). Understanding the dynamics of motivation in sport and physical activity: An achievement goal interpretation. In G. Tenenbaum, & R. Eklund (Eds.), *Handbook of research in sport psychology.* (pp 3-30) Boston: Wiley.

Sangiwa, G. M., van der Straten, A., & Grinstead, O. A. (2000). Clients' perspective of the role of voluntary counseling and testing in HIV/AIDS prevention and care in Dar es Salaam, Tanzania: The voluntary counseling and testing efficacy study. *AIDS and Behavior, 4,* 35-48.

Schueller, J., La Vake, S., Lugoe, W., Chuma, M., Mango F, & Humplick, B. (2003). *Summary review: YouthNet program assessment conducted for Tanzania.* Arlington, VA: Family Health International.

Sengendo, J., &. Nambi, J. (1997). The psychological effect of orphanhood: A study of orphans in Rakai district [Uganda]. *Health Transition Review, 7,* 105-124.

Stover, J. (2004). Projecting the demographic consequences of adult HIV prevalence trends: The spectrum projection package. *Sex Transformation Infection, 80,* 14 -18.

Swai, R. O., & Asten, H. V. (1991). Epidemilogy of HIV-1 infection in Tanzania. An update. *Tanzania Medical Journal, 6,* 33-39.

Talle, A., Biswalo, P. M., Schreiner, A. H., & Klepp, K. I. (1995). Introduction. In K. I. Klepp, P. M. Biswalo, & A. Talle (Eds.), *Young people at risk: Fighting AIDS in Northern Tanzania* (pp. xviii-xxviii). Oslo: Scandinavian University Press.

Tanzania Commission for AIDS. (2008). *Tanzania HIV/AIDS and Malaria Indicator Survey (2007-2008).* Dar es Salaam, Tanzania: Author.

Tanzania Commission for AIDS (2010). *Tanzania HIV/AIDS Indicator Survey (2007-2008)* Dar es Salaam, Tanzania: Author.

Tanzanian Ministry of Health and Social Welfare (1995). *National policy on HIV/AIDS/ STD.* Dar es Salaam, United Republic of Tanzania: Ministry of Health, National AIDS Control Program.

Tanzanian Ministry of Health and Social Welfare. (2009). *Document on HIV/AIDS surveillance.* Retrieved from http://www.noh.go.tz/document/HIV_surveillance_report_No_21.pdf

UNAIDS. (2003). *UNAIDS questions and answers.* Retrieved from http://application.fnu.ac.fj/classshare/Medical_Science_Resources/MBBS/MBBS13/PBL/Sexually%20Transmitted%20Infections/UNAIDS%20Questions%20and%20Answers.pdf

UNAIDS. (2006). *2006 Report on the global AIDS epidemic.* Geneva, Switzerland: Joint United Nations Programme on HIV/AIDS (UNAIDS).

UNAIDS. (2008). *2008 Report on the global AIDS epidemic.* Geneva, Switzerland: Joint United Nations Programme on HIV/AIDS (UNAIDS).

UNAIDS. (2010). *UNAIDS report on the global AIDS epidemic 2010.* Retrieved November 30, 2010, from http://www.UNAIDS.org/globalreport

UNICEF (2002). *The state of the world's children 2002.* Retrieved from http://www.unicef.org/sowc02/fullreport.htm

UNICEF (2004). *Girls, HIV/AIDS and education.* New York: United Nation's Children Fund (UNICEF).

United Nations (2003). *Inter-Agency task force report on sport for development and peace: Towards achieving the millennium development goals.* Geneva: United Nations.

United Nations General Assembly. (2003). *Sport as a means to promote education, health, development, and peace.* General Assembly Resolution 58/5, United Nations. Retrieved from http://www.un.org/ga/search/view_doc.asp?symbol=A/RES/58/5

Weiss, E. D., Whelan, D., & Rao Gupta, G. (2000). Gender sexuality and HIV: Making a difference in the lives of young women in developing countries. *Sexual Relationship Therapy, 15,* 233-245.

World Health Organization (1989). *Guide to planning health promotion for AIDS prevention and control.* (Rep. No. 5). Geneva: Switzerland: Author.

Future Directions in Youth Leadership Research in Sport

Daniel Gould, Dana K. Voelker, and Jed Blanton

> *"Ten soldiers wisely led will beat a hundred without a head."*
> *- Euripides*

> *"Our chief want is someone who will inspire us to be what we know we could be."*
> *- Ralph Waldo Emerson*

> *"An army of a thousand is easy to find, but, ah, how difficult to find a general."*
> *- Chinese Proverb*

As demonstrated by these opening quotes, society has viewed leadership as a critical component to success for centuries. It is therefore not surprising that leadership has been considered an especially important part of positive youth development. Historically, sport has been seen as an excellent training ground for developing leaders. For example, legendary football coach Vince Lombardi said, "Leaders aren't born, they are made. And they are made just like anything else, through hard work."

The emphasis on youth leadership is no less important today than in previous generations. Recently, increasing attention has been given to this topic in the scholarly literature.

For example, Gould, Chung, Smith, and White (2006) found that high school coaches believed that leadership was one of the most important life skills that young athletes must acquire and develop. Professionals in sport and physical activity fields have a number of reasons for desiring youth to learn leadership, including enhancing team performance and cultivating a life skill that may be applied to various contexts throughout their lives.

Many believe that sport and physical activity may be an excellent venue for developing leadership skills in young people. For example, Martinek and Hellison (2009) contended that sport and physical activity contexts are highly interactive and provide numerous leadership opportunities or "moments" for young people to gain leadership experience (e.g., enforcing rules for teammates). Furthermore, they believe that sport and physical activity provide an opportunity for youth to learn leadership in an enjoyable, motivating, and meaningful environment.

In light of the need and importance for youth leadership in sport, this chapter has four purposes: (a) to review the research and theory examining leadership in young people involved in sport and physical activity contexts, (b) to identify what has been learned from the current research and theory in the area, (c) to discuss future research directions, and (d) to discuss implications for professional practice. Importantly, before the youth leadership research can be reviewed, the construct must first be defined. Leadership has been described in many ways, especially as it pertains to youth development. For the purpose of this chapter, we have adapted a definition of leadership similar to that used by Northouse (2010): a complex process that involves the effort of an individual (i.e., a leader) to help groups identify and achieve personal and group goals.

THE SCALE AND SCOPE OF RESEARCH ON YOUTH LEADERSHIP

Leadership has been a research interest of psychologists for decades. Thousands of articles have been published on leadership in adult populations, and numerous theoretical orientations have been developed. Nevertheless, both books (e.g., Northouse, 2010) and comprehensive reviews of the literature (e.g., American Psychologist, 2007) show that although progress has been made, more research is certainly needed. In general, findings have revealed that leadership is a complex process that involves the interaction of leader characteristics, follower characteristics and needs, and situational influences. Avolio (2007) and other reviewers have concluded that future researchers must consider the leadership context while examining the dynamic interaction between leaders and followers. Due to the complexity of leadership, Hackman and Wageman (2007) called for a paradigmatic shift in the kinds of questions that investigators must examine so as to advance research in the area. More specifically, they stated that investigators should ask the following,

(1) Not do leaders make a difference, but under what conditions does leadership matter? (2) Not what are the traits of leaders, but how do leaders' personal attributes interact with situational properties to shape outcomes? (3) Not does there exist common dimensions on which all leaders can be arrayed, but are good and poor leadership qualitatively different phenomena? (4) Not how do leaders and followers differ, but how can leadership models be reframed so they treat all system members as both leaders and followers? (5) Not what should be taught in leadership courses, but how can leaders be helped to learn? (p. 43)

Reviews of adult leadership research in the sport psychology field typically parallel the general psychology and business psychology literature; however the body of work is more limited in both theoretical scope and sheer number of studies conducted (Chelladurai, 2007; Schonfeld, 2008). The bulk of the research has focused on coaching leadership from which two dominant models have emerged: Chelladurai's multidimensional model of leadership (Chelladurai; Chelladurai & Saleh, 1978) and Smoll and Smith's (1989) cognitive-mediational model. Some initial work has also focused on the application of transactional-transformational leadership models to sport (e.g., Rowold, 2006).

More recently, leadership research conducted on adults in sport has inspired the study of peer or athlete leaders. Although those interested in studying youth leadership should certainly consider the theoretical orientations, recommendations, and conclusions coming from the adult leadership research, these approaches should not be blindly applied. For example, van Linden and Fertman (1998) have identified specific needs that those studying youth leadership must address, such as physical and emotional changes and the development of self-acceptance and value systems occurring within and around young people. MacNeil (2006) has also argued that there are significant differences in the needs, practices, and styles of adult versus youth leaders. She stressed the importance of thinking about youth leadership from a broad perspective that integrates the developmental characteristics of youth; the larger leadership context; and the opportunities young people have for sharing a voice, having influence, and taking part in decision-making.

Specifically in youth sport, preliminary studies have suggested that the roles and responsibilities of adult versus peer leaders are fundamentally different. For example, Loughead, Hardy, and Eys (2006) found that peer, coach, and self-ratings of leadership roles were either not at all or only moderately correlated with one another. Similarly, Loughead and Hardy (2005) found that coach and peer leaders serve different roles on their teams. Dupuis, Bloom, and Loughead (2006) identified three categories of behaviors specific to peer leaders: interpersonal characteristics/experiences (e.g., maintaining a positive attitude and controlling emotions), verbal interactions (e.g., communicating with one's coach), and task behaviors (e.g., representing the team at functions). These studies emphasize the importance of moving beyond a single focus on the coach to other leaders in sport, and illustrate the need to study youth athlete leadership as a distinct construct. To date, youth leadership research in sport has focused less on how leadership works and more on how to develop leadership skills in young populations. Research efforts and programming have also focused on the degree to which leadership can and should be instilled in all young people versus a selected few.

General Psychology Research

Few studies have been conducted on youth leadership in general psychology, and systematic lines of research are lacking, which makes general conclusions difficult. Nevertheless, searches and reviews of the literature have helped us to determine which findings might best inform youth leadership development research in sport. The studies identified can be loosely organized under four general headings: (a) leadership and factors associated with becoming a leader, (b) advantages and consequences of being a leader, (c) the measurement of youth leadership, and (d) leader training effectiveness. Each of these will be briefly summarized below.

Leadership and factors associated with becoming a leader. A number of investigators have begun to examine characteristics of and factors associated with being a youth leader (e.g., Avolio, Rotundo, & Walumbwa, 2009; Dhuey & Lipscomb, 2008; Schneider, Ehrhart, & Ehrhart, 2002; Ward & Ellis, 2008). They have suggested that youth leaders tend to be older and have higher ability and emotional intelligence than their counterparts. When nominated by peers, they are judged to have social support, status, an effective personality, and motivational attributes that make them leaders. Finally, emerging research shows that early youth experiences are related to both later life leadership patterns and leadership styles used.

Advantages and consequences of being a leader. Other researchers have begun to explore the advantages and consequences of youth leadership (e.g., Extejt & Smith, 2009; Kuhn & Weinberger, 2005). Results from these studies suggest that merely being an athlete does not correlate to adult leadership, although practicing leadership as a captain or school leader does. Moreover, not all consequences of youth leadership may be positive. For example, Ferris, Zinko, Brouer, Buckley, and Harvey (2007) have forwarded the notion that bullying is a form of destructive leadership. Given concerns of bullying in sport, this topic would be particularly important to purse in future research.

Measurement of youth leadership. Measurement is a significant problem in the youth leadership research, especially the development of psychometrically sound instruments that are developmentally appropriate. Oakland, Falkenberg, and Oakland (1996) evaluated leadership measures used in youth populations and concluded that few good measures exist. They not only suggested validating adult measures for use with youth, but also developing measures specifically focused on youth leadership.

Leader training effectiveness. Understanding efforts to develop leadership in young people has been of interest in the general psychology literature. Several authors have discussed the components of effective programs as well as the lessons learned from implementing their programs in youth settings, such as 4-H (Head, Heart, Hands, Health) or Junior Reserve Officers Training Corps (JROTC) (e.g., Funk, 2002; MacNeil & McClean, 2006; Matsudaira & Jefferson, 2006). Funk, for example, described a multi-year Junior ROTC program for high school students emphasizing who leaders are and what they do. Four modules comprised the program, including character, life skills, leadership skills, and service learning. The program not only required the development of specific personal characteristics and skills in youth, but also reflective insight. Over the course of four years, younger participants observed their senior peers exhibiting leadership skills and making decisions. Gradually, these younger participants assumed more responsibilities as they gained leadership knowledge and experience. Following the principles of autonomy and empowerment, adult supervisors monitored the program while remaining in the background as much as possible.

Taking a different approach, Libby, Rosen, and Sedonaen (2005) described the San Francisco Bay Area's Youth Leadership Institute partnership with organizations to support community-change leadership opportunities for youth. Lessons learned over the course of 15 years have emphasized (a) the importance of creating pathways for youth to develop leadership over time, (b) engaging young people in the organizational structure, (c) giving them meaningful decision-making and planning responsibilities, and (d) ensuring extensive quality training and ongoing support for all program participants and facilitators.

Other investigators have studied youth leadership education and development efforts (e.g., Hoyt & Kennedy, 2009; Hynes, Feldhusen, & Richardson, 1978). Overall, the results of these leadership training effectiveness studies suggest that youth leadership training programs can effectively enhance leadership attitudes, behaviors, and skills in youth. Nevertheless, more research is needed, especially studies that further verify program outcomes and link demonstrated effects to specific theoretical contentions and intervention components.

Sport Psychology Research

Early research on youth leadership in sport has primarily focused on demographic and situational variables associated with being a team leader, including age, amount of sport experience, athletic skill (e.g., Tropp & Landers, 1979; Weese, 1983; Yukelson, Weinberg, Richard, & Jackson, 1983) and playing position (e.g., Lee, Coburn, & Partridge, 1983; Melnick & Loy, 1996). More recent research has closely examined the psychological factors associated with youth leadership in sport, as well as leadership roles, responsibilities, behaviors, and development. Because research in this area is so limited, key findings from selected studies examining both high school and college-aged youth will be discussed.

Psychological factors associated with youth leadership in sport. Psychological characteristics that researchers have shown to be associated with athlete leadership include an internal locus of control (Yukelson et al.), as well as high levels of aspiration, competitiveness, emotional expressiveness, responsibility, and acceptance as perceived by coaches (Klonsky, 1991). In a study investigating the leadership qualities of male preadolescents (ages 9 to 12), Pease and Zhang (2002) found a significant and positive relationship between self-esteem and coach and player perceptions of leadership roles. Another study, examining an older age group (male university-level team captains), found that athlete leaders were respectful, trustworthy, and optimistic, and had the capacity to effectively communicate and regulate their emotions (Dupuis et al., 2006).

Other studies demonstrate that important psychological components of youth leadership may vary by the perceptions of athletes, teammates, and coaches. For example, Glenn and Horn (1993) found that high self-esteem, perceived sport competence, a mixture of masculine (i.e., instrumental) and feminine (i.e., expressive) characteristics, and low competitive trait anxiety were important psychological predictors of self-perceived leadership in high school female soccer players. Coach and peer ratings of athlete leadership tendencies, however, were more strongly associated with player skill level than other psychological variables. Similar results were found by Moran and Weiss (2006) in a study of male and female high school soccer players. These studies suggest that athletic ability is an important factor in selecting youth sport peer leaders. Coaches and teammates may benefit, however, from a broadened definition of youth leadership that extends beyond athletic ability and performance. Understanding what youth leadership means to young athletes and adult coaches may help to inform and improve the captain or leader selection process.

Roles, responsibilities, and behavioral factors associated with youth leadership in sport. Qualitative methodologies have served as a particularly informative approach to understanding the specific roles and responsibilities of youth athlete leaders. In a qualitative study on former high school sport captains, the most frequently cited roles included organizational duties (e.g., calling the coin toss, organizing dress and uniforms, leading warm-ups and stretches), setting an example on and off the field, motivating and encouraging teammates, building relationships, and offering mentorship and support to teammates (Voelker, Gould, & Crawford, 2011). In a retrospective qualitative analysis by Wright and Côté (2003), Canadian university-level male athlete leaders reported physically working as hard as or harder than their peers in practices and games to improve their own skill competence and set a positive example for others. Athlete leaders also reported bonding and developing positive interpersonal relationships with all team members as opposed to only choosing a select few.

In another qualitative study, Dupuis et al. (2006) interviewed six former university male ice hockey captains. These researchers found that some of the primary roles of a team captain include serving as a liaison between coaches, fellow teammates, and referees; mentoring younger athletes by setting the appropriate team norms (e.g., promptness, work ethic); and executing a number of administrative and organizational duties (e.g., helping the coach plan the off-season, representing the team at special gatherings, talking to the media, sponsors, and fans, and organizing team meetings and fundraising events). Lastly, in a recent qualitative study examining athlete leadership on dyadic teams (elite ice dancing), communication, positive attitude, respect, leading by example, and discipline emerged as important leadership behaviors (Vincer, Baker, Loughead, & Monroe-Chandler, 2007).

Although the extant literature only provides a few studies on the specific roles and responsibilities of athlete leaders, the qualitative nature of these studies provides us with an exploratory view of the diverse range of duties that successful athlete leaders must fulfill. Nevertheless, much of the abovementioned research has focused on collegiate or elite level athletes. Future research may assess more traditionally defined youth, including pre-adolescent and high school athletes, because fewer studies have been conducted with these populations.

Other studies have examined the behavioral orientations of young leaders in sport. Findings have indicated that athlete leaders are not only concerned with accomplishing tasks (i.e., instrumental or task orientation—making plays, winning games), but also with increasing relationship quality among teammates (i.e., expressive or social orientation—establishing trust, enhancing communication; e.g., Rees, 1983; Rees & Segal, 1984; Todd & Kent, 2004). Loughead et al. (2006) found that athlete leaders fulfill a third leadership orientation known as the external function. More specifically, external leadership involves representing and promoting the team within the community, obtaining resources and support for the organization (e.g., planning fundraisers), and protecting teammates from external distracters (e.g., media).

In an examination of all three leadership functions, Eys, Loughead, and Hardy (2007) found that players who perceive a balance between task-, social-, and external-oriented leaders on their teams reported greater levels of satisfaction with team performance and team integration (e.g., the degree to which the team shares a common goal). These findings support the assumption that fulfilling task, social, and external-related roles are vital to establishing effective leadership on youth sport teams.

Youth leadership development and training in sport. Few studies have examined how youth athletes become leaders and develop their leadership abilities over time. Unfortunately, preliminary evidence suggests that sport captains at the high school level are receiving little to no training or preparation from coaches for their leadership roles (Voelker et al., 2011). Some high school captains even believe that their coaches inhibit them from developing into effective leaders by using intimidation, refusing to take suggestions, and limiting their opportunities to exercise leadership skills. In a qualitative study of ten high school coaches known for developing leadership in their captains, results suggested that the best youth leadership development methods are proactive, for example by developing ongoing communication with captains, providing them with feedback and reinforcement, holding coach-captain meetings, encouraging or conducting formal leadership training initiatives, and teaching and educating captains on concepts relevant to their leadership roles (Gould, Voelker, & Griffes, in press).

Other qualitative studies have begun to examine how early experiences contribute to leadership development in young adulthood. For example, Wright and Côté (2003) found that Canadian university-level male athlete leaders were competitive in their sports at an early age, often played with more highly skilled peers, and were positively influenced by their coaches (e.g., engaged in mature conversations) and parents (e.g., provided support and mentorship). In another qualitative study, Dupuis et al. (2006) found that Canadian university-level male team captains experienced early exposure to both sport and high levels of competition; held leadership positions in youth; and acquired knowledge from previous team leaders, relevant literature, and clinics. Thus, recent qualitative inquiry indicates that both the type and quality of early experiences may contribute to the emergence of athlete leaders.

Parents may play a particularly influential role in the leadership development of youth athletes. Zacharatos, Barling, and Kelloway (2000) found that transformational leadership observed in athletes' parents was positively associated with athletes' use of the same leadership style. These findings suggest that parents may play a significant role in the type of leadership developed in their children. Interestingly, findings from this study also indicated that adolescent athletes who used transformational leadership were perceived to be effective as rated by their peers and coaches.

A number of physical educators have also been interested in using recreational physical activity and out-of-school sports clubs to enhance the psychosocial development of underserved youth, particularly in the areas of personal and social responsibility (Hellison, 1995; Hellison & Walsh, 2002). To evaluate success in enhancing youth leadership, Hammond-Diedrich and Walsh (2006) assessed the effectiveness of a cross-age responsibility-based program designed to promote leadership in 11- to 15-year-old underserved boys who taught physical activity to fourth grade youth. Formal interviews, lesson observations, and field notes were used to measure leadership development. Results revealed that the program was effective in that the youth improved their leadership skills and became more confident as leaders. The authors noted, however, that consistency was problematic in some of the participants.

In an interesting set of four case studies, Martinek, Schilling, and Hellison (2006) described their evaluated efforts to develop compassionate and caring adolescent leaders who served as apprentice teachers in two after-school physical activity programs for underserved youth. Youth leadership was intentionally fostered by allowing participants to teach sport and life skills to younger children in the program. Based on the theorizing of Gilligan (1982) and Maslow's hierarchy of needs (1968), the authors conceptualized leadership as a four-stage developmental process. This process consists of youth (a) fulfilling their own needs rather then leading others; (b) focusing on planning, teaching, and leading others; (c) reflecting on their leadership experiences; and (d) developing compassion for those they lead. Evaluation criteria included individual and focus group interviews, written reflections on each participant, field notes, and informal observations of the program staff. Results revealed that the program was effective in helping youth to develop their leadership skills. Two of the youth reached the final stage and demonstrated compassionate leadership. Effects, however, were neither simple nor universal. For example, one participant showed difficulty demonstrating higher order leadership skills outside of the program because he was negatively influenced by non-program peers. Another youth attempting to move out of the first stage was not successful and left the program. The authors concluded that fostering leadership in underserved youth is a dynamic and fluid process and that helping youth progress requires high expectations, opportunities for reflection, recognition, and gentle nudging on the part of the program staff. Youth often progress to higher stages, but it is not uncommon for youth to regress as well (Martinek et al., 2006).

Those interested in studying peer leadership in competitive sport programs would do well to examine developing personal and social responsibility through physical activity research. Although the context is different, much can be gained from the lessons learned and evaluations conducted in these programs.

FUTURE RESEARCH DIRECTIONS

Given the paucity of youth leadership research conducted in psychology in general and sport psychology in particular, numerous opportunities for future research exist. Below is a brief discussion of a number of future research directions that are important to pursue.

Determining What Youth Leadership Involves

In the youth leadership literature, leadership has been defined in many ways. At times, youth leadership is viewed so broadly that it is difficult to distinguish it from positive youth development in general. At other times, youth leadership is seen as involving specific individual skills and attributes such as emotional intelligence, self-esteem, and moral character. Although current research and programming efforts are valuable, authors often do not precisely specify what youth leadership is and what it involves. In turn, reviewing the literature is a challenging and complicated process. As Baker (1997) indicated, it is also difficult to systematically develop youth leadership without precisely defining it. In sum, both researchers and practitioners must be clear about how youth leadership is characterized to effectively study and develop it in young people.

Identifying the Most Important Research Questions

In reviewing the general psychology leadership literature, Hackman and Wageman (2007) discussed the importance of asking the right questions when conducting studies in the area and not simply posing the same questions that have been examined over the last 30 years. Although recognizing that youth leadership research will need to differ from adult-oriented research in many ways, sport psychology youth leadership researchers should heed the suggestions of Hackman and Wageman and focus on many of the key research questions posed by these authors. In addition, there are a number of specific questions that should be pursued.

First, it would be helpful to know how coaches and athletes define leadership and what leadership roles they see as most crucial. Such information will help investigators to understand coaches' and athletes' views of leadership and how they match up with theoretical conceptions of the phenomenon. A second important question regards the factors that influence youth leader effectiveness. Currently, we do not know if males and females require different approaches to leadership development or if sport leadership differs by race, ethnicity, the developmental level of the young person involved, or sport type (e.g., team versus individual sports).

It is also important to identify what issues youth leaders face. For example, we know that peer leadership differs from coaching leadership but not precisely how. Moreover, it would be extremely valuable to know how adolescents in their mid-teens (who are characterized by peer acceptance concerns) maintain status with their peers while delivering unpopular information and difficult feedback. Another imperative question to study is how young people in sport and physical activity learn to lead. General psychology research shows that parenting practices influence young people's leadership behaviors, and initial descriptive research in sport shows that parents are an important influence on young athletes' leadership development. Pursuing this line of research through a more theoretical perspective by looking at parenting styles (Steinberg, 2001; Steinberg, Blatt-Eisengart, & Cauffman, 2006) would be a valuable way to learn more about developing leadership in youth. Looking beyond the contribution of parents may also be useful because van Linden and Fertman (1998) indicated that family, community, school, and work experiences interact to influence youth leadership development. These authors additionally suggested that youth learn leadership in a number of different ways: via trial and error, observation, prior life experiences, and formal programs (van Linden & Fertman). Most of the current research has examined the effect of formal training programs. Researchers may also longitudinally study youth involved in sport and physical activity leadership activities and identify the contributions of each of these varied ways of learning to the leadership development of young people.

Researchers might also examine the leadership capacity of youth. One major difference from adult leaders is that youth leaders are moving through various developmental stages. Movement through these stages may influence youth leadership development. For example, van Linden and Fertman (1998) indicated that youth must learn both transactional (e.g., communication techniques, motivation principles) and transformational leadership skills (e.g., the ability to assess feelings in others and integrate multiple perspectives) to be effective. With the exception of one initial study showing that high school students were able to demonstrate transformational leadership, we know little about the developmental and cognitive capacity of an adolescent to learn transactional and transformational leadership skills (Zacharatos et al., 2000). For example, can or to what degree can an early adolescent, who is egocentric in orientation, develop transactional and transformational leadership skills that require understanding and integrating the perspectives of others?

When we have more knowledge about how young athletes learn to lead, researchers can move towards examining the most effective methods of developing youth leaders. For example, intervention effectiveness studies must begin to tease apart what aspects of the program are most and least influential so as to begin developing the best programs possible. Identifying the most effective and efficient methods (those that can be implemented in the shortest amount of time and with the least expense) is important for program design and implementation.

Whether competitive youth sport is too adult-dominated for leadership to be cultivated is another critical question that must be examined. One consistent finding from current youth leadership training studies is that youth best learn to lead by gaining leadership experiences, making meaningful decisions, and engaging in planning efforts that have important consequences for the group (Martinek & Hellison, 2009; van Linden & Fertman, 1998). Reflection time is also seen as critical (Funk, 2002). These practices are much easier to implement in programs where all activities are designed to foster the single purpose of developing youth leadership. Competitive sport programs, however, often have multiple goals, such as enhancing fitness, achieving team success, and promoting prosocial behaviors. Coaches in these programs are often highly motivated to achieve and are held accountable for athletic success and a winning record. In turn, coaches may be hesitant to give young people the independence and agency needed to truly learn to lead. Given these constraints, it is critical to discover whether coaches will give up enough control to allow young athletes to engage in the planning efforts and meaningful decision-making that facilitates leadership development.

Finally, claims are often made that youth who have opportunities to lead in sport and other physical activity settings will develop leadership skills that transfer beyond sport to other life settings. Little research exists, however, to support these contentions. If and under what conditions youth sport leadership opportunities teach transferable skills is an important question in need of further study.

Creating Models of Youth Leadership Development in Sport

A need exists to develop models and theoretical explanations that can be used to help understand how leadership functions in youth contexts and how sport can be used to facilitate leadership development in young people. Two excellent places to start this process would be to further test the utility of Martinek and Hellison's (2009) stages of leadership development and van Linden and Fertman's (1998) developmental model of youth leadership.

The stages of youth leader development forwarded by Martinek and Hellison (2009) included (a) learning to take responsibility; (b) leadership awareness; (c) cross-age leadership; and (d) self-actualized leadership. The learning to take responsibility stage is based on Hellison's (1995) five-stage responsibility model (Level 1: Respecting rights and feelings of others; Level 2: Participation and effort; Level 3: Self-directions; Level 4: Helping others and leadership; and Level 5: Transferring what has been learned). According to this model, young people need to first learn how to take responsibility for their own actions before learning to lead. Responsibility serves as the foundation for becoming aware of their leadership potential, beginning to develop caring and compassionate leadership, and developing into self-actualized leaders where they extend their leadership skills to other domains. Although this model was developed for use in small out-of-school sports clubs, it would be useful for researchers to see if it applies to training captains in competitive youth sports settings across various age groups.

Similar to Martinek and Hellison (2009), van Linden and Fertman (1998) contended that leadership development in youth is a continuous process best viewed as unfolding in three stages: Awareness, interaction, and mastery. They further suggested that youth must learn numerous cognitive, emotional, and behavioral skills organized into five major dimensions and improve across the stages of development. These include (a) leadership information (e.g., what youth know about leadership and leaders), (b) leadership attitude (e.g., thoughts, dispositions, and feelings youth have about themselves as leaders), (c) communication skills, (d) decision-making skills, and (e) stress management skills. Moreover, within each dimension, youth must learn both transactional (e.g., what leaders do—make decisions, speak to groups) and transformational aspects of leadership (e.g., skills focused on helping followers transform themselves and their performances). This model could be tested in the sport setting to determine if youth progress according to the hypothesized stages and whether the five dimensions account for the major leadership skills that youth must learn. The model could also be used to determine which skills are best learned at certain ages.

IMPLICATIONS FOR PROFESSIONAL PRACTICE

Although more research is certainly needed, current youth leadership research and theory have a number of implications that can be used to guide practice. First, research has shown that leadership is a complex and continuous process. It involves the reciprocal interaction of both leader and follower characteristics as well as a host of situational influences. Hence, young people must develop an awareness that leadership is much more than one's personal characteristics or the implementation of certain techniques. It also involves reading the situation; working to understand follower preferences, notions, and characteristics; and empowering followers to accomplish their goals.

Leadership development involves a number of skills, dispositions, self and other perceptions, and regulatory skills that unfold over time. Young athletes must first understand and become aware of what leadership is and how it functions. They must then believe that they can lead and that they have the capacity and abilities to learn to do so. A number of basic transactional leadership skills must be learned (e.g., being able to speak to groups, making eye contact when communicating, focusing on positive reinforcement). Transformational skills that involve moving to abstract interpretations of and interventions into one's environment must also be acquired (e.g., understanding the complexity of leader-follower dynamics, developing and sharing a team vision, eliciting positive behaviors from followers). Finally, young leaders must self-regulate their own leader behaviors and develop the vision to see leadership possibilities beyond sport and transfer their leadership skills to new arenas of life.

Learning to lead is multi-faceted. It involves modeling, experiential learning, mentorships, trial and error, and formal education (e.g., Doh, 2003; Kempster, 2006; Kouzes & Posner, 1987; Martinek & Hellison, 2009). Experiential learning is an especially important component in the leadership development process. More specifically, young people in leadership roles must be empowered to make meaningful choices and become active agents in their own environment. Coaches and other supervising adults must allow young athletes to actually lead and not just assign them relatively mundane and meaningless roles. Cultivating leadership in young people is difficult when adults dominate their sport environment. Efforts to give high school captains real leadership opportunities are not occurring frequently enough and when they do occur, captains are often ill prepared to handle them. Coaches must do more to facilitate leadership training in the young people with whom they work. Not only will young athletes need training, but the coaches who mentor them must also be educated.

Based on their sport and physical activity leadership work with countless underserved youth, Martinek and Hellison (2009) and Hammond-Diedrich and Walsh (2006) have offered a number of specific guidelines for teaching leadership skills to young people. Some of these are summarized below.

- An empowerment approach is absolutely necessary for developing youth leadership.
- It is important for adult leaders to pinpoint and acknowledge examples of good leadership for young athletes.
- Cross-age teaching is an excellent way to help young people learn to lead.
- Students must be given numerous opportunities to reflect on their leadership experiences.
- Adult leaders must establish meaningful relationships with youth leaders and provide frequent opportunities for interaction and dialogue.
- Adult leaders should help young people engage in the broader community.
- Adult leaders should focus their attention on youth leaders' strengths rather than their weaknesses.
- Adult leaders should help youth learn to problem-solve by formally listing problems and discussing how to solve them.
- Adult leaders must regularly help youth leaders self-evaluate their leadership practices.
- Adult leaders must assist youth leaders in assessing current leadership abilities and identifying future goals.
- Adult leader guidance and feedback are critical to youth leader development.

Finally, it is important to note that developing youth leaders is an imperfect process. Although the research shows that young people can certainly learn to lead and become effective in leadership roles, some will struggle with taking on responsibility, mastering the skills needed, learning how to effectively interact with others, and following through on commitments. Coaches and other adults fostering youth leadership in young athletes must understand this fact, demonstrate patience, and be sure not to overreact by taking too much control when problems do occur. The key is to recognize that making mistakes, acknowledging them, and devising plans for improvement is an integral part of the leadership learning process, especially in young people. At the same time, the art of developing youth leadership is providing enough guidance and intervention to ensure that the overall experience is positive and that errors are treated as learning opportunities.

CONCLUSIONS

There is a strong societal belief that youth need to learn to lead and that the sport context is an excellent training ground for accomplishing this task. The initial research examining youth leadership development, both in general and within sport psychology, is encouraging. We now have a general understanding of what youth leadership involves and how it is developed. Nevertheless, many more questions remain unanswered. Future research should involve well-thought definitions of youth leadership, ask key questions that have both practical and theoretical importance, be guided by or test theoretical explanations for how leadership functions and develops in young people, and employ a range of quantitative and qualitative methods. Finally, it is important to consider youth leadership from a developmental perspective in light of the uniqueness of young people and their environments.

REFERENCES

American Psychologist (2007). Special issue: Leadership. *American Psychological Association, 62,* 1-70.

Avolio, B. J. (2007). Promoting more integrative strategies for leadership theory-building. *American Psychologist, 62,* 25-33.

Avolio, B. J., Rotundo, M., & Walumbwa, F. O. (2009). Early life experiences as determinants of leadership role occupancy: The importance of parental influence and rule-breaking behavior. *The Leadership Quarterly, 20,* 329-342.

Baker, R. A. (1997). How can we train leaders if we do not know what leadership is? *Human Relations, 50,* 343-362.

Chelladurai, P. (2007). Leadership in sports. In G. Tenenbaum, & R. C. Eklund (Eds.), *Handbook of sport psychology* (3rd ed., pp. 113-135.). Hoboken, NJ: Wiley.

Chelladurai, P., & Saleh, S. D. (1978). Preferred leadership in sports. *Canadian Journal of Applied Sport Sciences, 3,* 85–92.

Dhuey, E., & Lipscomb, S. (2008). What makes a leader? Relative age and high school leadership. *Economics of Education Review, 27,* 173-183.

Doh, J. P. (2003). Can leadership be taught? Perspectives from management educators. *Academy of Management Learning and Education, 72,* 54-67.

Dupuis, M., Bloom, G. A., & Loughead, T. M. (2006). Team captains' perceptions of athlete leadership. *Journal of Sport Behavior, 29,* 60-78.

Extejt, M. M., & Smith, J. E. (2009). Leadership development through sports participation. *Journal of Leadership Education, 8,* 224-237.

Eys, M. A., Loughead, T. M., & Hardy, J. (2007). Athlete leadership dispersion and satisfaction in interactive sport teams. *Psychology of Sport and Exercise, 8,* 281-296.

Ferris, G. R., Zinko, R., Brouer, R. L., Buckley, M. R., & Harvey, M. G (2007). Strategic bullying as a supplementary, balanced perspective on destructive leadership. *The Leadership Quarterly, 18,* 195-206.

Funk, R. C. (2002). Developing leaders through junior ROTC: Integrating theory with practice. *Journal of Leadership Studies, 8,* 43-53.

Gilligan, C. (1982). *In a different voice: Psychological theory and women's development.* Cambridge, MA: Harvard University Press.

Glenn, S. D., & Horn, T. S. (1993). Psychological and personal predictors of leadership behavior in female soccer athletes. *Journal of Applied Sport Psychology, 5,* 17-34.

Gould, D., Chung, Y., Smith, P., & White, J. (2006). Future directions in coaching life skills: Understanding high school coaches' views and needs. Athletic Insight: *The Online Journal of Sports Psychology, 18*(3), 1-11.

Gould, D., Voelker, D. K., & Griffes, K. (in press). Best coaching practices for developing team captains. *The Sport Psychologist.*

Hackman, R. J., & Wageman, R. (2007). Asking the right questions about leadership. *American Psychologist, 62,* 43-47.

Hammond-Diedrich, K. C., & Walsh, D. (2006). Empowering youth through a responsibility-based cross-age teacher program: An investigation into impact and possibilities. *Physical Educator, 63,* 134-142.

Hellison, D. (1995). *Teaching responsibility through physical activity.* Champaign, IL: Human Kinetics.

Hellison, D., & Walsh, D. (2002). Responsibility-based youth programs evaluation: Investigating the investigators. *Quest, 54,* 292-307.

Hoyt, M. A., & Kennedy, C. L. (2008). Leadership and adolescent girls: A qualitative study of leadership development. *American Journal of Community Psychology, 42,* 203-219.

Hynes, K., Feldhusen, J. F., & Richardson, W. B. (1978). Application of a three-stage model of instruction to youth leadership training. *Journal of Applied Psychology, 63,* 623-628.

Kempster, S. (2006). Leadership learning through lived experience: A process of apprenticeship? *Journal of Management and Organization, 12,* 4-22.

Klonsky, B. G. (1991). Leader's characteristics in same-sex sport groups: A study of interscholastic baseball and softball team. *Perceptual and Motor Skills, 72,* 943-947.

Kouzes, J. M., & Posner, B. P. (1987). *The leadership challenge: How to get extraordinary things done in organizations.* San Francisco: Jossey Bass.

Kuhn, P., & Weinberg, C. (2005). Leadership skills and wages. *Journal of Labor Economics, 23,* 395-436.

Lee, M. J., Coburn, T., & Partridge, R. (1983). The influence of team structure in determining leadership function in association football. *Journal of Sport Behavior, 6,* 59-66.

Libby, M., Rosen, M., & Sedonaen, M. (2005). Building youth-adult partnerships for community-change: Lessons from the Youth Leadership Institute. *Journal of Community Psychology, 33,* 111-120.

Loughead, T. M., & Hardy, J. (2005). An examination of coach and peer leader behaviors in sport. *Psychology of Sport and Exercise, 6*, 303-312.

Loughead, T. M., Hardy, J., & Eys, M. A. (2006). The nature of athlete leadership. *Journal of Sport Behavior, 29*, 142-158.

MacNeil, C. A. (2006). Bridging generations: Applying "adult" leadership theories to youth leadership. *New Directions for Youth Development, 109*, 27-43.

MacNeil, C. A., & McLean, J. (2006). Moving from "youth leadership development" to "youth governance": Learning leadership by doing leadership. *New Directions for Youth Development, 109*, 99-106.

Martinek, T., & Hellison, D. (2009). *Youth leadership in sport and physical education.* New York: Palgrave MacMillan.

Martinek, T., Schilling, T, & Hellison, D. (2006). The development of compassionate and caring leadership among adolescents. *Physical Education & Sport Pedagogy, 11*, 141-157.

Maslow, A. (1968). *Motivation and personality* (2nd edition). New York: Harper.

Matsudaira, J., & Jefferson, A. (2006). Anytown: NCCJ's youth leadership and social justice. In M. Klau, S. Oyd, & L. Luckow (Eds.), *New directions in youth leadership—Youth development* (pp. 107-115). San Franciso: Jossey-Bass.

Melnick, M. J., & Loy, J. W. (1996). The effects of formal structure on leadership recruitment: An analysis of team captaincy among New Zealand provincial rugby teams. *International Review of Sociology and Sport, 31*, 91-108.

Moran, M. M., & Weiss, M. R. (2006). Peer leadership in sport: Links with friendship, peer acceptance, psychological characteristics, and athletic ability. *Journal of Applied Sport Psychology, 18*, 97-113.

Northouse, P. G. (2010). *Leadership: Theory and practice.* (Fifth edition). Thousand Oaks, CA: Sage.

Oakland, T., Falkenberg, B. A., & Oakland, C. (1996). Assessment of leadership in children, youth, and adults. *Gifted Child Quarterly, 40*, 138-146.

Pease, D. G., & Zhang, J. J. (2002). Predictors of preadolescent athletic leadership behaviors as related to level of play. *International Sports Journal, 6*(1), 92-106.

Rees, C. R. (1983). Instrumental and expressive leadership in team sports: A test of leadership role differentiation theory. *Journal of Sport Behavior, 6*, 17-27.

Rees, C. R., & Segal, M. W. (1984). Role differentiation in groups: The relationship between instrumental and expressive leadership. *Small Group Behavior, 15*, 109-123.

Rowold, J. (2006). Transformational and transactional leadership in the martial arts. *Journal of Applied Sport Psychology, 18*, 312-325.

Schneider, B., Ehrhart, K. H., & Ehrhart, M. G. (2002). Understanding high school student leaders: II. Peer nominations of leaders and their correlates. *Leadership Quarterly, 13*, 275-299.

Schonfeld, A. (2008). Leadership development in athletes and coaches. In A. M. Lane (Ed.), *Sport and exercise psychology: Topics in applied psychology* (pp. 153-169). London: Hodder Education Group.

Smoll, F. L., & Smith, R. E. (1989). Leadership behaviors in sport: A theoretical model and research paradigm. *Journal of Applied Social Psychology, 19,* 1522-1551.

Steinberg, L. (2001). We know some things: Parent-adolescent relationships in retrospect and prospect. *Journal of Adolescence, 11,* 1-19.

Steinberg, L., Blatt-Eisengart, I., & Cauffman, E. (2006). Patterns of competence and adjustment among adolescents from authoritative, authoritarian, indulgent, and neglectful homes: A replication in a sample of serious juvenile offenders. *Journal of Research on Adolescence, 16,* 47-58.

Todd, S. Y., & Kent, A. (2004). Perceptions of the role differentiation behaviors of ideal peer leaders: A study of adolescent athletes. *International Sports Journal, 8,* 105-118.

Tropp, K. J., & Landers, D. M. (1979). Team interaction and the emergence of leadership and interpersonal attraction in field hockey. *Journal of Sport Psychology, 1,* 228-240.

van Linden, J. A., & Fertman, C. I. (1998). *Youth leadership.* San Francisco: Jossey-Bass.

Vincer, D. J., Baker, A. M., Loughead, T. M., & Monroe-Chandler, K. J. (2007). The role of athlete leadership in dyadic team sports. *Journal of Sport & Exercise Psychology, s209.*

Voelker, D. K., Gould, D., & Crawford, M. J. (2011). Understanding the experience of high school sport captains. *The Sport Psychologist, 25,* 47-66.

Ward, P. J., & Ellis, G. D. (2008). Characteristics of youth leadership influence adolescent peers to follow. *Journal of Park & Recreation Administration, 26,* 78-94.

Weese, J. (1983). *Peer rating and observable leadership behavior: The determinants of leadership emergence within high school baseball teams.* Unpublished master's thesis, University of Windsor, Windsor, Ontario.

Wright, A., & Côté, J. (2003). A retrospective analysis of leadership development through sport. *The Sport Psychologist, 17,* 268-291.

Yukelson, D., Weinberg, R., Richardson, P., & Jackson, A. (1983). Interpersonal attraction and leadership within collegiate sport teams. *Journal of Sport Behavior, 6,* 28-36.

Zacharatos, A., Barling, J., & Kelloway, E. K. (2000). Development and effects of transformational leadership in adolescents. *Leadership Quarterly, 11,* 211-226.

Youth Sports: What Counts as "Positive Development"?

Jay Coakley

"**S**port contributes to positive development." Worldwide, few people disagree with or qualify this statement about sport and development, regardless of whether it is applied to individuals, communities, or societies. The seldom-questioned link between sport and development is grounded in the dual assumption that sport has a fundamental essense that transcends time and place, and that sport is inherently good and pure, unlike most other activities.

The effect of this dual assumption is significant. It leads people at all levels of power to make wide-ranging policy decisions that allocate public and private resources to sports and sport programs. Similarly, it influences parental, peer, and personal decisions about sport participation and general support for local and national sport programs and teams.

At the same time, this dual assumption discourages scholars across disciplines, and especially in social sciences, from doing critical research and developing theories to inform policy makers and program managers about the conditions under which sports are most and least likely to produce outcomes that match popular assumptions. Scholars who have studied sport by asking critical questions and developing theories that do not match popular beliefs have traditionally been marginalized in their disciplines because their research and theorizing have not been taken seriously by colleagues, university administrators, or public policy makers. For example, there are fewer than a half dozen sociologists at major universities in the United States that declare the sociology of sport as a primary research area; grants to study sports are almost nonexistent; and status in sociology goes to those in traditional interest areas, such as demography, deviance and social control, race and ethnicity, family, education, work and organizations, health, community, and social stratification.

Although research on sports has increased in recent years, nearly all decision-making related to sport continues to be based on unquestioned and unexamined beliefs bolstered by wishful thinking and the personal testimonials of current and former athletes who idealize sport and sport experiences. This view is especially apparent when cities prepare bids to host sport mega-events. Local leaders give unqualified endorsements of the assumed developmental benefits of sports and highly visible former athletes tell local voters that sport participation rescued them from boredom or deviance and guided them into productive adulthood. Over time, these beliefs and testimonials are woven into the dominant everyday narratives in many cultures, making it difficult to seek support for doing critical research, developing theory, and making the argument that sport policies, programs, and personal decisions should be informed by systematic evidence.

In this chapter I focus mostly on issues of personal development and youth sports, although I will suggest that developmental issues in youth sports extend into the realm of community and civic engagement.

YOUTH SPORTS ACCORDING TO SPORT EVANGELISTS

The beliefs, wishful thinking, and personal testimonials that often influence sport-related policies, programs, and personal decisions are widely publicized and promoted by people who are best described as "sport evangelists" (Giulianotti, 2004). These people view sport as a site for many forms of development as well as remediation in cases when individuals need special socialization experiences to reduce their nonconforming or delinquent actions. For some sport evangelists, sport is presented as a perfect tool for avoiding or solving nearly all problems and improving the overall quality of life for individuals and society alike.

The claims of sport evangelists are many, but in the case of youth sports they can be grouped into two major categories: personal development and reforming "at-risk" populations (Coalter, 2007). They claim that the development of young people is promoted through sport participation because it

- enhances physical skills;

- improves health and fitness;

- increases self-esteem;

- builds character in the form of discipline, teamwork, and responsibility;

- fosters educational achievement; and

- creates a basis for future occupational success (Coalter, 2007; Donnelly, Darnell, Wells, & Coakley, 2007).

This claim that sport participation leads to positive character development is based on the assumption that for young people, sport has a *fertilizer effect*—that is, if you apply it to their lives, their character (and health) will bloom in socially desirable ways (see http://www.livestrong.com/article/136633-youth-sports-benefits/ for statements based on an assumed fertilizer effect; these statements are so common that they are used in everything from bids to host the Olympic Games to parent-teacher discussions of sports in elementary schools).

Similarly, sport evangelists claim that sport participation reforms "at-risk" young people, making them less likely to abuse drugs or engage in delinquent, criminal, or violent actions because sport

- structures their lives in constructive ways;
- takes them off the streets and puts them into controlled activities and environments;
- teaches them the importance of rules and discipline; and
- provides adult guidance and role models for positive development (Donnelly, Darnell, Wells, & Coakley, 2007; Hartmann, 2003; Hartmann & Depro, 2006).

This claim that sport participation reforms young people classified "at-risk" is based on the assumption that sport has a *car wash effect*—that is, participation cleanses their character and washes away problems so they look acceptable in mainstream society.

These claims about sport often take on the characteristics of ideology because they express and shape widely shared visions of what could and should be in the world. Like ideology, they also resist change because they are linked with emotions, identities, and larger interpretive frameworks for many people. Over the past century many men in policy-making positions have used these claims as a basis for their program and funding decisions at local and national levels. As a result, they seldom raise questions about the organization and culture of various sports, nor do they pay much attention to the conditions under which sport participation occurs.

STUDYING SPORT AND PERSONAL DEVELOPMENT

Taken as a whole and evaluated in terms of methodological quality, research findings have led scholars in the sociology of sport and other sport sciences to conclude that the relationship between sport and personal development is contingent. This conclusion means that, by itself, the act of playing a sport leads to no regularly identifiable pattern of development or specific developmental outcomes. Instead, developmental outcomes are related to and dependent on combinations of factors; among these are

- type of sport played;
- orientations and actions of peers, parents, coaches, and program administrators;
- the culture and norms associated with that sport;

- socially significant characteristics of those who play sport;

- material and cultural contexts under which participation occurs;

- meanings given to sport and personal sport experiences;

- social relationships formed in connection with sport participation;

- the ways that sport and sport experiences are integrated into a person's life; and

- re-definitions of sport experiences that become relevant at particular points in time and life course (see Côté & Fraser-Thomas, 2007; Donnelly, 2007; Miller, Melnick, Barnes, Farrell, & Sabo, 2005; Petitpas, Cornelius, & van Raalte, 2008; Trulson, 1986).

This conclusion that the sport-development relationship is contingent does not mean that playing sport is irrelevant in the lives of young people (Coalter, 2007; Holt, 2008). But it does mean that the influence of playing sport varies greatly depending on the cultural, situational, and relational contexts in which it occurs. In more specific terms, my review of research on socialization and sport has led me to conclude that sport participation is associated with positive socialization experiences when it expands or diversifies a person's identities, relationships, and experiences, especially beyond sporting contexts. Conversely, sport participation is associated with negative socialization experiences when it constricts or limits a person's identities, relationships, and experiences (Coakley, 2010). Those of us who have done this research now describe sport as a site at which developmental processes may occur, but sport is not a cause of particular developmental outcomes (Coalter).

Researchers interested in the developmental influence of sport participation on young people labeled "at risk" have reported findings that are consistent with general research findings on sport and personal development. Nevertheless, these findings emphasize that positive outcomes require that young people play sport under conditions where they are physically safe, personally valued, morally and economically supported, personally and politically empowered, and hopeful about the future (Martinek & Hellison, 1997).

Researchers also have suggested that sport participation is most likely to decrease the incidence of aggression and violence among young people when coaches are trained to teach them an explicit philosophy of nonviolence, respect for self and others, the importance of fitness and self-control as a part of overall development, confidence in physical skills, and a sense of responsibility to self and others (Trulson, 1986). Without these things being systematically taught, playing sports either has no effect or it increases aggression and the likelihood of violent actions.

After conducting a comprehensive review of methodologically sound research on sport and development, Fred Coalter (2007), a leisure studies scholar at the University of Stirling (UK), noted that positive developmental outcomes are most likely in what he described as *Sport Plus* programs and *Plus Sport* programs, each of which are explained below.

Sport Plus programs emphasize traditional sport development objectives such as increasing participation and building sport skills, but they are organized so that participants learn information and strategies for effectively dealing with challenges faced in their everyday lives. For example, a youth sport football program in Uganda may include carefully planned strategies to teach young people about HIV and AIDS prevention.

Plus Sport programs, on the other hand, involve existing educational or community organizations that use sport to attract, retain, and motivate young people in activities designed to build their personal resources or to provide them access to organizational or community resources; most often, the targeted participants in *Plus Sport* programs are young men. For example, a minister at a local church where there are weekly youth meetings may decide to organize and manage a sport program for young people to attract participants and create peer pressure to attend the weekly meetings.

In these two examples, sport serves as a site at which there are planned developmental experiences or intentionally facilitated social processes designed to promote relationships and actions unrelated to sport. In both cases, sport is part of a planned strategy to produce positive developmental outcomes.

DEFINITIONS OF POSITIVE DEVELOPMENT

Our understanding of sport and development is complicated by varying definitions of *positive development*. Researchers during the 1960s and 1970s often investigated the possible relationship between sport participation and attitudes and actions related to social and community issues (McPherson, 1981; Sage, 1980). Many scholars in the sociology of sport at that time defined positive development in terms of a person's civic engagement and support for civil rights and social justice; those who were uninvolved in the community and lacked concerns about civil rights and social justice were perceived as "in need of further development."

At the same time, there was general consensus among people in North America, where much of this research was done, that young people were a community resource and community programs were needed to foster their development. In this context, youth sport was seen as providing (mostly) boys and young men with the experiences and learning needed to become productive citizens with vested interests in maintaining community vitality and growth.

This community-based conception of development began to fade during the 1980s as neoliberal ideology increasingly informed economic and political policy as well as cultural attitudes and everyday forms of social organization (Coakley, 2009, 2010). This ideology highlights individualism, individual responsibility, the positive functions of economic inequality, and the moral necessity of individual self-interest as the primary source of motivation and guide for personal decisions in all institutional spheres, especially the economy.

Neoliberal ideology is grounded in the assumption that the moral and economic choices of individuals are the foundation for social order and overall quality of life. Community, society, public interest, and the common good are viewed as fabrications designed to support government entitlements and the ideological foundation of modern welfare states. In its political manifestations, neoliberalism was based on the belief that it was important to destroy all collectives because they did not give priority to individual responsibility and self-interest (Bourdieu, 1998).

Margaret Thatcher, England's Prime Minister during the 1980s, provided a classic neoliberal statement in a 1987 *Women's Own* magazine interview when she said, "...there is no such thing as society. There are individual men and women, and there are families" (Keay, 1987). This view of the world aligned her closely with then U.S. president Ronald Reagan (1980-1988), whose commitment to neoliberal policy was voiced in his first inaugual address (January 20, 1981) with his statement that "government is not the solution; government is the problem" (http://www.youtube.com/watch?v=IleiqUDYpFQ).

These two world leaders were among many powerful people worldwide who supported neoliberal ideology as the basis for economic and political policies and the foundation for cultural priorities and social organization. As this ideology was increasingly embraced, at least in narrative form, by many people in post-industrial societies, youth sport programs that had been publicly funded and defined as necessary community programs were privatized and funded by parents concerned with the personal development of their children. The idea that youth sport created citizens to maintain community vitality and growth began to fade as people increasingly saw youth sports as necessary for the future success of individual participants.

Along with this cultural shift, youth sports that previously were neighborhood based and publicly supported were eliminated or trimmed back as community resources became scarce as a result of policies that lowered taxes. In their place, people with personal resources created private, non-profit, or commercial entities organized mostly through the efforts of parents, youth sport entrepreneurs, and sport-oriented people in the social problems industry. Through the 1980s and 1990s, youth sport rapidly morphed into district, state, regional, and even national programs in which club/competitive/travel teams played extended schedules that usually were dedicated to achieving win-loss records to qualify them for high profile tournaments.

The narratives used to rationalize the parental commitment and family resources needed to sustain these new forms of youth sports emphasized developmental payoffs for the individual young people who participated in them. Positive development in many of these programs came to be defined almost exclusively in terms of individual growth and increased personal advantage in the form of status, academic success, scholarships to reputable high schools and colleges, and future material success on and off the playing field.

Sports for young people from low-income and at-risk populations became increasingly dependent on government and corporate grants and other forms of "soft" money that were not regular "line items" in community budgets. Funding required formal grant requests, and these often came from people in "the social problems industry"—a high growth industry as privatization occurred during the 1980s and 1990s. The narratives at the core of most grant proposals emphasized that youth sports would reduce character deficits in children perceived as potential threats to the status quo. For example, when the Midnight Basketball League was founded in Glenarden, Maryland, in 1986, it was noted in *Sports Illustrated* that the program would take "Black inner-city males off the streets by keeping them in the gym during … the hours when they would be most likely to get into trouble" (Bessone, 1991, p. 21). Subsequent grant requests for midnight basketball-like youth sports highlighted this narrative and often were linked with anti-crime programs and goals (see Chapter 6 in this book). Youth sports, as presented in these grant proposals were described as a means to control young people, especially Black, inner-city males—a population defined by corporate and government funders as an "urban other" in need of external policing (Hartmann & Depro, 2006; Pitter & Andrews, 1997).

Positive development in these grant requests was not defined as commitment to social justice, rebuilding strong community-based social institutions, reestablishing the resource base of the communities where these young people lived, or politicizing and empowering young people to be effective change agents on behalf of their communities. Instead, it was defined in terms of increasing individual self-esteem so that young people would have the desire to pull themselves up by their athletic shoelaces and escape from the communities where they had been labeled "at-risk." The goal of these programs was to "fix" the character of young people, while also providing the adult supervision and structure that would control them and eliminate their actions that might disrupt the social order (Hartmann, 2001, 2003, 2008).

The narratives supporting youth sports in the 1980s through the present day define positive development in terms of individual characteristics, but they have usually been mediated by the social class of the young people to whom they have been applied (Coakley, 2002). For example, programs for young people from families with higher-than-average incomes have consistently been described with narratives that emphasize building the strengths of the participants so they can take advantage of the relatively privileged status they already possess. The narratives were organized around the idea that these privileged young people needed confidence and opportunities to maximize their future success in life, especially as leaders in competitive work environments. At the same time, programs for young people from families with lower-than-average incomes have consistently been described by narratives that focus on eliminating character defects and making participants less likely to cause trouble. The narratives were organized around the need for social control and deficit reduction in the lives of these young people.

All these narratives framed youth sports around basic neoliberal assumptions, including the following (see Coakley, 2002):

- Change is grounded in maximizing individual freedom and choice (as opposed to maximizing social justice and equality).

- Progress is best measured in terms of individual achievement (as opposed to community development and sustainability).

- Problems are best solved through personal actions (as opposed to empowering neighborhoods and communities).

- Developmental programs should focus on increasing self-esteem (as opposed to empowering young people and community organizations to instigate structural and ideological transformation).

- Deviance and violence among young people are controlled by enforcing rules and promoting individual responsibility and accountability (as opposed to laws demanding corporate responsibility and accountability).

- Violence is associated with young people, especially those in gangs (as opposed to the corporate executives and political officials who make and enforce policies that have devastatingly violent consequences for low income, minority communities).

In line with this ideology, social and community problems were seen by many people to be results of individual irresponsibility and poor choices. At the same time, local governments became increasingly irrelevant as sponsors of youth sports. New club sports and travel teams were organized by parents or youth sport entrepreneurs who catered to young people whose parents had the resources to pay significant annual fees and drive their children long distances so they could participate on teams with the best coaches and develop elite skills that would lead to future rewards.

The growing emphasis on neoliberal ideas in North America and Western Europe often pressured parents to sponsor and support their children's participation and success in youth sports, regardless of cost and convenience. As publicly supported programs faded away, and parents became the sole source of support for a child's sport participation, parental moral worth was linked with the participation and success of their children in highly valued and visible programs (Coakley, 2009, 2010). Young athletes in neoliberal societies represented their families rather than their neighborhoods or communities. As a result, parents took much more seriously their roles as coaches, mentors, advocates, managers, and agents of their children's sport "careers." Parents were credited or criticized depending on the quality of those careers. For example, when the parents of United States gymnast Shawn Johnson made major financial sacrifices to continue supporting Shawn's Olympic gymnastic dreams, NBC commentators identified them as ideal parents to everyone viewing the 2008 Olympic Games in the United States.

During the 2008 and 2010 Olympic Games in Beijing and Vancouver, US media coverage often focused on athletes' parents. Commentators and journalists praised their dedication and willingness to subordinate their lives for the sake of their children's quests for sport achievements. Even Johnson & Johnson, a major sponsor of the US-NBC Olympic coverage, created a special advertising campaign called "Thanks, Mom" to remind everyone that "Behind every Olympic champion is a mom [who provides] love and care…to help their children achieve their goals" (see http://www.jnj.com/connect/NewsArchive/all-news-archive/20080729_113000 for the descriptions of the campaign and the families it highlighted). Olympic medals were won by sons and daughters, but they became moral worth merit badges for the moral worth of mothers and fathers who worked and sacrificed to support their children's training.

This cultural shift was based on the neoliberal notions that *there is no society, public programs are a problem,* and *positive development is exclusively an individual and family matter.* As these notions were increasingly accepted, the links between young people who play sports and their communities were increasingly weakened.

Although this observation-based hypothesis must be tested by methodologically rigorous research, it appears that as young people become increasingly skilled in a sport and compete at higher levels, they are viewed as creations of their parents with little or no reference to or awareness of their communities. When this focus on family occurs in neoliberal societies, youth sport participation does not lead young people to be integrated into their local communities or identify as citizens with vested interests in neighborhood and community. Instead, they often feel indebted to their parents and fear not being able to thank them enough through their performances and achievements. Positive development is now a matter of personal achievement and success and an indication of parental moral worth. In the United States, many people with children see an expensive trip to a national championship tournament hosted for profit at Disney World as unquestioned proof of positive development.

As I've assessed the potential merit of this hypothesis, I've been struck by public responses to the notable achievements of young athletes as they occurred between the mid-1980s and today (Opdyke, 2007). For example, in 1997, Earl Woods earned more money in 1997 telling people how he created his son than Tiger Woods made playing golf and winning the Masters in April of that year. The book, *Training a Tiger: A Father's Guide to Raising a Winner in Both Golf and Life* (1997) made Earl Woods a best-selling author. Like most parents of age group champions, he was seen as the raison d'être of his son's success, and people wanted to know how he did it. Consistent with neoliberal logic, personal development in and beyond youth sports was defined in terms of the individual and family, not the community.

EXCEPTIONS TO THE RULE AND A CALL FOR RESEARCH

Although sport evangelists regularly claim that sport creates social capital and builds communities, the hypothesis offered in this paper is that contemporary youth sports may do the opposite. When youth sports are supported exclusively with fees paid by parents who seek the most competitive and highly-regarded programs and coaches for their children, it is likely that the sport programs are organized in ways that characteristically separate young people from community-based contexts and forms of identification. The shift away from neighborhood teams for the sake of competitive excellence, the shift from public to private programs due to community resource shortages, the shift from recreational to performance-based goals in youth programs, and cultural shifts making parental moral worth dependent on the personal achievements of their children convert youth sport into a site for positive development having little to do with community and community engagement.

To the extent that youth sport participation depends on socio-economic status (SES), the social capital formed in connection with sports is characterized by exclusive forms of *bonding* rather than inclusive forms of *bridging* among people. Sport connects people who are similar to one another in terms of SES rather than bridging differences and connecting people who are unlike one another (Putnam, 2000; Putnam & Goss, 2002). This process raises questions that beg future research. For example, when youth sport programs are sponsored by local neighborhood and community organizations and are strategically linked with larger projects that are socially inclusive and designed to empower people to be meaningfully engaged in decision-making that affects their own lives and neighborhoods, do they inspire forms of community identification that lead to future forms of engaged citizenship? Similarly, when youth sport participation is sponsored exclusively by parents and occurs in privatized programs under the supervision of hired coaches with no links to the local community, does it undermine the forms of community identification that are associated with engaged citizenship in the future?

The sense-making framework presented in this paper requires systematic examination before it can be counted as knowledge in the sociology of sport. Unlike the claims of sport evangelists, this framework is presented as interrelated hypotheses, not assumed and unquestioned truths.

REFERENCES

Bessone, T. L. (1991). Welcome to night court. *Sports Illustrated 12*, 20-21.

Bourdieu, P. (1998). The essence of neoliberalism (trans. by Jeremy J. Shapiro). *Le Monde diplomatique*. December. Retrieved from http://mondediplo.com/1998/12/08bourdieu

Coakley, J. (2002). Using sports to control deviance and violence among youths: Let's be critical and cautious. In M. Gatz, M. A. Messner, & S. J. Ball-Rokeach (Eds.), *Paradoxes of youth and sport* (pp. 13-30). Albany, NY: State University of New York Press.

Coakley, J. (2009). The good father: Parental expectations and youth sports. In K. Tess (Ed.), *Fathering through sport and leisure* (pp. 40-50). New York: Routledge.

Coakley, J. (2010). The 'logic' of specialization: Using children for adult purposes. *Journal of Physical Education, Recreation and Dance 81*(7), 16-18, 25.

Coalter, F. (2007). *A wider social role for sport: Who's keeping score.* London: Routledge.

Côté, J., & Fraser-Thomas, J. L. (2007). Youth involvement in sport. In P. R. E. Crocker (Ed.), *Introduction to sport psychology: A Canadian perspective* (pp. 266–294). Toronto: Pearson Prentice Hall.

Donnelly, P., Darnell, S., Wells, S., & Coakley, J. (2007). The use of sport to foster child and youth development and education. In *Literature reviews on sport for development and peace* (pp. 7-47). Toronto, Ontario: University of Toronto, Faculty of Physical Education and Health.

Giulianotti, R. (2004). Human rights, globalization and sentimental education: The case of sport. *Sport in Society 7,* 355-369.

Hartmann, D. (2001). Notes on midnight basketball and the cultural politics of recreation, race, and at-risk urban youth. *Journal of Sport and Social Issues, 25,* 339–371.

Hartmann, D. (2003). Theorizing sport as social intervention: A view from the grassroots. *Quest 55,* 118–140.

Hartmann, D. (2008). High school sports participation and educational attainment: Recognizing, assessing, and utilizing the relationship. Report to the LA84 Foundation. Retrieved from http://www.la84foundation.org/3ce/HighSchoolSportsParticipation.pdf

Hartmann, D., & Depro, B. (2006). Rethinking sports-based community crime prevention: A preliminary analysis of the relationship between midnight basketball and urban crime rates. *Journal of Sport and Social Issues, 30,* 180–196.

Holt, N. L. (Ed.). (2008). *Positive youth development through sport.* Milton Park/New York: Routledge.

Keay, D. (1987). Aids, education and the year 2000. *Women's Own.* October 31, 8-10.

Martinek, T. J., & Hellison, D. R. (1997). Fostering resiliency in underserved youth through physical activity. *Quest, 49,* 34-49.

McPherson, B. D. (1981). Socialization into and through sport. In G. Luschen & G. H. Sage (Eds.), *Handbook of social science of sport* (pp. 246-273). Champaign, IL: Stipes.

Miller, K. E., Melnick, M. J., Barnes, G. M., Farrell, M. P., & Sabo, D. 2005. Untangling the links among athletic involvement, gender, race, and adolescent academic outcomes. *Sociology of Sport Journal 22,* 178–193.

Opdyke, J. (2007). Love and money: When a kid's game becomes your life. *Wall Street Journal Online,* May 6. Retrieved from http://online.wsj.com/article/SB117840716307293503.html

Petitpas, A. J., Cornelius, A., & van Raalte, J. (2008). Youth development through sport: It's all about relationships. In N. L. Holt (Ed.), *Positive youth development through sport* (pp. 61-70). New York: Routledge.

Pitter, R., & Andrews, D. L. (1997). Serving America's underserved: Reflections on sport and recreation in an emerging social problems industry. *Quest, 49,* 85-99.

Putnam, R. (2000). *Bowling alone: Collapse and revival of American community.* New York: Simon & Schuster.

Putnam, R., & Goss, K. A. (2002) Introduction. In R. Putnam (Ed.), *Democracies in flux: The evolution of social capital in contemporary society* (pp. 1–19). Oxford: Oxford University Press.

Sage, G. H. (1980). Socialization and sport. In G. H. Sage (Ed.), *Sport and American society* (pp. 133-142). Boston, MA.: Addison-Wesley.

Trulson, M. E. (1986). Martial arts training: A novel ``cure" for juvenile delinquency. *Human Relations, 39,* 1131-1140.

Woods, E. (1997). *Training a Tiger: A father's guide to raising a winner in both golf and life.* New York: William Morrow.

AUTHOR'S NOTE

A revised and extended version of this paper was previously published with the same title in the *Journal of Sport and Social Issues, 35*(3), 306-324.

Revelation at the Superdome: Race, Class, and Politics in Post-Katrina America

Michael D. Giardina and C. L. Cole

The Hurricane Katrina disaster... revealed a vulnerable and destitute segment of the nation's citizenry that conservatives not only refused to see, but had spent the better part of two decades demonizing.
—Henry A. Giroux, 2007

A racially divided, disorganized... falling-apart-at-the-seems New Orleans: this is George W. Bush and Karl Rove's gift to America.
—Norman K. Denzin, 2005

PROEM

It's the images that strike you first: The lifeless body of a fellow citizen cast off to the side of a street, a starving dog gnawing at a bloody limb. A mother gripping onto her infant daughter at the New Orleans Convention Center, begging—*pleading*—for someone, anyone, to whisk them away from their uncertain future. An elderly man in a wheelchair, clinging to his last shards of breath. A news reporter breaking down into frustrated tears on national television. People—fellow human beings—rummaging in garbage cans or blown-out storefronts for food because FEMA had yet to realize that New Orleans was, in fact, a city located in the United States.[i] The collapse of civil society: live and in unliving color.

The mood is somber. Reflective. Harsh. Sad. Depressing. Frustrating. A collision of emotions ready to explode. Kim Segal, a segment producer at CNN caught in New Orleans (henceforth the colloquial NOLA), recalls the scene unfolding through her journalistic eyes: "It was chaos. There was nobody there, nobody in charge. And there was nobody giving even water. The children, you should see them—they're all just in tears. There are sick people. We saw... people who are dying in front of you." A photojournalist from NBC concurs, declaring that a Third World country he once covered was in much better shape than the ramshackle conditions downtown. CNN's Sanjay Gupta, a medical doctor by trade, relays the shocking brute force of horror in one of NOLA's hospitals:

> [W]hen patients die in the hospital, there is no place to put them, so they're in the stairwells. It is one of the most unbelievable situations I've seen as a doctor, certainly as a journalist as well. There is no electricity. There is no water. There's [sic] over 200 patients still here remaining ("A big disconnect in New Orleans," 2005).

And hardened journalists such as CNN's Anderson Cooper and FOX's Sheppard Smith break down numerous times during live shots, the former snapping viciously at U.S. Senator Mary Landrieu (D-LA) during an on-air interview,[ii] the latter barking unexpectedly at his colleagues for not "getting" what he was physically witnessing and psychologically experiencing as they sat back in the comfort of their broadcast studio.

As the days turned to weeks, and the situation on the ground turned from atrocious to horrific to absurd, satirical headlines such as "Iraq to Deploy Troops in Louisiana, Mississippi"—which appeared in *Flak Magazine* and included such hard-hitting musings as "The Iraqi National Assembly, in an amazing display of solidarity between Kurds, Shiites, and Sunnis, unanimously voted to send 10,000 of its troops into America" and "The victims of the flood will greet [them] as liberators"—seemed almost plausible in the wikiality of Bush World (see Scott, 2006).[iii]

Contextualizing Katrina

Hurricane Katrina and the overwhelming flooding that followed has been called the most devastating natural disaster in recent US history, as well as arguably its most devastating bureaucratic disaster. For most Americans, it was television (and later video available online at sites such as YouTube) that drew attention to the crisis with shocking footage—primarily from New Orleans—of people suffering in nightmarish conditions. Viewers watched live as more than 20,000 people, many from New Orleans's historically Black, working-class Ninth Ward, were stranded—in some cases abandoned—without food, water, or sanitation; witnessed people who were sick and dying; saw homes and lives literally being destroyed in real time: the scene could very well have mirrored that of conditions in Baghdad, Kabul, or Darfur. With the massive structure of the Louisiana Superdome (home to the New Orleans Saints of the National Football League) as a soaring architectural backdrop, the world watched as one of the most vulnerable populations in this country—poor urban Blacks—were left without even the crudest necessities of life.

Most provocatively, the image of the Black mother and child, photographed in stark relief against the looming Superdome, figured prominently in the cable media's 24/7 live coverage. Indeed, the Superdome became the national media's reproductive stage for the very violences (racism, poverty, and federal neglect) it is typically deployed to conceal on any given Sunday. Some commentators appealed to discourses already in place to attempt to make sense of the scene: The repetition of the traumatized mother and child—the Black mother, helpless to do anything other than comfort her hungry infant (an image long-used by international aid organizations soliciting donations for Third World countries)—stood in for the poor Black community in distress. But the narrative of suffering was countered by a mediated spectacle of upheaval signaled by the apparent breakdown of law and order in and around the Superdome. A long familiar trope in the US, the always-already patholo-gized bodies of Black men, were used to signal "incomprehensible crimes." Some commentators repeated and then repeated again stories about "looters" who were stealing guns, alcohol, sneakers, athletic wear, and electronics (not to mention groceries, which figured prominently in one racialized storyline[iv]). Other commentators claimed that the city was under siege by "roving gangs" who were shooting at rescue helicopters, hospital supply trucks, and workers trying to evacuate the sick in hospitals. And still others repeated stories of children being raped in the Superdome, along with other atrocities normally reserved for dystopian horror movies. To listen to a medley of cable news reports, a *Mad Max*-meets-*New Jack City* shroud had become draped over a dark, twisted, evil city languishing in chaos. Along this line, and on his highly rated Fox News Channel spinfest, *The O'Reilly Factor,* host Bill O'Reilly (2005) blatantly inferred that the majority of NOLA's Katrina vic-tims—particularly those trapped in the Superdome—were uneducated, poor, drug addicts who lived a "Gangsta" lifestyle akin to that of the *Grand Theft Auto* video game world:

> Every American kid should be required to watch videotape of the poor in New Orleans and see how they suffered, because they couldn't get out of town. And then, every teacher should tell the students, "If you refuse to learn, if you refuse to work hard, if you become addicted, if you live a gangsta-life, you will be poor and powerless just like many of those in New Orleans."

And all of it was a pack of lies. As *Washington Post* columnist, Eugene Robinson (2005), pointed out, the prevailing mediated pedagogy of urban destruction dominating the Katrina landscape just wasn't entirely true in an empirical reality:

> I got there five days after the deluge, when the story, as the whole world understood it, was one of *Mad Max* depravity and violence. Hoodlums were raping and pillaging, I just "knew"—even shooting at rescue helicopters trying to take hospital patients to safety. So it was a surprise when I rolled into the center of the city, with all my foreign-correspondent antennae bristling, and found the place as quiet as a tomb. The next day I drove into the French Quarter and was struck by how pristine St. Louis Cathedral looked, almost like the castle at Disney World. I got out of the car and walked around the whole area, and I wrote in my notebook that except for the absence of tourists, it could have been just an ordinary Sunday morning in the Big Easy. Then I got back into the car, and on the radio a caller was breathlessly reporting that, as she spoke, a group of policemen were "pinned down" by snipers at the cathedral. I was right there; nobody was sniping at anybody. But the reigning narrative was *Mad Max,* not Magic Kingdom. Thanks to radio, television and the Internet, everyone "knew" things that just weren't true (p. A23).

However, as Ezra Klein (2005) reminds us, it isn't enough to simply point out that incendiary news coverage was just spotty work done by lazy or inept reporters. He stated:

> Those horror stories, now proved [mostly] untrue, were not simply mistaken, they were racist. From the widely reported but never confirmed rapes in the Superdome all the way to the false accounts of sniped rescue workers and roving gangs of looting blacks, Katrina exposed a latent cultural racism that many Americans assumed had vanished. These were tropes more suited to the Deep South of the 1800s than the cable networks of the 21st century.

So let's cut to the chase: as Gov. Howard Dean (2005), Chairman of the Democratic National Committee, stated in his address to the National Baptist Convention of America on the impact of Katrina, "We must… come to terms with the ugly truth that skin color, age, and economics played a deadly role in who survived and who did not" (Dean, quoted in Kalette, 2005)[v] William Jelani Cobb (2005) put it in more direct language: "Filter through the spin and you will meet a brutal truth: there are people who have died and people who are dying in Louisiana because they are black and they are poor" (n.p.). Correlatively, Mark Anthony Neal (2005) was correct in his observation that, while rap star Kanye West's nationally televised pronouncement that "George W. Bush doesn't care about black people" is accurate to a degree, it is a sentiment that we must complicate: "The initially tepid and lazy response to Katrina in New Orleans wasn't *just* a product of racist neglect, [but] it was *also* the product of the devaluation of whole communities because they didn't posses political capital" (n.p.). His strong words are echoed by former U.S. Senator and Ambassador to New Zealand, Carol Moseley-Braun (D-IL), who spoke out about the general neglect of poor and underprivileged citizens in New Orleans: "I think it's a sin of omission more than anything. They don't see poor people. They don't even think about them, they don't plan for them. How do you tell people to evacuate and then turn your back on those who don't have money for cab fare or who don't have cars?"[vi] On this point, Cobb's words again ring true: "The truth is that neglect is the racial default setting—which is why those people were left behind in the city literally and metaphorically."

Yet despite the federal neglect and disastrous bureaucratic rescue attempts by FEMA, an outpouring of charity came full-force from the American (and, indeed, world) public in droves not seen since the immediate aftermath of 9/11. How do we make sense of this apparent paradox? Perhaps it was the finely honed Madonna image that limited the impact of the criminalized looter image, as racialized pleas for help were translated into mainstream American compassion. In part, what made the Madonna-child image so powerful is both its long, political career and, given the recent coverage of the famine in Niger or the political unrest in Darfur, its immediacy in the collective imaginary of the United States. As scholars such as Christina Klein, Wendy Kozol, and Laura Briggs have illustrated, that image has figured prominently in US images of Third World poverty and hunger. Laura Briggs (2003) summarized its effects in her recent genealogy of the image:

> [The image] directs attention away from structural explanations of poverty, famine, and other disasters, including international, political, military, and economic causes... It has played a powerful role in shaping support in the US for a variety of public policy and foreign policy initiatives, from IMF loans to the globalization of an international force to US debates about the family... The visual and familial practices worked together to produce an ideology of rescue by white people of non-white people inside and outside the United States (pp. 180-181).

The prominent association of the image with the Third World can help us make sense of America's confounded puzzlement about the geopolitical context of the image. And the historic political work performed by the image helps us account for the atypical entrance of black women as mothers into the US public sphere. As well, it helps of make sense of the narrative of rescue that followed and facilitated the dramatic consumption of the event.

Already profoundly and intimately woven into the traumatized Madonna image, the narrative of rescue took its form in a national discourse of heroic *White* masculinity. White men, in military uniform, openly displaying weapons, stood in for the state as a moral actor meeting its obligations. Or, as political scientist Simon Darnell (2010) might say, the (re) development practices—in the form of rescue narratives—were predictably based on and reflective of "the construction and maintenance of hegemonic power relations and First World authority rather than international benevolence or a commitment to global social justice" (p. 71). Again with the Superdome in the background, rescuers were represented as All-American action heroes (in much the same fashion as first-responders on 9/11 or US Marines in Iraq have been portrayed). Rescues took on an extreme sport aesthetic as they appeared to be overcoming and redefining their bodily limits as they maneuvered through the wreckage, repelled from helicopters, or sped through flooded neighborhoods in powerboats.

While we don't want to dismiss the efforts of those who helped people to safety,[vii] we do want to draw attention to the way that the rescue efforts were framed to highlight a heroic White masculinity. The reader will no doubt recognize such a trope in charity, development, and aid campaigns as diverse as (Product),[RED] Charity: Water, and the United Nations Mine Action Service. In each of these instances, wealthy white men (e.g., Bill Gates, Bono, Michael Dell), upscale urbanites, or suburban nuclear families (soccer dads) respectively are deployed to both invoke a feeling of distant pity (what philosopher Hannah Arendt would term as the activation of a *politics* of pity) toward the less fortunate and recuperate a sense of faith in the neoliberal state to care for those very same individuals (see Giardina, 2009). Or to put it more simply, *white masculinity mediated the social relations between the spectators and those who were suffering.*

These masculine images quickly replaced what had begun dangerously as a threat to the American myth of colorblind plenty with a smug sense of White heroics and charitable opportunity. Most especially, sport—or, perhaps more appropriately, physicality and the site of the body—was front and center in these narratives. In one particularly striking example, framed under the guise of providing never-before-seen footage of the crisis, Discovery Channel recently opened its *SOS: Coast Guard Rescue Series* with three hours of Katrina rescues, or what it calls "close-up, you-are-there video" made possible by helmet-mounted cameras. Viewers, according to the framing by Discovery Channel, "swing through the window of a flooded house" and are there "as a desperate family reach out to embrace [the rescuer]" (Squires, 2005). And, Discovery Channel tells us, when the rescuer "climbs into the attic looking for a way to get the family onto the roof, viewers will find themselves peering into the darkness for an ax or a crowbar on anything that might help." "Viewers" coded as would-be heroic White men are helped by the Discovery Channel to overcome what was first played out as shock and even shame at the plight of Americans in poverty. This retelling of the Katrina story is symptomatic of yet another form of protecting the White public from so-called damaging media images—it is the story that will salvage White American innocence and allow for a cathartic adventure experience in place of activism to change the historical and political circumstances that led to such a crisis.

Racialized (Sporting) Bodies

The representation of Black bodies before, during, and after the hurricane hit is of particular relevance when we consider, for a moment, the Superdome during Katrina as itself a transient site for the mediation of Blackness in the United States. For a few fleeting days, the Superdome found itself openly officiating between two seemingly warring camps about 'urban' Blackness: the story of *productive* Black bodies disciplined through sport to entertain and profit privileged fans and owners, and that of *undisciplined* Black bodies that threaten the social good and burden the U.S. economy. Never mentioned was the irony that those people typically priced out of the Superdome as sport spectators were now trapped within it, being treated like dangerous animals, contained by armed National Guard troops. Indeed, the sort of taxing and finance priorities that build and maintain stadiums like the Superdome, rather than using resources for the entire public's good, are at least partially responsible for the poverty of the evacuees in the first place (more on this below).

That is to say, both public and popular disposition toward US urban centers has over the years followed a contradictory hyper-moral impulse. As Cameron McCarthy and Michael D. Giardina have argued (2005), 'urban' America has become discursively caught hanging in a liminal state between "all-out decay" and the possibility of social and economic "renewal," at various times emphasizing cold disinterest, at other times seen as the object of almost laboratory-like social experimentation and intervention. This pendulum of neglect and intervention swings, sometimes frenetically, one way or another, as the urban context continues to be viewed by bureaucratic and cultural elites through a paradigm of cultural deficit and moral underdevelopment (see, for example, CNN's recent multi-part exposé "CNN Presents: Black in America," which received widespread criticism despite its laudable efforts). Since the high point of the Civil Rights era and its culminating fruition in the ameliorative social programs of the Great Society/War on Poverty conceptualized under the John F. Kennedy administration in the early 1960s and put into practice by the Lyndon B. Johnson administration in the late 1960s (e.g., Head Start), the urban centers of the United States have been the target of revisionary strategies of both policy makers and policy intellectuals. This revisionary disposition has been, to give but one example, operationalized in the policies of benign neglect found during the Nixon/Carter years and the aggressive disinvestment of social programs during the Reagan/Bush era.

Up until the 1990s, continue McCarthy and Giardina, the dominant framework around which both public policy and the surplus popular social meanings were generated was the

Keynesian formula of (more or less) social welfarism. In the early 1990s, this overwhelming paradigm of Keynesianism was both rhetorically and practically overturned as the newly ordained Clinton administration sought to connect urban centers to its broad-scale global neoliberal initiatives vis-à-vis universalizing entrepreneurship. As the administration sought to spread the gospel of unfettered neoliberal capital around the world through the North American Free Trade Agreement, General Agreements on Tariffs and Trades (GATT), and the World Trade Organization, it simultaneously turned its brassy new corporatist gaze on the inner city by speaking the language of enterprise zones, self-help, and community voluntarism. The urban center was/is thus a piece of a much larger puzzle of the proliferation of new social meanings that translate the capitalist enterprise form of modern conduct to the conduct of organizations (e.g., charter schools, corporate partnerships, and voucher programs in education) and the conduct of individuals; the problems of inner-city life have become the new targets of self-management, regulation, the restraint of individual appetites, and the moral purposive voluntaristic investment of the inner-city dweller himself or herself (see Giardina & McCarthy, 2005, for more on this topic).

This governing practice we see instantiated within public policy maneuvers such as those related to so-called "Empowerment Zones" generally and the Gulf Opportunity Zone (or GO Zone; H.R. 4400) as related to Katrina-afflicted areas specifically, the latter of which portends to offer lower tax rates, expand private investment incentives, and promote regulatory relief in the hurricane-devastated region. If the neoliberal economic policies/politics that have informed empowerment zones heretofore are carried through in the "GO Zone" (which is highly likely), issues of crime and criminality will be centrally located within its make-up. Such was the language of the 1993 *Building Communities Together: Guidebook for Community-Based Strategic Planning for Empowerment Zones and Enterprise Communities,* authored by the President's [Clinton] Community Enterprise Board of the Department of Housing and Urban Development, which stated in part,

> If this program is to stabilize and reinvigorate neighborhoods, residents must be free from the fear of crime and violence. Job creation, improved housing, and enhanced service delivery are crucial in most potential empowerment zones and enterprise communities, but a commitment to the reduction of crime and violence through coordinated law enforcement is necessary to community stability, the delivery of health education, and other social services and economic development… *Unchecked violence, gun and drug trafficking, drug use, and other serious felonies will stifle investment, development and community building emphasis of the initiative* (pp. 45-46, emphasis ours).

Yet, upon closer inspection of such supposedly high-minded rhetoric, as we (2005) pointed out in our case-study analysis of the New York City/Upper Manhattan Empowerment Zone project, such (de)moralizing jingoism is eerily reminiscent of something President Reagan said in 1982;

> We must make America safe again, especially for women and elderly who face so many moments of fear… Study after study shows that most serious crimes are the work of a relatively small group of hardened criminals. Let me give you an example—subway crime in New York City. Transit police estimate that only 500 habitual criminal offenders are responsible for nearly half of the crimes in New York's subways last year… It's time to get these hardened criminals off the street and into jail… We can and must make improvements in the way our courts deal with crime… These include revising the bail system so that dangerous offenders, and especially big-time drug pushers, can be kept off our streets ("Radio address to the nation on crime and criminal justice reform," 1982).

Though writing in response to Reagan's quote above, David L. Andrews's (1993) words remain applicable to the 1993 guidebook: "Without ever referring to race or ethnicity, it is manifest that the threat to American society he vocalized was a black male inhabitant of American's anarchic urban jungles" (pp. 114-115). The outcome is that security becomes mobilized around economic stability and corporate investment opportunities: incarcerating or evicting young Black (or Latino) men becomes the naturalized, accepted—in some cases, even promoted—outcome of "cleaning up" the so-called inner city and paving the way for corporate expansionary measures (a fate we have witnessed in empowerment zones from New York to Cleveland to Los Angeles).

While New Orleans will most certainly be rebuilt (at least, from a structural point of view), does anyone expect the "new" Big Easy to be anything more than an expansion of the Time Square Lite, consumerist façade that already existed—a place where jazz music, Cajun/Creole food, and French historical inflections are reduced to banal touristic caricatures that see "neighborhood radicalism and protest as entertainment, myth, human-interest story, or a peculiar spectacle to be gazed at by a curious middle-class?" (Mele, 2000, p. 308) Of course not! If anything, the new branding dynamic sure to take place in NOLA will be "embedded in highly marketable, sanitized styles and signs of subversion, anti-authoritarianism, and experimentation that designate it as an 'alternative' space" (Cole, 2001, p. 117). As Friedman, Andrews, and Silk (2004) have contended, one of the primary results of such "consumption-based, visitor-oriented redevelopment could be in creating little more than a veneer of change and vitality within the city" in which, beneath the shiny new façade of an improved national image, "the underlying realities of urban life frequently remain unaltered" (p. 130). As "tourist bubbles" or "islands of affluence" as Judd referred to them as, these re-written, white-washed landscapes actively work to "project a reassuringly dislocated experience and perception of safety, fun, and vitality for downtown areas" (Eisinger, 2000). Sarah Vowell (2003) got it right when she said "There are few creepier moments in cultural tourism than when a site tries to rewrite its past" (p. 36).

Not only that, but if the powers-that-be have their way, *New* New Orleans certainly won't *look* much like *Old* New Orleans. Rep. Richard Baker (R-LA) admitted as much when he told the *Wall Street Journal,* "We finally cleaned up public housing in New Orleans. We couldn't do it, but God did" (quoted in Babington, 2005). Of course, by "cleaned up public housing," Rep. Baker means that he is thankful that the hurricane displaced those (largely poor, primarily Black) residents who were living in impoverished dwellings, in effect making the now-abandoned or destroyed land prime for real estate (re)development. In fact, Alphonso R. Jackson, Secretary of Housing and Urban Development, has already predicted that New Orleans will be "whiter" now that its pre-Katrina population of more than 500,000 African Americans has predictably dispersed across the country, many to Houston, Texas, and other neighboring areas.[viii]

Says Mark Krasnof, a co-founder of the Civic Center Shelter on the Louisiana-Texas border, which helped house many who were lucky to escape Katrina's wrath, "The very soul of Louisiana is now at stake… If our 'leaders' have their way this whole goddamn region will become either a toxic graveyard or a big museum where jazz, zydeco and Cajun music will still be played for tourists but the cultures that gave them life are defunct or dispersed" (quoted in David & Fontenot, 2005, p. 1). Let us not forget, as Gloria Ladson-Billings (2003) reminded us in her recent address to the American Educational Researchers Association meetings in New Orleans, that the cultural history of NOLA has *already* been white-washed numerous times over, re-narrated through capitalism's ghoulish eyes: "They sold slaves in this city. They made a tourist stop out of the place where they sold slaves!" Fighting against this trend, Glen Ford and Peter Gamble (2005) of *The Black Commentator* plead that:

> Priority must be given to the right to preserve and continue the rich and diverse cultural traditions of the city, and the social experiences of Black people that produced the culture. The second line, Mardi Gras Indians, brass bands, creative music, dance foods, language and other expressions are the "soul of the city." The rebuilding process must preserve these traditions. THE CITY MUST NOT BE CULTURALLY, ECONOMICALLY OR SOCIALLY GENTRIFIED INTO A "SOULLESS" COLLECTION OF CONDOS AND tract home NEIGHBORHOODS FOR THE RICH [formatting in original].[ix]

These diverse traditions, points out Matt Sakakeeny (2006) can be found in the fact that,

[a]s a French, Spanish, and American city, New Orleans has always maintained a significant Black population that has continuously and resourcefully created a coherent yet flexible collective identity through the combination of what Stuart Hall (2003) calls "presences": the *présence Africaine*, *présence Européene*, and *présence Américaine*.

Likewise, if present history holds true to form, the latest "sanitizing" will be done by underpaid laborers, because Bush and his ilk—always ready to capitalize on what Naomi Klein (2007) refers to as "disaster capitalism" (the profit-based privatization of relief efforts in disaster-stricken environs)—went so far as to temporarily suspend the Davis-Bacon Act of 1931 for the Gulf Coast reconstruction effort (see "Proclamation by the President to Suspend Subchapter IV of Chapter 31 of Title 40, US Code," 8 September 2005).[x] In response to this suspension of Davis-Bacon, President Edward C. Sullivan, Building and Construction Trades Department, AFL-CIO, criticized President Bush for taking away critical wage protections from struggling Gulf State workers. He stated in a press release: "Once again the poorest workers are exploited in this disaster. This Administration's continued disregard for the victims of this tragedy is evident in the President's proclamation suspending Davis-Bacon protection for workers in the hurricane torn Gulf." Sullivan further stated:

Once again this Administration is looking out for corporations eager to profit from a national emergency. They want to pay the poorest workers the lowest wages to do the most dangerous jobs. Suspending Davis-Bacon protections for financially distressed workers in the Gulf States amounts to legalized looting of these workers who will be cleaning up toxic sites and struggling to rebuild their communities while favored contractors rake in huge profits from FEMA reconstruction contracts. This is a shameful action and a national disgrace. It's time for this Administration and those members of Congress who blatantly carry the water for corporate gougers during a disaster to realize that denying fair wages to Gulf State workers is no way to help them get back on their feet (Quoted in Corbett, 2005).[xi]

In line with the proposals such as the suspension of Davis-Bacon, Paul Teller, then-Legislative Director of the House Republican Study Committee, circulated an e-mail containing a list of pro-free-market ideas for responding to Katrina. Included among the suggestions were: make the entire area a flat-tax free-enterprise zone; waiving the so-called death tax for anyone in the affected area who died between August 20, 2005, and December

31, 2005; repeal or waive environmental regulations for building contractors; eliminate faith-based regulatory blocks; give school-choice vouchers to displaced children and their families (this was especially promoted by Milton Friedman in the *Washington Post*); and make the entire region an economic competitiveness zone.[xii]

And so here we have it: At the core of this nascent form of disaster capitalism emerges the overriding market logic of the Bush administration as revealed during and after Hurricane Katrina. As Adolph Reed Jr. (2006) suggests, "The goal of this [neoliberal ideological position] is acceptance, as the unquestioned natural order of things, that *private* is always better than *public*, and that the main functions of government are to enhance opportunities for the investor class and suppress wages for everyone else. Hurricane Katrina and reactions to it throw into relief how successful that program has been" (p. 1).

Returning for a moment to the Superdome itself, we would do well to remember how its 'rebirth' was heralded when, a year later, the stadium reopened to national fanfare, with the Saints football team and its players depicted as shining beacons of a redeveloped New Orleans. The gathered, partying throng of 68,000+ fans—primarily White—jammed the stadium, this time in celebration. Signs could be seen bearing phrases such as "Dome is Where the Heart Is," "Welcome Home," "America's Help: Priceless," "Thanks, y'all," "Our Home, Our Team," and "No Place Like Dome." Sports reporters and television news crews were in abundance (hundreds of media credentials were made available), all promoting a 'successful' if not landmark event—quite a departure from the last assembly of bodies in the Superdome.

Additionally, and as part of the $185 million in repairs, the Federal Emergency Management Agency (FEMA) contributed $115 million (out of an initial $1.2 billion in funds awarded to Louisiana by FEMA in the year following Katrina). Said Federal Coordinating Officer Scott Wells, "[The Superdome's] rehabilitation is *essential* to New Orlean's recovery" ("Superdome returns with glitz, glamour, and Monday Night Football," 2006, emphasis ours). Yet the Superdome wasn't just *repaired*; it received numerous technology upgrades in the form of state-of-the-art LED scoreboards; fan comfort was stressed, as Club-level seats (among the most expensive in the stadium) were replaced with leatherette seats; all 137 luxury suites were remodeled (including the addition of plasma televisions in each); and so forth. How is this outlay "essential" to New Orleans? Perhaps one can make the civic pride argument (and, when the Saints won the Super Bowl a few years later and gained a national following, it would have been hard to deny such an argument), but remodeling luxury suites owned by corporations and wealthy patrons while schools remained closed in the Ninth Ward raises questions regarding such a, to spin a word, development—the racialized juxtaposition of aid could not be more stark. And, as Christopher Caldwell has noted, moments such as these "make explicit the privileges of the haves and the envy of the have-nots in a way that is embarrassing for both" (quoted in Klein, 2007, p. 509).

Thus, and although one could credibly argue that the above is a particularly striking example of sport development gone wrong, we would side with Naomi Klein in stating that this is, sadly, disaster capitalism at its best (which, of course, means the very worst): And, increasingly, it is getting harder and harder to tell the two apart!

CODA

As the days following Katrina turned into weeks, and the weeks into months, two more powerful hurricanes slammed into the southern coast of the United States. This time, the discourse was in place, the hero-narratives well-planned. The appearance of law and order was back, up and running, organized. News reports focused on federal help that actually managed to arrive. Racial issues, of course, were soon ignored once again in the mainstream media. (The running "joke" becoming, "Well, two weeks for a national conversation on race seems about right.") Critical discussions about poverty and class silently receded into the mist as attention was once again focused on such pressing infotainment issues as the Tom Cruise-Katie Holmes marriage, supermodel Kate Moss's arrest on drug charges, or Terrell Owens's suspension from the Philadelphia Eagles football team.

In working through and unmasking this latent, systemic cultural racism, we must reject outright such outlandish claims that the people of New Orleans brought this tragedy upon themselves, or that those who did not have the means to vacate the city failed of their own volition. Alongside O'Reilly in the domain of public demagoguery, Senator Rick Santorum (R-PA) heartlessly suggested *punishing* those who are unable to leave a disaster-stricken area, as when he stated: "I mean, you have people who don't heed those warnings and then put people at risk as a result of not heeding those warnings. So there may be a need to look at tougher penalties, candidly, on those who decide to ride it out and understand there are consequences to not leaving."

Additionally, we must also be mindful of the disturbing corollary to Rep. Baker's aforementioned the conservative blame-the-victim statement that, in effect, 'God cleaned up public housing in NOLA': a nationwide poll of 1,003 Americans conducted several weeks after Katrina hit found that 23% of Americans believe that "hurricanes are a *deliberate* act of God" (see also Miller, 2006).[xiii] This absurd implication—that Katrina was a deliberate, punitive act by "God" unleashed against the citizens of NOLA—was propagated *en masse* by those on the far right, such as Michael Marcavage, Director of Repent America (a Philadelphia-based ministry), who stated in a press release: "Although the loss of lives [sic] is deeply saddening, this act of God destroyed a wicked city. From 'Girls Gone Wild' to 'Southern Decadence,' New Orleans was a city that had its doors wide open to the public celebration of sin" (http://www.repent america.com/pr_hurricanekatrina.html). Rev. Bill Shanks, pastor of the New Covenant Fellowship of New Orleans, touched a similar chord: "New Orleans now is abortion free. New Orleans now is Mardi Gras free. New Orleans now is free of Southern Decadence and the sodomites, the witchcraft workers, false religion—it's free of all of those things now… God simply, I believe, in His mercy purged all of that stuff out of there—and now we're going to start over again" (http://headlines.agapepress.org/archive/9/22005b.asp). And, not to be outdone, the Irreverend Pat Robertson claimed on his September 12 broadcast of *The 700 Club* cable program that Katrina was punishment for the 'legalization of abortion.'[xiv]

A year after Katrina came ashore, New Orleans remained an empty shell of its past glory. As Spike Lee's (Lee & Nevins, 2006) documentary, *When the Levees Broke,* so powerfully detailed, decomposed bodies were still being pulled from the wreckage; garbage and debris remained strewn in the streets; the local economy continued its faltering slide. To mark the one-year anniversary, President Bush spun empty platitudes about how the hurricane launched "a moment of great sadness" and how "although a year has gone by, it's really the beginning of the renewal and rebuilding" ("Bush Sees Rebirth from 'Sadness' of Katrina: As Bells Toll on Anniversary, President Says New Orleans 'Still a Mess,'" 2006).

Yet it is poet Andre Codrescu (2006)—not Bush—who offered perhaps the most spot-on commentary of the yearlong fiasco when he stated:

> Katrina was just a storm, but what followed was so hideous that one year later, we can only shake our heads and vomit…In the space of one year, our commander-in-chief has evolved from a flyover disaster to a profligate dispenser of cash…[in which] the only thing wrong with the vast billions that are supposedly heading our way is that they may actually be handed out in the form of checks instead of being thrown down from helicopters so the groveling masses can wrestle for them like a proper Mardi Gras crowd [because] hurling cash into the streets would, in fact, be a more equitable way of dispensing treasure than handing it over to people like Congressman Jefferson or a mayor who has been invisible since his re-election.

Contra Bush, and in the spirit of Codrescu's stinging narrative, the words of Howard Dean's (2006a) address marking the Katrina anniversary makes us imagine an alternative to the sorrows of the Bush imperium, of the divisiveness knocking on our door:

> Katrina was a terrible tragedy, not just for New Orleans and Mississippi, not just for the people who died or still have not been able to move home. Katrina was a tragedy for America. Because one thing people believed throughout the world, throughout this country but throughout the world, whether they liked us or not, they believed that Americans could fix anything. And we believed that about ourselves. That if something really bad happens, call in the Americans,

they're the best-organized people and the best managing people—they can fix anything. Something really bad happens, call in the Americans.

And what we experienced in 2005 was not just the personal loss and tragedy to all of our lives, because so many of us knew people or had family in New Orleans or Mississippi. What we experienced was a tragedy. But seeing, unmasked, the incompetence, and failures, and indifference, of the president and the Republican majority, we need a new direction for America where no one is left behind!

REFERENCES

Andrews. D. L. (1993). *Deconstructing Michael Jordan: Popular culture, politics, and postmodern America.* Unpublished doctoral dissertation. Champaign, IL: University of Illinois.

Babington, C. (2005, September 10). Some GOP legislators hit jarring notes in addressing Katrina. *Washington Post.* Retrieved from http://www.wash-ingtonpost.com/wp-dyn/content/article/2005/09/09/AR2005090901930.html

A big disconnect in New Orleans. (2005, September 2). *CNN.com.* Retrieved from http://www.cnn.com/2005/US/09/02/katrina.response/

Briggs, L. (2003). Mother, child, race, nation: The visual iconography of rescue and the politics of transnational and transracial adoption. *Gender & History, 15,* 179-200.

Brown, J., & Martin, A. (2005, September 2). New Orleans' residents: God's mercy evident in Katrina's wake. AgapePress.com. Retrieved from http://headlines.agapepress.org/ archive/9/22005b.asp

Bush sees rebirth from "sadness" of Katrina: As bells toll on anniversary, President says New Orleans "still a mess." (2006, August 29). *MSNBC/NBC.* Retrieved from http://www.msnbc.msn.com/id/14567350/

Cobb, W. J. (2005). It is about race. *Black Voices.* Retrieved from http://www.blackvoices.com/black_news/resurrecting_neworleans/_a/it-is-about-race/20050906072209990001

Codrescu, A. (2006). Mourning for a flooded crescent city. *NPR Radio.* Retrieved from http://www.poynter.org/column.asp?id=52&aid=109898

Cole, C. L. (2001). Nike goes Broadway. *Journal of Sport & Social Issues, 25,* 115-117.

Cole, C. L. (2005). Katrina's wake-up call. *Journal of Sport & Social Issues, 29,* 367-368.

Cole, C. L., & Giardina, M. D. (2005, October). Revelation at the Superdome: The "other" America. Paper presented at the annual conference of the North American Society for the Sociology of Sport, Winston-Salem, NC.

Controversy over New Orleans photo captions. (2005, September 2). *WikiNews Service.* Retrieved from http://en.wikinews.org/wiki/Controversy_over_New_Orleans_photos_captions

Corbett, H. (2005, September 9). Building trades blast administration for suspension of worker wage protections in hurricane stricken gulf counties. *Building and Construction Trades Department press release.* Retrieved from http://www.buildingtrades.org/news/newsreleases/2005/09.09.05.html

Darnell, S. (2010). Power, politics and "Sport for Development and Peace": Investigating the utility of sport for international development. *Sociology of Sport Journal, 27*(4), 54-75.

Davis, M., & Fontenot, A. (2005, October 20). Hurricane gumbo. *The Nation.* Retrieved from http://www.thenation.com/doc/20051107/davis/6

Dean, H. (2006a, 18 August). Speech to the Democratic National Committee, Chicago, IL.

Dean, H. (2006b, 23 August). Interview with Wolf Blitzer. Cable News Network.

Denzin, N. K., & Giardina, M. D. (Eds.). (2006). *Contesting empire, globalizing dissent: Cultural studies after 9/11.* Boulder, CO: Paradigm.

Department of Housing and Urban Development (1993). *Building communities, together: Guidebook for community-based strategic planning for empowerment zones and enterprise communities.* Washington, D.C.: Government Printing Office.

Dreier, P. (2006). Katrina and power in America. *Urban Affairs Review, 41,* 528-549.

DuBose, B. (2005, September 30). HUD chief foresees a "whiter" Big Easy. *The Washington Times.* Retrieved from http://www.commondreams.org/headlines05/0930-07.htm

Eisinger, P. (2000). The politics of bread and circuses: Building the city of the visitor class. *Urban Affairs Review, 35,* 316-333.

Ford, G., & Gamble, P. (2005, October 27). The battle for New Orleans: Only a real movement can win this war. *The Black Commentator.* Retrieved from http://www.blackcommentator.com/156/156_cover_battle_for_no.html

Friedman, M., Andrews, D. L., & Silk, M. L. (2004). Sport and the façade of redevelopment in the postindustrial city. *Sociology of Sport Journal, 21,* 119-139.

Giardina, M. D. (2005). *Sporting pedagogies: Performing culture & identity in the global arena.* New York: Peter Lang.

Giardina, M. D. (2009). One day, one goal? PUMA, corporate philanthropy, and the cultural politics of brand 'Africa'. *Sport in Society, 13,* 130-142.

Giardina, M. D., & Cole, C. L. (in press). Race, class, and politics in post-Katrina America. In M. Silk & D. L. Andrews (Eds.), *Sport and neoliberalism.* Philadelphia, PA: Temple University Press.

Giardina, M. D., & Hess, L. A. (2007). If not us, then who? Performing pedagogies of hope in post-Katrina America. *Cultural Studies/Critical Methodologies, 7,* 169-187.

Giardina, M. D., & McCarthy, C. R. (2005). The popular racial order of urban America: Sport, identity, and the politics of culture. *Cultural Studies/Critical Methodologies, 5,* 145-173.

Giroux, H. A. (2007). Violence, Katrina, and the biopolitics of disposability. *Theory, Culture, & Society, 24,* 305-209.

Goldberg, M. (2006). *Kingdom coming: The rise of Christian nationalism.* New York: W. W. Norton & Co.

Grieve, T. (2005, September 3). Halliburton gets its share, where has Cheney been? *Salon. com.* Retrieved from http://www.salon.com/politics/war_room/2005/09/03/halliburton/index.html

Hamill, S. D. (2005, September 7). Santorum retreats on evacuation penalty remarks. *The Post-Gazette* (Pittsburgh). Retrieved from http://www.post-gazette.com/pg/05250/566844.stm

Hedges, C. (2007). *American fascists: The Christian Right and the war on America.* New York: Free Press.

In Katrina's aftermath, Duke responds. (2005). *Duke Magazine* (91,6). Retrieved from http://www.dukemagazine.duke.edu/dukemag/issues/111205/depgaz2.html

Kalette, D. (2005, September 7). Dean: Race played a role in Katrina deaths. *The Associated Press.* Retrieved from http://www.breitbart.com/news/ 2005/09/07/D8CFNMPG0.html

Kaplan, E. (2005). *With God on their side: George W. Bush and the Christian Right.* New York: Free Press.

King, S. J. (2005, October). Sport culture, the "War on Terror," and the emergence of jockocracy. Paper presented at the annual conference for the North American Society for the Sociology of Sport, Winston-Salem, North Carolina.

Klein, E. (2005, October 30). The media of 100 years ago, today. The *American Prospect Online.* Retrieved from http://www.prospect.org/archives/archives/2005/10/index.html

Ladson-Billings, G. (2003, April). Egon Guba distinguished lecture. Paper presented at the annual meeting of the American Educational Research Association, New Orleans, LA.

Lee, S. (Director), & Nevins, S. (Executive Producer). (2006). *When the levees broke: A requiem in four acts* [Motion picture]. United States: 40 Acres & a Mule Filmworks in association with Home Box Office.

Marcavage, M. (2005, August 31). Hurricane Katrina destroys New Orleans days before "Southern Decadence." *Repent America.* Retrieved from http://www.repentamerica.com/pr_hurricanekatrina.html

Mele, C. (2000). *Selling the lower east side: Culture, real estate, and resistance in New York City.* New York: New York University Press.

Miller, T. (2006). The American people cannot be trusted. In N. K. Denzin & M. D. Giardina (Eds.), *Contesting empire, globalizing dissent: Cultural studies after 9/11.* (pp. 121-135). Boulder, CO: Paradigm.

Neal, M. A. (2005, September 6). Race-ing Katrina. *NewBlackMan.* Retrieved from http://newblackman.blogspot.com/2005/09/race-ing-katrina.html

New Orleans is sinking. (2005, November 20). *CBS.com*. Retrieved from http://www. cbsnews.com/stories/2005/11/18/60minutes/main1056304_page2.shtml

O'Reilly, B. (2005). *The O'Reilly Factor*. Retrieved from http://www.pfaw.org/pfaw/general/ default.aspx?oid=19453

Phillips, K. (2006). *American theocracy: The peril and politics of radical religion, oil, and borrowed money in the 21st century*. New York: Viking.

Proclamation by the President: To suspend Subchapter IV of Chapter 31 of Title 40, United States Code, within a limited geographic area in response to the national emergency caused by Hurricane Katrina: A proclamation by the President of the United States of America. (2005, September 8). Office of the Press Secretary of the President of the United States. Retrieved from http://www.whitehouse.gov/news/ releases/2005/09/20050908-5.html

"Radio address to the nation on crime and criminal justice reform." (1982). *The public papers of President Ronald W. Reagan*. Ronald Reagan Presidential Library. http://www. reagan.utexas.edu/archives/speeches/1982/91182a.htm

Reed, Jr., A. (2006, 31 August). Undone by neoliberalism. *The Nation*. Retrieved from http://www.thenation.com/doc/20060918/reed

Robinson, E. (2005, October 7). Instant revisionism. *Washington Post*, p. A23.

Redmcclain. (2006, May 29). Six flags over Jesus [Web log post]. Retrieved from http:// www.dailykos.com/story/2006/5/29/193711/698

Scott, A. (2006, September 3). Iraq to deploy troops to Louisiana, Mississippi. Retrieved from http://www.flakmag.com/rejected/louisiana.html

Squires, C. (2005, October 9). *If it were any closer, one would need a life jacket*. St. Petersburg Times. Retrieved from http://www.sptimes.com/2005/10/09/news_pf/Artsandentertainment/Discovery_was_there.shtml

"Superdome returns with gliz, glamour, and Monday Night Football" (2006). *CBSsports. com*. Retrieved from http://www.cbssports.com/nfl/story/9673908/1

Vowell, S. (2003). *The partly cloudy patriot*. New York: Simon & Schuster.

Wallace, M. O. (2005, September 7). "Our tsunami": Race, religion and mourning in Louisiana, Mississippi, and Alabama. *NewBlackMan*. Retrieved from http://newblackman. blogspot.com/2005/09/our-tsunami-race-religion-and-mourning.html

Weisman, J., & VandeHei, J. (2005, September 15). Bush to request more aid funding: Analysts warn of spending's impact. *The Washington Post*. Retrieved from http://www. washingtonpost.com/wpdyn/content/article/2005/09/14/AR2005091402654_pf.html

The wound of Katrina slowly festers. (2005, November 21). *DailyKos.com*. Retrieved from http://www.dailykos.com/story/2005/11/21/152843/01

AUTHORS' NOTE

We thank Laura Vaughan (née Hess) for our conversations regarding her time spent volunteering and providing humanitarian relief in Louisiana in the aftermath of Katrina. This chapter draws on, updates, and revisits arguments in Giardina and Hess (2007) and Cole and Giardina (2005), and appears in slightly different form in Giardina and Cole (in press).

ENDNOTES

[i] *The New York Times,* among other media outlets, reprinted former FEMA director Michael Brown's shocking emails from the time when New Orleans was first under siege. These emails contained, among other statements, Brown telling to one staffer: "If you'll look at my lovely FEMA attire you'll really vomit. I am a fashion god [sic]." Other emails revealed Brown and his staffers to be more concerned with his dinner reservations in Baton Rouge and a dog sitter for his house than with anything of any consequence. Brown was also credited with perhaps the most bizarre comment of the situation, when he stated: "Considering the dire circumstances that we have in New Orleans, virtually a city that has been destroyed, things are going relatively well."

[ii] After introducing Sen. Landrieu (D-LA), Cooper immediately asked her, "Does the federal government bear responsibility for what is happening now? Should they apologize for what is happening now?" Landrieu responded that, "there will be plenty of time to discuss those issues," and proceeded to begin thanking various government officials for their disaster relief support. Cooper then interrupted her and passionately stated:

> Senator, I'm sorry... for the last four days, I have been seeing dead bodies here in the streets of Mississippi and to listen to politicians thanking each other and complimenting each other—I have to tell you, there are people here who are very upset and angry, and when they hear politicians thanking one another, it just, you know, it cuts them the wrong way right now, because there was a body on the streets of this town yesterday being eaten by rats because this woman has been laying in the street for 48 hours, and there is not enough facilities to get her up. Do you understand that anger? [...] There are people that want answers, and people want someone to stand up and say: we should have done more.

[iii] For more, see Aemilia Scott's (2006) essay at http://www.flakmag.com/rejected/louisiana.html

[iv] The sharply mediated divide of public opinion toward "Black" and "White" survivors was vividly captured in the main of America's popular-public sphere when *Agence-France Presse*

and the *Associated Press* news agencies became embroiled in a case of image-captioning that set off a mini-firestorm of debate. The first photo, from *Agence-France Press,* highlighted a picture of two White individuals (a man and a woman) wading through water carrying bags of food with the description: "Two residents wade through chest-deep water after *finding* bread and soda from a local grocery store after Hurricane Katrina came through the area in New Orleans, Louisiana." The second photo, from the Associated Press, highlighted a picture of an African American man carrying similar items with the description "A young man walks through chest-deep flood water after looting a grocery store in New Orleans on Tuesday, Aug. 30, 2005."

[v] According to the 2000 census, the per capita annual income for "Whites" in New Orleans, $31,971, was $10,000 above the national average. The per capita income for African Americans, $11,332, was $10,000 below the national average. This $20,000 gap between White and Black residents of New Orleans compared to a gap of less than $10,000 nationwide.

[vi] Former First Lady Barbara Bush summed up the view of many on the Right when she callously stated with respect to evacuees who had fled to Houston, Texas: "What I'm hearing which is sort of scary is that they all want to stay in Texas. Everybody is so overwhelmed by the hospitality. And so many of the people in the arena here, you know, were underprivileged anyway so this (chuckle)–this is working very well for them." A close second in terms of callousness can be attributed to George W. Bush himself who, in touring the region several days later, stated: "We've got a lot of rebuilding to do...The good news is— and it's hard for some to see it now—that out of this chaos is going to come a fantastic Gulf Coast, like it was before. Out of the rubbles of [Senator] Trent Lott's house—he's lost his entire house—there's going to be a fantastic house. And I'm looking forward to sitting on the porch" (Laughter).

[vii] For example, three Duke University students drove to New Orleans from Durham, North Carolina, forge a set of media credentials, gain access into the cordoned-off city, and rescue several people ("In Katrina's Aftermath, Duke Responds," 2005); Davy Jones Locker, a volunteer-run store serving Navy and civilian personnel and their family members at Stennis Space Center in Mississippi, distributed basic sundries such as soap, dishes, and cat food free of charge; Kuwait donated US$500 million for Katrina relief, and the Red Cross likewise raised more than US$750 million in aid; Web sites such as http://www.katrinaconnections.com, http://katrina.im-ok.org, http://hurricanekatrinasurvivors.com, and http://katrinasafe.com quickly sprung up, connecting thousands of lost and displaced families; Internet blogs such as DailyKos.com played a similar role in disseminating crucial information (as well as critically informed commentary); a medical team from Anne Arundel

County, Maryland, traveled to and operated a makeshift hospital in Jefferson Parish, Louisiana, and ended up treating more than 1,000 patients; and the National Football League hosted an historic Monday Night Football double-header featuring the now-homeless New Orleans Saints in a part-game/part-telethon that raised over US$25 million (see King, 2005). See also Giardina and Hess (2007) for an ethnographic account of on-the-ground volunteer rescue efforts.

[viii] And still, twelve weeks after Katrina hit, "no one [had] an answer to where people [who want to return to NOLA] should go. An estimated 80,000 homes had no insurance, and for now, the biggest grant a family can get from the federal government is $26,200."

[ix] For more, see Ford and Gamble's (2005) "New Orleans Citizen's Bill of Rights," available online at http://www.blackcommentator.com/156/156_cover_battle_for_no.html

[x] The Davis-Bacon Act of 1931 established the requirement for paying the "prevailing wage" on public works projects. All federal construction contracts and most contracts for federally-assisted construction over $2,000 must include provisions for paying workers on-site no less than the "locally prevailing wages," including fringe benefits. It is recognized by workers both inside and outside the construction industry as an important milestone in the history of organized labor.

[xi] Pressured by numerous sides, Bush eventually relented and dropped the suspension of Davis-Bacon.

[xii] For a full list see the email at http://www.naomiklein.org/shock-doctrine/resources/part7/chapter20/pro-market-ideas-katrina

[xiii] It is important to point out that the division between income/education levels and responses is quite stark: 31% of respondents with a high school diploma or less reported believing that hurricanes are a *deliberate* act of God (compared with 61%, who said no) whereas only 11% of those with a college degree or higher reported believing hurricanes are a deliberate act of God (79% said no). [The key word here being deliberate.]

[xiv] With this context in mind, we side with Rev. Dr. Maurice O. Wallace (2005) in being "grievously troubled by the popularity of a commercial Christianity that romanticizes… faith for the sake of capital campaigns, political favor and box office receipts" (n.p.). For more on the collision of religion and politics during the Bush era, see Goldberg (2006), Hedges (2007), Kaplan (2005), and Phillips (2006).

Investing in Communities: Sporting Events and Social Responsibility

Laura Misener and Daniel S. Mason

The use of sporting events, as a means of marketing and promoting cities, has become a widely recognized strategy to attract capital, retain inward investment, and market a positive image. Mega-events such as the Olympic Games, World Cup, and Commonwealth Games are large-scale cultural events with mass popular appeal that garner international recognition (Roche, 2002). The strategy of hosting mega-events is increasingly being incorporated into broader economic initiatives designed to celebrate and promote cities (Andranovich, Burbank, & Heying, 2001; Whitson & Macintosh, 1996), foster tourism within and around cities (Hall, 2004), and, more generally, garner media attention (Horne, 2007). Concerns over the returns cities receive from hosting such events continue to grow, with claims that events privilege only elites within the city (Whitson & Horne, 2006), and that economic benefits are grossly overstated (Baade, 2007; Mules & Faulkner, 1996; Porter & Fletcher, 2008). As a result, there is a growing demand that events also show that they positively influence other groups within the communities where games are hosted.

Cities that stage large-scale sporting events invest substantial human, financial, and physical capital, and thus need to be accountable to the communities that host them (Whitson, 2004). In response to this need, scholars have recently begun to focus on strategically identifying and capitalizing on the leverageable assets of events as a means of fostering sustainable social and economic benefits (Chalip, 2006; Kellett, Hede, & Chalip, 2008). This perspective shifts focus away from evaluating event outcomes, such as social and economic impacts, and allows cities and local businesses to focus on what they can do to position themselves within the context of socially responsible, sustainable legacy planning for events.

The purpose of this chapter is to examine ways in which sporting events can and should make a socially responsible contribution to civic and community development. Corporate social responsibility (CSR) is about businesses conscientiously giving back to society above and beyond profits for shareholders. Research on events has shown that sport organizations are attempting to articulate a commitment to CSR by engaging in "cause-related" marketing and participating in community outreach programs (Babiak & Wolfe, 2006; Filo, Funk, & O'Brien, 2009). Nevertheless, little is known about how corporations can tie the events agenda to broad-based community initiatives. In the present chapter, we draw upon the concept of corporate community involvement (CCI), which is a prominent facet of corporate social responsibility (Chapple & Moon, 2005), to offer ways in which corporations might develop programs and activities surrounding events to foster positive social outcomes. As corporations have increasingly been faced with a heightened expectation of accountability of the role they play in the community (Muthuri, 2007), CCI has developed as an avenue to support the community through corporate donations, strategic philanthropy, employee volunteering, and community driven development (Moon & Muthuri, 2006). The chapter is organized into three sections. We begin with a brief overview of the literature on sport and corporate social responsibility, and introduce the concept of CCI, particularly as it relates to the concept of community development. We then present two case studies of cities that have used sporting events as part of a larger civic development strategy demonstrating the potential links between the sporting events agenda and community development —Manchester, UK, and Melbourne, AU. Finally, we suggest that event organizers and companies associated with events have a unique opportunity to foster community development activities and actively engage citizens in responsible and sustainable development activities. Our focus is on developing mechanisms for ensuring community collaboration and the maximization of positive benefits for local communities.

CORPORATE SOCIAL RESPONSIBILITY AND SPORT

Corporate social responsibility (CSR) is concerned with what managers believe their businesses need to give back to society to meet the various needs/demands of their stakeholders. It is defined broadly as a set of actions that appear to further some social good, extend beyond explicit pecuniary interests of the firm, and are not required by law (Godfrey, Merrill, & Hansen, 2009). The concept implies that companies' efforts be directed to benefit society, above and beyond the interests of shareholders. Organizations have become aware of the importance of making a positive contribution to society, extending their mandate beyond profit maximization to include responsibility to the community (Carroll, 1991, 1998; Moir, 2001). Engaging in CSR activities can also benefit organizations in many ways, such as differentiation from competitors, engendering employee loyalty, generating favorable publicity, and building corporate reputation (Foley, 1998; Godfrey, 2005). Although CSR began as a form of charity, it is now viewed as part of the integrated set of strategies designed to add value to businesses (Porter & Kramer, 2006).

The concept of CSR is also gaining traction in the sport industry. For example, more professional sport organizations are engaging in CSR initiatives (Babiak & Wolfe, 2006, 2009), and most professional franchises have community affairs or outreach programs focused on supporting social causes. CSR research related to sport has been limited and focused primarily on three areas: cause-related marketing, corporate citizenship, and civic engagement (Bradish & Cronin, 2009; Smith & Westerbeek, 2007). Cause-related branding and marketing occurs where firms donate to non-profit organizations as charitable donations through sponsorship opportunities, which have been examined from both organizational and consumer perspectives (Irwin, Lachowetz, Cornwell, & Clark, 2003; Lachowetz & Gladden, 2003; Roy & Graeff, 2003; Walker & Kent, 2009). The recent works of Babiak and Wolfe (2006, 2009), and Sheth and Babiak (2010) demonstrate how CSR activities are being used by professional franchises as a form of corporate citizenship to signal their strategic philanthropic initiatives. Finally, some scholarly attention has been given to civic engagement. In particular, a focus has been on how sport entities associated with sporting events participate in community outreach programs (Babiak & Wolfe, 2006; Seguin, Parent, & O'Reilly, 2009), or partake in charitable giving to local agencies (Filo, Funk, & O'Brien, 2008, 2009). CSR research on sporting events has focused primarily on the potential role of CSR in event management (e.g., Babiak & Wolfe, 2006), and spectators' attitudes towards CSR initiatives (cf. Irwin et al., 2003; Walker & Kent, 2009).

CORPORATE COMMUNITY INVOLVEMENT

Corporate community involvement (CCI) has developed as a means for companies to engage in CSR activities that tie directly to local community interests (Moon, Crane, & Matten, 2005). CCI is typically part of a broader CSR strategy and managed by a CSR department or community relations personnel. CCI has evolved from broader notions of business philanthropy into its current form of accountability and responsibility to stakeholders and communities giving rise to new modes of discretionary benevolence through community involvement, community partnerships, and strategic community investments (Moon & Muthuri, 2006). Many corporations have long traditions of CCI through corporate donations and corporate philanthropy (Cowton, 1987). More recently, other forms of CCI, such as strategic philanthropy (Saiia, Carroll, & Buchholtz, 2003), cause-related marketing (Varadarajan & Menon, 1988), employee volunteering (Muthuri, 2007), and strategic partnerships with community groups (Seitanidi & Ryan, 2007), have become commonplace for organizations seeking socially responsible business opportunities.

The motives for partaking in CCI range from altruistic (for the greater good of society) to self-interest (profit maximization). Although much debate remains over the motivations of firms and their claimants, it is relatively clear that most companies seek entrepreneurial opportunities such as CCI to gain a competitive advantage, comparative advantage, or meet the demands of a new moral marketplace (Hess, Rogovsky, & Dunfee, 2002; Waddock & Boyle, 1995). In addition, the rise in corporate social auditing, accounting, and reporting through organizations such as the *Global Reporting Initiative* (GRI, 2010) and the *Institute of Social and Ethical AccountAbility* (ISEA, 2010) has increased pressure for businesses to focus on social performance.

Research on CCI has demonstrated that communities have limited influence due to power differentials between corporations and the community. As Muthuri (2007) argued, when corporations attempt to engage in community development activities, communities can become "victims of community initiatives that advance patronage and placation of community needs" (Muthuri, 2007, p. 185). To ensure that communities receive maximum benefit from the programming offered by corporations, power needs to be shifted to communities to allow participation and collaboration in CCI activities. Community participation refers to the opportunities, processes, and mechanisms in which community stakeholders take part and their sharing in the decision-making in CCI programs. We argue that community participation and consultation is the key to successful CCI.

SPORTING EVENTS AND COMMUNITY DEVELOPMENT

Sporting events demand vast amounts of resources from local communities, and concerns continue to be raised about the sustainability and viability of events for local communities (Jones, 2001; Misener & Mason, 2006, 2008; Rowe & McGuirk, 1999). Some commentators have suggested that the practices surrounding the use of large scale sporting events for civic and economic development are divorced from the everyday practices of local communities, neighbourhoods, and local development activities (Horne & Manzenreiter, 2006). If sporting events are to become a vehicle for greater social inclusion and healthier communities, more attention needs to be focussed on strategically leveraging assets of events to foster lasting community benefits (Chalip, 2006; Kellett, Hede, & Chalip, 2008). Thus the concept of CCI offers organizations the opportunity to be involved in the events process to meet their social responsibility agendas while helping to ensure sustainable outcomes for communities.

CASE STUDIES: SPORT AND THE POTENTIAL OF CCI

The following cases have been developed from a broader study on the use of sporting events in entrepreneurial cities. This study centered on how community development and social responsibility have been considered as part of the sporting events agenda in a number of cities around the world. Extensive public documentation, books, websites, newspaper accounts, and journal articles were collected through online, library, and archival searches, and during site visits to each of the cities between August 2003 and July 2006. Each case draws upon the multiple sources of evidence, including national, regional, and local policy documentation; media reports; bid documentation; and other city documents. Interviews with personnel such as city mayors, chief executives, marketing officers, community development officers, and private industry professionals were also performed in each city. Thus, the direct quotes herein represent those gleaned from industry stakeholder interviews.

Case Study #1: Manchester, United Kingdom

Manchester is the largest economic region in England outside of London. It is often considered to be the world's first city of the industrial revolution (Quilley, 1999; Williams, 2003). Following World War II, Manchester experienced severe economic decline due to the downfall of the industrial-manufacturing sector. Between 1951 and 1981 the inner city lost over 52% of its inhabitants and the rate of unemployment grew dramatically. By 1981, inner city unemployment was over 20%, and the city was characterized by dilapidated housing, industrial wasteland, abandoned factories, and out of work residents. In 2000 the Federal Department of the Environment, Transport and the Regions (DETR) commissioned a study of poverty, health, and social exclusion, which resulted in the Index of Multiple Deprivation. The study demonstrated that a number of areas in and around Manchester were among the most deprived areas in the country (Office of National Statistics, 2001).

In 1996, the Manchester city center was devastated by an IRA bomb, which proved to be a turning point in the redevelopment efforts for the city, because a substantial amount of money was spent on rebuilding the city's infrastructure. Manchester set about its attempt to use sport as part of its regeneration agenda in the mid 1980s. The city bid unsuccessfully for the 1996 and 2000 Summer Olympic Games, which began the efforts to tie sporting events to the regeneration of deprived and devastated areas of the city. In February 1994, Manchester City Council successfully bid for the 2002 Commonwealth Games, and committed to build a new 65,000-seat stadium. Leading up to the 2002 Games, Manchester hosted several other high profile events such as the 1996 and 2000 World Track Cycling Championships, the 1997 World Table Tennis Championships, and the 2002 British Diving Championships. Since hosting the 2002 Commonwealth Games, Manchester has hosted events such as the 2003 UEFA Champions League Final, the 2004 World Track

Cycling Championships, the 2006 Paralympic World Cup, the 2008 FINA World Swimming Championships, and the 2009 European Masters Track Championships.

Manchester's growth agenda has been centred upon urban revitalization in numerous areas in and around the city. The Events Unit in the Manchester City Council has helped to focus on a unified approach to the use of sporting events as part of the city's overall growth ideology. Development groups, government organizations, and private companies have been working cooperatively in the process of bidding for and staging major events with many efforts focused on developing opportunities for sustainable development and viable community development. An example of this cooperative process is in the area of East Manchester, a region that had undergone significant post-industrial decline and was the focus of the major regeneration efforts surrounding the hosting of the 2002 Commonwealth Games. Generally, there have been strong ties between the city's events agenda and local community development interests. As indicated by the Deputy Head of Manchester, "Manchester's agenda has [focussed on] grassroots community benefit rather than just simply the event." Regeneration initiatives have been at the heart of socially responsible community programming in and around Manchester.

The inclusion of community organizations such as New East Manchester Ltd.[2] as an integral and ongoing partner in the event's strategy is demonstrative of the efforts towards social inclusion. *Beacons for a Brighter Future,* which is East Manchester's New Deal for Communities' program, a Government strategy aimed at addressing social exclusion and bridging the gap between the poorest neighborhoods and the rest of the country, was integral in ensuring local residents were part of the decision-making processes throughout the lead up to the Commonwealth Games. Community-based organizations such as these have been integral in helping to ensure that the communities in New East Manchester would receive positive community benefits from the hosting of events. Nevertheless, these socially responsible activities have primarily occurred as a result of the UK government's focus on regeneration through addressing social exclusion and promoting growth in local economies, and have not been part of a larger strategy to ensure community involvement and socially responsible programming surrounding all sporting events in the UK.

Several lessons regarding the potential for corporate community investment can be gleaned from the case of Manchester. First, it is necessary to have comprehensive community involvement in decision-making processes for planning, event staging, and event-related programming for communities to be truly engaged in the developmental outcomes of events. Public opinion polls are often cited during the bid process for sporting events as evidence of tacit public support, yet for the most part citizens have neither been consulted nor involved in event processes. It is only through the practice of engaging in comprehensive consultation strategies at all stages of the event development process that we can begin to empower members of communities. Empowerment processes such as community involvement in decision making start during the strategic visioning and planning phase of the event process. Efforts to build a strategic vision with marginalized communities that have experienced sustained periods of economic and social declines require careful planning.

Second, full public disclosure and transparency regarding event processes need to be central to community involvement initiatives. Openness is integral to ensuring opportunities for social participation, for democratic involvement at the local level, and thus for active citizenship. Although community forums held by New East Manchester Ltd. were one means of attempting to guarantee that information regarding the event process in Manchester was accessible, representatives of local neighborhood groups have voiced concern over the limited transparency surrounding events. An example of one concern of local groups was the development of the Manchester City Stadium within the Sportcity complex in East Manchester. Upon completion of the infrastructure developments and the staging of the 2002 Commonwealth Games, the perception among local community members was that the stadium was merely handed over to the professional football club, Manchester City, without local residents sharing in any of the benefits of the new stadium. In fact, the lease agreement between the city and football club provided numerous benefits to the local community in terms of community use, public access, and social development. Nevertheless, because the process lacked the necessary transparency, many citizens were troubled by the arrangement (Manchester 2002 Ltd., 2002).

Finally, mobilization and engagement of local community and interest groups are essential to leveraging event resources for community benefit. The lack of policy regulations regarding the engagement of communities in the development of sporting event processes has resulted in problems for local businesses, governments, and development groups alike because the balance of power lies with elite groups, and communities' members and local development groups have little power to affect decision making. Although each of the desired outcomes mentioned here seeks to address the interests of communities through the engagement of local citizens, the mobilization of grassroots planning—particularly around event legacies—is vitally important in promoting and reinforcing community-centered values. Despite a perceived focus on community, much of the work that has been done in Manchester has used a top-down approach where local government and corporations have developed policies and legacy plans that do not necessarily reflect the needs and interests of communities. It is through partnering and active inclusion of grassroots groups that events can truly tie to the needs and interests of communities.

Case Study #2: Melbourne, Australia

Melbourne garnered enough global recognition in the first half of the 20th century to convince the International Olympic Committee to move the 1956 Summer Olympic Games to the southern hemisphere for the first time ever. By the 1980s, however, the city had experienced substantial economic decline; in 1989, a severe market crash forced the closure of the State Savings Bank of Australia, and Melbourne's population declined as unemployment grew and the city went into a recession. Melbourne's growth and re-development agenda began during the 1990s, and sporting events and entertainment venues have been a central part of planning and redevelopment in Melbourne. For example, Melbourne Park was built in 1988 to host the now annual Australian Open Tennis Tournament, and the annual Formula 1 Australian Grand Prix moved to its permanent home to Melbourne in 1996. Melbourne Major Events Company[3] was set up to attract large-scale events to the city. Thus, Melbourne's leaders positioned the city as the "Sporting Capital," with an illustrious record of hosting events and sporting activities. The city has hosted events such as the 2005 World Artistic Gymnastic Championships, the 2006 Commonwealth Games, the 2007 FINA World Championships, and the 2009 World Masters Games. The Melbourne Spring Racing Carnival is one of the biggest horse racing events in the world and is one of the world's largest sporting events with crowds often exceeding 700,000 for the four-day event.

In addition to its distinction as a well-established city for successfully hosting sporting events, Melbourne's developmental agenda has focused on significant connections between events and community development activities. The strategies and examples of ties between sport and local community interests are unique and a model often studied by other cities. Interest in linking sporting events to community development issues, however, has not always been strong in Melbourne. Problems with some of the sporting development initiatives in the city have been well documented (Lowes, 2004; Mules, 1998), and there continues to be opposition to event activities in the city. Local government officials have focused on attempting to ensure events are tied to the needs of community members and are used for capacity building. This process has occurred through collaboration with local community groups and attempts to ensure good knowledge. The method in which the infrastructure for sporting events has developed continues to be an integral part of the event process and has been a key factor in the engagement of communities. For example, Melbourne Olympic Trust, owned by the people of Victoria, runs the sporting precinct. The role of the trust is to examine what is good for the people of Victoria with each and every decision. The model of building infrastructure in the city is often considered to be about developing community infrastructure first, that can also be used for major event hosting.

A key to ensuring local community interests and needs are better served through events is the engagement of various organizations in event-related developments. As a result, not only do event organizers consist of the typical public and private groups such as local and state government, marketing organizations, and tourism industry professionals, but also others, including local neighborhood coalitions and grassroots organizations such as the Melbourne Development Board (MDB). The role of the MDB is to be an advocate for individual communities and regions by ensuring that community issues and local business concerns are front and center in developmental discussions. An example of this involvement occurred with the MDB's involvement in job training, social housing initiatives, and local procurement programs tied to the 2006 Commonwealth Games.

From the case of Melbourne we can learn some important lessons about the structuring of corporate community investment opportunities. First, the use of comprehensive social and community impact assessments are necessary to ensure a collaborative, community-centred agenda. In Melbourne, when the Labor government came into power in 1999 at the state level, policies were implemented that helped to ensure communities were better served by the events. In this case, it was the state government that tried to implement impact assessments and develop events with stronger ties to issues of community and community development. A proactive approach to social assessments and providing guidelines for communities seeking to host events might benefit communities seeking to leverage community resources.

Second, procurement programs/opportunities and business providers need to ensure maximum deployment of local knowledge and community-based suppliers. This strategy focuses on local communities' knowledge and resources to support developmental efforts associated with events. In response to concerns about the ability of events to attain widespread economic and social well-being, different levels of Australian government have begun moving towards a policy framework that maximizes the virtues of community in the delivery of services and local development. Local community knowledge is not something that can simply be tapped into through arms-length consultation (Bauman, 2000). Rather, engagement activities are essential to the creation and nurturing of knowledge, which helps communities focus attention on local needs and capacities. Where event organizers typically tend to seek outside resources and knowledge structures to organize events—such as hiring outside experts with experience in event hosting in other cities—local communities need to be part of the process as providers and purveyors of local knowledge capital. In the past, government policy has placed little emphasis on community organizations and local governance structures. Yet, these institutions help foster the use and distribution of assets and skills. An investment strategy that facilitates access for local organizations to developmental capital would seem to have the potential of not only stimulating a physical revitalization of distressed areas, but also supporting the growth of social capital within communities (Daniels, Barbe, & Seigle, 1981).

In terms of ensuring that local companies benefit from the development and staging of events, the Government of Victoria has a policy that demonstrates its commitment to local development. The *Victorian Industry Participation Policy* (VIPP) tenders for major projects to meet specific requirements related to level of local content, the number of new local jobs created, and possible skills and technology transfer (Victorian Government Purchasing Board, 2007). In the lead-up to the 2006 Commonwealth Games, the Melbourne Cricket Ground (MCG) underwent a $434 million redevelopment. This redevelopment was undertaken by the Industry Capability Network, which is an independent, not-for-profit consultant service funded by the state government, providing free sourcing and business matching to manufacturing and engineering service sectors. The goal was to ensure the maximum provision of opportunities for local companies and facilitate knowledge transfer. This policy represents an example of being proactive and seeking to ensure that local businesses and communities benefit from development. These types of policies can be scaled down to require all developments associated with the staging of a major event to undergo similar evaluations focused on local development.

Third, cross-sector management of event strategies and programs needs to ensure a cohesive community agenda. It is perhaps this strategy that offers the most promise for corporations with partnership experience seeking to be more involved in positive community experiences. To ensure cohesive community-centered strategies, there is a need for strategic planning that includes various sectors involved in, and affected by, events in the mobilization of community interests. Local authorities in Melbourne work alongside other public, private, and voluntary organizations not only in providing services for a locality, but also in making strategic decisions influencing the local conditions for community development. This approach does not necessarily ensure, however, that the various public and private sectors affected by the event process will play a role in community development and event planning outcomes. Policy and community investment activities that guarantee representation from the various sectors, particularly local grassroots organizations, remain of key importance to ensuring comprehensive community-centered strategies. When event outcomes focus on economic and tourism returns, local community organizations are left out of the planning process. To ensure fair planning that is both informed by and informs communities, all sectors must be represented.

MOVING FORWARD: CORPORATE COMMUNITY INVESTMENT AND SPORTING EVENTS

Strong communities are built by community members being engaged, participating, and feeling supported by strong networks (Gilchrist, 2004). Typically, these elements are missing in sporting event agendas, and more specifically from the policy discourse surrounding the events process in the cities in the study. Much of the criticism surrounding the negative effect events have on communities stems from the limited community engagement and the power differential between elite groups organizing large events and local communities. The aim of engaging corporations in socially responsible activities through CCI is underpinned by the notion that businesses can deliver maximum benefit by involving local communities in decision making and drawing upon a corporation's wealth of resources. As Trebeck (2008) argued, the most effective influence on community development is achieved through sustainable private-sector contributions that are multifaceted and exploit the strengths of the local community. The cases presented here demonstrate that, in some instances, policies regarding community development and engagement strategies do exist, but often get sidestepped due to the complicated nature in which the event process develops. Economic development is a much easier process to coordinate, whereas community development requires greater amounts of coordination, grassroots mobilization, and extensive long-term strategies. Thus, for corporations seeking to engage in CCI, their social responsibility strategies need to be embedded in the principles of community engagement and grassroots organization involvement.

From the two cases presented above, a number of guidelines regarding corporations' socially responsible involvement in events have been developed:

1. Comprehensive community-based decision-making processes.

2. Full public disclosure and transparency of strategic initiatives.

3. Mobilization and engagement of local community and interest groups to leverage event resources for community benefit.

4. Comprehensive social and community impact assessments that ensure a collaborative, community-centered agenda.

5. Procurement and business providers to ensure maximum deployment of local knowledge and community-based suppliers.

6. Cross-sector management of event strategies and programs to ensure a cohesive community agenda.

These guidelines can serve as the basis for developing CCI strategies that will engage communities and present meaningful opportunities for socially responsible engagement of corporations.

CCI seeks to exploit companies' core competencies to maximize positive influence in collaborative social initiatives. Based on the preceding discussion, we argue that there are three primary issues that can be addressed by corporations developing socially responsible activities surrounding events: a) leveraging social resources, b) local economic development, and c) community-based partnerships.

Leveraging Social Resources

As Chalip (2006) has argued, with commercial activities so often cluttering the event landscape, the challenge is to differentiate commercial activity that supports social leverage from commercial activity that may undermine it. It is at this juncture that corporations seeking positive effects from the social outcomes of events can play a significant role. For example, it has been argued elsewhere (Misener & Mason, 2009) that all infrastructure developments—such as housing for an athletes' village—associated with an event should be dedicated to social housing units, low-income housing units, and accessible community recreation complexes. In addition, these infrastructure developments should ensure that housing units are built prior to the event and fit the needs of the local community interest. In Melbourne, leading up to the 2006 Commonwealth Games, the development of the Commonwealth Games Village in Parkville (Department of Victorian Communities, 2005) was controversial and met with opposition from groups such as the Royal Park Protection Group for the limited public consultation prior to the site selection (Royal Park Protection Group Inc., 2005). After much mediation, the government negotiated with the private developer that 20% of the units would be earmarked for social housing. What did not surface until after the completion of the Games was that a large portion of the houses slated for social housing had not been built (Bell, 2006). This problem underscores the need to ensure that local communities are informed about and understand the processes and effects of hosting a large-scale event such as the Commonwealth Games. Corporations with the political and economic will can strongly influence the outcomes of such developments by making socially responsible investments in housing and infrastructure projects that ensure representation and voice by members of the local community.

Local Economic Development

All too often events are criticized for privileging elite groups with few true economic benefits accruing to local communities (Andranovich, Burbank, & Heying, 2001; Dwyer, Mellor, Mistilis, & Mules, 2000). To ensure that local communities benefit from events and the associated developments and cultural activities, corporations can help to ensure that local providers and local companies are part of the planning and development processes. Ideally, event organizers should establish a predetermined minimum percentage of all contracts that will be awarded to, or at least partnered with, local providers, ensuring equitable community representation. When external providers are employed to run local events, the potential exists for event activities to be hijacked in the interests of global capital and economic rewards that can supersede the interests of the local community. Helping to ensure that local organizations are part of the process is not only a way to help reduce the potential for disregarding community interests, but makes good business sense. Policies such as the VIPP discussed above represent a step in the direction of ensuring that local communities benefit from the vast investment opportunities available through events. Through this type of socially responsible investment strategy, corporate community investment and local social development can be achieved to the greater benefit of communities.

Community-Based Partnerships

The development of community partnerships warrants significant attention from corporations seeking to be involved in positive community experiences and ensure socially responsible activities. Rather than elites structuring opportunities for event-related participation and community development activities, these should be developed in partnership with local community members. The groups most often left out of the development of events are in all likelihood those principally affected by the developmental activities. For example, in Manchester and Melbourne, there appears to have been opposition from community coalitions and local grassroots organizations despite the rhetoric of integrated community-driven management. Lowes (2004) examined one particular group that continues to lobby against the Australian Grand Prix being held in a prominent Melbourne park. A more informed process that ensures the inclusion of the local community, public agencies, and private interests in shaping events will result in better ties to local developmental activities and community needs. Multisector involvement, including local community-development groups is vital for improving the positive role of events in communities. It is through partnering and active inclusion of the community that events can truly tie to the needs and interests of communities. The involvement of community and grassroots organizations can enhance the opportunities of individuals within communities to gain skills and access links to ensure community well-being; these practices are truly at the heart of CCI.

CONCLUSION

Chalip and Leyns (2002) argued that local businesses need to work to leverage event resources for economic benefit. We extend that argument further to suggest that local businesses and corporations can make socially responsible investments in conjunction with event resources for both the benefit of the business and the local community. CCI offers a socially responsible approach for businesses to leverage event resources and help further the agenda of local community development. As businesses seek opportunities to make socially responsible contributions to the community and events move more towards ensuring sustainable development efforts, the suggestions provided in this chapter present a point to begin to further the discussion about socially responsible programming for events. It is our hope that the agenda of social responsibility continues to be at the forefront of event agendas and that local businesses take advantage of these opportunities to make greater contributions to local social and community development.

REFERENCES

Andranovich, G., Burbank, M. J., & Heying, C. H. (2001). Olympic cities: Lessons learned from mega-event politics. *Journal of Urban Affairs, 23,* 113-131.

Baade, R. A. (2007). The economic impact of mega-sporting events. In W. Andreff & S. Szymanski (Eds.), *Handbook on the economics of sport* (pp. 183-196). Cheltenham, UK: Edward Elgar.

Babiak, K., & Wolfe, R. (2006). More than just a game? Corporate social responsibility and Super Bowl XL. *Sport Marketing Quarterly, 154*, 214-224.

Babiak, K., & Wolfe, R. (2009). Determinants of corporate social responsibility in professional sport: Internal and external factors. *Journal of Sport Management, 23*, 717-742.

Bauman, Z. (2000). *In search of politics.* Cambridge: Polity Press.

Bell, J. (2006, June). A legacy of the Commonwealth Games. *North and West Melbourne News, 1.*

Bradish, C. L., & Cronin, J. L. (2009). Corporate social responsibility in sport. *Journal of Sport Management, 23*, 691-697.

Carroll, A. (1998). The four faces of corporate citizenship. *Business and Society Review, 100/101*, 1-7.

Carroll, A. B. (1991). The pyramid of corporate social responsibility: Toward the moral management of organizational stakeholders. *Business Horizons, 34*, 39–48.

Chalip, L. (2006). Towards social leverage of sport events. *Journal of Sport & Tourism, 11*, 109-127.

Chalip, L., & Leyns, A. (2002). Local business leveraging of a sport event: Managing an event for economic benefit. *Journal of Sport Management, 16*, 132-158.

Chapple, W., & Moon, J. (2005). Corporate social responsibility (CSR) in Asia: A seven country study of CSR website reporting. *Business and Society, 44*, 115-136.

Cowton, C. J. (1987). Corporate philanthropy in the United Kingdom. *Journal of Business Ethics, 6*, 553-559.

Daniels, B., Barbe, N., & Seigle, B. (1981). The experience and potential of community-based development. In R. Friedman & W. Schweke (Eds.), *Expanding the opportunity to produce* (pp. 176–185). Washington, US: The Corporation for Enterprise Development.

Department of Victorian Communities (2005, February 25). *Public consultation process begins for the Commonwealth Games village.* Retrieved from http://www.dpc.vic.gov.au

Dwyer, L., Mellor, R., Mistilis, N., & Mules, T. (2000). A framework for assessing "tangible" and "intangible" impacts of events and conventions. *Event Management, 6*, 175–189.

Filo, K. R., Funk, D. C., & O'Brien, D. (2008). It's really not about the bike: Exploring attraction and attachment to the events of the Lance Armstrong Foundation. *Journal of Sport Management, 22*, 501–525.

Filo, K., Funk, D. C., & O'Brien, D. (2009). The meaning behind attachment: Exploring camaraderie, cause and competency at a charity sport event. *Journal of Sport Management, 23*, 361-387.

Foley, J. (1998). Picking a philanthropic partner. *Marketing Magazine, 103*, 16-20.

Gilchrist, A. (2004). *The well-connected community. A network approach to community development.* Bristol: Polity Press.

Global Reporting Initiative. (2010). *About GRI.* Retrieved from http://www.globalreporting.org/AboutGRI/

Godfrey, P. C. (2005). The relationship between corporate philanthropy and shareholder wealth: A risk management perspective. *Academy of Management Review, 30,* 777–798.

Godfrey, P. C., Merrill, C. B., & Hansen, J. M. (2009). The relationship between corporate social responsibility and shareholder value: An empirical test of the risk management hypothesis. *Strategic Management Journal, 30,* 425-445.

Hall, C. M. (2004). Sports tourism and urban regeneration. In B. Ritchie & D. Adair (Eds.), *Sports tourism. Interrelationships, impacts and issues* (pp. 192-205). Toronto: Channelview.

Hess, D., Rogovsky, N., & Dunfee, T. W. (2002). The next wave of corporate community involvement: Corporate social initiatives. *California Management Review, 44,* 110-125.

Horne, J. (2007). The four 'knowns' of sports mega events. *Leisure Studies, 26,* 81-96.

Horne, J., & Manzenreiter, W. (2006). *Sport mega-events: Social scientific perspectives of a global phenomenon.* Oxford: Blackwell.

Institute of Social and Ethical AccountAbility (2010). *About us.* Retrieved from http://www.accountability.org/default2.aspx?id=54

Irwin, R. L., Lachowetz, T., Cornwell, T. B., & Clark, J. S. (2003). Cause-related sport sponsorship: An assessment of spectator beliefs, attitudes, and behavioural intentions. *Sport Marketing Quarterly, 12,* 131-139.

Jones, C. (2001). Mega-events and host-region impacts: Determining the true worth of the 1999 Rugby World Cup. *International Journal of Tourism Research, 3,* 241-251.

Kellett, P., Hede, A., & Chalip, L. (2008). Social policy for sport events: Leveraging (relationships with) teams from other nations for community benefit. *European Sport Management Quarterly, 8,* 101-121.

Lachowetz, T., & Gladden, J. (2003). A framework for understanding cause-related sport marketing programs. *International Journal of Sport Marketing and Sponsorship, 4,* 313-333.

Lowes, M. (2004). Neoliberal power politics and the controversial citing of the Australian Grand Prix Motorsport event in an urban park. *Loisir et Société / Society and Leisure, 27,* 69-88.

Manchester 2002 Ltd. (2002). *Lessons learned review of the 2002 Commonwealth Games in Manchester for DCMS, Sport England and Manchester City Council.* Manchester 2002 Ltd.

Misener L., & Mason, D. S. (2006). Creating community networks: Can sporting events offer meaningful sources of social capital? *Managing Leisure, 11,* 39-56.

Misener, L., & Mason, D. S. (2008). Urban regimes and the sporting events agenda: A cross-national comparison of civic development strategies. *Journal of Sport Management, 22,* 603-627.

Misener, L., & Mason, D. S. (2009). Fostering community development through sporting event strategies: An examination of urban regime perceptions. *Journal of Sport Management, 23,* 770-794.

Moir, L. (2001). What do we mean by corporate social responsibility? *Corporate Governance, 1,* 16-22.

Moon, J., Crane, A., & Matten, D. (2005). Can corporations be citizens? Corporate citizenship as a metaphor for business participation in society. *Business Ethics Quarterly, 15,* 427–451.

Moon, J., & Muthuri, J. N. (2006, December). An evaluation of corporate community investment in the UK: Current developments, future challenges. *A report of Charities Aid Foundation, United Kingdom.*

Mules, T. (1998). Events tourism and economic development in Australia. In D. Tyler, Y. Guerrier, & M. Robertson (Eds.), *Managing tourism in cities* (pp. 195-214). Chichester, UK: John Wiley & Sons.

Mules, T., & Faulkner, B. (1996). An economic perspective on major events. *Tourism Economics, 12,* 107-117.

Muthuri, J. N. (2007). Participation and accountability in corporate community involvement programmes: a research agenda. *Community Development Journal, 43,* 177–193.

Office of National Statistics (2001). Indices of deprivation. Retrieved from http://www.neighbourhood.statistics.gov.uk/dissemination/Info.do?page=aboutneighbourhood/indicesofdeprivation/indices-of-deprivation.htm

Porter, M. E., & Kramer, M. R. (2006). Strategy and society: The link between competitive advantage and corporate social responsibility. *Harvard Business Review, 84,* 78-92.

Porter, P. K., & Fletcher, D. (2008). The economic impact of the Olympic Games: Ex ante predictions and ex poste reality. *Journal of Sport Management, 22,* 470-468.

Quilley, S. (1999). Entrepreneurial Manchester: Elite genesis of consensus. *Antipode, 31,* 185-211.

Roche, W. M. (2002). The Olympics and global citizenship. *Citizenship Studies, 6,* 165-181.

Rowe, D., & McGuirk, P. (1999). Drunk for three weeks: Sporting success and city image. *International Review for the Sociology of Sport, 34,* 125-141.

Roy, D. P., & Graeff, T. R. (2003). Consumer attitudes toward cause-related marketing activities in professional sports. *Sport Marketing Quarterly, 12,* 163–172.

Royal Park Protection Group Inc. (2005). *Annual report of the Royal Park Protection Group Inc. (RPPG).* Retrieved from http://www.royalparkprotect.org.au.htm

Saiia, D. H., Carroll, A. B., & Buchholtz, A. K. (2003). Philanthropy as strategy when corporate charity "begins at home". *Business and Society, 4,* 169–201.

Séguin, B., Parent, M. M., & O'Reilly, N. (2010). Corporate support: A corporate social responsibility alternative to traditional event sponsorship. *International Journal of Sport Management and Marketing, 7,* 202-222.

Seitanidi, M. M., & Ryan, A. M. (2007). A critical review of forms of corporate community involvement: From philanthropy to partnerships. *International Journal of Nonprofit and Voluntary Sector Marketing, 12,* 247-266.

Sheth, H., & Babiak, K. (2010). Beyond the game: Perceptions and practices of corporate social responsibility in the professional sport industry. *Journal of Business Ethics, 91,* 433-450.

Smith, A. C. T., & Westerbeek, H. M. (2007). Sport as a vehicle for deploying social responsibility. *Journal of Corporate Citizenship, 25,* 43–54.

Trebeck, K. (2008). Relative advantages. Exploring private-sector impact on disadvantaged groups and deprived areas. *The Journal of Corporate Citizenship, 32,* 79-95.

Varadarajan, P. R., & Menon, A. (1988). Cause-related marketing: A coalignment of marketing strategy and corporate philanthropy. *Journal of Marketing, 53,* 55–78.

Victorian Government Purchasing Board (2007). *Procurement and local industry participation (VIPP).* Retrieved from www.vgpb.vic.gov.au

Waddock, S. A., & Boyle, M. (1995). The dynamics of change in corporate community relations. *California Management Review, 37,* 125–140.

Walker, M., & Kent, A. (2009). Do fans care? Assessing the influence of corporate social responsibility on consumer attitudes in the sport industry. *Journal of Sport Management, 23,* 743-769.

Whitson, D. (2004). Bringing the world to Canada: 'The periphery of the centre.' *Third World Quarterly, 25,* 1215-1232.

Whitson, D., & Horne, J. (2006). Underestimated costs and overestimated benefits? Comparing the outcomes of sports mega-events in Canada and Japan. In J. Horne & W. Manzenreiter (Eds.), *Sport mega-events: Social scientific perspectives of a global phenomenon* (pp. 73-89). Oxford: Blackwell.

Whitson, D., & Macintosh, D. (1996). The global circus: International sport, tourism, and the marketing of cities. *Journal of Sport and Social Issues, 20,* 278-295.

Williams, G. (2003). *Enterprising city center: Manchester's development challenge.* London: Spon Press.

AUTHOR NOTE

We would like to acknowledge the Social Sciences and Humanities Research Council of Canada for supporting the research discussed herein.

ENDNOTES

[1] New East Manchester Ltd is a partnership initiative between Manchester City Council, English Partnerships, the North West Development Agency, and the communities of East Manchester. Its mandate is to lead the physical and social regeneration of East Manchester, recognized as one of the most deprived areas in the country.

[2] In 2001, MMEC became the Victoria Major Events Company.

Intercollegiate Athletics' Role in Donor Development in Higher Education

Jeffrey L. Stinson and Dennis R. Howard

Intercollegiate athletic programs have a long history of involvement with the development programs associated with higher education in the USA. Whether raising money specifically for athletics or assisting in the solicitation of gifts supporting the academic mission, athletic programs are increasingly integral to American university fundraising. According to the latest data released by the National Collegiate Athletic Association (NCAA), private giving continues to grow as a revenue stream for athletic programs (Fulks, 2009). At schools competing at the top level of NCAA competition (NCAA Football Bowl Subdivision), private donations now account for 18% of the average athletic department's revenues. Donations account for 27% of the earned revenues at the second level of competition (NCAA Football Championship Subdivision). The importance of athletics in fundraising is not limited to NCAA Division I schools. For example, at my home institution, Central Washington University (NCAA Division II), athletic programs directly raised a record amount of nearly $340,000 in 2009 (Anderson, 2010).

By almost any measure, athletic programs are increasing their fundraising efforts. It is less clear whether those efforts are integrated with overall institutional development. Throughout this chapter, our primary focus will be to focus on the development and cultivation of the donor through sport. First, we will examine the role sport programs can play in the philanthropic development of the donor. For many donors, sport plays an important role in the development of their giving patterns over the life course. Second, we explore the value intercollegiate athletic programs add to the institutional development effort, building a case for the active use and leveraging of sport to increase giving to the university as a whole. Finally, we will provide some recommendations on integrating the athletic and academic fundraising efforts to maximize the value of institutions' donor bases.

COMMERCIAL VERSUS ADOPTIVE PHILANTHROPY

Charitable donations are not always altruistic or philanthropic in the traditional sense. Schervish (1997), acknowledging that much charitable behavior is in fact self-serving, divided philanthropy into two categories: commercial philanthropy and adoptive philanthropy. Commercial philanthropy occurs when an individual donor is motivated to make a gift in exchange for some benefit that has commercial value to the donor. The primary motivation is the benefit the donor receives in exchange for a gift. For example, a donor motivated to make a gift to a university athletic department to access ticket or parking privileges would be participating in commercial philanthropy. Adoptive philanthropy, on the other hand, occurs when a donor makes a gift with the primary purpose of benefiting the non-profit organization or its beneficiaries. The motivation is to provide benefit to others, rather than benefit to self. A donor making a gift to a scholarship fund motivated by the desire to provide educational access is participating in adoptive philanthropy.

Both types of philanthropy can provide revenues to the organization. Nevertheless, commercial philanthropy may be limited by ceiling effects that are not present in adoptive philanthropy (Stinson & Howard, 2010). The amount a donor is willing to give in exchange for commercial benefits appears to closely mirror the financial value of those benefits. With adoptive philanthropy, the ceiling is set by the donor's perceived capacity to give, as opposed to the commercial value of benefits. Thus, adoptive philanthropy may result in the potential to attract larger gifts. An organization focused solely on adoptive philanthropy, however, may not realize its fundraising potential.

Effective fundraising organizations must appropriately understand the use of each type of philanthropy in the solicitation and cultivation of donors. Offering tangible or social benefits designed to meet the self-benefit motives of commercial philanthropy may be an ideal strategy for attracting new donors to the organization. New donors, particularly those with little or no direct connection to the organization, are unlikely to have high levels of involvement and identification typically associated with adoptive philanthropy. Nevertheless, they may be inspired to make a gift in exchange for a desired commercial benefit. That commercially motivated gift, in turn, may allow the organization to begin developing a relationship with the donor that may evolve to include larger gifts motivated by adoptive philanthropy. We will detail this donor transition in the higher education context below.

We expect that over the period of a sustained relationship with an organization that donors will transition from giving for primarily commercial to primarily adoptive reasons.

Likewise, we expect that identification (Bhattacharya, Rao, & Glynn, 1995; O'Reilly & Chatman, 1986) and involvement (Wunderink, 2002) levels with the organization will increase, supporting the transition to adoptive philanthropy. This motivational transition is often associated with increases in financial capacity as the donors move through their careers (Olsen, Smith, & Wunnava, 1989). The combination of greater financial capacity to give and adoptive motives may result in gifts that are larger than commercially motivated gifts. Figure 16.1 visually depicts motivational transitions as well as the likely types of gifts associated with the move from commercial to adoptive philanthropy (Greenfield, 1999). The transitions are consistent with a donor transitioning from a conventional to post-conventional moral social orientation (Kohlberg, 1984). A donor's behavioral motivation for gift-giving changes from social norms and felt obligations (conventional moral orientation, where a donor gives because it is expected or the "right" thing to do) to sincere concern for the welfare of others in an interdependent social structure (post-conventional moral orientation, where the donor gives out of concern for and the benefit of society).

If over their lives, donors change motivations when making gifts, fundraising organizations must be prepared to match those changing donor motivations to be successful in attracting and retaining donors. In the remainder of this chapter, we will examine the role sport may play in donor solicitation and cultivation for higher education institutions.

FIGURE 16.1. Developmental model of giving (based on Greenfield, 1999)

Although we focus primarily on higher education, we have no reason to believe the contributions of sport to donor development must be limited to a single context. The thousands of charity athletic events employed by nonprofit organizations of all types attest to the role sport can play in donor development across sectors (See Filo, Funk, & O'Brien, 2009).

THE EFFECTS OF ATHLETIC PROGRAM FUNDRAISING ON THE INSTITUTION AT LARGE

Historically, research on the role of intercollegiate athletic programs in higher education fundraising has been quite equivocal. Proponents of athletics argue that fundraising for athletic programs enhances universities' fundraising for academic programs. Critics assert that athletics fundraising "crowds out" or reduces donor support for academic programs. Yet it has been shown in other studies that there is no relationship between sport and university development. McCormick and Tinsley (1990) were among the first to empirically find a symbiotic relationship between sport and academic fundraising. In a study of donors at Clemson University, the authors estimated that a 10% increase in giving to athletic teams was associated with a 5% increase in academic fundraising. Increased attention to and investment in athletic fundraising stood to benefit the academic mission of the institution. Recently, researchers have indicated that the results may have to do with the ability of sport to attract new donors to the institution (Daughtrey & Stotlar, 2000; Stinson & Howard, 2008). Several other researchers have also documented a significant, positive influence of athletics on giving (Cunningham & Conchi-Ficano, 2002; McEvoy, 2005; Rhoads & Gerking, 2000; Sigelman & Carter, 1979). Together, the aforementioned researchers suggest that athletics can have a positive influence on both athletic and institutional fundraising.

Although from the studies reviewed there is indication that sport has the potential to contribute positively to donor and institutional development, in other studies, researchers have demonstrated that the realization of that potential may not be automatic. Sperber (1990, 2000) asserted that "crowding-out" effects were responsible for a reduction in academic support at many colleges and universities with high-profile athletic programs. He argued that as athletic programs significantly increased fundraising efforts to support their own operations, donors would give to those programs rather than academic programs (at least in part due to the commercial benefits associated with giving to athletic programs). Subsequent empirical research supported the presence of "crowding-out" effects at some institutions. Stinson and Howard (2004) identified potential "crowding-out" effects at the University of Oregon following the opening of the newly renovated Autzen Stadium (football) in 2002. As part of the fundraising effort to pay for the stadium project, donors were asked to contribute more for their football tickets and associated benefits. Empirical analyses indicated that the increased giving to athletic programs was associated with significant decreases in academic giving, particularly for non-alumni. To make larger athletic gifts, many donors, at least in part, reduced their academic giving. Thus, from an institutional perspective, the increases in athletic fundraising were offset by declines in academic support.

With a third set of studies, researchers concluded that athletic programs do not have a significant influence on the overall fundraising activity at the institution (e.g., Frank, 2004; Gaski & Etzel, 1984; Shulman & Bowen, 2001). Notably, Frank (2004) concluded that inconsistent research results across the literature were indicative of a lack of relationship between sport and university giving. We interpret the disparate research results somewhat differently. The studies finding a symbiotic effect of sport on institutional development are indicative of intercollegiate athletic programs having the potential to play a positive role in donor and institutional development. Particularly positive is the apparent ability of inter-collegiate athletic programs to attract new donors to the institution (Daughtrey & Stotlar, 2000; Stinson & Howard, 2008). The positive influence, however, is not guaranteed and has not been realized at all institutions, suggesting that athletic programs must be actively managed and leveraged if they are to benefit institutional fundraising efforts.

Over the past decade, we have focused much of our research effort on understanding the causes of disparate research results. In those studies we have considered the strategic use of athletic programs in donor and institutional development. We first sought to understand the potential factors resulting in the inconsistent conclusions documented in previous research. Subsequently, we pursued greater knowledge as to how sport influences donor-giving decisions to both athletic and academic programs. Finally, we have attempted to integrate our findings to demonstrate how the positive potential of sport to develop donors can be realized. The remainder of the chapter will focus heavily on the results of our research. By understanding both the positive and negative influences of sport on donors and their giving decisions, athletic development officers can best position themselves to maximize the value of donors toward both athletic and academic programs.

In an effort to identify relevant factors explaining when sport has a positive or negative influence on institutional development, we conducted two studies on a national (U.S.) dataset (See Table 16.1 for mean gift patterns). Although this dataset (the Voluntary Sector in Education database) only maintains institutional level data, as opposed to the individual donor-level data available in the University of Oregon study referenced above, the results shed significant light on the institutional effects of increased athletic fundraising. During the first of the two studies, we examined giving at schools competing in NCAA FBS Football (Stinson & Howard, 2007). Several important conclusions were drawn from the empirical analysis:

1. Alumni and non-alumni donors are not differentially affected by the onfield performance of sports teams with respect to giving decisions.[1]

2. Shifting gift patterns favoring athletics over academics (or crowding-out effects)

TABLE 16.1. Mean Giving Patterns to NCAA FBS Schools and other NCAA Division I Schools (FCS and DI Basketball) by *US News & World Report* Academic Ranking

Non-Alumni	1998 Avg. (% Ath)	1999	2000	2001	2002	2003
All FBS	4,069,517 (12.41)	4,019,814 (14.30)	5,072,682 (12.54)	5,670,842 (14.61)	5,931,355 (15.49)	5,469,002 (18.54)
US News 1 FBS	8,572,057 (6.11)	7,640,521 (5.55)	10,262,615 (6.26)	12,166,394 (6.22)	13,241,626 (7.20)	11,411,457 (9.86)
US News 2 FBS	4,467,503 (16.95)	4,697,924 (18.20)	4,952,128 (17.10)	5,890,598 (19.75)	6,026,017 (20.89)	5,395,652 (24.19)
US News 3 FBS	2,815,608 (8.62)	2,972,614 (17.84)	3,717,669 (15.42)	3,839,572 (16.79)	3,675,048 (19.75)	4,314,843 (22.89)
US News 4 FBS	1,930,597 (13.39)	1,949,832 (18.87)	2,135,969 (18.56)	2,489,811 (18.56)	2,424,032 (21.37)	1,942,618 (15.26)
ALL Other (BB)	1,323,865 (4.33)	1,479,182 (4.34)	2,234,973 (3.20)	1,828,869 (4.65)	1,767,039 (4.93)	2,000,939 (4.25)
US News 1 BB	6,609,435 (2.43)	7,563,093 (1.52)	14,479,006 (0.87)	10,094,194 (0.92)	8,067,694 (1.39)	8,420,399 (1.21)
US News 2 BB	1,204,168 (2.26)	1,120,603 (4.67)	1,264,387 (4.71)	1,476,591 (6.09)	2,426,096 (3.05)	1,954,801 (5.09)
US News 3 BB	1,140,674 (3.90)	1,236,339 (3.67)	1,582,343 (3.30)	1,158,501 (5.02)	1,246,891 (6.56)	1,932,508 (3.02)
US News 4 BB	1,118,913 (4.64)	746,307 (15.81)	846,643 (5.29)	1,093,028 (11.74)	858,026 (7.20)	696,921 (5.97)
US News 5 BB	822,137 (6.22)	568,715 (9.04)	675,491 (10.45)	715,753 (10.50)	860,570 (12.57)	947,494 (13.76)
Alumni						
All FBS	5,841,124 (14.70)	6,337,790 (16.90)	7,330,109 (16.88)	8,683,508 (17.77)	7,327,726 (22.86)	8,095,027 (26.01)
US News 1 FBS	15,948,940 (7.76)	16,869,950 (7.65)	18,341,812 (9.67)	22,319,110 (11.64)	18,708,838 (18.95)	19,908,272 (17.35)
US News 2 FBS	6,388,074 (22.14)	7,043,307 (22.35)	7,299,773 (23.45)	8,193,533 (23.72)	7,164,917 (24.02)	7,534,334 (33.34)
US News 3 FBS	2,813,529 (14.97)	3,413,462 (29.07)	3,894,292 (22.30)	6,003,788 (18.78)	4,205,463 (28.71)	5,836,203 (32.70)
US News 4 FBS	1,258,578 (17.95)	1,254,674 (27.39)	1,596,628 (25.15)	1,554,787 (38.02)	1,356,498 (35.68)	1,494,753 (37.24)
ALL Other (BB)	2,311,223 (6.27)	2,475,515 (6.90)	2,969,444 (7.18)	3,029,666 (7.17)	2,846,036 (7.47)	3,319,769 (7.83)
US News 1 BB	13,506,680 (5.13)	14,039,313 (5.84)	18,454,930 (6.15)	16,135,580 (5.93)	15,654,481 (5.77)	17,923,664 (6.01)
US News 2 BB	1,109,048 (6.41)	1,250,756 (7.55)	1,879,052 (5.82)	2,045,377 (7.39)	1,825,577 (8.33)	1,993,923 (9.56)
US News 3 BB	1,487,405 (6.24)	1,726,436 (6.08)	1,717,156 (6.26)	2,628,489 (3.69)	1,453,706 (7.47)	1,951,626 (6.00)
US News 4 BB	592,901 (6.23)	689,845 (3.54)	891,490 (1.95)	861,106 (3.62)	815,604 (8.52)	801,228 (8.30)
US News 5 BB	1,781,252 (9.13)	1,444,637 (10.69)	1,369,746 (11.43)	1,643,170 (10.23)	1,468,543 (10.13)	1,857,966 (10.57)

are weaker at academically elite institutions (as measured by *US News & World Report* academic rankings) than at schools falling outside the top tier of academic rankings. Nevertheless, the trends are towards increased preference for athletic giving (as opposed to academic giving) at all levels of higher education.

3. Although success on the field significantly influences giving to sport programs, it does not directly influence giving to academic programs. The crowding-out effect on academic gifts appears to be indirect, perhaps a result of donors' perceived financial capacity constraints.

4. Onfield success increases the donor base (i.e., attracts new donors), though most new donors make only sport-related gifts.

Within the second of the two studies, we empirically examined giving at NCAA FCS schools and schools without football programs competing in Division I basketball (Stinson & Howard, 2008). Again, the data were limited to institutional level (as opposed to individual donor) data. We found sport programs a significant influence on giving patterns at these schools. Several notable results:

1. At schools where football is offered, its influence on giving is stronger than basketball. In the absence of a football team, basketball becomes the primary athletic influence on giving.

2. As opposed to the FBS schools where crowding-out effects appeared to predominate, in this sample of schools, athletic success appears to increase both athletic and academic giving, particularly by alumni.

3. Athletic success again increases the donor base and the new donors, particularly new alumni donors, make both athletic and academic gifts.

Combined, the two studies present a sobering review of changes in giving patterns to higher education institutions. Donors, alumni and non-alumni alike, increasingly have indicated a preference for supporting sport programs, in many cases at the expense of support for academic programs. Yet, from the analysis there is also suggestion that crowding-out effects are not an inevitable outcome of increased sport fundraising. The key for development officers seeking to position the sport development effort as a contributor to university fundraising is to actively use the sport platform to not only support athletic giving, but academic giving as well. For example, at The Ohio State University, donors receive sport-related benefits (i.e., access to tickets) for academic as well as athletic giving. This program encourages donors to support both the sport and academic programs at the institution. Many institutions do not pursue such strategies. The results of our studies indicate that simply operating at the status quo, for many institutions, may result in the crowding-out of academic gifts.

A starting point for more closely aligning athletics fundraising efforts with institutional development is to focus on the new donors who are attracted to the institution by successful athletic programs. In both national studies we conducted, successful football and basketball teams were associated with an increase in the number of donors making gifts to the university. For some institutions, up to 70% of new donors made their first gift to the athletic program (Stinson & Howard, 2010). Whether those new donors subsequently give only to support sport or whether they also give in support of the academic mission is an important determinant of the overall institutional benefit. Implementing specific strategies designed to encourage and cultivate academic gifts from new donors, such as The Ohio State University strategy, allows athletic development officers to position themselves as valuable assets in overall institutional development efforts.

THE ROLE OF ATHLETICS DEVELOPMENT IN INSTITUTIONAL DEVELOPMENT

To effectively cultivate donors, institutional development officers must have a deep understanding of their donors and how those donors make giving decisions. We sought this deep understanding by interviewing major donors (i.e., donors giving $1,000 or more annually) at three NCAA Division I FBS Schools. We chose to focus on donors making gifts to both athletic and academic programs because we were interested in understanding their changing gift patterns, particularly whether crowding-out occurred as athletic giving increased. In contrast to the entirely quantitative analysis of previous research, we recognized that we would need to personally interview donors to fully understand why and how they were making their respective giving decisions. Face-to face, semi-structured interviews were conducted with over 70 donors at three universities. Interviews were conducted in donor's homes, offices, or in the athletic department offices at the participating universities. The interviews ranged from 45 to 90 minutes. All data were transcribed and analyzed independently and iteratively by the researchers. We found several consistent patterns that help explain not only the changing gift patterns, but also how donors can be best cultivated to maximize their total institutional support (Stinson & Howard, 2010). We review four of those conclusions below.

Conclusion #1: Intercollegiate Athletics Socialize Both Alumni and Non-Alumni to the University Creating a Strong Emotional Connection to the Institution

Many authors have asserted that one contribution of intercollegiate athletic programs is to serve as a "window" to the university (e.g., Duderstadt, 2000; Shulman & Bowen, 2001; Toma, 2003). It is through this window that the general public understands the mission and vision of the institution. Our research has supported the "window contribution" of intercollegiate athletics and extended the analogy even further to include intercollegiate athletics' ability to generate strong emotional ties with the institution.

A significant number of donors commented on sport's role in developing an emotional connection with the university. That emotional connection in turn provided the foundation for the donor's propensity to financially support the institution. The emotional connection rooted in athletics appears to be equally strong for alumni and non-alumni. Many non-alumni donors reported that their emotional connection to the universities they were supporting charitably was stronger than the emotional connection to their respective alma maters. The ability of intercollegiate athletics to establish this emotional connection is not easily replicated by academic programs. From both the qualitative and quantitative data we have studied there is an indication that when forced to choose one or the other, donors will support the institution and program to which they have the strongest emotional ties. Athletic programs consistently establish and strengthen the emotional ties for many donors.

Athletic programs are well suited for establishing, maintaining, and strengthening the emotional connection to the school. Almost 75% of the donors we interviewed made their first gift to athletics, not academics. Even for alumni, athletics served as the primary emotional connection to the university. Although we cannot be certain that the donors interviewed would not have eventually supported academic programs without the sport connection, it is clear that the emotional connection to sport established and strengthened their connections to academic programs. The spillover connections that are fostered through sport are an important contribution of intercollegiate athletics to the institutional development effort.

Conclusion #2: Initial Support of Athletics (and Institutions) Is Often Commercially Motivated, Resulting in Ceiling Effects on Gift Amounts

With nearly 75% of donors making their first gifts to the institution in support of sport programs, we wanted to know how those initial gifts influenced later giving to both athletic and academic programs. In almost all cases, donors reported that their initial gifts to athletics were the result of the donors' desires to access tickets or other privileges associated with the athletic gifts. The athletic gifts were motivated by commercial philanthropy; the donors made gifts to obtain desired commercial benefits (Schervish, 1997). Even more telling, when asked what alternative uses they would consider for the money donated to athletics, donors reported mostly entertainment and leisure-related expenses. Travel, boats, and purchasing other forms of entertainment were commonly cited as "competition," further supporting the commercial nature of the initial athletic gifts. This finding is not surprising given that material incentives are well suited to attracting commercial philanthropy (Barnes & McCarville, 2005). Given the commercial motivation for the athletic gifts, it is also not surprising that ceiling effects were present. Gifts were commonly capped at the amount of commercial benefit received by the donor in exchange for the gift. For a significant majority of donors, the required gift necessary to secure ticket benefits was the amount the donor gave to support athletics (Stinson & Howard, 2010a).

Several important implications result from this finding. First, if the perceived value of tickets or other benefits provided by the athletic department decreases (e.g., the football team has a prolonged period of losing), athletic giving may be withdrawn in favor of other discretionary expenses that would then be valued more highly. Second, the commercial nature of the giving places a ceiling on the amount a donor is willing to give. A commercially motivated donor can only be expected to give up to the perceived value of the tickets or other benefits received in exchange for giving. Although athletic programs can attract new donors to the institution (Daughtrey & Stotlar 2000; Stinson & Howard, 2008), many of the new donors may be motivated by the commercial benefits and give only the minimum amount necessary to receive desired benefits. Thus, the university must work to effectively leverage the emotional connection with the sport program to motivate adoptive philanthropy. For many donors, the preference in making adoptive philanthropic gifts is for non-athletic programs (Stinson & Howard, 2010b). Thus, for the university, a key success factor in fundraising is whether the institution can leverage commercially oriented athletic giving to foster donor intent to make adoptively motivated academic gifts.

Conclusion #3: Donors Can be Successfully Cultivated to Transition from Commercial to Philanthropic Giving, Reducing or Removing Ceiling Effects

Donor involvement and identification with an organization have been cited as strong influences on gift decisions (Bhattacharya et al., 1995; Wunderink, 2002). Leveraging donors' emotional connections to sport to increase donor involvement and identification with the university, athletically and/or academically, is critical in soliciting gifts that are more adoptive than commercial in motivation. Developing adoptive motivations for giving is essential to both athletic and academic development officers because adoptive philanthropy does not appear to be subject to the same ceiling effects as commercial philanthropy. Recognizing that a substantial subset of athletic donors may not view intercollegiate athletics adoptively (Stinson & Howard, 2010), institutions should be encouraged to cultivate athletic donors in an attempt to secure adoptively motivated gifts for other, usually academic, programs. Athletic donors have strong emotional connections to the university, predisposing them to consider additional institutional information positively. Thus, athletics can provide a vehicle for communicating relevant academic information, in a context where it is likely to be evaluated positively by the donor. The potential exists to cultivate commercially motivated donors beyond their donations to sport to include adoptive philanthropic support for the university's academic programs. Certainly, some donors can be cultivated to make adoptive gifts to support athletics, but others cannot. For the institution to benefit, athletic development officers must help cultivate donors to make additional philanthropic gifts to the university's academic programs.

Conclusion #4: Academic Units May Benefit from Leveraging the Emotional Connection to Athletics to Cultivate Gifts

Interviewed donors revealed that with few exceptions, academic programs and development officers have not been able to generate the same strong, personal connections with the donors as the donors have with sport. Again, the emotional connection established by athletics may be an important point of leverage for the institution attempting to develop connections to academic programs and to increase donor commitment and retention (Sargeant & Woodliffe, 2007). Because many donors are reluctant to make adoptive philanthropy gifts to sport programs, academic programs have the potential to provide an adoptive outlet for athletic donors. By not cross-cultivating and soliciting athletic donors, institutions may under-realize the potential of their donor base. To successfully cross-cultivate and solicit donors will require athletic and academic development staff to put aside the all-too-frequent competitive disconnects that divide the two groups (Howard & Crompton, 2004). Instead of operating as competitive, independent entities, athletic development officers will need to be integrated into the larger fundraising efforts of the university. Outcomes of such integrated efforts may lead to larger gifts and higher retention rates, maximizing the value of donors to the institution (Stinson & Howard, 2010a,2010b).

CULTIVATING AND DEVELOPING DONORS

Understanding donor decisions and gift patterns from the quantitative and qualitative research described above provides a foundation for examining the potential benefits of integrating intercollegiate athletics into university fundraising efforts. Additional empirical examination of detailed giving records to three NCAA Division I FBS schools highlighted the positive outcomes of integrated development efforts designed to cross-solicit and cultivate donors (Stinson & Howard, 2010a). Most notably, donors who made gifts to both athletic and academic programs gave larger gifts and were retained at higher rates than their counterparts (See Table 16.2). We now turn our attention to these positive outcomes and to consideration of how sport can contribute to the philanthropic development of a donor.

As previously noted, successful athletic programs have been effective in attracting new donors to universities (Daughtrey & Stotlar, 2000; Stinson & Howard, 2008). Nevertheless, many new donors give for what appear to be primarily commercial reasons (e.g., access to tickets). As a result, they donate only up to the perceived value of the benefits

TABLE 16.2. Year-to-Year Retention Rates and Average Gift Sizes

Year	Athletic Donors		Academic Donors		Split Donors	
	Retention Rate (%)	Average Gift ($)	Retention Rate (%)	Average Gift ($)	Retention Rate (%)	Average Gift ($)
1992	76.26	4150.73	68.01	6252.25	97.41	6591.56
1993	92.28	2036.26	78.17	6905.49	94.40	3979.02
1994	99.87	2013.50	89.99	9398.90	101.30	4067.52
1995	85.54	1937.12	63.55	9622.17	73.55	4986.73
1996	85.27	2060.99	70.80	8091.04	82.14	7034.68
1997	88.65	2395.47	74.10	9337.74	90.59	7831.58
1998	94.82	6591.87	74.66	11439.50	97.75	9903.34
1999	87.37	2622.80	79.02	13758.31	87.75	9103.16
2000	92.15	2715.41	79.19	13230.05	97.24	9724.36
2001	95.93	2579.47	74.88	11400.97	100.70	10434.17
2002	91.10	3146.13	80.34	11778.88	87.50	9222.15
2003	90.61	2993.05	76.16	14090.49	98.77	21591.33
2004	89.47	3145.41	75.49	9804.51	87.02	11842.40
2005	75.59	3307.42	84.40	12805.44	88.47	9131.63

**Retention rates over 100 possible given renewed donations of lapsed donors.

received in exchange for their gift (Stinson & Howard, 2010a). Unless new donors can be cultivated to give for adoptive as opposed to commercial reasons, ceiling effects limit their giving. Almost all donors in the interview study reviewed above indicated that their academic gifts were adoptively motivated (Stinson & Howard, 2010b). Thus, cultivating donors to make adoptively motivated academic gifts, in addition to their commercially oriented athletic gifts, maximizes the donors' value to universities. Several important implications result and are discussed below.

Donors making gifts to both athletic and academic programs (split donors) make larger total gifts to the university than their counterparts making only athletic gifts. We have theorized that split donors give more because they access financial resources allocated to different mental budgets, increasing their perceived capacity to give (e.g., Heath & Soll, 1996). When athletic support is primarily driven by a desire to gain access to tickets, the gift may not be considered charitable by donors. As a result, donors account for the gift as an entertainment/leisure expense. For example, one donor stated that, "The English department should not be upset that I give so much to athletics. I will tell you who should be upset. The boat dealer down the road won't be making a sale to me this year as a result of the increased amount we have had to give to get our tickets" (Stinson & Howard, 2010b, pp. 321). Sentiments such as this one are consistent with commercial philanthropy.

The academic giving of split donors, on the other hand, appears to be more adoptively motivated. Motives for academic gifts were commonly centered on either repaying the institution for benefits previously provided to the donor (often as a student) or on the adoptive support of current students. For example, one split donor explained his academic giving, "The hand-written notes from students are so moving. I just got a note from a gal stating that 'without this help I would not have been able to attend (the institution).' This makes you think you have really been able to help change a kid's life" (Stinson & Howard, 2010b, pp. 319). Further, donors frequently cited other non-profit organizations as the competition for their academic gifts, not athletic programs. As a result, academic donations typically were allocated against a charitable or philanthropic budget.

Drawing on two budgets potentially expands the perceived capacity of the donor to support the institution (Morewedge, Holtzman, & Epley, 2007). The interviews with split donors are clearly supportive of this possibility. Due to donors' ability to draw upon different motives and budgets, their perceived availability of financial resources for making gifts increases. When more resources are available, spending may increase (Cheema & Soman, 2006). By attracting both commercially and adoptively motivated gifts, universities are able to secure donations from both leisure/entertainment and philanthropic budgets.

Donors making gifts to both athletic and academic programs are also retained at significantly higher rates than academic-only donors and at equal or higher levels than athletic-only donors. Within this chapter we have theorized that the strong emotional connection and social opportunities associated with giving to sport are important in maintaining high levels of donor retention. Developing the emotional and social connections appears to be another significant contribution that intercollegiate athletics can make to overall university fundraising efforts. We think higher retention rates may result from the multiple levels of attachment split donors have with an institution (see also Wunderink, 2002). It is possible that broader involvement immunizes donors, to an extent, from negative information or poor performance in one program. For example, intercollegiate athletic donors may withdraw if the football team has a sustained period of losing. Donors making both athletic and academic gifts may be less sensitive to onfield performances because they are offset by positive academic performances. The opposite relationship may be true as well (i.e., positive athletic performances may help mitigate negative academic program news). In any event, the combination of larger gifts and high retention rates makes split donors extremely valuable to institutions.

There is a tremendous amount of potential to increase the cross-cultivation of donors. Less than a third of donors make both athletic and academic gifts to the universities we have studied. Further, the observed conversion rates of athletic-only donors to split donors are only about 10% on average (Stinson & Howard, 2010a). Given the high value of split donors, evidenced by gift size and retention rates, efforts to increase cross-cultivation efforts have great potential for significant institutional return.

When a donor converts from making an athletic-only gift to making both athletic and academic gifts, there is often a small reduction in the athletic gift (less than 5% in most cases). Institutionally, this decrease is offset by what is often more than a two-fold increase in the total gift (Stinson & Howard, 2010a). Thus, it is important to recognize that as individual agents, athletic department fundraisers may not have an incentive to cross-cultivate donors. Institutional strategies to overcome barriers to cross-cultivation of donors, as opposed to independent athletic and academic fundraising strategies, can more fully leverage the athletic fundraising function within university development and reap the benefits (i.e., larger gifts and higher retention rates) of split donors.

Donors making gifts to both athletic and academic programs are quite valuable to institutions. Intercollegiate athletic programs have important roles to play in recruiting and cultivating split donors. Successful sport programs may be the most effective tools on campuses for attracting new donors, both alumni and non-alumni, to universities. Sport also may play a critical role in the high retention rates of donors. Yet, in many cases, sport alone cannot realize the full value of donors to universities. Many donors are not motivated to make adoptive philanthropic gifts to sport programs. Nevertheless, donors may be motivated to make adoptive gifts to academic programs. The athletic programs that attracted the donors may become key vehicles for communicating an academic message and cultivating academic gifts.

Recognizing that for many donors the motives for athletic giving are quite different from the motives for academic giving can break down the competitive barriers that sometimes prevent athletic and academic fundraisers from working in concert to maximize donors' potentials. It is no surprise to us that the schools that have the highest percentages and conversion rates of these donors are those that have integrated, cooperative fundraising efforts (Stinson & Howard, 2010a). Too often, the barriers between independent athletic and academic fundraising units prevent the communication and cooperation that allow for successful cross-cultivation of donors. Actively overcoming those barriers will allow athletic development officers to not only support the intercollegiate athletic programs, but to become key contributors to larger university fundraising efforts.

CONCLUSION

Universities are in a unique position to develop strong, mutually beneficial relationships with donors throughout donors' lives (Brady, Noble, Utter & Smith, 2003). The tangible, commercial benefits that can be offered early in the donor-institution relationship (e.g., football tickets, theatre tickets) attract new donors to institutions (Daughtrey & Stotlar,

2000; Stinson & Howard, 2008). From a donor perspective, commercial benefits allow donors to participate in philanthropy at a time when they may not have significant financial capacity to give (i.e., early in careers). Thus, offering an attractive program that will benefit donors, yet allow them to make a philanthropic gift can provide a foundation on which to build stronger levels of involvement and identification over time (Bhattacharya et al., 1995; Wunderink, 2002). These programs also create a propensity to give in donors who may not otherwise make gifts to support an institution. As donors increase their involvement and organizational identification, they may expand their giving beyond commercial philanthropy to also include adoptive philanthropy. In our research there is indication that the transition from commercial to adoptive philanthropy results in both additional gifts to the organization and greater retention of the donors. As donors gain financial capacity, they increasingly seek to make adoptive gifts to organizations and causes that resonate personally. Because of the foundational relationships and emotional connections created with universities through sport, universities may be at an advantage in soliciting and cultivating adoptive gifts for athletic and academic programs.

Of course, cultivating donors from commercial to adoptive philanthropy is easier said than done. To successfully develop donors, institutions must recognize the different segments of donors and match their respective motives for giving with appropriate solicitations. The institutions must maintain relationships with the donors to increase involvement and identification, and ultimately transition the donors into new areas for giving. Success will require athletic and academic development officers to work in partnership rather than competition. Establishing integrated development units, creating incentives for cross cultivation and solicitation, and coordinating sport and academic fundraising efforts may be required. The return, however, of undertaking such challenges appears to be quite positive and will maximize the value of donors to institutions over their lives.

REFERENCES

Anderson, M. (2010). *2009 CWU athletic fund raising sets new record.* Ellensburg, WA: CWU Athletics.

Barnes, M., & McCarville, R. (2005). Patron or philanthropist: Charitable giving to a performance-based leisure provider. *Journal of Park and Recreation Administration, 23,* 110-134.

Bhattacharya, C. B., Rao, H., & Glynn, M. A. (1995). Understanding the bond of identification: An investigation of its correlates among art museum members. *Journal of Marketing, 59,* 46-57.

Brady, M. K., Noble, C. H., Utter, D. J., & Smith, G. E. (2002). How to give and receive: An exploratory study of charitable hybrids. *Psychology & Marketing, 19,* 919-944.

Cheema, A., & Soman, D. (2006), Malleable mental accounting: The effect of flexibility on the justification of attractive spending and consumption decisions. *Journal of Consumer Psychology, 16,* 33-44.

Cunningham, B. M., & Cochi-Ficano, C. K. (2002). The determinants of donative revenue flows from alumni of higher education. *Journal of Human Resources, 37,* 540-569.

Daughtrey, C., & Stotlar, D. (2000). Donations: Are they affected by a football championship? *Sport Marketing Quarterly, 9,* 185-193.

Duderstadt, J. J. (2000). *Intercollegiate athletics and the American university: A university president's perspective.* Ann Arbor, MI: The University of Michigan Press.

Filo, K., Funk, D. C., & O'Brien, D. (2009). The meaning behind attachment: Exploring camaraderie, cause, and competency at a charity sport event. *Journal of Sport Management, 23,* 361-387.

Frank, R. H. (2004). *Challenging the myth: A review of links among college athletic success, student quality, and donations.* New York: Knight Foundation Commission on Intercollegiate Athletics.

Fulks, D. L. (2009). *2004-08 NCAA revenues and expenses of division I intercollegiate athletic programs report.* Indianapolis, IN: The National Collegiate Athletic Association.

Gaski, J. F., & Etzel, M. J. (1984). Collegiate athletic success and alumni generosity: Dispelling the myth. *Social Behavior and Personality, 12,* 29-38.

Greenfield, J. M. (1996). *Fundraising cost effectiveness: A self-assessment workbook.* New York: John Wiley & Sons.

Heath, C., & Soll, J. B. (1996). Mental budgeting and consumer decisions. *Journal of Consumer Research, 23,* 40-52.

Howard, D. R., & Crompton, J. L. (2004). *Financing sport.* Morgantown, WV: Fitness Information Technology.

Kohlberg, L. (1984). *The psychology of moral development: The nature and validity of moral stages.* San Francisco: Harper & Row.

McCormick, R. E., & Tinsley, M. (1990). Athletics and academics: A model of university contributions. In B. L. Goff & R. D. Tollison (Eds.), *Sportometrics* (pp. 193-206). College Station, TX: Texas A&M University Press.

McEvoy, C. (2005). Predicting fundraising revenues in NCAA division I-A intercollegiate athletics. *The Sport Journal.* Retrieved July 26, 2007 from http://www.thesportjournal.org/2005Journal/Vol8-No1/Chad_McEvoy.asp

Morewedge, C. K., Holtzman, L., & Epley, N. (2007). Unfixed resources: Perceived costs, consumption, and the accessible account effect. *Journal of Consumer Research, 34,* 459-467.

Olsen, K., Smith, A. L., & Wunnava, P. V. (1989). An empirical study of the lifecycle hypothesis with respect to alumni donations. *American Economist, 33*(2), 60-63.

O'Reilly III, C., & Chatman, J. (1986). Organizational commitment and psychological attachment: The effects of compliance, identification and internalization on prosocial behavior. *Journal of Applied Psychology, 71,* 492-499.

Rhoads, T. A., & Gerking, S. (2000). Educational contributions, academic quality and athletic success. *Contemporary Economic Policy, 18,* 248-259.

Sargeant, A., & Woodliffe, L. (2007). Building donor loyalty: The antecedents and role of commitment in the context of charity giving. *Journal of Nonprofit & Public Sector Marketing, 18*(2), 47-68.

Schervish, P. J. (1997). Inclination, obligation and association: What we know and what we need to know about donor motivation. In D. F. Burlingame (Ed.), *Critical issues in fund raising* (pp. 110-138). San Francisco: Jossey Bass.

Shulman, J. L., & Bowen, W. G. (2001). *The game of life.* Princeton, NJ: Princeton University Press.

Sigelman, L., & Carter, R. (1979). Win one for the giver? Alumni giving and big-time college sports. *Social Science Quarterly, 60,* 284-294.

Sperber, M. (1990). *College sports inc.* New York: Henry Holt.

Sperber, M. (2000). *Beer and circus: The impact of big-time college sports on undergraduate education.* New York: Henry Holt.

Stinson, J. L., & Howard, D. R. (2004). Scoreboards vs. mortarboards: The impact of intercollegiate athletics on donor behavior. *Sport Marketing Quarterly, 13*(3), 73-81.

Stinson, J. L., & Howard, D. R. (2007). Athletic success and private giving to athletic and academic programs at NCAA institutions. *Journal of Sport Management, 21,* 235-264.

Stinson, J. L., & Howard, D. R. (2008). Winning does matter: Patterns in private giving to athletic and academic programs at NCAA division I-AA and I-AAA institutions. *Sport Management Review, 11,* 1-20.

Stinson, J. L., & Howard, D. R. (2010a). Athletic giving and academic giving: Exploring the value of SPLIT donors. *Journal of Sport Management, 25.*

Intercollegiate athletics as an institutional fundraising tool: An exploratory donor-based view. *Journal of Nonprofit and Public Sector Marketing, 22,* 312-335.

Stinson, J. L., & Howard, D. R. (2010b). Intercollegiate athletics as an institutional fundraising tool: An exploratory donor-based view. *Journal of Nonprofit and Public Sector Marketing, 22,* 312-335.

Toma, J. D. (2003). *Football U.* Ann Arbor, MI: The University of Michigan Press.

Wunderink, S. R. (2002). Individual financial donations to charities in The Netherlands. *Journal of Nonprofit and Public Sector Marketing, 10,* 21-39.

ENDNOTE

[1] Athletic performance was measured by the won-loss performance of football and men's basketball teams, post-season appearances, and by tradition of appearance in final season rankings (similar to Rhoads & Gerking, 2000).

Corporate Philanthropic Activity Related to Sport: What Works and What Doesn't

Shane Pegg and Ian Patterson

lobalization, technological innovations, and a changing consumer focus have dramatically affected the way that sporting agencies and associations operate in today's turbulent business environment. For example, in recent years, sport managers have been increasingly compelled to rethink their business strategies to optimize their operations' competitive advantages. At the same time however, they have also been required to identify ways to reduce their vulnerability to any prospective external threat from other sport and/or entertainment-based businesses. As noted by Aaker (2005), each industry sector in the modern economy is either already hostile (i.e., characterized by overcapacity, low margins, and intense competition) or increasingly becoming so. In such a marketplace it has become imperative that any sport business (regardless of its size) continually seek out ways to improve its services so as to fulfill the holistic needs of its customers in today's experience economy (i.e., businesses focused on delivering experiences for consumers cased in terms of affective memories, sensations, and symbolism rather than services or goods) (Hosany & Witham, 2009; Ritchie, Mules, & Uzabeaga, 2008).

These commercially oriented or non-profit-based sport operations have designed staged events (which may be as diverse as a youth sports "come and try" program offered during the school holiday recess at the community and recreational sport level or an annual internationally staged tournament such as the Hong Kong Sevens at the professional end of the sports spectrum) as central pillars of their operations, while at the same time they must continuously adopt new and innovative strategies to improve or maintain their competitiveness in the marketplace (Pegg & Patterson, 2010; Rumelt, 2008). Because of these changing trends, sporting operations need to be proactive in seeking to differentiate themselves to remain competitive. By necessity, the changed business environment entails that the management team needs to be willing to provide better value (as perceived by the various stakeholders) than their competitors. Thus, customer-focussed service activities that are highly regarded as being of value are essential in gaining loyalty and market leadership. Businesses must therefore effectively engage themselves in an ongoing process whereby the internal mechanisms of an operation are tailored to meet the changing needs of consumers while simultaneously allowing each business to differentiate itself from its competition through the services that it offers. Such a process necessitates the identification and adoption of a range of service-oriented activities that are seen to be of value to the consumer on a regular basis (Solnet & Kandampully, 2008). Certainly, how and why a philanthropic group or individual could benefit from linking in some manner or other with a sport organization, or how the sporting entity itself could positively engage in philanthropic activities should now be a central interest for that operation's management.

REPOSITIONING SPORTS OPERATIONS AS BUSINESSES IN THE EXPERIENCE ECONOMY

As noted by Pine and Gilmore (1998), an experience is not an amorphous construct. Rather it is as real an offering as any service, good, or commodity. It is an unfortunate reality, however, that in today's service economy, all too many sport operators simply wrap experiences around their traditional offerings in an effort to add extra value to sell them. To realize the full benefit of staging experiences, businesses must attempt to deliberately design new and engaging experiences that command a fee (Pine & Gilmore, 1998, 1999, 2000). Such practices, however, are something that to date has not been well demonstrated by many operators in the sport and events sector, where much of the focus has remained on the setting, rather than better catering for people's multiple needs and/or desires (Packer, Small, & Darcy, 2008).

Lusch, Vargo, and O'Brien (2007) argued that services were more than simply adding value to products. Rather, service has to do with the entire organization viewing and approaching both itself and the market with a service-dominant philosophy. This logic needs to be grounded effectively in a commitment to collaborative processes, where due recognition is given to the organization and its exchange partners (i.e., corporate benefactors, sponsors, spectators, players) effectively engaging in the co-creation of value through reciprocal service provision (Lusch et al.). This issue is critically important to the sports industry, because not only is it quite specialized, but the type of benefits that are sought, and the motives and needs that drive engagement, are very much related to other areas of business activity. As a result, the services offered and the type and range of opportunities provided to the full gamut of stakeholders in these types of settings must be suitably blended and balanced accordingly. Critically, such fine-tuning needs to include a detailed consideration by sports managers about the role and positioning of philanthropic groups or individuals in the community. These same groups and individuals are often seeking out positive outcomes from market relationships that reflect well on their brand and perceived standing in the community. It also means that today sports managers need to fully consider the strategic benefits that the sporting entity itself might derive from direct involvement in philanthropic activities as part of its overall business plan.

UNDERSTANDING CORPORATE PHILANTHROPY: THE WHO, WHAT, AND WHY

There are an increasing number of businesses that are seeking to weave philanthropy into the very fabric of their operations (Bianchi, 2006). It is important to recognize from the outset that corporate philanthropy has traditionally been cased in the notion that it is based on some form of patronage whereby support is given principally for an altruistic benefit, with little contribution in return beyond perhaps some recognition of good standing in the community (Arthur, Scott, Woods, & Brooker, 1998). This concept is not entirely discrete from that of sponsorship, which has been described as a commercial activity designed to achieve business objectives (Masterman, 2007). Although it can be argued that philanthropy has been viewed as being oriented more towards being a provider of a service for the general welfare of members of the community, this provider may nevertheless still gain a number of commercial advantages from such an effort. As noted by Sasse and Trahan (2007), each business and each individual has their own giving philosophy. For some, it is a case of enhancing their public image. In other cases, however, the determining factor may well be related to the personal views of the company owner or the collective interests of the staff. Regardless, for any sporting entity in today's highly competitive marketplace, an understanding of why corporations seek to engage in corporate philanthropy and how they do so, is of critical importance to their own business operations. Such knowledge can significantly assist managers to better align their own sport and recreation operations with philanthropic activities so that they can take full advantage of the resources and connections that come hand in hand with the development of such relationships.

As Saiia (2001, p. 58) noted,

> when a corporation engages in philanthropy it is confronted with the task of allocating corporate resources for activities that are not directly related to its immediate business objectives and thus must consider what is important enough for the corporation to support as an institution within a community.

For many corporate entities that engage in philanthropic activities, the benefits can be varied. For example, above and beyond any benefit that society might derive from this activity, the company itself may see "improvements in staff morale, a stimulation of customer demand, an enhancement of their attractiveness in the labor market, and even an opportunity for the organization to learn how to apply their core competencies in new areas" (Bianchi, 2006, p. 13). There are also benefits to be derived by the recipient agency. For example, the recipients of any act of corporate philanthropy benefit first and foremost from the additional public exposure they receive for the particular cause they are championing. The organization also benefits from the credibility that comes with being identified as a worthy recipient by a discerning business corporation. Benefits may also accrue more broadly to the local region in which the support is targeted because such activity can often serve to offer encouragement to other businesses and individuals to engage in a similar manner. For example, in Australia, it is no surprise that both the Coles Group and Woolworths (major supermarket chains), who are fierce competitors in the marketplace, are each heavily involved in supporting junior sporting initiatives in a wide variety of regions throughout Australia through their philanthropic activities.

By and large though, philanthropic efforts have been viewed to date as being cased in terms of either philanthropic strategies or strategic philanthropies (Campbell & Slack, 2008). Saiia, Carroll, and Buchholtz (2003) contended that a philanthropic strategy entails developing an orderly set of procedures and systems that are established so as to give money away. Strategic philanthropy on the other hand is considered to be "the synergistic use of a firm's resources to achieve both organizational and social benefits" (Thorne, Ferrell, & Ferrell, 2003, p. 360). Thus, and as noted by Campbell and Slack, the latter has "a dual objective of corporate value added and charitable benevolence" (p. 188).

Traditionally, much of the corporate activity with respect to support of community endeavors has been cased as being principally under the banner of a philanthropic strategy. Under such an approach, it has historically been the case that funds or other resources were often distributed ad hoc at best, with the choice of successful recipients largely determined by staff engaged in the localized decision-making process. The consequential flow-on effect of such a process was that the funds and/or other resources distributed to particular communities resulted in being only of diminished value to the recipients. Perhaps the best recent example of this can be found in Indonesia with respect to the survivors of the 2008 tsunami. Immediately after the tragedy, aid agencies were quick to supply rice and clothing to support communities that had been affected by the natural disaster. It appears, however, that limited thought was given to the range of on-the-ground needs for the survivors. Because of this minimal planning, the provision of any form of shelter was extremely limited in many regions, there were no pots provided to store or cook the rice that was supplied, potable water for drinking or cooking was extremely limited, and much of the donated clothing provided from overseas was inappropriate for the tropics and the rough coastal landscape of the Indonesian provinces. Although grounded in good intent, the harsh reality for many aid recipients was that they derived a reduced benefit from what was supplied via many philanthropic agencies.

Bruch and Walter (2005) argued that although many businesses appreciate the relevance of philanthropy, few actually achieve any significant form of long-term societal benefit because most lack a cohesive strategy with respect to how they should go about the task. Bruch and Walter contended that businesses need to run their philanthropic activities in the same professional manner as other elements of their core business. In effect therefore, the one-size-fits-all mentality is ill suited for today's dynamic and ever-changing sport business environment. As noted by poet and singer Bob Dylan, the times most certainly are a changing as more and more corporations today attempt to align their philanthropic activities with other sections of their overall operations.

Because of this change, businesses are increasingly focusing attention on a strategic approach to philanthropy aligned with their business operations to obtain the most bang for their buck. Certainly, there has been a great deal of support for this notion that it makes good business sense to strategically use their philanthropic activities to create win-win situations for both the businesses and the beneficiaries of the activities (Bruch & Walter, 2005). This position was also espoused by Fombrun, Gardberg, and Barnett (2000) who asserted that companies have quickly come to the realization that in today's modern marketplace, a strategically focused corporate social responsibility (CSR) portfolio assists the operation to build for itself a great amount of reputational capital. The authors contended that "by doing good, managers generate reputational gains that improve a company's ability to attract resources, enhance its performance and build competitive advantage" (Fombrun et al., p. 105). These types of endeavors, however, do not come without some level of business risk. This risk exists because, increasingly, the values and expectations of consumers are changing and with these changes have come higher expectations of individual businesses with regards to ethical standards, governance procedures, and socially acceptable practices consistent with that of the "triple bottom line" philosophy. A triple bottom line philosophy is grounded in the notion of expanding the evaluation of business operations beyond the traditional company reporting framework based around financial performance to a broader assessment of operations that also encapsulates environmental and social performances aspects of the business (Darcy, Cameron, & Pegg, 2010; Dwyer, 2005). Therefore, businesses must now walk something of a consumer-driven tightrope to balance their operations.

There is now clear evidence to indicate that those organizations that are perceived by consumers as engaging in CSR on the basis of it being driven largely by self-interest or as little more than a public relations exercise can actually damage their brands and corporate images. On the other hand, being totally passive (or perhaps ignorant) about such activity is also untenable. Thus, a business that does not adequately engage in and promote its CSR initiatives may well fall short in the public eye and consequently lose consumer support for its products and services. Clearly, therefore, it is important to fully understand that there are significant differences between the two positions, and knowing how and when to successfully implement philanthropic strategies has become a critical factor for those in the sport and recreation sector to acknowledge and act upon accordingly. There can be no doubt that the changing focus of many corporations towards the incorporation of strategies of philanthropy as part of their broader CSR agendas will most definitely serve to effectively differentiate and reposition various sporting entities in the marketplace.

KEYS TO RETHINKING CORPORATE PHILANTHROPY IN A SPORTING CONTEXT

There can be no argument that the landscape of sport has dramatically changed over the last few decades, particularly in the Asia-Pacific region where the development of a range of professional and semi-professional national sporting leagues has come to the fore as the premier form of regularly scheduled entertainment in the region. Although it is evident that only a limited amount of research has been undertaken to date with respect to corporate social responsibility in the sports industry, one need look no further than the World Wide Web and the social network pages (i.e., Facebook) of sports organizations to appreciate that CSR, with corporate philanthropy as one key form of activity, has become a critical element of the day-to-day marketing activities of operations. Evidence to this effect is not hard to find. For example, in Australia and New Zealand the individual clubs that make up the National Rugby League have demonstrated a long-term commitment to youth initiatives and, more recently, social issues such as breast and prostate cancer. Similarly, a rival competition in effectively the same consumer market, the Australian Football League (AFL), has sought to (successfully) reinforce its strong connections with Indigenous youth initiatives and healthy lifestyle choices for children through their sport development programs. In North America, the National Football League has in recent years continued and enhanced its long association with the charitable group, United Way, and particularly its initiatives with respect to ethnic minorities and disadvantaged children. The National Basketball Association (NBA) has also developed its own "NBA Cares" campaign as a means of highlighting their commitment to addressing social issues in the communities in which the various franchise operations are located.

A more recent phenomenon is that individual players negotiate their own player contracts allowing them access to venues or services so that they are better positioned to participate personally in some form of philanthropic activity. For example, Kinzie (2010) reported that Ryan Zimmerman, a popular third baseman who has recently negotiated a new contract with his club, the Washington Nationals, a major league baseball team based in Washington, D.C., included in the terms and conditions a clause where he had full access to the team's ballpark so he could use it to stage his own charity event. In Australia, the ongoing support by individual high-profile sports people, such as Brisbane Bronco rugby league stars Darren Lockyer and Sam Thaiday, for children receiving treatment in oncology wards of regional hospitals is similarly noteworthy. Importantly, Kinzie has indicated that this behavior will become more the norm than the exception in the immediate future with individual athletes and teams alike placing a much greater emphasis on donating funds, volunteering their time, and helping local communities as part and parcel of their sport business involvement.

Interestingly, for all of the activity that is being undertaken in the area of corporate philanthropy in sports, it remains a relatively unexplored area of research inquiry. This current situation is unfortunate to say the least because CSR, and corporate philanthropy in particular, have emerged as topics of some significance to the sports sector as more individual operations are being called upon to operate within a framework cased by stringent modern day business practices. Although it is true that many sporting organizations have played a significant social role in their local communities for many years, little attention has been drawn to the critical importance of corporate philanthropy in a setting that continues to grow to become more commercialized, commodified, and business-model driven. Considering that the sport industry continues to grow globally in both size and complexity, it has become imperative that today's sport managers are aware of the importance of CSR so that their organizations will be in the best position now and into the future. To that end, many businesses are now seriously reviewing their positions with respect to strategic philanthropy. This type of philanthropic engagement is part of a broader CSR framework that encompasses ethical business conduct, but also meets the organization's economic and legal obligations (Bianchi, 2006; Bruch & Walter, 2005). Strategic philanthropy in sport is an area that, despite its importance in a business sense, has received relatively little academic attention to date although it must be said that several authors have recently begun the process of better understanding the socially responsible business efforts of organizations generally (Bruch & Walter; Ricks & Williams, 2005; Saiia, 2001, Saiia, Carroll, & Buchholtz, 2003).

Such research has revealed that corporate social responsibility, and philanthropy as a critical pillar of a broad strategic approach to it, is now playing an increasingly important role in today's business world (Baughn, Bodie, & McIntosh, 2007). As noted by Pava and Krausz (1997), a key tenet of CSR is that the business entity has a responsibility to society beyond that of mere profit maximization because "corporations possess the power to control and influence the quality of life of employees, customers, shareholders and residents of local communities in which they operate" (p. 357). This notion was supported by Sagawa and Segal (2000) who contended that any modern business must today operate with the knowledge that it needs to act in a manner that contributes in a positive manner, for the benefit of its stakeholders as well as the broader community in which it exists. Furthermore, there is now clear evidence that business operations are refocusing their attention not only on a changed business environment post the global financial crisis but also towards a range of societal issues of growing concern to society. For example, in the Westernized world, issues such as childhood inactivity and obesity, the growing prevalence in society of lifestyle related type 2 illnesses, and the ongoing need to support research and development with respect to a range of diseases have become focal points of activity for communities and individual businesses alike. In such an environment, sport generally and sporting bodies as the administrative arms of sports activities in particular have become a conduit for much of this philanthropic activity. Increasingly, important social and economic issues such as rapid technological change, the declining health of children and youth, environmental concerns, a diverse and aging population, and mounting concerns regarding the growing social divide have resulted in a refocusing on the responsibility of firms to the communities in which they operate (Foster, Meinhard, Berger & Krpan, 2009; Margolis & Walsh, 2003; Sagawa & Segal, 2000).

It is perhaps a little surprising to note that it has been only recently that attention has again been drawn to the unique characteristics of sport operations that make them somewhat different in comparison with many other types of businesses; a situation that in part has evolved because several entrepreneurial leaders have begun to question whether or not the nature and role of corporate social responsibility are in any way different in a sporting context to other business settings. Are the nature and role of CSR in the sports industry fundamentally different to other settings because of the nature and scope of the relationship with the consumer, and if so, how? Certainly Smith and Westerbeek (2007) thought they were because they have asserted that the sports industry has a range of factors that are discrete to the area and positively influence the nature and scope of CSR efforts of business arrangements in this setting. They suggested these factors include the sport industry's mass media distribution and communication power, the positive health and lifestyle messages it conveys, the social interaction it fosters, and the overall appeal it has to a diverse range of consumer markets such as today's youth (Smith & Westerbrook). It is equally clear, however, that business operations that have no obvious links with sport need to become involved so as to use it as a vehicle for promoting themselves as worthy corporate citizens in the local community. In the Australian setting, Woolworths, for example, has used its community grants initiative to emphasize its role of supporting local communities, and junior sporting teams in particular. The National Australia Bank, via its support of a range of AFL initiatives, has taken a similar road. Importantly, sport today is also seen as having an impact on the natural environment because it is often practiced outside or via the use of a large amount of infrastructure (i.e., sport complexes) such that the environment is affected when any form of development occurs. Given the growing concern being expressed globally about a range of social and environmental issues affecting our everyday quality of life, many organizations in the sport industry have begun to reinforce their commitment to socially responsible endeavors. In so doing, and often directly via their philanthropic activities, sport operators have grasped the opportunity to increase their organizations' social standing in the community. Surfaid International is an example of one such sports-based group to orient itself in this manner in recent years. Although its membership is based around a common passion for the sport of surfing, the efforts of the group to provide medical aid in undeveloped areas of need in the Asia-Pacific region has not gone unnoticed by many in the community. The outcome of such efforts has resulted in the organization continuing to garnish strong community support for itself and its charitable operations as a consequence.

CONCLUSION

It is clear that the full potential of corporate philanthropy as a vehicle for community development has yet to be fully explored in the true business sense. Untapped marketing applications aside, there is clear evidence that healthy and vibrant communities support and encourage socially minded businesses. Therefore, a thorough understanding of the pros and cons of corporate philanthropic activity, and how and why such activity can be successfully encapsulated into the strategic vision of a sports-driven operation, is a critical and necessary attribute for today's entrepreneurial and business focused sports manager. This notion was supported by Kotler (1999) who argued that successful operators "must identify, evaluate, and select market opportunities and lay down strategies for achieving eminence if not dominance in target markets" (p. 17).

Although social and community development are not yet perceived as areas of high priority for many businesses, the stark reality that must now be embraced by sports managers is that corporate giving is increasingly becoming a popular and strategic tool in the market place. So much so that this form of niche marketing is rapidly becoming one of the few effective means available to maintain (or perhaps enhance) business operations so as to obtain a distinctive community image. Corporate giving can promote name recognition and facilitate market penetration where other strategies might fail or be largely ineffective. Importantly, such actions can also engender consumer loyalty and serve to improve the bottom line performance of the business as a whole. Without doubt, corporate social responsibility and corporate philanthropy as central pillars of such endeavors provide a clear direction for astute business managers who want to increase their operations' social and economic performances (Wolcott & Lippitz, 2007).

In this context, it is worth noting that the various associations formed by any organization in the business world today must play a significant role in determining its reputation;

how its brand, product, or service is evaluated; the purchase intent of consumers; and even customer identification with the operation itself (Ellen, Webb, & Mohr, 2006; Pitts & Stotlar, 2007). Johnson, Morgan, and Summers (2005) argued that any alliance between a sport operation and a prospective benefactor of one form or another should be firmly grounded in an arrangement that provides positive marketing opportunities for both partners. In effect, Johnson, Morgan, and Summers suggested that such an alliance should be constructed though sport with the mindset that it be entered into as a joint venture. They argued that by approaching sports alliances in a strategic manner, a business is better positioned to determine whether the personality and identity of its own brand are compatible with the sport entity (and vice versa). As a result, organizations can make more reasoned decisions about partner suitability (Johnson, Morgan, & Summers, 2005). Page (2009) contended that "it is critical to understand not only the dimensions of demand but also the market segments and the behavior and expectations of consumers that they will need to accommodate in providing a high quality experience" (p. 144). This notion was also supported by Pitts and Stotlar (2007) who argued that sport businesses must seek to constantly evaluate what is affecting their industry because such trends or influences may affect the success or failure of a product, service, or business. Failing to keep pace with the dynamic and ever changing business environment results in what Dwyer, Edwards, Mistillis, Roman, and Scott (2009) referred to as "strategic drift" whereby the organization inadequately matches the changing consumer needs in the external environment with their strategies. This point is of considerable importance for sports managers to note because the savvy and better-informed consumers of today tend to "respond most positively to corporate socially responsible efforts they judge as values driven and strategic while responding negatively to efforts perceived as stakeholder driven or egoistic" (Ellen et al., 2006, p. 147).

REFERENCES

Aaker, D. (2005). *Strategic market management* (7th ed.). New York: John Wiley.

Arthur, D., Scott, D., Woods T., & Brooker, R. (1998). Sport sponsorship should...A process model for the effective implementation and management of sport sponsorship programmes. *Sport Marketing Quarterly, 7,* 49-60.

Baughn, C. C., Bodie, N. L., & McIntosh, J. C. (2007). Corporate social and environmental responsibility in Asian countries and other geographical regions. *Corporate Social Responsibility and Environmental Management, 14,* 189-205.

Bianchi, A. (2006). Rethinking corporate philanthropy. *Stanford Social Innovation Review, 4,* 12-13.

Bruch, H., & Walter, F. (2005, Fall). The keys to rethinking corporate philanthropy. *MIT Sloan Management Review, 47*(1) 49-55.

Campbell, D., & Slack, R. (2008). Corporate "philanthropy strategy" and "strategic philanthropy": Some insights from voluntary disclosures in annual reports. *Business Society, 47,* 187-212.

Darcy, S., Cameron, B., & Pegg, S. (2010). Accessible tourism and sustainability: A discussion and case study. *Journal of Sustainable Tourism, 18,* 515-537.

Dwyer, L. (2005). Trends underpinning global tourism in the coming decade. In W. Theobald (Ed.), *Global tourism* (pp. 529-545). Burlington, MA: Butterworth Heinemann.

Dwyer, L., Edwards, D., Mistillis, N., Roman, C., & Scott, N. (2009). Destination and enterprise management for a tourism future. *Tourism Management, 30,* 63-74.

Ellen, P., Webb, D., & Mohr, L. (2006). Building corporate associations: Consumer attributions for corporate socially responsible programs. *Journal of the Academy of Marketing Science, 34,* 147-157.

Fombrun, C. F., Gardberg, N. A., & Barnett, M. L. (2000). Opportunity platforms and safetynets: Corporate citizenship and reputational risk. *Business and Society Review, 105,* 85-106.

Foster, M., Meinhard, A., Berger, I., & Krpan, P. (2009). Corporate philanthropy in the Canadian context: From damage control to improving society. *Nonprofit and Voluntary Sector Quarterly, 38,* 441-466.

Hosany, S., & Witham, M. (2009). Dimensions of cruisers' experiences, satisfaction and intention to recommend. *Journal of Travel Research, 20,* 1-14.

Johnson Morgan, M., & Summers, J. (2005). *Sports marketing.* Melbourne: Thomson.

Kinzie, S. (2010, August 14). D.C. teams boosting focus on charitable giving. *The Washington Post.* Retrieved from http://www.washingtonpost.com/wp-dyn/content/article/2010/08/14/AR2010081402783.html

Kotler, P. (1999). *Kotler on marketing: How to create, win and dominate markets.* New York: The Free Press.

Lusch, R., Vargo, S., & O'Brien, M. (2007). Competing through service: Insights from service-dominant logic. *Journal of Retailing, 83,* 5-18.

Margolis, J., & Walsh, J. (2003). Misery loves companies: Rethinking social initiatives by business. *Administrative Science Quarterly, 48,* 268-305.

Masterman, G. (2007). *Sponsorship for a return on investment.* London: Butterworth-Heinemann.

Packer, T., Small, J., & Darcy, S. (2008). *Tourist experiences of individuals with vision impairment.* Gold Coast: Sustainable Tourism Commonwealth Research Centre.

Page, S. (2009). *Transport and tourism. Global perspectives* (3rd ed.). Essex: Pearson Education.

Pava, M. L., & Krausz, J. (1997). *Corporate social responsibility and financial performance: The paradox of social cost.* Westport, CT: Quorum Books.

Pegg, S., & Patterson, I. (2010). Rethinking music festivals as a staged event: Gaining insights from understanding visitor motivations and the experiences they seek. *Journal of Convention & Event Tourism (11)*2, 1-15.

Pine, B., & Gilmore, J. (1998). Welcome to the experience economy. *Harvard Business Review, 76,* 97-105.

Pine, B., & Gilmore, J. (1999). *The experience economy.* Boston: Harvard Business School Press.

Pine, B., & Gilmore, J. (2000). Satisfaction, sacrifice, surprise: Three small steps create one giant leap into the experience economy. *Strategy & Leadership, 28,* 18-23.

Pitts, B., & Stotlar, D. (2007). *Fundamentals of sport marketing* (3rd ed.). Morgantown, WV: Fitness Information Technology.

Ricks, J., & Williams, J. (2005). Strategic corporate philanthropy: Addressing frontline talent needs through an educational giving program. *Journal of Business Ethics, 60,* 147-157.

Ritchie, B., Mules, T., & Uzabeaga (2008). *Visitor attractions satisfaction benchmarking project.* Gold Coast: Sustainable Tourism Commonwealth Research Centre.

Rumelt, R. (2008, December). Strategy in a 'structural break.' *The McKinsey Quarterly,* December, 10-18.

Sagawa, S., & Segal, E. (2000). *Common interest, common good.* Boston: Harvard Business School.

Saiia, D. (2001). Philanthropy and corporate citizenship: Strategic philanthropy is good corporate citizenship. *Journal of Corporate Citizenship, 1,* 57-74.

Saiia, D., Carroll, A., & Buchholtz, A. (2003). Philanthropy as strategy: When corporate charities begin at home. *Business and Society, 42,* 169-201.

Sasse, C., & Trahan, R. (2007). Rethinking the new corporate philanthropy. *Business Horizons, 50,* 29-38.

Smith, A., & Westerbeek, H. (2007). Sport as a vehicle for deploying corporate social responsibility. *Journal of Corporate Citizenship, 25,* 43-54.

Solnet, D., & Kandampully, J. (2008). How some service firms have become part of "service excellence" folklore, *Managing Service Quality, 18,* 179-193.

Thorne, D., Ferrell, O., & Ferrell, L. (2003). *Business and society: A strategic approach to corporate citizenship.* Boston: Houghton Mifflin.

Wolcott, R., & Lippitz, M. (2007). The four models of corporate entrepreneurship. *MIT Sloan Management Review, 49,* 75-82.

Conclusions and Future Directions

Stephanie J. Hanrahan and Robert J. Schinke

18

This book was structured with four separate sections: (a) peace and reconciliation, (b) sport and social justice initiatives, (c) promoting health and well being through sport and physical activity, and (d) sport and social corporate responsibility/philanthropy. We will briefly review what we see to be the main take-home messages from each section and then provide our thoughts on what all these messages may mean in terms of future research and practice. We acknowledge that some readers may have different viewpoints in terms of what is most important or what this information might mean in terms of future directions; we enthusiastically encourage readers to reflect on what they have read and consider how the material may be of benefit in terms of future actions. We are happy that you, the reader, have actually read the book (or at least part of it), but feel that its take-home messages are only successful if they lead to reflection and action among those working in the general area of community and personal development through sport (or, better yet, inspire people new to the area to become actively involved).

Peace and Reconciliation

The section about peace and reconciliation contained four chapters. Three of the chapters include descriptions of existing sport-based intervention programs designed to "develop skills and attitudes that help build a just, peaceful society" (Chapter 2, multi-ethnic South Africa); "facilitate character development and promote social inclusion" (Chapter 3, Greek and Turkish Cypriots); and "[use] the game of soccer as a mediator for peace building" (Chapter 4, Jewish, Arab, and Palestinian children).

All of the authors mentioned positive outcomes from their existing programs: "[T]he participants indicated the program helps them to 'get to know one another, to respect other players and people, to learn trust and work as a team, to be peaceful and communicate with respect'" (Chapter 2); "[P]articipants increased their (a) social perspective taking, (b) cross-cultural friendship and tolerance, (c) self- and academic-efficacy, and (d) global citizenship knowledge, attitudes, and behaviors" (Chapter 3), and "[T]he non-profit bodies that ideologically, and more importantly financially, supported the educational programs considered that these programs had a positive influence on the social interactions among Jewish and Arab children" (Chapter 4).

The authors were also unanimous, however, in the belief that research is needed in the area: "[T]here is too little research and therefore too little recognition of how both recreational and professional sport at the community level are used as a positive force for reconstruction, development, reconciliation, and peace (Chapter 2); "[T]here is an absence of substantial evidence regarding (a) the process of the development of positive emotions and cognitions toward out-group members, and (b) the extent to which the positive outcomes from cross-group contact can be generalizable to people with similar characteristics" (Chapter 3); and "[Practitioners] should document their practical work and collect relevant data that can help them assess the usefulness of their programs" (Chapter 4).

Sport-based youth programs were not the only method to develop peace and reconciliation mentioned by authors in this section. The authors of Chapter 4 described a sport psychology intervention aimed at fostering relationships and building peace among Jewish and Arab players, both youth and adult. The authors of Chapter 5 portrayed the seven year-long research collaboration between Wikwemikong and researchers from Laurentian University on projects related to sport and physical activity. The experiences they shared reflect efforts where the goal had been to progressively create research projects with practical components meaningful within their region for Aboriginal youth participants. The collaborative processes also created social change locally, from within the reserve. Although they did not originally envision that their project would serve as a resistance strategy to the oppression that can sometimes occur in mainstream research, they realized that this may have occurred. The authors of Chapter 5 advocated using coalition-building (mainstream university academics and Aboriginal community members as co-researchers) as a resistance strategy against the usual "divide-and-conquer" mentality that has been in place historically when White mainstream researchers have entered First Nation spaces.

In addition to indicating that intervention and research programs can result in developing peace and reconciliation, and that additional research is needed in this area, the authors in this first section of the book provided some useful guidelines for those who may be instigating similar programs. In no particular order, some of the recommendations:

- Have equal status among the members of groups.
- Establish common goals for the people involved with the program.
- Use inter-group cooperation to help diverse groups reach their goals.
- Obtain support from the authorities, structures, and institutions.
- Apply scientific monitoring and evaluation methodology.
- Collect data from multiple sources.
- Create inclusive mixed teams (ethnicity, gender, competence level) with similar interests.
- Use inclusive decision making.
- Encourage coaches and instructors to serve as educators, positive role models, and agents of positive change.
- Use Olympism as a framework of inclusion, inspiration, and engagement.
- Facilitate conditions for optimal engagement by keeping a balance between skills and challenge.
- Make mental and practical associations between sports and real life experiences.
- Embrace local culture and promote global perspective and appreciation.
- Create a professional dialogue between players (at the elite level).
- Discuss the relationship between players and fans.
- Talk about the playing of the national anthem or other behaviors or customs that may be challenging for some minority team members.
- Systematically observe practices and games to follow patterns of overt behavior.
- Persuade coaches, schoolteachers, and policy makers to encourage children from different populations to participate together in sport activities.
- Participate in programs with practitioners from different populations.
- Provide practitioners (as well as participants) the opportunity to interact professionally and socially to (a) get to know each other, and (b) establish trust and open relationships with each other.

Sport in Social Justice Initiatives

The first chapter in this section focused on using sport, specifically midnight basketball, for community-based crime prevention. Midnight basketball has involved older participants than most youth-oriented programs and has been largely dominated by African American males. The unquestionable success of sports programs such as midnight basketball is their ability to recruit and retain otherwise hard-to-reach populations. Sport is definitely an effective hook. There is less agreement about why these intervention programs may be successful or if indeed they are effective in reducing crime. Some believe that the sports programs are beneficial because they keep participants in a controlled physical activity and off the street where they might be involved in delinquency and offending. Others assume that simply playing sport builds self-esteem and social skills that teach otherwise undisciplined and disorderly young people principles of social order and self-control. Although crime rates have dropped in areas with these sport programs, the results cannot simply be due to the physical containment of would-be offenders. The programs serve a minimal number of youth and only operate a few days a week for a limited number of weeks in a year.

It would be naive, however, to believe that sport participation is automatically a positive social force. It can be that, but if a program is not properly run or has poor leadership and role models, it can also have the opposite effect. The success of a sport-based social intervention program is largely determined by the strength of its non-sport components, what it does with individuals once they are brought into the program through sport. The authors of Chapter 6 suggested that, "The creation of popular, community-based programs such as midnight basketball might incline all community members (not just those in the program) to be less likely to commit crimes, not for fear of being caught, but because they feel more directly connected to their communities and more positively served by law enforcement and social services." Sport-based social intervention programs may contribute to improving the lives of urban youth, but we must not treat them as a miracle cure for all that ails these communities.

The authors of the second chapter in this section also cautioned against sport being seen as a cure-all for the ills of society, but this time through a postcolonial and feminist critique of sport for development. The authors acknowledged that excellent sport and development initiatives exist, but argued that some programs continue imperial and colonial legacies, particularly in terms of uneven relations of power. Sport can bring diverse groups of people together (as discussed in the first section of the book) and can create positive change, but sport also has a darker side. Sport has been tied to issues of drug abuse, homophobia, marginalization of women, masculine privilege, and intensifying social conflict and social inequality. Given these negatives it may be unrealistic to expect sport for development initiatives to ameliorate problems for marginalized peoples and communities.

Sport for development programs should follow the lead provided by Schinke et al. in the first section. Instead of having donors and funding agencies drive these programs, the communities involved should be active participants in identifying their own needs and shaping interventions. After all, buy-in is far more likely when the participants have an active stake in the creation of programming, from the ground up. The authors of this chapter argued for the need to go beyond just participation to true empowerment that addresses core power issues that inform development initiative. They also suggested using a strengths-based approach rather than a deficit model to focus on the emotional and behavioral skills that can help people feel accomplished, improve relationships, enhance coping skills, and promote development.

The third chapter in this section provided an overview of the situation for LGBT individuals in sports. Ravel argued that men's sport is often a space where heterosexual masculinity is reinforced through homophobic and misogynistic discourses, non-heterosexual athletes are not welcome, and women are denigrated. She acknowledged, however, that men's sports may be transitioning from a homophobic space to one that is somewhat more open to the presence of gay athletes. The case of women's sports, on the other hand, has been a bit more complex with it often seen as being both homophobic as well as a refuge for non-heterosexual women.

The author of this third chapter also reported on a study with women with non-conventional sexualities. The participants in the study constructed sport as a space of resistance to heterosexism and emphasized the enjoyment related to being "out" in sport. She also emphasized the great acceptance, and sometimes, even celebration of non-conventional sexualities in their sport environment, even though most played in mainstream leagues. The author highlighted that although sport can be open to those who challenge heteronormativity, it is less so to those who transgress gender boundaries. Sexuality may not be as fixed as once believed in terms of hegemonic categories of sexuality. Including diverse sexual minorities in research/interventions related to LGBT issues may therefore be preferential to focusing on gay men or lesbians.

The final chapter in this section focused on the need to construct sporting opportunities for people with disabilities. Fay and Wolff indicated that, similar to race and gender, disability identity is a socially constructed paradigm promulgated through cultural and sport classification systems that can become an internalized, as well as externalized, paradigm. Ableism devalues people with disabilities and results in segregation, social isolation, and policies that limit their opportunities for full societal participation (including sport). Persons with disabilities often internalize these stereotypes and negative beliefs. At the organizational level, who is currently allowed (or not) to participate at certain levels is based in part on the fear that economic resources that are currently prioritized to able-bodied individuals might be somehow diverted to athletes with disabilities. Limited awareness, education, and expertise on the part of management professionals within sport governance structures in fully understanding the capability and level of athletic ability of a person with a disability perpetuates these unequal opportunities in sport. The authors argued that work needs to be done in all sectors of society to help improve access, inclusion, equality, respect, legitimacy, and opportunity for people with disabilities in sport. New and more diverse opportunities in sport within the existing mainstream system will only begin to emerge through a combination of research, education, and advocacy activities.

What follows are a summary of some of the take-home messages from the chapters in the second section:

- Recognize the value of sport in recruiting and retaining participants to education or social change programs.

- Do not expect sport on its own to be a miracle cure for what ails society.

- Include communities in the planning of sport for development programs.

- Conceptualize the programs within the communities and give those targeted by projects a voice when it comes to evaluating them.

- Don't get caught up in a deficit-based approach where the focus is on a problem believed to be in need of fixing and then develop or support a program that is designed to fix that problem, particularly if the "problem" is that recipients do not mimic privileged Westerners in their cultures, beliefs, and associated practices.

- Increase research on athletes with non-conventional sexualities and genders.

- Increase the visibility of results from studies on LGBT issues in sport (e.g., interviews with the media, publications intended for a large audience).

- Educate yourself about LGBT issues in sport (e.g., consult electronic resources, attend workshops).

- Denounce all derogatory comments (e.g., homophobic, sexist, racist).

- Be inclusive when you speak and do not assume that everybody is heterosexual.

- Create a welcoming climate where diversity is valued and everybody can feel comfortable. For example, invite partners of LGBT individuals when partners of heterosexual individuals are invited.

- Develop initiatives that bring people with disabilities from the margins to become integral members of the sporting community.

- Conduct ongoing research examining the inclusion of people with a disability in sport.

- Develop educational awareness training and resources on inclusion in sport to support sport organizations regarding the process of inclusion.

Promoting Health and Well-being through Sport and Physical Activity

This section contained four chapters, with the first two contributions reflecting programs that were implemented in at-risk communities and the latter two reflecting conceptual submissions, built from a synthesis of literature pertaining to youth development. Stephanie Hanrahan, the first contributing author in the section, is an avid traveler. Each year she works with underprivileged youth in economically disadvantaged regions. For this book, she chose to feature applied work in Mexico and Argentina. The lives of financially poor children and adolescents are not easy, and given their early disadvantages of limited education and limited access to positive life skills, she crafted a lifeskills program with a focus on confidence, resilience, control, and self-worth. The program was taught through the development of mental skills, in association with sport and games. From the author's experiences, adolescent youth at risk are a worthwhile audience to target with positive life-skill programs.

There is evidence from Stephanie's experiences that it doesn't take much to inspire youth at risk. Motivators seem to include rewards that the middle class child might take for granted, such as stickers. The cost to run such programs is not necessarily finance heavy, but rather requires a commitment of time and expertise in terms of content and context. For example, contextually, discussions about family in the traditional sense may not be relevant or appropriate when working with orphaned children. Some middle or upper-class SD providers might not initially understand that the concept of family can be totally different to the program participant than to the staff member(s) providing the program. Contextual sensitivity, then, seems to be an important piece of expertise that SD staff ought to acquire before they engage in the provision of programming. If one attempts the delivery of an SD project without first knowing the intended participants, there may be a discrepancy between what might work conceptually and how it might be distilled and made accessible for a community.

Sport and physical activity can also be employed to impart a message relating to disease awareness, such as in the prevention of AIDS. In the continent of Africa (and elsewhere), children and adolescents sometimes engage in sexual activities before their teenage years. Precautions such as condom use seem to be less readily available and even if available are, sometimes regarded as unorthodox or against the norm. Sexual activity in some communities is a rite of passage. With early sexual activity regarded as typical, the children and youth in some communities are at risk for disease. Glyn Roberts, Cyprian Maro, and Marit Sorensen have worked together for several years on relevant projects in Tanzania, Africa, where HIV prevalence among youths is high. Given the high prevalence of AIDS in his country, Cyprian sought to combine his interest of sport with the social challenge posed by AIDS and develop an intervention program upon which he could propose a form of disease prevention and with it, the reduction of an at-risk behavior among youth, through sport.

Cyprian implemented a program where coaches were engaged through the sport of soccer to impart sport-specific skills, and also, information and buffering strategies to reduce risky sexual behavior, via HIV/AIDS education. Similar to the work of Hanrahan, important skills were taught in a physical activity context. Beyond their applied focus, the co-authors developed a research component to assess the potency of their program. Measures included "attitude to condom use, condom knowledge and experience, subjective norms about condom use, abstinence, having an exclusive sexual partner, perceived behavior control in using a condom, and behavioral intention (intended condom use)." Confirming the importance of sport as a conduit to awareness, it was found that the sport environment was a better context to impart preventative messages than a formal education environment, such as a sex education course. Should Cyprian and his colleagues be correct, then on a larger scale, sport and physical activity contexts, if carefully structured, can become a strong line of defense for disease prevention. Consequently, SD programs might prove to be the best medium through which to impart messages about at-risk behavior among youth.

The two aforementioned chapters open us up to a more general discussion regarding what sorts of opportunities might be accomplished through the promotion of health and well-being, starting with youth. Gould and colleagues proposed a number of possible areas where researchers and practitioners might begin their work. First and foremost, the authors proposed that we need to understand what youth leadership is by definition before we attempt to create programs that place youth in leadership positions. In addition, the authors realized that leadership skills are taught not only in sport contexts, but also through family and friends. Though the aforementioned two chapters did not extend fully to family, it makes intuitive sense that practice and research be broad-based to ensure the consistency of the message within and also away from sport and physical activity contexts. With guidance from adaptive social support, it becomes more likely that consistently good decisions are made in the short-term, with obviously longer-term implications. After all, take-home messages are taken home, and so they need also to be reinforced away from the intervention context.

More globally, we asked Jay Coakley to consider what might "count" as positive youth development. Clearly, the work of Hanrahan, and Roberts, Maro, and Sorensen are good examples of how sport and physical activity might be used as paths to positive youth development, but they are very much the tip of the iceberg. As Coakley re-affirmed, there are a vast number of possible *Sport Plus* programs that can "emphasize traditional sport development objectives such as increasing participation and building sport skills, but they are organized so that participants learn information and strategies for effectively dealing with challenges faced in their everyday lives." These challenges might be socioeconomic hardship, a lack of parenting, risk for disease, substance abuse, negative peer associations, and/or obesity. In all circumstances, sport contexts can become the answer (or at least part of the answer), directly through the activity, and indirectly, through a healthy context with good messaging. There can also be *Plus Sport* programs, that in contrast "involve existing educational or community organizations that use sport to attract, retain, and motivate young people in programs designed to build their personal resources or to provide them access to organizational or community resources." Both types of programs can contribute to positive youth development.

Though it would seem that sport and physical activity can become a context where solutions to social and personal challenges can be found, perhaps we are dreaming if we believe that such opportunities are provided for youth across cultural, racial, and socioeconomic lines. Coakley suggested that access to health and well-being opportunities is often restricted in terms of access. In some communities, there are the financial and technical resources to make effective programs happen. In other communities, such as those described by Hanrahan and Roberts and colleagues, access is most often restricted to those with resources and means. And yet, the applied examples aforementioned (in this section and in other sections) suggest that even when there are limited resources, programs can be created from within the community—all it takes is one or a few enthusiastic people. We propose that access needs to be opened to sectors in communities where SD programming is unlikely to be provided. Granted, the challenges of developing and then sustaining such programs will be taxing. Nevertheless, without such programs, academics and professionals alike will be developing their programs for populations where they might be beneficial, but not most beneficial.

What follows are a summary of some of the take-home messages from the chapters in the third section:

- Small rewards tend to motivate youth at risk.
- There must be a good understanding by SD staff members and researchers of the social context in advance of any program implementation.
- Concepts of family and friends might vary with each context, and an understanding of these concepts in situ will enhance program delivery.
- Intervention strategies delivered through sport and physical activity contexts are sometimes more successful than the same messaging delivered in formal educational contexts.
- Intervention strategies should sometimes be broad-based and include not only youth, but also their peers and family members.
- Sport and physical activity intervention programs should be delivered to youth across socioeconomic, racial, cultural, and gender lines.

Sport and Corporate Social Responsibility/Philanthropy

The final section of this book was devoted to corporate social responsibility and philanthropy. Venture on to most any large corporation's website and you will find that each reflects some sort of effort where community partnerships and programs are in existence. Corporations including Rolex, Pepsi Cola, and Johnson & Johnson are a few examples where efforts have been made to bridge companies with communities. These relationships are meant to contribute to better living, while at the same time position products or product lines to prospective consumers. After all, corporations need a positive image. Whatever the agenda behind communities and corporations, the opportunities that avail from such partnerships can be meaningful. Nowhere is the partnership between a community and a company better illustrated, for better and for worse, than when the New Orleans Saints allowed homeless people to reside within its Superdome's confines. Michael Giardina and C. L. Cole considered the days following Hurricane Katrina and what the context was like for residents relocated to the arena. From their writing, we are left to consider that people who were typically priced out of the arena, as a result of a natural disaster became, in a sense, prisoners of the arena. Sometimes, efforts on the part of a city, a professional sport team, or a corporation are intended in one way, but instead illustrate and reinforce the separation of people along racial and socioeconomic lines. From the New Orleans chapter, it becomes apparent that how information is illustrated in the media might not truly depict what is happening. In the Superdome people were homeless and most often, these people were from marginalized populations (i.e., African Americans, Hispanic Americans). These people might have been offered temporary refuge in the confines of the arena, but at the same time, perhaps the objective was also to confine such people to reduce perceived risks such as looting and violence.

As an afterthought from the chapter, you might be left wondering why an awareness of this supposed SD endeavor is important to you, the reader. Although we do not really know the case-by-case outcomes of people who experienced the SD strategy that took place in the Superdome, we do know that the people who resided in the Superdome were in some cases relocated after the natural disaster to another part of the city while their previous community was reconstructed into a new community built for people from a higher socio-economic class. Hence, there are strategies initially packaged as SD that, over time, become something entirely different and far removed from the agenda of community betterment. The bottom line is that SD projects must better communities and, within these communities, the lives of people who are at most risk for mistreatment, abuse, and displacement. As we stop and consider the words of Giardina and Cole, it becomes clear that refuge in the Superdome might not be a SD initiative, at all. Perhaps the reasons behind the shortcomings of the project have something to do with effective communications and transparency of the project's administration and the community at large. Liaising and communication among groups of people influenced by SD projects is central to project success over the long-term.

From the work directly above, we must also consider closely how cities and their governance use and misuse big sporting events, sporting arenas, and essentially all resulting infrastructure (e.g., buildings, equipment). Laura Misener and Daniel Mason did exactly that. Precisely, the authors considered two cases where big sport events were completed and how much the outlying communities benefited after the events. One case cited within their chapter was the city of Manchester. Over the last decade, Manchester has hosted international tournaments and also the 2002 Commonwealth Games. In the wake of the events, housing has been created and in many cases, sporting facilities have been upgraded. As the authors noted, what was initially proposed to better the city district of Manchester seems to have been disconnected from the start with the needs of its residents. One consistent message that most every author has made throughout this compilation is that for community betterment to happen, consultation with that community must be ongoing, from the beginning of the SD initiative, onward to its culmination. Trust must be developed and sustained throughout such initiatives through the practice of transparency. When we look closely at what has been left behind from the legacy of international sporting events in Manchester, there are clearly some shortcomings in the aftermath of the events.

Contrasted with Manchester are the sporting activities that have been hosted in Melbourne, Australia. Unlike Manchester, there appears to have been a much closer partnership among the organizations that administrate the sporting events and the residents of the city. In Melbourne, there were transparency and community consultation before, during, and after sporting events, enhancing community engagement and buy-in. Clearly, people can be engaged in the high-profile activities that happen within their communities. All it takes is consultation and effective liaising. Not unlike high-quality participatory action research, the active involvement of interest groups facilitates a sense of ease and is also beneficial for the long-term development of a community, in the cases above, through sport projects.

The importance of an ongoing relationship among people in relation to financial resources accrued through sport was also illustrated by Jeffrey Stinson and Dennis Howard, who focused on donor behavior in universities. Similar to Misener and Mason's work about high-profile sporting tournaments/games, this chapter focused on university sport as a business. From sport, there can be a trickle down effect with the entire university community benefiting from sport programs. Nevertheless, once more, the interests of athletics and the larger community can be different and, therefore, divided. In the university context, the divide was between the varsity programs, regarded as those who have financial resources, and the larger community (i.e., university)—people with limited access to financial resources and direct benefits. In the United States sometimes high-profile academics and programs gain paltry financial support when compared to high-profile varsity coaches and their teams. So, what might be done to share financial resources and improve the university community as a whole?

For a university community buy-in to happen, the relationship between sport and the larger community must be looked at closely. Ties can (and should) be made that bridge interests among sport programs and the communities where they reside. The emotional connections developed with a university through sport teams can potentially lead to financial gifts eventually also being directed toward academic programs. For example, people accustomed to supporting an athletics program might look within the university and notice some of the academic program in which their favorite varsity athletes are enrolled. Hence, initial giving behavior could eventually shift from exclusively varsity athletics to a balance with academic program support. Partnerships among groups in a community are often undeveloped, perhaps due to limited understanding of how their interests can intersect. And yet, a community's interests often do correspond with a sponsor's interests; it is only a matter of jointly understanding where the commonalities are.

Finally, we look beyond the direct benefits derived from the sponsor and a single community to the broader image derived by supporting SD projects. In some cases the sponsor/philanthropist is an individual, in other instances, a company. Regardless, the image created through a philanthropic act and how it is perceived reflects upon the gift giver. For companies or government agencies to consider whether they wish to engage in an SD project, that project must in part reflect their core values. Although sponsors have their own responsibilities to their communities, communities also must consider how sponsoring agencies can benefit. When the SD project is carefully positioned to match with the corporate philosophy of the sponsor, sponsorship becomes more likely, both in the present and over the long term. Conversely, when communities do not consider how their needs might align with the needs of the corporation, incompatibility will likely result. As Shane Pegg and Ian Patterson have suggested, the relationship between community and sponsor is bi-directional, with both parties requiring some benefit.

What follows is a summary of some of the take-home messages from the chapters in the fourth section:

- Projects that do not include active engagement from communities cannot be considered SD programs.
- SD programs should target those who need them most.
- Successful community-based decision-making processes are required among sport organizations, municipalities, companies, and communities.
- Effective programs at the community level require full public disclosure and the transparency of strategic initiatives.

- The mobilization and engagement of local community and interest groups are needed to leverage event resources for community benefit.

- Comprehensive social and community impact assessments ensure a collaborative, community-centered agenda.

- SD projects should take into account the needs of the sponsor as well as the community.

Concluding Remarks

Sport on its own is not a miracle cure for the ills of society, nor a magic elixir for the effective positive development of youth. Nevertheless, when sport development programs involve active engagement with communities, account for the needs of all parties involved, are accessible by all interested potential participants, promote the development of skills and abilities beyond sport-specific skills, and consider the specific context, multiple positive benefits can result for both individuals and communities, We encourage you to look beyond the featured work of the authors in this book and engage in existing SD projects or work with others to develop new programs that are relevant to your community. There is much that can be done to better communities and individuals through sport and physical activity projects.

Index

About the Editors

Robert J. Schinke, EdD, is the Canada research chair in multicultural sport and physical activity and professor of sport psychology in the School of Human Kinetics at Laurentian University in Canada. As a Canadian Sport Psychology Association certified practitioner, Schinke has extensive experience working with national teams and professional athletes of North America, South America, Europe, Asia, Africa, and the Caribbean. Robert has authored more than 100 academic and applied articles in publications, including *The Sport Psychologist, International Journal of Sport and Exercise Psychology, International Journal of Sport Psychology, Journal of Clinical Sport Psychology,* and the *Journal of Sport Science and Medicine* and co-edited five textbooks, beyond authoring three. His research is supported by the Social Sciences and Humanities Research Council of Canada, the Indigenous Health Research Development Program, and the Canadian Foundation for Innovation. In addition, Robert serves as editor of *Athletic Insight* and has guest co-edited the *Journal of Sport and Social Issues* and the *International Journal of Sport and Exercise Psychology.* In addition, a former Canadian equestrian team member and Pan American Games medalist, Robert still enjoys equestrian pursuits in addition to hiking and cross-country running. He, his wife Erin, and their two sons, Harrison and Pierce, reside in Sudbury, Ontario.

Stephanie J. Hanrahan, PhD, is an associate professor in the Schools of Human Movement Studies and Psychology and the director of the sport and exercise psychology program at the University of Queensland in Brisbane, Australia. As an author and researcher, Hanrahan has obtained 20 grants and published seven books, 26 book chapters, and over 85 articles. She has made hundreds of presentations at professional meetings and to community clubs and organizations, and has served as the editor of the *Journal of Applied Sport Psychology* from 2006 to 2009. Hanrahan is a fellow of the Australian Sports Medicine Federation and the Association for Applied Sport Psychology. She is also a member of the Australian Psychological Society, Sports Medicine Australia, and the International Society of Sport Psychology. As a registered psychologist, she has worked with individuals and teams from all levels of sport (both with and without disabilities), Aboriginal performing artists, Mexican orphans, and teenagers living in poverty. Hanrahan resides in Queensland and enjoys traveling within Australia and abroad.

Contributing Authors

Jed Blanton

Jed Blanton, MS, earned his bachelor's degree in sports administration from Fort Lewis College, and his master's degree in sport psychology from Georgia Southern University. Currently, he is enrolled in the doctorate program at Michigan State University, specializing in sport psychology. As a competitive distance runner, he served as a cross-country captain in both high school and college. Jed participates in research and outreach efforts at the Institute for the Study of Youth Sports geared toward the development of youth leadership, with an emphasis on team captain selection and education, and relationship analysis.

Amy T. Blodgett

Amy T. Blodgett, MHK, is a graduate student at Laurentian University in Sudbury, Canada. Her research and practical interests pertain to culturally reflexive approaches in sport psychology and social justice issues within marginalized sport populations. Presently, she is part of a multicultural research team working to develop culturally sensitive leadership training programs in Wikwemikong Unceded Indian Reserve in order to inspire active lifestyles among Aboriginal youth. Amy has presented her research at national and international conferences, including the Eastern Canada Sport and Exercise Psychology Symposium, the annual congress of the Association for the Advancement of Applied Sport Psychology, and the North American Indigenous Games Education Symposium.

Boris Blumenstein

Dr. Boris Blumenstein is the director of the Department of Behavioral Sciences and Methodology at the Ribstein Center for Sport Medicine Sciences and Research, Wingate Institute, Netanya, Israel. He was a sport psychology consultant and advisor to the Soviet National and Olympic teams and since 1990 has served as head of psychological services in the Elite Sports Unit of the Israel Olympic Committee (including the delegations to the last four summer Olympic Games—1996, 2000, 2004, and 2008). He has authored over 100 refereed journal articles and book chapters, and was senior editor of two books.

Jay Coakley

Jay Coakley is professor emeritus of sociology at the University of Colorado in Colorado Springs, USA. He received a PhD in sociology at the University of Notre Dame and has since taught and done research on play, games, and sports, among other topics in sociology. Dr. Coakley has received many teaching, service, and professional awards, and is an internationally respected scholar, author, and journal editor. His text, *Sports in Society: Issues and Controversies* is in its 10th edition with adaptations published in Canada, Australia, and the United Kingdom, and translations in Japanese, Chinese, and Korean. Coakley continues to critically examine social phenomena and promote changes that will make social worlds more democratic and humane.

C. L. Cole

C. L. Cole is a professor of media and cinema studies and gender and women's studies at the University of Illinois at Urbana-Champaign. She has been the editor of the *Journal of Sport & Social Issues* since 2000, and currently is at work on several projects related to the media, sport, and national culture.

Lawrence Enosse

Lawrence Enosse, BA, is a former elite athlete in both ice hockey and track and field. As a community member from Wikwemikong, Lawrence has been the assistant coach for the Manitoulin Wild and the Blind River Bears, both Junior A ice-hockey teams. In addition to his interests in coaching, he is a sport and activity enthusiast. He has also worked with Duke Peltier and Robert Schinke in several federally funded research grants. He has co-authored publications in *Sport Psychologist, International Journal of Sport and Exercise Psychology, International Journal of Sport Psychology,* and *Journal of Clinical Sport Psychology.*

Ted Fay

Ted Fay is a professor and former chair of the Sport Management Department at the State University of New York (SUNY) at Cortland. He holds a PhD from the University of Massachusetts at Amherst. Dr. Fay also served as a senior research fellow at the Center for the Study of Sport in Society at Northeastern University and as a strategic consultant related to the Center's research and academic program initiatives from 1999-2010. Fay has an extensive background in international sport including the Olympic and Paralympic movements. Fay is recognized as an international expert on issues related to the integration and inclusion of athletes with a disability in mainstream sport. He was involved in the drafting of Article 30.5 of the United Nations Convention on the Human Rights for Persons with a Disability that addresses involving culture, leisure and sport. Fay has also worked with, or for, a number of national and international sport governing bodies including the US Ski & Snowboard Association, the US Biathlon Association, USA Hockey, US Team Handball Federation and the International Paralympic Committee. Fay was a member of the 1988 US Winter Olympic Team in Calgary, Alberta.

Leslee A. Fisher

Leslee A. Fisher is an associate professor in the Department of Exercise, Sport & Leisure Studies at the University of Tennessee. Leslee holds a PhD in sport psychology from the University of California at Berkeley and an MS in counselor education from the University of Virginia. She is currently serving as secretary/treasurer of the Association for Applied Sport Psychology (AASP). Leslee's primary research interests focus on the social psychological experiences of female athletes, including the intersectional identities of gender/race/class/ sexual/moral orientation, body issues, and the ways in which a cultural sport psychology can be used to enhance research and applied work within sport and exercise psychology.

Michael D. Giardina

Michael D. Giardina is an assistant professor of sport management at Florida State University. He is the author or editor of 10 books, including *Sporting Pedagogies: Performing Culture & Identity in the Global Arena* (Peter Lang, 2005), *Contesting Empire/Globalizing Dissent: Cultural Studies after 9/11* (with Norman K. Denzin, Paradigm, 2006) and *Sport, Spectacle, and 'NASCAR Nation': Consumption and the Cultural Politics of Neo-liberalism* (with Joshua I. Newman, Palgrave Macmillan, 2011). He is also the associate editor of the *Sociology of Sport Journal* and a member of the editorial board for *Cultural Studies/Critical Methodologies*.

Audrey R. Giles

Audrey R. Giles is an associate professor in the School of Human Kinetics and Faculty of Health Sciences at the University of Ottawa. In general, her research interests include Aboriginal peoples' involvement in physical practices in Canada's north. She is particularly interested in contested understandings of "tradition"; cross-cultural examinations of understandings of gender and development; and emerging qualitative research methods and methodologies.

Daniel Gould

Daniel Gould, PhD, is the director of the Institute for the Study of Youth Sports at Michigan State University. Dan has published more than 150 articles on applied sport psychology. He is best known for conducting applied research and for his efforts in coaching education. Dan's current research focuses on the role that parents play in junior tennis, how coaches teach life skills to young athletes, youth leadership in sport, and an assessment of the most pressing issues involved in high school athletics. He has been invited to speak on sport psychology and coaching topics in over 25 countries.

Douglas Hartmann

Douglas Hartmann, PhD, (University of California, San Diego, 1997) is a professor and associate chair of sociology at the University of Minnesota. Hartmann is author of *Race, Culture, and the Revolt of the Black Athlete: The 1968 Olympic Protests and their Aftermath* (Chicago, 2003), and co-editor of *Contexts,* the American Sociological Association publication devoted to bringing sociology to public visibility and influence. His contribution to this volume is based upon the final chapter of his forthcoming book (also with Chicago) *Midnight Basketball: Race and the Realities of Sports-Based Crime Prevention.*

Dennis R. Howard

Dennis R. Howard is a Philip H. Knight professor of business in the James H. Warsaw Sports Marketing Center at the University of Oregon's Lundquist College of Business. Considered the leading authority on sports finance, Howard has authored three books and more than 100 articles in sports and leisure management and marketing publications. Most notably, his book *Financing Sport* (coauthored with John L. Crompton) pioneered the application of business and financing principles to the sports industry.

Marion Keim

Marion Keim is an associate professor at the University of the Western Cape, South Africa, directing the University's Interdisciplinary Centre of Excellence for Sports Sciences and Development. She is also the chairperson of the Western Cape Network for Community Peace and Development, a civil society peace and development network consisting of 40 NGOs working in the field of community and youth development, conflict transformation and peace building, and she is an advocate of the High Court of South Africa. In addition to book chapters and articles in international academic journals, she has published *Nation Building at Play* (2003) by Meyer & Meyer Sport (UK) and *Umama, Recollections of South African Mothers and Grandmothers* (2009) by Umuzi (Randomhouse).

Ronnie Lidor

Dr. Ronnie Lidor is an associate professor at the Zinman College of Physical Education and Sport Sciences at the Wingate Institute and in the faculty of education at the University of Haifa (Israel). His main areas of research are cognitive strategies, talent detection, and early development in sport. Dr. Lidor has published over 90 articles, book chapters, and proceedings chapters, in English and in Hebrew. He is the senior editor of several books, among them *Sport Psychology: Linking Theory and Practice* (1999) and *The Psychology of Team Sports* (2003) published by Fitness Information Technology (USA). A former basketball coach, Dr. Lidor now provides psychological consultation to young and adult elite basketball players. He focuses mainly on attentional techniques used before the execution of free-throw shots.

Meghan Lynch

Meghan Lynch is a PhD student in the social and behavioral health sciences division of the Dalla Lana School of Public Health at the University of Toronto. She completed her MA in the University of Ottawa's School of Human Kinetics.

Alexis Lyras

Alexis Lyras is an assistant professor currently working at the College of Education and Human Development at the University of Louisville, focusing on global sport for development and peace policy, governance, strategic planning, and impacts assessment. Dr. Lyras has 20 years experience in youth sport, program and policy development, and consulting, and has worked with national sport development federations, ministries of education, NGOs and universities in Greece, Cyprus, Africa, the USA, and the Caribbean. Dr. Lyras also holds adjunct professor positions at the University of Trinidad and Tobago and the University of Nicosia and holds a faculty fellowship position at the Mohammad Ali Institute of Peace and Justice. Dr Lyras is a co-founder of the International Sport for Development and Peace Association (ISDPA), where he currently holds the pro-bono position of the ISDPA secretariat's scientific advancement director.

Cyprian Maro

Dr. Cyprian Maro is currently lecturer of sport and exercise psychology at the University of Dar es Salaam in Tanzania. He received his PhD in 2008 from The Norwegian University of Sport Science in Norway. Dr. Maro is the founder of the EMIMA program that began in 2001. EMIMA is a community-based sport program to deliver life skills for HIV/AIDS prevention to at-risk children. Dr. Maro's research interests are in life skill development and in the determinants of motivation for children.

Daniel Mason

Daniel Mason is a professor with the faculty of Physical Education and Recreation and an adjunct with the School of Business at the University of Alberta. His research takes an interdisciplinary approach to understanding the relationships between sport organizations, cities, events, and the stakeholders impacted by them. His work has been published in various journals, including the *Journal of Urban Affairs, Economic Development Quarterly, Journal of Sport Management, American Behavioral Scientist, Contemporary Economic Policy,* and *Tourism Management.*

Laura Misener

Laura Misener is an assistant professor in the faculty of Human Kinetics at the University of Windsor. Her research focuses on sport as a vehicle for social and community development, with particular emphasis on the relationship between event hosting and leveraging strategies for cities and communities. She takes a community-based multidisciplinary approach to her research and her work has been published in variety of outlets, which include journals such as the *Journal of Sport Management, Managing Leisure, Current Issues in Tourism,* and the *Journal of Management and Organization.*

Ian Patterson

Ian Patterson is an associate professor in the School of Tourism at the University of Queensland, Australia. He teaches courses in leisure, tourism, and sport management and has published over 50 peer-reviewed scholarly articles and 15 book chapters. He is primarily interested in researching the leisure experiences of older people who are undertaking events, travel, and attending sporting events as spectators or participants. He wrote the textbook *Growing Older: Toursim and Leisure Behaviour of Older Adults* in 2006 with CABI Publishing House. He is currently an editor of the journal *Annals of Leisure Research.*

Shane Pegg

Shane Pegg is a senior lecturer with the School of Tourism in the faculty of Business, Economics and Law at The University of Queensland, Australia. He has an active and ongoing involvement in research and consultancy projects related to the effective management of sport and tourism services, experience management, and volunteerism. Shane has published over 50 refereed papers and 15 book chapters related to the field. Recent projects he has been involved in have included an assessment of participant engagement in the Australian University Games and an exploration of the visitor experience at the Shanghai World Expo.

Duke Peltier

Duke Peltier is a member of the Wikwemikong Unceded Indian Reserve Band and Council. A former NCAA Division 1 ice hockey player, Duke has coached elite junior ice hockey for several years in Northern Ontario, Canada. As director of recreation in Wikwemikong, Duke oversees the sport programming for youth provided by Wikwemikong. In addition to his professional capacities, Duke has also collaborated on two successive SSHRC funded research projects with Robert Schinke and his colleagues from Laurentian University. The articles resulting from such work have been published in *The Sport Psychologist, International Journal of Sport and Exercise Psychology, Quest, Journal of Sport and Social Issues, Journal of Physical Activity and Health,* and *International Journal of Sport Psychology.* Duke has also co-authored several academic book chapters.

Barbara Ravel

Barbara Ravel, PhD, is an assistant professor in the School of Human Kinetics at Laurentian University in Canada. She received her MSc (sport psychology) and PhD (sport sociology) from the Université de Montréal after receiving a BA (psychology) and an MA (social psychology) from the Université Lyon 2 Lumière (France). Her research interests focus on non-conventional genders and sexualities in sport using queer theory, feminist post-structuralism and qualitative methodologies (e.g., conversations, discourse analysis). She has co-authored publications in *Sociology of Sport Journal, International Review for the Sociology of Sport,* and *Journal of Sport and Social Issues.*

Glyn C. Roberts

Glyn C. Roberts is professor emeritus from both the Norwegian University of Sport Science and the University of Illinois. Glyn 's research has focused on the motivational determinants of achievement especially of children in the competitive sport experience. He has been on research grants for over 2 million dollars, has over 200 publications, 15 books and over 70 book chapters. He has several distinguished scholar awards, including ISSP (1997), NASPSPA (1998), and AASP (2008). Dr Roberts is a past president of NASPSPA, FEPSAC, Division 12 of IAAP, and AASP. He is a Fellow of AAK, AASP, and IAAP. Dr Roberts is a certified consultant of AASP.

Marit Sørensen

Marit Sørensen is a professor in sport and exercise psychology at The Norwegian School of Sport Sciences in Oslo, Norway. Her research has focused on exercise and psychosocial health, empowerment through sport, and inclusion of disability sport in the regular sport organizations. She was primary investigator on a National Science Foundation grant to study empowerment for athletes with a disability through sport and has led a research team evaluating a process to integrate disability sport in the National Sport Confederation. She has served as president of Division 12, Sport Psychology in IAAP, and as vice–president of the International Society of Sport Psychology.

Jeffrey L. Stinson

Jeffrey L. Stinson is an assistant professor of marketing and associate director of the Northwest Center for Sport Business at Central Washington University. Over the past 10 years, Stinson's research has centered on the nexus of sport and fundraising. He has published in *Journal of Sport Management, Sport Marketing Quarterly, Sport Management Review, Journal of Services Marketing,* and *Journal of Nonprofit & Public Sector Marketing.*

Dana K. Voelker

Dana K. Voelker, earned her bachelor's degree in psychology with honors from the Pennsylvania State University. She is currently enrolled in the doctorate program in sport psychology and masters program in counseling at Michigan State University. She was a competitive figure skater for 11 years and also a captain of both her high school and college ice hockey teams. As one of only a few doctoral university fellows at MSU, Dana participates in numerous research and outreach efforts at the Institute for the Study of Youth Sports. She is particularly interested in student-athlete leadership development and women in sport issues.

Mary Jo Wabano

Mary Jo Wabano is the director of the Youth Center at Wikwemikong Unceded Indian Reserve. She and her staff provide sport and activity services to youth in collaboration with the recreation program at Wikwemikong. Presently, Mary Jo has partnered with faculty members from Laurentian University and is serving as a community contact person. The nature of her present collaboration involves PAR and the ongoing provision of youth leadership training through an adventure leadership excursion, in which traditional teachings are provided as part of the experience. Mary Jo has contributed to peer-reviewed publications authored in *Journal of Physical Activity and Health, Qualitative Research in Sport and Exercise,* and *Journal of Sport and Social Issues.* She lives in Wikwemikong with her husband Mike, their two children and their grandchildren.

Eli A. Wolff

Eli A. Wolff is a sport and human rights fellow at the Brown University Watson Institute for International Relations, and is also the co-director of the Sport and Development Fellowship program at Brown University. From 2001-2010, Wolff was the manager of research and advocacy at the Center for Sport in Society at Northeastern University. Wolff was also a member of the US Paralympic Soccer Team in the 1996 and 2004 Paralympic Games. He is a graduate of Brown University.